BEYOND FEAR

Dorothy Rowe, born in Australia in 1930, worked as a teacher and as a child psychologist before coming to England where she obtained her PhD at Sheffield University. From 1972 until 1986 she was head of the North Lincolnshire Department of Clinical Psychology. She is now engaged in writing, teaching and research. Her work is concerned with the questions of how we communicate and why we suffer.

Her other books are *The Experience of Depression* (1978) reissued as *Choosing Not Losing* (1988), *The Construction of Life and Death* (1982) reissued as *The Courage to Live* (1991), *Depression: the Way Out of Your Prison* (1983), *Living with the Bomb: Can We Live Without Enemies?* (1985), *The Successful Self* (1988) and *The Depression Handbook* (1990) reissued as *Breaking the Bonds* (1991).

Dorothy Rowe

BEYOND FEAR

Fontana

An Imprint of HarperCollinsPublishers

Fontana
An Imprint of HarperCollins*Publishers*
77–85 Fulham Palace Road,
Hammersmith, London W6 8JB

A Fontana Original 1987
9 8

A catalogue record for this book is
available from the British Library

ISBN 0 00 637101 9

Set in Linotron Times

Printed in Great Britain by
HarperCollinsManufacturing Glasgow

To my dear friends
Helen, Galen, Marc and Naomi

Contents

Acknowledgements

The author and publishers would like to thank the following for permission to reproduce copyright material:

Michael Heath and Posy Simmonds for their cartoons; United Feature Syndicate, Inc. for the Peanuts cartoon; Routledge & Kegan Paul for *Images of Destruction*/D. Wigoder; A.D. Peters and Co. for *Walking Away*/C. Day-Lewis; The Society of Authors for *The Welsh Marches*/A.E. Houseman; Basil Blackwell for *Caring for Your Children*/M. Herbert; *The British Journal of Psychiatry* for 'A Psychotherapist Looks at Depression'/A. Storr; Tavistock Publications for *The Child, the Family and the Outside World*; *New Society* for 'Is Alcholism a Disease?'/N. Heather and I. Robinson; Olwyn Hughes for *Mirror*/S. Plath; David Hencke for the quotation from his article in *The Guardian*; Connie Bensley for the quotation of *Self Selection*; Virago Press for *The Art of Starvation*/S. Macleod; Faber & Faber and Farrar, Straus and Giroux for *The Drama of the Gifted Child*/A. Miller; Farrar, Straus and Giroux for *Thou Shalt Not Be Aware*/A. Miller; and John Wiley and Sons for *Wounded Healers*/V. Rippere and R. Williams.

Preface

This book is about a secret. It is a secret which all of us, men and women, children and adults, the powerful and the weak, the happy and the unhappy, conspire to keep.

It is a secret which we keep from one another. It is a secret we keep from ourselves. The secret is fear.

We can admit to all sorts of things about ourselves – that we don't like talking about death, that some things make us anxious, that we worry a lot – but we try never to say, even to ourselves, 'I am afraid'.

Fear is too fearful to be discussed. We talk about what we do to protect ourselves from our fear – we worry about practical things or unlikely eventualities, or we work hard, or become bad-tempered or extremely powerful, or we cling tenaciously to some religious or political faith, or we drink too much, or become ill or depressed, and so on – but we do not talk about the total, annihilating terror we feel whenever we as much as glimpse our own insignificance, vulnerability, helplessness, isolation, weakness and fragility in this limitless, incomprehensible cosmos. We fear death, but far worse than death is the annihilation of our self. In this our body might survive but that which was our self has vanished into chaos and nothingness.

So much of what we do, and all the theories we have created about why we do what we do, are defences against this fear, but the fear itself is not acknowledged. To talk about this fear is to risk being considered weak and despicable. Those people who might disclose the secret because they have to resort to desperate defences to guard against this fear are labelled 'mad' and treated with contempt. 'Lunatics' may no longer be herded and confined within the walls of an asylum, but the 'mentally ill' are still regarded as inferior and dangerous, and, under the guise of care, are often treated inhumanely and sometimes very cruelly. It is said that nowadays people with a 'mental illness' are no longer discriminated against, but in practice prejudice against psychiatric patients is still very strong.

So many of the theories about what we do to defend against the unnamed and unacknowledged fear have to do with behaviour which is a problem, such as being addicted to drugs, or refusing to eat, or being unable to cope with your responsibilities, or being a danger to yourself or to other people. 'Sane' behaviour is not seen as being a defence against the unacknowledged fear. Yet it is, for every moment of the day each of us is engaged in creating, maintaining and defending a structure which we call 'myself, my life, my world'. Continual defence is necessary, for the ever-moving, ever-changing cosmos can reveal to us at any moment that our precious structures are as fragile as a matchstick house, and can be swept away like matchsticks in a stream.

We react to any threat to our structures with fear and then with anger, and we use this anger to try to hold our structures in place. We insist that our perception of our self, our life and our world is the only true reality. Threats to our structures usually come when other people insist that their constructions are the correct ones. A power struggle ensues, and the winner is the person who makes his structure prevail.

One power struggle may be:

'Mummy, I'm hungry.'
'No you're not, dear. You're tired. You're going to bed.'

Or:

'Now that the children are all going to school I think I might take a course in computing.'
'Don't be silly. Women are no good with computers. Who's going to get my meals if you're out gallivanting around?'

Or:

'Doctor, ever since I retired I've felt useless and life seems meaningless.'
'You're obviously depressed. It's an illness which unfortunately is common at your age. I'll give you a prescription.'

All the theories about the defences against the unacknowledged fear are theories about the losers in these power struggles, the 'mad' people. (If you keep losing the contests over whose definitions of reality should prevail, you lose confidence in yourself, become increasingly prey to fear, and have to defend yourself with what the medical profession calls 'the symptoms of mental illness'.) Yet there can't be a loser without a winner, and the winner is as much a part of the pattern as the loser.

The winners have tried to ensure, so far very successfully, that 'madness' is explained solely in terms of the losers. Thus, psychiatrists, as winners, insist that 'madness' is a result of some fault within the person's body. Psychoanalysts, as winners, insist that 'madness' is a result of some fault within the 'mad' person's mind. Behavioural psychologists, as winners, insist that 'madness' is a result of some fault in the behaviour of the 'mad' person. Losers don't just lose. They get blamed for losing.

When I wrote about one kind of loser, those people who get depressed, I tried, in my *Depression: The Way Out of Your Prison*, to redress the balance a little by showing how some winners, like the depressed person's spouse, help create and maintain the state of depression while at the same time trying to help the depressed person to cease to be depressed. In *Living With the Bomb* I wrote about winners, those people who are so devoted to creating and combating enemies that they are likely, in the end, to make us all losers in every sense of the word.

In this book I have written about winners and losers together, and how we lose as children so as to win as adults. But to win as adults, or even just get by, we have to deny that we lost as children, and, to do this, we must not acknowledge in any way the terrible fear which we felt as children when we lost and which comes back to us now whenever we are in danger of losing.

In writing about this I am very much indebted to Alice Miller and to all those people, chiefly women, who have courageously revealed the extent of the physical and sexual abuse of children in our society. The effects of such abuse, as some of my clients reveal in this book, are passed down from generation to generation. The degree to which all children, even if not sexually or physically abused, suffer punishments and humiliations is greatly under-estimated and, even when revealed, dismissed as unimportant because 'children don't remember'. Adults like to be winners.

Winners can be very cruel. Part of being a winner, even if you are not cruel yourself, is not to acknowlege that cruelty exists. Of course, we are all good, caring people, and we are greatly distressed at news of the starving children in Africa, or of tortured prisoners in Chile, or of people confined for political reasons in Soviet psychiatric hospitals. That cruelty is far away and we are not threatened personally by it. What we don't want to acknowledge is that good, caring parents can be cruel to children, and that good, caring psychiatric staff can be cruel to their patients. But they are, and such cruelty creates the conditions which provoke the worst experience of all, that of total, annihilating fear.

Winners and losers alike don't want to acknowledge this fear because not only is it terrible but it is a problem incapable of a once-and-for-all solution. One American publisher rejected this book immediately because I have not given a recipe for abolishing fear. Yet a moment's reflection would surely reveal that there can be no recipe for ridding us of this fear. Fear is an inevitable part of what it is to be human.

The fragility of our structures is always a cause for fear. Even if other people do not threaten our structures, the world itself is full of sudden, uncontrollable dangers, and we cannot guard ourselves completely against illness and injury, loss of loved ones and possessions, old age and death. Even when we feel healthy and physically secure we have, every day, to find some optimum balance between our need to be an individual and our need to be a member of a group. If we go too much one way we are threatened with loneliness and isolation, and if we go the other way we are threatened by being swallowed up in the group. So, too, every day we have to find an optimum balance between freedom and security. We cannot have both. The more free we are, the less secure; and the more secure, the less free.

So, I have provided no recipe for abolishing fear. But I hope that within these pages (I am sorry there are so many of them;

writing about winners and losers and fear is a lengthy task) you will find some useful clues to the acquisition of courage.

The courageous person does not deny fear, but acknowledges it and faces it. Only through courage can we find a sustaining happiness.

Many courageous people have contributed to this book. They have shared with me, and now with you, the reader, some of the most fearful parts of their lives. They agreed to becoming part of this book because they hope that out of their mistakes and pain other people might find something of value.

It is only out of our imperfections that we can help one another and protect one another from fear.

Dorothy Rowe
Eagle, Lincolnshire
August 1986

Fear and the Fear of Fear

Chapter One

The Nature of Fear

Fear comes to us in many guises. It can come as a shiver in the delight of anticipation; or as the drenching, overwhelming, annihilating terror, known by the inadequate names of existential anxiety or dread. It can come suddenly, life-savingly to danger, when it is known as fear; or it can gnaw away endlessly with little apparent cause, and we call it anxiety; or it can come with a sense of having the eyes of the world upon us when we are naked and alone, and we call it shame; or it can loom darkly, threatening punishment, and we call it guilt.

Fear, like death, is the great unmentionable. We maintain a conspiracy of silence so as to pretend we are not afraid. In the aftermath of great physical danger everyone claims that everyone was brave and no one panicked. After the fire aboard a British Airways aircraft at Manchester Airport in 1985, those surviving passengers who spoke of terror and panic and the rush for the exits as smoke filled the rear of the plane soon ceased to be reported in the newspapers as other people, important people who were not aboard the plane, took over to commend the passengers on the plane for their bravery. Yet would not anyone, trapped in the narrow space of a crowded plane, watching the flames and breathing the acrid smoke, feel afraid and try desperately to escape?

The memory of such fear can stay with us for the rest of our lives, leaving us unable to enter any place which will remind us of our fear, or returning in our dreams of terror when we find ourselves re-enacting, helplessly, the scenes where we once successfully escaped destruction. Some people, to give themselves freedom to go and do what they wish, put themselves through the painful process of therapy, in the hope that re-learning a skill or talking about the events will remove the fear and with that the shame of being afraid. Most people, however, adapt their life to an avoidance of certain situations and activities, like never entering an enclosed space or flying again, or they fog their sleeping brain with drugs to blot out the dreams, or become what is known as 'a light sleeper', someone who is often awake while others sleep. They invent all sorts of excuses for not doing certain things, proneness to illness, or allergies, logical reasons for following one course of action rather than another, all to hide the fact that they are afraid. They must do this because they know, correctly, that to be afraid is to be scorned.

The fear we feel when faced with an external danger – fire or flood or a terrorist bomb – is bad enough, but what is far, far worse is the fear we feel when the danger is inside us. When the danger is outside us we know that at least some people will understand how we feel, but when the danger is inside us, when we live our lives in a sweat of anxiety, shame and guilt, we find ourselves in the greater peril that if we tell other people about our fear they will think that we are weak, or, worse, mad. So we take drugs to drown our fear and maintain the conspiracy of silence.

Edith is a very good woman who has devoted her life to others. She often acted as chauffeur for one of my clients, and while this client was talking to me Edith would visit some of the elderly patients in the hospital. One day she phoned me and asked if, when she came next day, she could have a quick word with me. I agreed, and so the next day she came into my room, apologizing for taking up my time and sitting nervously on the edge of her chair. What she wanted to know was whether she was going mad. The evidence that she might be was that she would often waken at 2 a.m. and lie there worrying. The fear that pervades her being comes as the fear that no one will look after her when she is old. What if she becomes senile and incontinent, like the old women she visits on the psychiatric ward? She has done enough nursing to know that I cannot truthfully say that her old age will not bring indignities and inadequacies, but there is one truth I can tell her.

Waking in the early hours of the morning in a sweat of terror is an extremely common experience. It might be some comfort to her to know that, as she lies there, all across the country are people experiencing that terrible loneliness of being. They have woken suddenly to the greatest uncertainty and loneliness a human being can know. There is no shape or structure to hold them. They are falling, dissolving, totally, paralysingly helpless without hope of recovery or of rescue. Sickening, powerful forces clutch at their heart and stomach. They gasp for breath as wave after wave of terror sweeps over them.

We all knew such terror when, as small children, we found ourselves in a situation which filled us with pain and helpless rage. We screamed in fear and in hope that our good parents would rescue and comfort us. Now grown up, we know the extent of our loneliness and helplessness. Some of us wake, like Edith, completely alone. Some of us have a figure sharing our bed, but it is effectively insensate, a log refusing to acknowledge our misery. Others of us, more fortunate, share our bed with a kindly person who switches on the light, makes us a cup of tea, and holds us close. Such love can make our terror recede like the tide, but, like the tide, it can return, and there is no good parent there to pick us up and cuddle us and assure us that the world is a safe place and there is no reason to be afraid. We are grown up now, and, try as we might to deny it, we know the loneliness of being. We long for good parents who will rescue and love us, but we know that there are no good parents and, while we might believe in God the Father, in these times of terror He is far away.

For some people the waves of terror and the sense of annihilation last for many minutes. Some people move very quickly to turn the terror into all kinds of manageable worries – manageable not because the worries are about problems which can be solved but because they turn a nameless terror into a named anxiety. Thoughts like 'Who will look after me when I get old?', 'I can't manage the tasks I have to do at work today', 'The lump on my groin is certain to be cancer', 'If my daughter goes to that school she'll get mixed up in drugs', 'I won't be able to meet this month's bills', 'I should have done more for my parents before they died' are indeed terrible, but they give a sense of structure and have a common, everyday meaning. With them we can pretend that the terror does not exist and that we belong to the everyday world.

But not everyone can do this. For some people, lying there in the dark, the terror goes on and on. When Edith described to me how this happened to her she said, 'It gets so bad that I think that I shall run outside the house in my nightie and stand in the middle of the road so I'll get run over and that'll stop it.'

'Not in your street at two a.m. you won't,' I said, knowing how empty her town is at night. I went on to tell her that the terror she felt is called 'existential angst'. She laughed and laughed at this ridiculously pretentious name. 'I'll remember that next time,' she said, 'I'll lie there and think, "I'm experiencing existential angst."'

I do hope she does, and finds her laughter in the midst of her terror. It would be so monstrously unfair if Edith followed the path of a woman whose inquest was reported in the paper recently. She was an elderly patient, not long discharged from a psychiatric hospital. A nurse told the coroner that she had looked in the patient's room at midnight and seen the patient sound asleep. When she returned at 6 a.m. she found the patient floating in the bath. The coroner returned an open verdict. There was no mention of the terror which the poor woman could bring to an end only by filling the bath with water and, all alone, immersing herself in it. When fear is terrible, all we can do is run away.

Fight or Flight

Fear has a vital life-saving function. It is the means by which our body mobilizes itself to move swiftly and efficiently to protective action. Our heart rate increases, we breath more quickly, taking in extra oxygen, and adrenalin enters our bloodstream. We see the danger and we act immediately. If we act physically, by striking out at the source of the danger or by taking to our heels and running away, then we make use of our body's preparations. But if we neither fight back nor run away we are left with the effects of the body's preparations and these effects can be most unpleasant.

Our heart beats fast and we feel shaky, sweaty and tingly. Some people experience severe headaches, some feel nauseous, some feel dizzy and close to fainting. When these reactions occur in company, where we need to be calm and collected, we can feel very ashamed of ourselves. When these reactions occur and we don't know why, we can feel frightened and so start on the sickening cycle of fearing fear itself.

Faced with an external danger such as a man carrying a gun or a runaway bus we can stand and fight or flee. That is not difficult to do. But sometimes the people around us will not let us do either. Children who are frightened of their parents or teachers may be prevented from either fighting to protect themselves or running away. Lacking the means to support themselves or their children, women may be unable to flee from husbands who frighten them. Needing to support their families, men may be unable to fight or flee from employers who frighten and mistreat them.

Thus it is very easy to find ourselves in a situation where we wish to fight or to flee, but we feel that we can do neither. Such a conflict leaves our mind in a turmoil and our body reacting appropriately to our reading of the situation (danger) and inappropriately to our reaction to our reading of the situation (neither fighting nor fleeing).

If we can make such a conflict explicit, by thinking about it very clearly and honestly and by discussing it with understanding friends and counsellors, then we can often find a way to solve the conflict or to live with it more easily. But if we dare not make the conflict explicit to others or even to ourselves then we cannot resolve it and our misery goes on.

Shirley came to see me because she was nervous. She had given up driving in a car because she was frightened she would have an accident and hurt someone.

'I'm not worried about hurting myself. It's other people that I worry about.'

She felt nervous when she had to go into a room where there were other people.

'I worry that they'll all look at me. Yet I like going out and having a social life. It's just, I sort of feel ashamed. I don't know why. I do go out, like we go out for a drink, and I find my hands shaking.'

She said that what she wanted was to feel more confident.

'I've never felt confident,' she said.

Her brothers, all older than her, used to tell her that as she was a girl, she couldn't play with them. At school her teachers told her that she wasn't bright.

'I mightn't be brainy but I'm intelligent. That's what I'm always telling my husband. He treats me like I'm stupid and don't know anything. But you can't tell him. He's one of those men who always have to be right. Don't get me wrong, he's a wonderful husband and thinks the world of me, but he does put me down.'

She spoke of how important it was to her to be herself, to have a small job so she had some money of her own, and how annoyed she got with herself when she became too nervous to do the things that she wanted to do. Yet, when she spoke of being confident, there was some sense of reservation. She wouldn't want to be totally confident.

Why was that? Well, totally confident people have a great deal expected of them. People expect them to be able to cope with everything. The problem was that if she became totally confident, she would be asked to do things which she couldn't or wouldn't do and she did not want to say no to people.

'I don't like to upset people. I want to be liked.'

Unavoidable Conflicts

Shirley's conflict is one which many people experience. We want to be ourselves, but we fear that if we do express our own wishes, needs and attitudes, then people will not like us. Some people aren't all that bothered about whether they are liked or not but for many people being liked is a matter of life and death. More of this later, but here I want to point out that all of us, however we feel about being liked, are for ever involved in finding a balance somewhere between

Being		being a
an	....	member
individual		of a group

Being a complete individual, ignoring all the demands of family and friends, means complete loneliness and risking the destruction of the self, which comes from complete isolation. Being nothing but a member of the group means giving up being a person and becoming an empty space. This is complete powerlessness and complete vulnerability.

In finding a liveable balance between being an individual and being a member of a group, you have to arrive at a balance between regarding yourself as

Completely		Completely
valueless and	....	valuable and
imperfect		perfect

The more you regard yourself as valueless and imperfect (which you might describe to yourself as being bad or evil or unacceptable to you and other people), the more you fear, hate and envy other people, the more you feel frightened of doing anything and the more you fear the future. Regarding yourself as bad brings a lot of troubles. Yet if you regard yourself as perfect you delude yourself and make it difficult for other people to get along with you. No one's perfect. We all make mistakes, get things wrong and aggravate other people and fail to make the most of our talents.

So we have to arrive at a realistic assessment of ourselves, with no false modesty, seeing ourselves as ordinary people, like all other people, yet at the same time as individuals who are valuable to ourselves and to other people, even though other people may not value us in the way that we want them to value us.

It can take us many years to arrive at an assessment of ourselves which provides a realistic and hopeful balance between imperfection and perfection. We can be plagued by doubt, confused by the conflicting demands that people make on us, and hurt by criticism. To find out who we are and how we should assess ourselves we need to explore, to meet new people, to try out new situations and to see how we feel and react and deal with the strange and the new. But to do this, we need freedom, and to have freedom we have to give up security.

From the moment of our birth, we have to find a balance between

Freedom   ....   Security

The more freedom we have, the less security. The more security, the less freedom. Total freedom means total uncertainty and great danger. Total security means total certainty and total hopelessness, for hope can only exist where there is uncertainty.

We all try to hold on to a measure of security. Most of us do this by having possessions (what's that line from a song, 'Freedom's just another word for nothing left to lose'?), just as most of us find security by keeping close to a group of people (why else would we put up with awful relatives?). Some people seek security not just in possessions and people but in a set of beliefs which makes everything that happens part of a pattern. The pattern may be in terms of Heaven and Hell, or Allah's will, or karma, or fate or a constellation of stars or the eventual victory of the proletariat, but whatever the pattern is, it gives us a sense of fixity in what would otherwise seem to be a meaningless chaos.

However, while having a belief in some kind of grand design can give a sense of security, it can make the person who holds the belief feel hopeless. If the pattern of your life is already determined by God or by your stars, or by your genes as some doctors would have us believe, or by your parents or by a series of rewards and punishments as some therapists would have us believe, then there is nothing you can do to change it. You are helpless and hopeless.

On the other hand, if nothing is fixed, if anything can happen, at any time, then you have an infinite number of choices about what you do with your life. Such freedom can be exciting if you have lots of confidence in yourself, but if you don't, then such freedom is very scary. So, somehow we all have to make a balance between

An		Having no
infinite	....	choice
choice		at all

Along with the question of choice comes the question of responsibility. How much are we responsible for what happens? If we are just acting out a pattern which was determined and fixed before we were born then we are not responsible if we turn out to be murderers or thieves and it is not our fault if our children turn out badly or millions of people starve. Such a release from responsibility can seem quite attractive, but, equally, if we are not responsible for when things turn out badly we cannot take the credit for when they turn out well. You cannot praise yourself when you become rich, famous and powerful, when your children lead happy, successful lives and when you solve the problems of world hunger and nuclear war. So, being responsible does have its benefits.

But where does that responsibility end? You might be responsible for doing your work properly but are you responsible when the firm you work for goes bankrupt and you lose your job? You might be responsible for looking after your children, but are you responsible when your daughter's marriage breaks up or your son gives up his job to go surfing in California? You might be responsible for organizing your finances so that you have some money to give the charities but are you responsible for those world events which give rise to hunger, terrorism and war?

So we have to find a balance between being

Not		Totally
responsible	....	responsible
for anything		for everything

Even though from the moment of birth we need other people, as small children we soon learn that other people can reject and punish us, and this can be very painful. We protect ourselves from this pain by becoming very careful in our relations with other people. We withdraw from them and when we deal with them we put on some sort of social front. Being close to other people is risky, but then we also run the risk of loneliness.

So we have to find a balance between

The risk		The risk
of	....	of
rejection		loneliness

Thus in these six vital aspects of our lives we are for ever trying to achieve a balance between two opposites. There is no textbook we can consult which will tell us what is the right balance because what is right for one person is wrong for another. We cannot when we are, say, fifteen, arrive at a set of balances which will suit us for the rest of our lives and stick with that, because what is a good balance at fifteen is not so good at twenty and quite disastrous at forty. So we have to keep trying to find the right balance and we always run the risk of getting it wrong. We are always in the position of the juggler who is trying to keep eight oranges in the air while balancing on a ball which is on a chair, which is resting on a plank which is supported by two rolling drums which are on a raft floating in deep water. Any minute, something could go wrong. It is no wonder that we often feel frightened.

We struggle on, meeting what seems an endless stream of difficulties and problems. When we meet yet another setback, we often look at other people and see them being like those people in the telly ads who are always beautiful, knowledgeable, organized, intelligent, happy, loved, admired and suffering no greater problems than choosing the right margarine and coping with the weather. Then we can feel just like Alice when she met a couple at a dinner party.

'They've got three children,' she told me, 'and they're all brilliant, marvellously musical, getting excellent degrees, entering wonderful careers. He's done terribly well, she's got this marvellous part-time job and she's got paintings in this new exhibition. Everything that family does is just right. Urgh!'

It is hard not to feel envy for people whose lives seem to go along more easily, more successfully than ours. But this is the price we pay for clinging to the hope that it is possible for us to find a way of life where we are happy, trouble free and never have to make a mess of things. Without this hope many of us would find life very difficult indeed. The alternative version of life, that all of us suffer one way or another, have heavy burdens and often make a mess of things, can rob us of hope and make us feel very frightened.

Many of us, as we get older, come to agree with Samuel Johnson that, 'Human life is everywhere a state in which much is to be endured and little to be enjoyed', and try to meet this view of life with courage and hope. But those of us who have read about Johnson know that during his life he was often depressed and that he was always afraid of dying.

Fear of Life and Death

Most of us go through a large part of our lives not thinking about death. 'When it comes, it comes' we say and secretly think that it won't. Other people die in earthquakes or car accidents or of cancer or of old age, but not me. I'm the exception. Then one day something happens and we know. Death means me.

Then all the careful security we had built up comes crashing down. We are all alone, without protection, open to great forces which we cannot and do not understand. We ask in our anguish, 'Why me?' 'Why death?' 'Why life?' 'What is it all about?' There are no satisfactory answers.

All the answers that we had before, which in all their forms meant 'If I am good, nothing bad can happen to me', are swept away. There is nothing that we can cling to.

Rose's lawyer asked me to prepare a report on how Rose had been affected by her accident. She was having difficulty in getting back to work.

Rose said to me, 'The car pulled out of the driveway and hit me as I was cycling past. My bike was caught under the front of the car and I was pushed across the road. I could see the lights of other cars coming towards me. I remembered how, when I was eight, we left our beautiful home in the country and moved to London. And then I thought, 'I won't have any more holidays.' I ended up in the gutter on the other side of the road. A man came to pick me up and I thought he was the driver of the car. I gave him a mouthful. I was angry and then I found that he wasn't the driver . . . I feel so guilty about all of this, putting all you people to so much trouble. You've got people who need your help far more than I do. I'm all right, really, just my back's a little sore and I get a bit weepy now and then. I usen't to be like that. Always self-controlled, really. Now I think why me? Why do I go on living and those babies die?'

Rose wasn't all right. She was shaken to the very core and guilty that she was alive. That sounds crazy but it is what many people think when they have survived a terrible disaster. 'Survivors' guilt' is now a common term, derived from studies of the people who survived the concentration camps of the Second World War or Hiroshima and Nagasaki (the *hibakusha*) or the fighting in the Vietnam War[1]. Such people feel not joy at being alive but fear, fear that they have done something wrong, for they *ought* to have died like their companions, fear that they have been given something which they do not deserve and that they will be punished for holding on to it or that it will be suddenly taken away from them. They may have survived, but death as retribution is imminent.

Rose's question 'Why me?' was the question of an ordinary woman who was nearing sixty who had worked diligently all her life, looking after her family, being competent in her office work, enjoying a quiet life in a country town, never expecting that her life would have any other significance than in the pattern of the lives of her family and friends.

Then suddenly she was flung, not just across a road in the path of oncoming cars but into the vast mysterious universe of being. Why me? In all this vastness, why me? Alone in all that vastness she trembles with fear. Has she been saved for some purpose? Is there some pattern, some Grand Design, where she has to play a significant role? If there is, why is she, an ordinary woman, chosen to play it? Will something be asked of her that she cannot perform, where she will fail and be punished for her failure? Or is there a Grand Design and the Grand Designer has got it wrong? Was she saved by mistake? Has she been given something that she doesn't deserve? Should she be dead, and some little baby, now dead, be alive? Or is there no design, just a random universe where some people live and others die, with no justice or fairness or reward for goodness and punishment for badness? Just randomness, chance without significance, life without meaning? Is 'Why me?' a question flung against the stars and the stars shine coldly back with no answer?

To contemplate the significance of one's life against the limitlessness of space and the infinity of time is to create a powerful sense of awe and dread. Sometimes this is a very sensible thing to do. It certainly helps in keeping a sense of proportion about our own anxieties and ambitions. But at other times such a contemplation brings a sense of powerlessness and insignificance which can be quite overwhelming.

We all first had this experience when we were children and learning about space and time. By then we had all come across death through the death of grandparents or pets or stories on television or simply the unspoken threat of death in the instruction 'Be careful crossing the road'. As young children we puzzled over the problem of what death is and we arrived at an answer.

Over the centuries of human life, death has been given many meanings. Yet in all, such explanations fall into two categories. Death is either the end of the person's identity or it is a doorway into another life. 'Another life' can be described in a multitude of ways, but whatever the description given, it implies that some significant part of the person goes on existing after death.

The curious part of arriving at an answer to the question, 'What will happen to me when I die?' is that even though we may use scientific methods in seeking an answer ('Has anyone come back from death to tell us about it?' 'Are there such things as ghosts?' 'How many people could fit in Heaven?') the answer we arrive at is in terms of *meaning*. We discover a meaning for death which then gives meaning to our life. We say, 'There has to be something after this. Otherwise, what's the point?' or 'This life's all we've got. It doesn't make sense, the idea of an afterlife.'

In giving death a meaning, the end of identity or doorway to another life, we fix the purpose of our life.

If death is the end of my life, then to be able to accept my death I have to live my life in a way that I feel is satisfactory. There are a multitude of ways of seeing life as satisfactory, by becoming rich, or famous, or having a good marriage, or having children, or just getting by without too much trouble.

If you see death as the end of life and find yourself failing to make your life satisfactory in the way that you want it to be, you feel fear. Death looms menacingly, you see time running out and you feel the pain and guilt we all feel when we know that we have wasted our talents and thrown away our opportunities.

If we see death as a doorway to another life we are immediately confronted with the problem of justice. If the afterlife means that there is the possibility of going somewhere better than this present world with its troubles and pain, then the questions are, 'Does everyone go there? Is it fair that everyone goes somewhere better irrespective of the kinds of lives they lead? Should Hitler enjoy the same kind of afterlife as Mother Teresa?' The answer that most people give to these questions is no. So the idea of an afterlife, whatever form it takes, contains some notion of justice. If you see your life as a doorway to another life you then feel that you have to achieve a certain standard of goodness and excellence which will allow you entry to a better life. When you see yourself as failing to meet the standards and rules of life beyond death's doorway, you feel great fear.[2]

Seeing death as the end of existence or as a doorway to another life are ways of trying to understand not just our own life, but to see it in relation to space and time. When we contemplate the vastness of the ocean or the immensity of the heavens, we feel great awe, a mixture of respect, fear and incomprehension. To reduce our fear and increase our understanding, we develop theories to explain, in the words of the *Hitchhiker's Guide to the Galaxy*, 'Life, the universe and everything.'[3]

Some of us frame our explanation in scientific terms, and are left with puzzling things like curved space, black holes, and whether there is life in other parts of the universe. A scientific description of life, the universe and everything is just as strange as a metaphysical or magical description. It gives rise to many fantasies, as the popularity of science fiction shows. In the end, a scientific explanation of life gives neither comfort nor security. To hold such beliefs and not be afraid requires courage and the ability to tolerate much uncertainty.

Not all people can manage this and so they turn to metaphysical or magical beliefs in order to find greater comfort and security. The scientific view of life and the universe sees us humans as just a small part of a vast complexity which will go on being itself with no more special regard for human life than it has for asteroids, atoms and the fourth dimension. Metaphysical and magical views of life place human beings at the centre of the universe where everything that happens relates to us and where we can influence vast forces and powers by our prayers, rituals and other actions.

Holding beliefs which place us at the centre of the universe under the control of a beneficent power can create a sense of security and increased self-esteem. Knowing that God loves you, or that your ancestors are watching over you, or that you are party to the forces of goodness which rule the world can make day-to-day living simple and secure. But the trouble is that everything in life has both good and bad implications. You win a lot of money in a lottery, which is good, and then all your impecunious relatives want to share your good fortune, which is bad. As an adolescent you look forward to being an independent adult, which is good, but as an independent adult you'll have no one to look after you, and that can be quite bad. In the same way, our beliefs about the nature of life and death, whatever they may be, have good and bad implications. To rest secure in God's love, or in the approbation of our ancestors, or in the power of the forces of goodness, we have to live our lives following certain rules and if we fail to follow those rules then we are in great danger. The power which we perceived as protecting us can be turned against us and can threaten us with death and damnation.

In a group discussion about the experience of depression one woman described how when she was badly depressed she would waken during the night with the conviction that she should check whether her children were safe in their beds. She would get out of her bed to do this, but as she entered the hallway, all familiarity with the hallway vanished and she found herself faced with a vast black hole. She knew that if she took a step forward she would plunge down the hole, so she would stand there frozen with terror. The group discussed this in terms of how easy it is in the dark to lose contact with the most familiar of surroundings, and how the image of being depressed (frequently expressed as falling down into a bottomless pit) is experienced as something real and palpable. The woman listened to this and then said, 'I think that your feelings summon up powers – good powers or evil powers – out there. If you feel terrible, inside you, then you somehow draw this terrible blackness towards you. If you feel good and happy, then you draw this goodness out there to you.'

So depression for her was not merely the pain of the depression itself, and perhaps the guilt about being depressed, but also the fear that the darkness within her had summoned up greater and malevolent powers over which she had no control. But perhaps she was prepared to endure this fear because when she was not depressed she felt that she had access to a special power of goodness.

We may try to deal with our fear of death by imagining that it will not occur for a long, long time. But if that is the case we have to travel through old age to meet death, and the prospect of old age can be full of terrors. No one likes the idea of becoming deaf, weak- sighted, forgetful, frail and incontinent. No one wants to be treated like a foolish child by patronizing doctors and nurses and disrespectful relatives. Yet that is the fate which awaits many of us, and no matter what plans we may make to avert such a fate – by looking after our health, or making financial provision for a place in a superior nursing home, or threatening our relatives wth guilt and retribution if they don't look after us properly – we can still be frightened.

Sometimes our fear of old age is more than just a fear of the practical problems it creates. Sometimes there is a magical dimension to our ideas about youth and old age.

Sylvia came to see me distraught after her husband of fourteen years had left her for another woman. All her conversation was about him, and if her description of him was in any way accurate I wouldn't have given him houseroom. But she desperately wanted him back.

They had met and married when she was thirty-four and he was twenty. I asked her what had made her fall in love with him.

'Chemical reaction. He made me feel so good. Young. Some women don't get older, do they? Like in those films, you've seen them, haven't you, where there's this woman and she's young and very beautiful but really she's hundreds of years old, and then something happens and she gets old, real old, suddenly, and her body starts to break up, uh, it's horrible, and she just crumbles up and her body sort of falls in on itself.'

If this is what she feared old age would be, then it was no wonder that she wanted to hang on to a man who had the power to preserve her, even though he did beat her when he got angry.

Until Sylvia told me this I had not thought of old age in this way (despite a standing joke amongst my friends that anyone who is not ageing as quickly as might be expected is 'on to his third picture', as in *The Picture of Dorian Grey*). My image of my old age was caught by Sylvia Plath in her poem 'Mirror': '*In me she has drowned a young girl and in me an old woman/Rises toward her day after day like a terrible fish.*'[4]

Fear of Not Being Good Enough

When we came into the world as babies we were quite pleased with ourselves and did whatever we wanted to do. We slept when we were sleepy, cried when we were hungry or uncomfortable, and, when offered a nipple, sucked only if we wanted to suck. We had no notion of good or bad. We just were. Then society stepped in and said, 'This won't do. You are not satisfactory as you are. You have to be different.'

This all came as a terrible shock to us. We discovered that we weren't masters of our own universe. There were greater powers out there and they were insisting that we had to be what they wanted us to be. We had to eat when they wanted and not just when we were hungry. We had to empty our bowels and bladder at the time and place they wanted and not just when we felt the need. We resented this interference, but we knew that the powers that demanded this from us were also the people on whom we depended for survival, and so we acquiesced. We became obedient, and, even more than that, we accepted our family's definition of us as not being good enough and needing to improve.

Having accepted this as a child, we moved into adult life fearing that we were still not good enough and ready to react with shame and guilt whenever some parental figure chided us for not doing well enough. The editor of *Good Housekeeping* can write, 'The other visual treat is the second in our series of Norman Parkinson spectaculars photographed in Tobago. This time it's summer evening clothes – silky, slinky, sexy numbers. The models look wonderful – very Fifties, very Parkinson – and should inspire many of us to take stock and try a little harder,'[5] and the readers react with greater effort to lose weight or sink deeper into a feeling of inadequacy and despair. It is no wonder that so many women get caught in the round of starvation, binge eating and vomiting which now has the medical label of *bulimia nervosa*.

Men don't escape this sorry state of for ever trying to do better to justify one's existence. They have, in some way, to 'make it', and when they don't, or when what they have 'made' is taken away from them, they become very frightened. Some young men set themselves the goal of having 'made it' by the time they are thirty, and so, if they fail, enter their thirty-first year in a state of rage and despair. Others set the vital age at forty, and when the failure to be rich and famous combines with a lessening of sexual performance, they sink into depression, or seek denial in alcohol or in the arms of a much younger woman. Forty is indeed a dangerous age.

When we were small babies we had no concept of ourselves as separate entities. We were contiguous with the rest of our world which presented itself to us as a continuously changing phantasmagoria. Then, by about eight months, most of us made that curious transition to the belief that what we saw was not a display of an infinite range of spectacles, coming fresh to our eyes every moment, but a limited range of spectacles which came and went and then returned. We acquired the belief that we did not have an infinite number of mothers but just one who came and went and then returned and who was somewhere else when we couldn't see her. When a favourite toy disappeared, we had some idea of where to look to see it reappear. Making things disappear and appear became a great delight as we rejoiced in our power to control our universe. We weren't always successful at this. Sometimes mother disappeared and did not reappear, no matter how we tried to get her back.

With the belief that objects go on existing even if they are out of sight came the understanding that if objects do do this, then it is worth the bother of having some sign that stands for them when they are out of sight. There's no point in having a system of signs if there is an infinite number of things in our universe and their appearance is never repeated, but if events are repeatable then we may as well have some sort of language which we can use about them and to them. So babies who acquire 'object permanence', as Piaget called it, go on to acquire language.

As we went through this extraordinary process, something which seems to be to a large extent peculiar to the human species, we were learning that our world consisted not just of ourselves but of ourselves and other objects. Some of these objects were very important to us, especially our mother in whose warm and loving gaze we bathed in ease and delight. Then one day, when we were absorbed in some activity, we discovered this loving gaze had vanished and had been replaced by something cold and rejecting. Suddenly we were wrested out of the state of being ourselves and we became an object in another person's eyes, an object of disgust and contempt. We were exposed, vulnerable and frightened. We had discovered *shame*.

Few of us can remember our first experience of shame, but we know when a small child has discovered it. The child ceases to be frank and open in all situations and to all people. The little child squirms and hides his face. If he does not look then perhaps no one will look at him.

Experiences of shame which end with affirmations of love and reconciliation – a good cuddle – can be extremely helpful to the small child who is in the process of creating his sense of self, but when there are too many such experiences, or when such experiences never end with affirmations of love and reconciliation the child can be left with the belief that he is, in his very essence, bad and unacceptable. Shame is about our identity, what kind of person we are, and when we are small and having the world defined for us by our parents, then if we are shown over and over again that we are unacceptable, that we should be ashamed of ourselves, we come to believe that this is one of the facts of the universe, as immutable and unchangeable as the pattern of night and day. As we get older such a belief about ourselves gets confirmed again and again by other events.

Margaret cannot bear to be touched. She cannot bear to be alone, but when she is with people she cannot bear them to come too close. When she first came to see me she told me that she knew she was a bad person. She had known this ever since she was a small child. She knew that she was bad through and through. She spoke of herself as a child without any sympathy or concern, because, as she told me when I asked, she did not deserve any. She said that as a child she had done something terrible but she would not tell me what it was. If she told me what it was I would see how bad she was and then I wouldn't want to have anything to do with her.

This was the theme of our meetings, every fortnight for more than two years. She would sit, head down, saying nothing, or speaking so softly that I could not hear what she was saying. She wore glasses which darkened in the light, but when I eventually challenged her on this she changed them to lighter ones so I could at least see where she was looking.

Again and again she would say, 'If you knew what I was like you wouldn't want to know me.' Sometimes I would mock her gently, saying, 'That's right, I'd throw you out – tell you never to darken my door again.' But most times I would say, 'That's just how you feel about yourself.'

For the first year she resisted fiercely my idea that no one is intrinsically bad but that we can learn through what happens to us to experience ourselves as bad. Then she started to experiment with this idea. She would say to me, 'I say to myself, "Margaret, you're all right", but it doesn't work.'

She found our sessions together very painful. Silences forced her to writhe in embarrassment and say, 'I don't know what to say.' My travel caused her tremendous anxiety. When I discovered that she was one of those worriers who believe that worrying about something prevents it happening, I would ask her to be sure to worry about me when I was away and I would be sure to be safe. Postcards from me in far away places with the message 'Keep worrying' might make her laugh, but still she worried that I might leave her.

So the months rolled by. Then one day she arrived looking very miserable. She had phoned me the previous week when she was upset and unable to talk. Now I asked her what had happened, and she told me how she had been to the dentist and he had yelled at her and she had cried and cried. She told me how she thinks all the time of death. 'We're all going to die. What's the use? What's the use?' Then she told me about how she had dreamed that she had died. She had been run over by a huge car and then, as she walked up the street outside her home with her mother, her mother told her she was dead.

She mentioned the terrible thing she had done when she was a child, the thing which meant that the children in her street were forbidden to play with her. She told me how she had risked telling about one childish misdemeanour, something which shamed her, to her friend Sue and Sue had not rejected her. She had told Sue how her schoolfriend Betty had given her twopence to mind and she had spent it. Once she had told Sue about this and how ashamed she had been when her act had been discovered she found that the memory of this deed and the shame which accompanied it was not so painful.

Now she wanted to risk telling me about the greatest crime, the most shameful, terrible deed. But this was not easy. She looked at the clock and said, 'It's time to go.' It was into my lunchtime when I had planned to do some shopping, but I sat still and silent. Such a moment for Margaret might never come again.

Head down, speaking softly, with many blocks and hesitations, she said, 'We lived on the corner, the end of the terrace. Then there was Shirley and Peter, then Betty and her brothers, then Carol and Mary and Ann – they were Betty's cousins – and then the Smiths, and then my grandmother's house, at the other end of the terrace. We all used to play together. They all went to the

Protestant school and I went to the Catholic school. At school my best friend was Bernadette. I thought she was my best friend. She had a boyfriend Barry, and I thought I'd like to have a boyfriend, but there wasn't anyone, only Paul and he was awful. I didn't like him at all. He lived in a big house. We used to go there. He used to do things to me. I didn't like it but I let him. He said I'd like it but I didn't. We weren't the only ones, all of them did it – together – all of them.'

She remembered all their names. A roll call of former playmates.

'There was one boy, George, he used to tease me, and I didn't like it. I told Paul and he said he'd get George. He did, he got him, he tied him up and he did terrible things to him. I watched him – I didn't stop him – and afterwards, when George's parents found out, and the police came, I saw George's mother put her arms around him, and I thought, 'My mother won't do that to me.' When I got home, and the police took me home, my mother did put her arms around me, but I knew she didn't mean it. There was a policewoman and she took me and asked me lots of questions. She asked me who else did it, and I knew they all did but I couldn't say. She went on and on at me and I had to give her one name. I told her Betty and then they went to see her. Then we had to go up to the police station and there was this policeman there and he told me I was wicked. And afterwards, the parents, they wouldn't let their children play with me. Betty could play with them but I couldn't. I'd go and watch them, but I couldn't play with them. Sometimes Bernadette would let me play with her and her sisters, but if anyone came I had to hide. And if I had to go down the street to my grandmother's, they'd all call out to me, say things to me, it was terrible. They never played with me, not ever again. And they told other people about me. When I went to secondary school, some of the boys from the boys' high school knew, and they'd say things. That's why, when I left, I went right away. But I'm always frightened they'll find out where I am and they'll tell people and I'll lose my job and nobody will talk to me.'

She was crying. I gave her a tissue and said, 'That's the saddest story I've ever heard. That poor little girl.'

Margaret didn't believe me. For her the shame was never ending.

But the pain for Margaret was not simply the shame she continued to feel for a misdemeanour the like of which many children at that age commit. If it is not sexual exploration it is stealing, or joyriding, or, more recently, glue sniffing. It would be a rare adult who could put their hand on their heart and swear that between the age of six and sixteen they had never broken the law or transgressed the moral code. For Margaret there was a greater problem.

One day Margaret took me to task for never using her name when I was talking to her. I had to admit this. My conversational style is never to use the name of the person I am talking to except when I want to attract the person's attention, as in 'Hey, you'. I wish I could get in the habit of using people's names. That way I might remember them better. But I don't, and I apologized, and asked her why it was important that I used her name.

She said that it showed that I had not forgotten her name and thus had not forgotten her. She told me how she feels that when she vanishes from a person's sight she vanishes from that person's memory. Whenever she returns to work she is surprised to find that the people there remember her.

I said, 'I always remember who you are when you arrive', and she said, 'That's because you've written it in your diary.'

It is not just that she believes she is so insignificant that people do not remember her. She has a lurking suspicion that if everyone forgets her then her existence will cease. Most of the time she knows that believing that she exists only because other people think of her and that she might vanish at any time is nonsense, but being left alone is a fate to dread. Shame might make her want to hide away, but shame also gives her the feeling that other people are observing her and so she continues to exist. Shame gives her her sense of existence and so she dare not relinquish it.[6]

Many of us define ourselves in terms of our sense of guilt. A sense of impending punishment can hang over us, like a Damoclean sword, ready to smite us for deeds done or failed to be done. While shame relates to our identity, the person that we are, and guilt to what we do, we can come to believe that everything we do is wrong and that we can never do anything properly, so that a sense of guilt, a pervasive sense of fear, can so absorb our being that it becomes one of the structures by which we define ourselves. If we didn't feel guilty we wouldn't know what to do. As Constance once said to me, 'I was born guilty.'

Some children acquire this sense of guilt when they come to feel that it was their fault that their mother died or their parents split up, even though these events occurred when the children were far too young to understand them. Most of us acquired our sense of guilt when, as small children, we found ourselves locked in combat with a parent over where and when we should defecate, or whether we would eat, or because we had done something which made our parent very angry. We defended ourselves with anger and protest against a parent whom we saw as interfering and unjust. But we could not win the battle and bring it to an end. We went on battling, and as we did we recognized that the situation was becoming increasingly dangerous. We felt very keenly that our parent was wicked to do this, but if that were so it meant that the person on whom we depended was wicked. That realization undermined our security, and the fear that that brought was too much to bear. How could we get out of this situation and go back to feeling safe?

The solution was to accept our parent's definition of the situation. Power is always about who does the defining and who accepts the definitions. So we acquiesced, and instead of defining the situation a 'I am being unfairly punished by my wicked parent', we defined it as 'I am bad and am being justly punished by my good parent'.

This acceptance of our parent's definition might have extricated us from that dangerous situation, but the price we paid was a lifelong sense of guilt. The sins of commission and omission became an integral part of our relationships with others and, knowing our badness, we have to strive to be good. Or else what will happen to us if we are not good? We shall be abandoned.

This, as small children, is what we feared most of all, that our parents would abandon us and leave us alone, weak and defenceless in an alien world. We had learned what this was like when we were abandoned in our cot through a long dark night and no one came to comfort us, or our mother left us with strangers and did not return for aeons of time. We heard the threat of abandonment when our parents told us of bad children being sent to children's homes or of parents being driven to leave or die by their children's wickedness ('I can't stand you a moment longer', 'You'll be the death of me').

Threats of abandonment do not get less as a child gets older. A friend told me how when he was nine and causing his mother some bother she had packed a bag with his clothes and ordered him out of the house. He spent the day sitting at the front gate hoping to be let back in again and promising to be so very good. He is a man of unsurpassed goodness.

The fear of abandonment can underlie the whole of our experience of our existence and because it is always there, allowing no contrast with periods without it, we do not conceptualize it clearly and consciously. Without doing this we do not ask why we have this fear now and from whence it came.

Lorna had a nasty, life-threatening disease, cystic fibrosis, but she showed that by bravely and sensibly following a strict health regime this disease need not cut short one's life nor prevent one from leading an ordinary life. She had had to give up her work as a nurse but she had a loving, supportive husband, a wonderful daughter, a pleasant home, and a strong Christian faith which assured her that there was no reason to fear death. She could not understand why she should waken during the night consumed with panic nor why a black depression should immobilize her in a way that her illness never did.

Neither could she understand why her GP wanted her to talk to me. But she dutifully came along, and discovered that talking to me gave her something important that was missing from her life. At home she was addressed as wife, mother, daughter, daughter-in-law. Nobody talked to *her*. Now she had found someone who talked to her as her.

We talked about many things, the worry of her illness, the peculiarities of the medical profession, the responsibilities she carried for her family because she had always been the 'sensible, well-organized, reliable one'. We talked a great deal about her need to do everything perfectly. Visitors had to be entertained with hot meals and home-made cakes. The garden must be trim and neat, the house immaculate. 'I wouldn't dream of going out and leaving the washing up not done or a bed unmade,' she said.

I argued that she should let visitors fend for themselves and that housework should be kept to a minimum so that she had time and energy to do things which she found interesting and pleasant. At first she was doubtful, but one morning she told me, with triumph and laughter, 'I went to church on Sunday without making the bed first – but I closed the curtains so the neighbours couldn't see.'

Why did she set herself such high standards and always strive to meet them? True, she had a mother who always expected her daughter to be perfect and a credit to her, but why had she accepted the enormous demands that her mother made on her?

One day when she was telling me how fiercely she resisted going into hospital whenever her illness produced some complication and how miserable she felt when she was in hospital, she mentioned going into hospital when she was a child. I asked her about this and she described how she had been sent to a hospital when she was about seven. The hospital was housed in a castle and run with military efficiency. Parents were not allowed to visit and children had to do what they were told. They had to be neat and tidy, obedient and reliable, and there were punishments if they were not. When her parents left her there she dared not cry because her mother disapproved of tears. She thought that she might never see her parents again, but when, at last, after many months, she did go home she worried that she might be sent away again, abandoned and alone. So she tried very hard to be good.

Until we talked about these events in her childhood and uncovered the meaning these events had for her, Lorna had not seen the connection between these childhood experiences and her drive for perfection, her fear of hospitals and the terrible panics which came whenever she felt that she was completely and absolutely alone. Buried further was her anger at her parents who had abandoned her in the hospital and at her family who expected her to give up being herself and to be what they wanted her to be. She had not acknowledged this anger, lest it burst forth and her family, who would not tolerate anger, rejected her.

The sense of being abandoned arises from its opposite, the sense of being totally and securely held, which we felt in the womb. Expelled into the world, the baby has the first experience of being abandoned. Wise mothers wrap their baby in a cloth and hold it close, for babies who are never so held, though they may be fed and sheltered, grow grey and still, and die.

The need to be totally and securely held stays with us all our lives, and the ways in which the need can be met range from being physically held to knowing ourselves to be an accepted and loved member of our group. Important though this need is to all of us, there is no word for it in English. The closest word is 'dependence', from the Latin 'to hang from', but in our society to be dependent is not an admirable quality. Only weak and despicable people are dependent; strong, admirable people are independent. So we have to keep hidden our longing to be held secure in loving arms.

Not so in Japan. The Japanese language contains an important

from M. Heath, *Love All*, Blond and Briggs, London, 1982, p. 8.

word, *amae*, which has the root 'sweet'[7]. Sweet it is to rest secure in loving arms. Sweet it is to *amaeru*, to presume upon the secure and indulgent love given by another person. It is that sense of snuggling up, of coming home, not to shouts and yells and coldness and criticism, but to welcome, of being yourself and knowing that the people around you accept you as you are. The toddler who climbs on to an adult's lap, confident of a cuddle, the teenager who throws his dirty football shorts on the bathroom floor, confident that they will reappear in his drawer, clean and pressed, the wife who snuggles up to her husband in bed and confidently places her cold feet on his – all *amaeru*. We all long to *amaeru*, but so often we cannot do this.

The Greatest Fear

We need to be able to *amaeru*, but we need to be able to choose when to express this need and not to be for ever caught and held in arms, however loving, which do not give enough freedom for us to be our individual selves. As tiny babies we needed to *amaeru* for most of the time, but as we grew we needed those experiences which helped us to develop our sense of self. As we asserted our personal freedom in sitting unaided, crawling and walking, and experienced the joy of exploring the world outside the arms of indulgent love, we built within ourselves a structure which we came to know as our *self*.

As small children we knew that our self was a fragile structure. To maintain it we had to position ourselves between two dangerous extremes. One was the completely enclosing source of *amae*. The other was the danger of being completely and absolutely alone.

Both these extreme positions have the power to destroy our self, but each of us regards one of these extreme positions more dangerous than the other.

We live and have our being in two separate realities. One is the reality of what goes on outside us, what we call the world. The other is what goes on inside us, our thoughts, feelings, images, sensations and perceptions. To cope with living we have to be able to distinguish what goes on inside us from what goes on outside us, and to knit together in some consistent way our inner and outer realities so that we can find a meaning which enables us to carry our life forward and so that we can communicate with other people. We have to relate our thoughts and feelings to our perception of the outside world and we have to relate our perception of the outside world to our thoughts and feelings. This two-way process is what psychologists call 'reality testing', and the inefficiency of this process is their measure of madness.

Knitting these two realities together is not easy because to each of us they do not appear to be equally real. For some of us our inner reality is more real than our outer reality. For some of us our outer reality is more real than our inner reality.

Not only does one reality appear less real, but it also contains a danger.

For those people for whom outer reality is more real than inner reality, inner reality contains a danger which is felt as an emptiness, a vacancy from which all kinds of unknown and unknowable things can arise. Such people will express this by saying, 'It's not wise to introspect too much' or 'I spend too much time trying to understand myself'. For them *amae*, being held close by outer reality, is not dangerous. What is dangerous is for outer reality to drop away and for one to be left alone and isolated, a vacancy in an emptiness.

For those people for whom inner reality is more real than outer reality, outer reality contains a danger which is felt as an unknown and unknowable territory from which all kinds of uncontrolled and uncontrollable forces can arise. Such people have no anxiety about introspection, for within themselves is where they live their life, but they often speak of needing peace, which means a quietening down of, or distancing oneself from, outer reality. For them outer reality dropping away and leaving them isolated is not dangerous, for they live within their inner reality. What is dangerous is *amae*, being held close by outer reality, because out of outer reality can come the forces which confuse, overwhelm and destroy.

When we are coping with our lives and having no difficulty in knitting the outer and inner realities together we can be unaware of the differences in the qualities of the realities we perceive. But once we come under stress the differences in the two realities become more pronounced, and if the stress continues and increases we become less and less effective in knitting our inner and outer realities together. Some of us run away from the emptiness we find within and busy ourselves with the outside world, while some of us withdraw into ourselves and shut out the confusion outside.

A simpler way of discovering which reality is more real and how we experience our existence and our annihilation of our self is to go through a procedure of questions and answers which is called 'laddering'. This is a technique which I use in teaching and rarely in therapy. For a television programe, *The Mind Box*, I demonstrated this method with Sandy, a psychiatric nurse. While Sandy and I were seen looking at and driving cars in some dashing and bizarre sequences of film made on an empty airstrip, our conversation went as follows:

DOROTHY Sandy, we're going to play a little game. It's called laddering, and in this we'll start with something quite trivial, and then go on to something very important, but the first thing I'm going to ask you is, can you give me the names of three kinds of cars?

SANDY Yes, Rover, Triumph and Ford.

DOROTHY Now can you tell me one way in which two of them are the same and the other one is different?

SANDY Yes, Rover and Triumph are all part of British Leyland and Ford is an independent company.

DOROTHY And which would you prefer, a car from British Leyland or one from an independent company?

SANDY I'd prefer a Ford from an independent company.

DOROTHY Why is it important to have a car from an independent company?

SANDY I think I prefer something that's somewhat unusual, something different.

DOROTHY   And why is it important to have something that's different?

SANDY   In some way, I suppose, I get admiration from other people.

DOROTHY   Why is it important to have the admiration of other people?

SANDY   The admiration of other people makes me feel good. I suppose it makes me feel . . . it helps to establish my existence.

DOROTHY   What would you do if there wasn't anyone to give you admiration, if you were completely isolated?

SANDY   Completely isolated? I can't actually foresee myself in total isolation at all.

DOROTHY   But suppose you were completely and absolutely isolated for an indefinite period?

SANDY   In that case I should think I would be withered up, I'd die away. That would be the end of my existence, I think.[8]

With that Sandy was seen alone in a vast empty space. He looked miserable, but that was because he found making a television programme a nerve-racking experience. In ordinary life he knows he needs people and he is effective in meeting this need by having a talent for friendship and doing a job which involves people.

We use the term 'laddering' because in this process of question and answer we begin with a trivial decision and value judgement and proceed to more and more general, abstract value judgements until we reach the top of the ladder, the ultimate value judgement, which is how we experience our existence and how we experience our annihilation.

Annihilation of the self is our greatest fear. It is worse than bodily death, for after death we can imagine our self, or some important aspect of our self, our children, our work, the remembrances of friends, continuing on, but after annihilation there is nothing of our

self to carry on. We have gone, brushed aside like chalk off a blackboard, engulfed like a raindrop in an ocean, consumed like a dead leaf in a fire, swirled away like a puff of smoke when the wind blows. After annihilation our body may continue to function but that which was our self has gone.

Sandy was one of those people who experience their existence as being part of a group and their annihilation as isolation. His outer reality is more real for him than his inner reality. Had Sandy been one of those people for whom inner reality is more real than outer reality our producer, Angela Tilby, would have had greater difficulty in finding images to accompany our words. Sandy may have made the same choice of cars on the same grounds of wanting something unusual, but he would have gone on from there to talk in terms of personal development and achievement. I would have asked him what would happen to him if he were unable to do this and he would have spoken about his self (not his body) being overwhelmed and destroyed by chaos. Not easy images for television to supply, but a fate very real for those of us who experience our existence as the continual development of individual achievement, clarity and authenticity and our annihilation as chaos.

All of us fall into one or other of these groups. We are either, as my friend Sue Llewellyn refers to herself, a 'people junkie' or we are absorbed in the study and development of our inner experience. The words that are used to distinguish these groups are most unsatisfactory. Those people who experience their existence as the development of individual achievement, clarity and authenticity are called introverts and those who experience their existence as being part of a group and their annihilation as isolation are called extraverts. 'Introvert' and 'extravert' are words which are used in many different connections, but here it is well to remember that introverts can acquire excellent social skills and can appear to be greatly 'extraverted' while there are many lonely and shy extraverts.

In teaching sessions on laddering I find that one or two people will say, 'But I'm both an extravert and an introvert.'

In the final analysis we are either an extravert or an introvert, and when our backs are to the wall, in the extremes of danger, there is just one construction of our existence and annihilation that we know. But in ordinary life we have to make conscious attempts to learn the skills in which we are naturally deficient. Many introverts learn to be highly skilled in social interactions; many extraverts learn to be highly skilled in experiencing, labelling and understanding their inner reality.

Unless we come across a psychologist who is keen on laddering we rarely make conscious and explicit how we experience our existence and our annihilation. We simply use our experience of our existence and annihilation as the basis of everything we do. Sometimes it is hidden. Sometimes it comes out clearly in what we say about ourselves.

Linda Evans, Krystle Carrington of *Dynasty*, revealed herself as an extravert when she said:

> My main purpose as a child, and as a young adult, was to be loved. I was passive and submissive at any cost. The idea of rejection was frightening to me. I've broken out of that mould by now; but I still have this feeling for anyone who is *warm* . . . There's an old Chinese saying, which I apply in my everyday life, that 'everyone you meet is your mirror'.[9]

In contrast, Edna O'Brien, when interviewed by Miriam Gross, revealed herself as an introvert.

> *To what extent did she feel that writing was a way of explaining oneself, of making up for the failure to communicate fully in ordinary life?*
>
> It's a stab at it. I think it was Beckett who said – I'm paraphrasing – that you write in order to say the things you can't say. It's a cry, or a scream, or a song. Whatever form it takes, it is definitely an attempt to explain things and put them right.
>
> *Did she feel that if women had more confidence and a more active role in the affairs of the world, they would invest less energy in their emotional life?*

I do. But, ironically, I think that much as our longings might hurt us, they also enrich us. Because finally, when the curtain is down, I mean, when one is dying, what really matters is what took place inside, in one's own head, one's own psyche. And people who acknowledge the relative failure or paucity in areas of their lives – either in love or in work – are in a way more blessed than the others who pretend or who put on masks. Though you suffer by not being confident and you suffer by not being befriended or loved as you might like to be, you are the sum of all that need and at least you're alive, you are not a robot and you are not a liar.[10]

These are two successful people, successful not only in fame and wealth but in developing a way of life which allows them *to be themselves*, to live within and to extend that which gives them their sense of existence. Linda Evans is eminently lovable, on screen and off, as they say. Edna O'Brien uses everything that comes to her, whether it causes her pain or not, to develop her own clarity and understanding in ways which meet with enormous public approval. But when we do not develop a way of life which allows us to be ourselves, when we cannot live within and extend that which gives us our sense of existence we suffer great fear.

Ken had come to be cured. As soon as he sat down he announced, 'I have a good, secure job. I've got my own house and no money worries. I'm forty-two and I'm in good health. There is no logical reason why I should be anxious.'

He had been off work for six months. He was so overwhelmed by anxiety that he could not attempt the simplest task. He spent most of his time going over in his mind technical work he had done in past years in the homes of neighbours and friends, trying to convince himself that he had not made any mistakes and that the people living there were not in danger.

He was an engineer, a practical problem solver. 'That's my job,' he said. 'When there's a problem, they come to me to solve it.'

The miners' strike had created a series of problems. As he would solve one, another would be created. There was no way all these problems could be solved simultaneously. He couldn't afford to let his staff and his superiors see that there were practical problems which he couldn't solve.

A friend, 'the most logical and competent chap I know', had committed suicide. Ken had found him. 'It didn't upset me particularly,' he said. But, in fact, inside he was greatly upset.

He helped people. I asked him why. 'It gives me satisfaction.'

In later discussions Ken told me how his mother, a very strong-willed woman, had insisted that he achieve and that he help people. He had to accept what she said because she had ways of enforcing her orders. He told me how one day, when she discovered that he had lost his best sweater on his way home from school, she had come to the cinema where he was happily watching a film and, in front of all those people, had hauled him home to look for his sweater. The shame he felt then was the shame he feared if, through his own carelessness, he caused the people he had tried to help any suffering.

He had come on his own. I asked after his wife.

'She says I'm getting her down.' No, they didn't discuss things much.

At that first meeting it was not until he was near to leaving that he said, 'My sons have their own friends now. They don't need me any more.'

Ella nearly died in a road accident. Four years later she is still weak and shaky and prone to tears. She had not returned to work, and she found driving a car a frightening experience.

'I just want to hide myself away,' she said. 'I don't want people to see me like this. I used to be so confident and in control.'

She had always had to be competent, but only in the feminine skills of housekeeping. 'My mother thought that a girl didn't need an education. A woman's fulfilment was to be a wife and mother. I won a scholarship to grammar school but she wouldn't let me take it up. I got married and had a family, but I've always done something more. I've always worked. But now, I'm back to where I started. I've achieved nothing. I'm weak and frightened, and I'm just what my mother wanted, a wife and mother and nothing else. No personal achievement. And that's what life's about, isn't it?'

Ella's statement that life is about personal achievement is just what an introvert would say, though introverts cover a wide range of activities in what they call personal achievement. Extraverts say that life is about other people, though they cover a wide range of possible relationships with other people. But both extraverts and introverts need to achieve and they both need other people.

When we are small children we are aware that we have certain talents and powers. We may not be able to put a name to them, but we know that whenever we used them we felt an enormous joy. The passionate pleasure of acting creatively and successfully in and upon the world has always given puny human beings the will and power to go on striving in a vast and dangerous universe. As children, if we are lucky, our talents and powers are approved of and encouraged by the adults around us. If so, we can then use our talents and powers to develop and make safe our self. If we are extraverts we use our talents and powers to gather people around us and keep them there and to fill the empty space within us. If we are introverts we develop our talents and powers to gain clarity and personal achievement and to relate our inner reality to the outer world.

But if as children the adults around us do not recognize or approve of our talents and powers, we are forced to neglect and to deny them and to learn skills which we know are not in us. This leaves us with a sense of feeling 'not right', in some way always an imposter. We are left with a sense of longing. We might not be able to put a name to the object of the longing, or we might know the name but be too ashamed to admit it. How could this delicate wife and mother admit that all she ever wanted was to sail her own boat round the world? How could this rugby-playing company director admit that all he ever wanted was to be principal dancer in a ballet? How their families would laugh if they said these things! Perhaps they dare not even admit these longings to themselves. Then all they become aware of are certain passionate dislikes. She 'cannot stand' Claire Francis, while he refuses to accompany his wife to the ballet, saying that he has better things to do than watch 'those poofs'. The prevalence of envy in our society shows just how many children have been prevented from developing their talents and powers and being themselves.

Both extraverts and introverts need other people. Extraverts need other people to establish and maintain their existence. Introverts need other people to help them gain clarity by setting standards and giving approval. When I was discussing this with Mick McHale, I asked him which for him was the more real, his internal or external reality, what went on inside him or what went on outside him?

He said, 'Internal reality is far more real. I tend to believe that far more than my external reality.' He went on to say that while he wanted approval, when he did actually gain it it no longer meant anything to him. 'I think the difference is, if I've got things sorted out and I know I've done a good job, I can reward myself, but if it's on the periphery of that, if I'm not sure whether I've done a good job or taken the right direction, then it's very important and I really appreciate it.'

'So getting approval makes things more clear for you.'

'Yes.'[11]

If extraverts are left in isolation they are in danger of being overwhelmed by the emptiness within them. Under stress they continue to perceive their outer reality as ordinary, but it becomes oddly distant. If introverts are left in isolation they are in danger of retreating into their inner reality and losing the ability to distinguish inner from outer reality. Under stress they find that outer reality becomes increasingly strange. We need other people to help us structure ourselves and our world, but it is other people who threaten the structures we create.

How We Create and Defend Ourselves

Everyone knows that no two people are the same and no two people see things in the same way. This knowledge not only enables us to see every person as a unique individual but also to understand that the meaning we give to ourselves and our world is made up of structures which we have created. Reality, whatever that may be, does not come directly to us but is shaped and structured by the way our senses and our language create the structures which we call meaning. We live and have our being in meaning. Everything we perceive has a meaning, even though sometimes the meaning we give is 'This is meaningless'. Perception is meaning: meaning is perception. We cannot step outside our world of meaning for we cannot conceive of an existence where meaning does not exist. We each have to live in our own world of meaning where, as the Talmud says, '*We do not see things as they are. We see them as we are.*'

We use the meaning we create to predict. The predictions are implicit in the meanings we use. If someone says to me, 'You'll find a chair in the next room', I expect that I shall find the chair standing on the floor. I would be surprised to find the chair floating near the ceiling because my meaning 'chair' contains the meaning that chairs are found on the floor, not on the ceiling.

Sometimes the predictions we have created turn out to be wrong. This is always disturbing. Chairs which float in space may not meet my needs, while if I predict that 'Edward will be home before me', I feel uneasy when I turn into our lane and see our house in darkness. I immediately create other meanings – 'He's been delayed at work', 'There'll be a message on the answer phone', 'He's had an accident'. All these new meanings, which may calm or alarm me, have one reassuring effect. They aim to show that I can still create structures which give the world I live in a sense of regularity and predictable patterns.

Whenever our predictions fail or appear to have failed we feel frightened, not simply because this part of our experience is different from what we thought it was but also it shows us that ourselves and our world which we believed was so real is nothing more than the structures which we have created. It is frightening to be reminded of the insubstantial world we inhabit. It is frightening to discover that we got part of it wrong, for if we are wrong in this we could be wrong in everything. If you discover that the one person you regarded as your true and everlasting love has been unfaithful then it is not just your marriage you have to reconstrue. You have to reassess every aspect of yourself and your life. That is why the ending of any intimate relationship can be so painful.

When we discover that our structures do not conform to and predict reality we can simply reconstrue. We can say, 'I was wrong' and go on to develop new structures which we hope have a closer fit to reality. But we don't always do this. More frequently we hang on to our structures and try to hammer reality into fitting them. If the door we predicted to be open won't budge when we touch it we give it a shove and a kick. When people won't accept that our definition of reality is right we argue with them, or abuse them, or injure and kill them. When we discover that there is a discrepancy between the structures we have created and the reality presented we react with fear, frustration, anger and aggression (and, sometimes, depression).

Aggression, like everything else in our world, has good and bad implications. Bad, because the expression of aggression can create more danger, and good, because aggression gives us the drive to be creative, to find solutions and to survive.

A baby who is not aggressive does not survive. Our aggression first appears as greed, the impulse of a baby to suck. It is this impulse which pushes the baby forward into growth and development as a person.

The impulses of greed and aggression seem not just to be concerned with finding ways of relieving hunger pangs. Developmental psychologists who study young babies describe them as being very interested in their environment. Babies are curious about the world around them, and they seem to be carrying out experiments of their own so as to make sense of what is happening to them. It may be lights, or sounds, or things that move which interest them, but, most of all, it is 'conversations' with other people. Daniel Stern described how, in the first six months of life,

> the baby will have learned how to invite his mother to play and then initiate an interaction with her; he will have become expert at maintaining and modulating the flow of a social exchange; he will have acquired the signals to terminate or avoid an interpersonal encounter, or just place it temporarily in a 'holding' pattern. In general, he will have mastered most of the basic signals and conventions so that he can perform the 'moves' and run off patterned sequences in step with those of his mother, resulting in the dance which we recognize as social interactions. This biologically designed choreography will serve as a prototype for all his later interpersonal exchanges.[12]

Babies find such 'interpersonal exchanges' to be great fun, but these activities have greater meaning and purpose than just fun. In the first six months of life babies have the most important task of their life to achieve, the task of becoming a person. If they fail to achieve it they never enter the company of the human race, but wander, bizarre and fragmented, alone in a world they can never comprehend. If they do not achieve this task well enough, if they just cobble together an end result instead of creating something firm and permanent, they build the project of their lives on shifting sands, and when in later years life deals them blows, as life is wont to do, their shaky edifice crumbles, and they find themselves again in the disjointed, fragmented world of the infant, only now it is filled with terror.

Some babies fail to achieve this task or perform it badly because they lack the intellectual equipment to do so. Some of the neurological deficits which prevent a baby from carrying out this task are understood, such as a damaged cerebral cortex, while others, as suggested by genetic studies of schizophrenia, are no more than inspired guesses.

But neurological deficits cannot be a total explanation as to why some babies become autistic or schizophrenic children and why others in later years become psychotic. Many babies of undoubtedly limited intellectual ability develop a very clear sense of their own self. This has become abundantly clear in recent years when most mentally handicapped children in wealthy countries are no longer herded into blank, regimented hospital wards but are brought up in ordinary homes as ordinary children with a few special needs. It seems that no matter what kind of intellectual ability and genetic endowment we bring into the world, it depends very largely on what the world gives us as to whether or not we achieve a coherent sense of self.

Our present understanding of the importance of the first six months of life came first from psychoanalysis, in the observation and analysis of small children and in the analysis of psychotic adults, and second from the developmental psychologists who make detailed analyses of the behaviour of babies and their 'caregivers'. Both psychoanalysts and developmental psychologists have their own obscure jargon, but a translation of each into ordinary language reveals that they are, to a very large extent, saying the same things.

Babies come into the world with what Daniel Stern called 'formidable capabilities to establish human relatedness'.[13] They can unite their gaze, their facial expressions, and their movements in ways which attract adults to respond. That is, from birth they are aware of their external reality and can act upon it. Initially babies cannot discriminate their external from their internal reality because they have no concept of the passing of time with the reappearance of certain experiences. They live entirely in the present, and so are aware only of their present state. Thus, for the first few months a baby, as the psychoanalyst Donald Winnicott said, 'does not know *he is the same as himself*' when he is feeling hungry, or being bathed, or asleep, or awake.[14]

Small babies are in what Winnicott called an 'unintegrated state'. He wrote, 'There are long stretches in a normal infant's life in which a baby does not mind whether he is many bits or one whole being . . . providing that from time to time he comes together and feels something.'[15] It is the process of sensitive mothering which allows a baby to gather the bits together and become one person.

This capacity to exist in one state and then in another, and to perceive no connection between one and the other allows us to create the defence mechanism of disassociation which is an essential part of all the defence mechanisms which we use. We can deal with our fear by in some way disassociating ourselves from it.

Stern described how babies combine sensations, movements and feelings into a 'sensori-motor-affective unit' of experience which then combines with other such units to form the schemas or structures by which we know ourselves and our world and act in our world. While particular sensations, movements and feelings belong together, we have little difficulty in uncoupling the parts of these units. 'For instance, the memory of an emotional scene with a loved one can be recalled in exquisite visual and verbal detail, but the feelings associated with the incident remain out of awareness.' (This is the defence mechanism of isolation, much favoured by introverts.) 'The reverse is also found, where strong feelings are experienced or recalled but are unattached and disintegrated from their sensori-motor context.'[16] (This is the defence mechanism of repression, much favoured by extraverts.)

We may have existed quite contentedly in our unintegrated state, but once we gain even a modest degree of integration a possible return to this unintegrated state becomes extremely frightening. We perceive it, not as unintegration, but disintegration, the annihilation of our *self*. Winnicott wrote of this threat of annihilation as being 'a very real primitive anxiety, long antedating any anxiety that includes death in its description'.[17]

Babies are naturally sensitive to the dangers of disintegration. They come equipped with a means of avoiding unpleasantness. If, for instance, an adult is busily and insensitively playing with a baby and the baby finds it all too much, he 'averts his gaze, turns his face away rapidly, and may also withdraw rapidly'.[18] Babies will also make this kind of withdrawal when they try to attract their mother's attention and fail. This reaction is a precursor to the way we, when older, withdraw when we feel rebuffed and rejected.

Such withdrawals are a necessary part of a baby's experience, the kind of trial and error from which we can learn so much. But when the environment impinges on the baby in ways which go beyond the capacity of the baby to deal with them, or when the environment persistently fails to respond to the baby's attempts to engage it in discourse, then the baby cannot get on with the business of gathering the experiences of different states into one coherent rule.

Part of the coherence which the baby has to achieve is to locate this sense of wholeness which we call the self in the body. As adults we may take for granted the idea that our self and our body are conterminous, but it is something that we have learned, and, having learned it, we can choose to forget it or doubt it. We can easily imagine, and we often do, our self, or our soul, leaving our body and travelling to other places. We might regard this as fantasy, just a story to delight children, or as a literal, unquestioned truth. We can believe that when we die we go to Heaven, or remain on earth as a ghost or spirit, or, having slipped inside a newborn baby, live another life.

I spoke of us experiencing our self as having the same physical boundaries as our body, but in fact people vary in how they see their self relating to their body. The self can be valued more than the body, the spirit being of more value than crude, animal flesh and base matter. There are many people who hold the opposite view. For many people who regard themselves as scientific thinkers, it is nonsense to talk of 'the self' or 'the soul'. We are bodies, bio-machines, and all talk of selves, soul and spirits is nothing more than froth or bubble. If such scientific thinkers meet up with someone who has been influenced by the concepts of psychotherapy they can be accused of having a 'headtrip', or living only in their head. This accusation reflects one of the ways we specifically locate ourselves in our bodies.

For some of us our self is very much in our brain and, from the power controls there, directs the rest of our body. This concept of the brain as the seat of the self is largely a post-Renaissance Western European idea. In earlier times and in other cultures the vital centre of the self lies in other parts of the body. In the Hindu tradition 'the psychic energy activates the seven *chakras*, or "centres of psychospiritual consciousness" which . . . control our physical, emotional, mental and spiritual "bodies". . . The *chakras* (pour) their respective virtues into the human body-mind system . . . Upset *chakras*, on the other hand, are responsible for much psychic and physical distress.'[19] Within Western culture different functions of the self are located in different parts of the body. Our heart becomes the location of love ('I was brokenhearted when he died'), or of truth ('He spoke from the heart'), our stomach the location of our disgust ('You make me sick'), and our bowels the location of our hate ('You give me the shits').

The way in which we learn to locate our self in our body lays down the foundation for later psychosomatic illnesses where how we perceive ourselves and our world plays a major part in the creation of a physical illness. Perhaps, too, in those out-of-body experiences which some people who have barely escaped death through illness or injury have later described, the person has, in an effort to preserve the self, relinquished without fear the belief that the self resides in the body and returned to the knowledge that a small baby has, that our experience of consciousness need not be located in our body. Perhaps this is why so many people, despite their previous physical suffering, become in the moments of dying so peaceful. Life has a continuity and a oneness.

A much less benign return to the infant state of an insecure location of the self in the body is classified by psychiatry as one of the symptoms of schizophrenia. If a baby does not have these regular, reassuring experiences which are necessary for the baby to learn to locate his self in his body, so that there is always some doubt and uncertainty about his self and his body, then in later life, in periods of stress, this doubt and uncertainty can intrude and overwhelm. Often the first sign that a person is having difficulty in holding his self together is anxiety that his body is changing. A person might feel that his nose has grown to a grotesque size, or that his genitals are disappearing and that he is changing sex.

In psychosis, too, a person makes a painful return to the state where we do not know whether what we are feeling is located inside or outside us. Is this unpleasant sensation coming from outside me (the bathwater is too hot) or inside me (hunger pangs)? As babies we have to learn to experience and locate our feelings (pain, fear, anger, aggression, greed, love) inside us and with the recognition and response to these feelings from people outside us we build up a notion of our self as a person. A baby who has not received sufficient regular, reassuring experiences to build up a secure concept of what is inside himself and what is outside can in later life, when greatly frightened, lose this distinction and so experience himself as empty of feeling while his environment is charged with malign forces.

Developmental psychologists and psychoanalysts, when observing the interactions of mothers and babies, in feeding, bathing, changing and playing, have noted that, while taking account of the baby's feelings and expectancies, mothers organize these interactions so they have some temporal patterning, a beginning, a middle and an end, a kind of total happening. 'Total happenings', wrote Winnicott, 'enable babies to catch hold of time.'[20]

He went on, 'Do you see how the middle of things can be enjoyed (or, if bad, tolerated) only if there is a strong sense of start and finish? By allowing your baby time for total experiences, and by taking part in them, you gradually lay a foundation for the child's ability eventually to enjoy all sorts of experiences without jumpiness.'[21]

Mothers who organize their caregiving activities without regard to their baby's feelings and expectancies, or who are themselves so disorganized that their activities rarely form a total happening, make it very difficult for the baby to develop a sense of time and with that a sense of self. They also create in their baby great fear. We all know how anxious we can become when we are waiting for some event to come to a conclusion, and babies are no exception. Some of us, in later life, deliberately create a conclusion to an event, no matter how painful and destructive this may be, rather than endure the pain and fear of waiting. A man may say to himself, 'I love my wife but I know that she will eventually leave me when she discovers how really awful I am, so I'll do something terrible to her now and get it over with.' A schoolchild, perhaps less consciously, expecting punishment for some misdeed which her parents or teachers have yet to discover, may walk in front of a moving bus or fall down a flight of stairs, and count herself as punished for her misdeed. Perhaps those depressed and anxious adults who are convinced that the future holds nothing for them but pain and disappointment, that every good event is inevitably followed by something bad, had as babies so many inconclusive happenings that they could never develop the wisdom of knowing that all things come to an end.

Of course, we can never know for certain that *all* things come to an end until we have observed all things, and we can never live long enough to do that. So 'all things come to an end' is an *hypothesis*. While we are waiting for something to come to an end, like waiting for someone we love to return home, or deciding what we shall have for dinner, we have a *fantasy* of this waiting coming to an end. In our mind's eye we see the door opening and our loved one coming in, or we attend to the current state of our digestive organs and imagine the particular food which will satisfy that state. Sometimes our digestive organs say 'steak' and at other times 'a nice salad'. So in some way our *hypothesis* and our *fantasy* are the same. It is just a matter of which word we wish to use.

Developmental psychologists, being scientific thinkers, use the word *hypothesis*. Babies, they say, create hypotheses and test them out. Every baby is born a scientist. Psychoanalysts, being primarily interested in what goes on inside individuals, use the word *fantasy*. Babies, they say, create images. Every baby is born an artist.

They are both right. We are born both scientists and artists, and if we are extremely lucky, the world lets us continue being both scientist and artist for the rest of our lives. Most people are not so lucky.

Our first hypothesis and fantasy has to do with hunger and being fed. Winnicott wrote:

Imagine a baby who has never had a feed. Hunger turns up, and the baby is ready to conceive of something; out of need the baby is ready to create a source of satisfaction, but there is no previous experience to show the baby what to expect. If at this moment the mother places her breast where the baby is ready to expect something, and if there is plenty of time for the infant to feel around, with mouth and hands, and perhaps a sense of smell, the baby 'creates' just what there is to be found. The baby eventually gets the illusion that this real breast is exactly the thing that was created out of need, greed, and the first impulses of primitive loving. Sight, smell, and taste register somewhere, and after a while the baby may be creating something like the very breast the mother has to offer. A thousand times before weaning a baby may be given just this particular introduction to external reality by one woman, the mother. A thousand times the feeling has existed that what was wanted was created, and was found to be there. From this develops a belief that the world can contain what is wanted and needed, with the result that the baby has hope that there is a live relationship between inner reality and external reality, between innate primary creativity and the world at large which is shared by all.[22]

For the baby 'the world at large' is represented by the mother. Just as the baby has to build up one coherent hypothesis or fantasy which we call the self ('I am the same person over time and in different places') so he has to build up one coherent hypothesis or fantasy (here the developmental psychologists talk of an 'internal repres- entation' and psychoanalysts talk of an 'internal object') of the mother. At first, babies know only 'the feeding mother', 'the bathing mother', 'the playing mother', and only gradually do these images merge. It may be, as Stern suggests,[23] that the appearance of 'the playing mother' during the appearances of 'the feeding mother' and 'the bathing mother' gives the baby the idea that there is just one mother who comes and goes but does not change.

However, some mothers rarely play. They may be withdrawn into their own psychotic world, or they may be too depressed to take delight in their baby, or they may be distracted by poverty and overwork, or they may have husbands who are jealous of the baby, or powerful mothers and mothers-in-law who warn against 'spoiling' the baby. What do babies do then, when they need to play in the same way as they need to eat and sleep?

Some babies, said Winnicott, use their intellect to try to extract from an inadequate environment the sustenance they need. This may protect the baby initially, but it can have long-term de- leterious effects, for such intellectual effort may prevent the natural development of other intellectual and creative talents.

If we are born either extravert or introvert, if our nervous system predisposes us to be more keenly aware of either our internal or our external reality, then there could be significant differences in how extravert and introvert babies deal with an inadequate environment. Extravert babies may be better than introvert babies at attracting attention, when the environment does not stimulate them enough (extraverts are always such likeable people, are they not?), and may be able to tolerate higher levels of stimulation in a very stimulating environment than can introvert babies. Perhaps this is why those people who later in life when under great stress suffer a disintegration of the self and become schizophrenic tend to be introverts.

Whatever the cause, when a baby has failed to make a satis- factory integration of his self he is always in danger of disin- tegration, and the possibility of the annihilation of the self is a terrible fear. No matter how well integrated we are, we all know about this fear because we know that the cruel world can take away the conditions which are necessary for our self to survive. We all fear having disintegration and annihilation thrust upon us. However, if we are satisfactorily integrated we can enjoy choosing to return occasionally to an unintegrated state where we can simply *be*, without regard to past or future or elsewhere. On this, Winnicott wrote:

> It is sometimes assumed that in health the individual is always integrated, as well as living in his own body, and able to feel that the world is real. There is, however, much sanity which has a symptomatic quality, being charged with the denial or fear of madness, fear and denial of the innate capacity of every human being to become unintegrated, depersonalized, and to feel that the world is unreal. Sufficient lack of sleep produces these conditions in anyone. Through artistic expression we can hope to keep in touch with our primitive selves where the most intense feelings and even fearfully acute sensations derive, and we are poor indeed if we are only sane.[24]

The way to be 'only sane' is to deny fear.

Chapter Two

Fear denied

We can't live without denying. We have to shut things out. We have to say to ourselves, 'No, no, that's not there. It didn't happen. I'll take no notice.' If we didn't do this we'd be overwhelmed by the multitude of stuff going on around us and inside us.

We ignore the noise of the traffic outside our house while we concentrate on watching television. We ignore our sense of tiredness while we push on to finish an important task. We ignore our fear as we rush to save someone else from danger, and when we are commended for our bravery we say, 'It was nothing. Anyone would have done the same.'

We all know that such denial is necessary in times of stress. By denying painful facts and emotions we become brave. But such denial is just for a brief period of time. Later we can acknowledge the noise of the traffic, or our tiredness, or, in the privacy of our own home, feel the fear unfelt at the time of danger. Now our experience accords with reality and all is well.

But if we don't do this, if we go on and on denying what is happening, then we start to get into difficulties because our experience accords less and less with reality. Denying the aggravating noise of the traffic we get angry with our children for being unruly. (Our unadmitted thought is, 'I bought this house and I'm not going to admit I made a mistake.') Denying awareness of tiredness, we refuse to rest and so become ill. (Our rule for living is, 'It is my responsibility to see that my family are perfectly happy all the time.') Denying awareness of fear, we feel pain and breathlessness, suspect a faulty heart and await imminent death. (Our conscience knows, 'My father would despise me as a coward if I admitted being afraid.')

Denying Fear as 'Character'

Long-term denial puts us further and further out of touch with reality. If we start this kind of denial early enough and practise it assiduously enough we forget that we are denying and this way of living becomes our character. The long-term denial of fear produces a number of different kinds of 'characters'.

There is the person who is always *practical, sensible and down-to-earth*. Such people never indulge in fantasy or consider those questions for which there are no practical answers. I meet these characters frequently in the National Health Service. There are the administrators who divide the number of patients attending by the number of staff in a psychotherapy department, decide that the resulting figure is 'uneconomic' and close the department, all without taking the trouble to find out what actually goes on in such places. And there are the psychiatrists who assure a frightened, depressed woman that she has a good husband, a nice home, and that she should count her blessings, without once pausing to consider what it must be like to be forced by an unwanted pregnancy and poverty to share a house with a man who beats you up on a Friday night and enjoys his marital rights on a Saturday night and to know that such a future stretches ahead with death as the only escape. I have tried to explain the subtleties and complexities of such matters to such administrators and psychiatrists, but it is like trying to explain colour to the innately blind.

From what I have seen of politicians, I suspect that many of them are such 'characters'. Sometimes such people do good and useful work, but all too often their no-nonsense attitude makes other people feel not understood as their fears are belittled. Such 'characters' maintain their peace of mind at the expense of other people.

There is the person who is always *busy keeping busy*. This is not a successful denial of fear, because the busy person is well aware that stopping being busy means becoming frightened. But rather than face this fear, the busy person keeps dashing around, doing things, at the expense of loved ones who would dearly like to be given a generous share of the busy person's time or be allowed to order their own lives, and their bedrooms, in their own way, not the busy person's way. Busy people dash around, doing things, at the expense too of their own needs and health.

Betty's husband Roy had come to see me because he could not work. Betty was surprised when I asked if she would come along to one of our meetings. There was nothing wrong with her. But if it would help Roy she would come. So she did, and talked about herself.

'I've always got to be doing something. I can watch television, if I'm knitting, but I can't settle to reading, and I just couldn't sit doing nothing. It annoys me to see people doing nothing. I vacuum and dust right through every day. I'd feel the house isn't cleaned properly if I vacuumed one day and dusted the next.'

'She's always doing housework,' said Roy, who, depressed and unemployed, often sat doing nothing.

'I've always worked,' said Betty. 'I brought home my first pay packet the week before I turned fourteen. My mother expected us to work. There were six of us. You couldn't leave one job before you had the next lined up.'

But she shouldn't work so hard now. She has angina, and the doctor says she should rest.

'He says I should rest and put my feet up every afternoon. But I can't do that. It wouldn't be right.'

'Why wouldn't that be right?' I asked.

'I don't know. I've always been like that. I'm that sort of person.'

She said that she was frightened of dying, frightened of having a stroke and ending up like her mother, a helpless invalid. She was no stranger to fear. She knew what it was like to be swept by sudden, drenching fear. 'I need to be out of the house and with people.'

She spoke of her childhood. 'I was the third of three daughters and my mother didn't want me. She told me that. She said when she had me she didn't look at me for three days.'

So Betty learned early the dread of annihilation, and the way of keeping it at bay by earning her right to exist by working hard. She preferred to risk death by heart failure than face the greater fear of being annihilated by abandonment and rejection.

Betty worried a good deal but she dealt with her worries by working. There are many 'characters' who deny their fear by worrying. '*I'm a worrier*,' they say, in the same way as they would say, 'I'm a left-hander' or 'I'm a Gemini', something you are born with, something you can't change.

Worrying is not good for the health. A churning stomach, tense muscles, and an inability to concentrate on the task in hand can produce stomach ulcers, backache and accident injuries. But worrying does have advantages, and committed worriers are reluctant to give them up.

First, being a worrier allows you to concentrate on small worries rather than a big fear. A worrier can avoid thinking about her fear that her husband is being unfaithful to her by worrying about the state of the carpets in her home, or avoid thinking about the fear that the economic recession will make his firm bankrupt by worrying about the state of his car. This way of worrying uses a lot of energy, but it does allow you to shut out a great deal of unpleasant reality and saves you from having to bother about the needs of other people.

Second, a worrier usually believes that the sign that you love someone is that you worry about that person. (In the worrier's way of thinking, worrying is a sign of virtue because worrying means that you care, and caring means that you are good.) Thus the worrier will often say to loved ones, 'I worry about you' and then feel hurt because loved ones do not always react with warmth and affection to such statements. In fact, they often get quite huffy. They also become very secretive about their activities, so as to spare themselves the guilt of having made the worrier worry. Not that that makes the worrier any happier. Secrecy by the loved ones about their activities allows the worrier to expand the range of options about which to worry. Moreover, the worrier usually marries someone who never admits to anxiety, someone who takes pride in being imperturbable, someone who never says 'I worry about you'. So the worrier has to find more and more trivial things to worry about in order to avoid the big fear that 'Nobody loves me'.

But then the worrier might feel that the third advantage can make up for not being loved. If you feel that the people around you are too selfish and uncaring to love you, or if you suspect that you are unlovable, you can try to make up for this loss by controlling the people around you. You cannot make your loved ones love you but you can make them feel guilty by showing them that they have given you cause to worry. Then they, trying to avoid the imposition of guilt, will carry out your wishes. They will come home early, wrap up warmly, not smoke (at least when you're around), drive carefully (with you in the car), not swear, work hard, pass their exams and so on. A determined worrier can make the injunction 'Don't do any-thing which will cause me to worry' the basic and absolute moral imperative in a family and thus become the most powerful person in that family. I recall my father showing me a cartoon from the *Saturday Evening Post*. It showed a middle-aged couple in bed. The husband is settling down to sleep but the wife is sitting bolt upright and saying, 'You go to sleep. I'm going to sit here and worry.' It was the story of his married life.

The fourth advantage extends the worrier's powers even further, into the realms of magical power. There are many worriers who believe that 'If I worry about something it won't happen'. Since so many of the things we worry about never eventuate it is impossible to disprove that worrying is an effective way of controlling the universe.

Margaret, who has protected me from death, illness and injury on all my travels in recent years by worrying about me, gave me this Peanuts cartoon.

Daily Mail, 30 September 1985

All worriers agree that the most worrying thing is not having anything to worry about. Heaven must prove to be a most worrying place for worriers.

Many worriers, I find, regard their habit of worrying as something they have inherited from a parent, like the colour of their eyes or the shape of their nose. It has not occurred to them that worrying was something they had learned. One thing which parents are always teaching their children is how to become aware of a particular situation, how to define it, how to identify certain elements in it, and how to predict what will follow. Thus one parent will say, 'You've been invited to a birthday party. Won't that be fun?' and another parent will say, 'You've been invited to a birthday party. Don't eat too much or you'll be ill.' The ability to identify every doom and disaster element of a situation and to worry about it is a skill which passes from one generation to another.

Regarding the ability to worry as an inherited characteristic is one example of denying fear by *keeping things the same*. 'I'm a worrier, my parents are worriers, my grandparents were worriers, my children will be worriers.' There are many 'characters' who devote their efforts to stopping life changing. As life *is* change, such efforts produce little success. Nevertheless, that does not stop 'characters' who want to keep everything the same from trying to do this. Such extravert 'characters' try to maintain relationships no matter how damaging or empty these relationships may be. As Rachel said, 'I can't stand severing a relationship. It wounds me.' Such introvert 'characters' try to prevent their organization and their control of situations from changing. They insist that things have to be kept in a certain way, that actions have to be performed in a certain way. The contents of their rooms must never be changed around, or they must always dress in a particular style, or ceremonies, like the family's celebration of Christmas, must always be carried out in the same way.

The belief that by repeating our actions we prevent life from changing is as magical as the belief that if you don't talk about a thing that thing has not happened. This belief often underlies the thinking of those 'characters' who take great pride in *keeping things to yourself.* Such people believe that talking about worries makes them worse, or that admitting fear to yourself and to others shows you to be weak and despicable. This can end in tragedy, as the story of Willie Peacock shows:

The widow of Willie Peacock yesterday accused his fellow miners of hounding him to his death.

It was his wife Elizabeth who found him when she got home from work.

She opened the front door and saw him hanging from a rafter – unable, she believes, to face one more day's torment in the pit.

Yesterday union delegate David Hamilton ordered 1,200 men at Willie's colliery to stop work for 24 hours as a 'mark of respect' but Mrs Peacock is not impressed. 'As far as I am concerned,' she said, 'the NUM can send them back.'

Willie's friends say that men who stayed out on strike for a year picked on him because he went back after nine months sickened by the murder of a Welsh taxi driver taking a miner to work. His lunch box was contaminated with urine and excrement. His safety was threatened in whispered phone calls that taunted him for 'being a scab'. His injured foot was stamped on until it was bruised.

But Willie never said a word about it to his wife because he did not want to worry her. 'I knew nothing of what he was going through,' she said yesterday. 'That's the way he was.'

Only since his death, at 41, has she learned of the harrassment he suffered . . .

Willie, married 16 years, will be buried today. His last words to his wife were 'See you later' and his last present was a model of a miner pushing a coal truck.[1]

We might wonder why Mrs Peacock had not noticed that something was amiss with her husband, but then many women collude with their husbands in pretending that the husband is a strong, imperturbable, silent man. Such a collusion relieves the wife of the responsibility of taking her husband's feelings into account. Many women believe without question the John Wayne myth that men never get frightened. Thus they can ignore the suffering that some men undergo and collude with the denial of fear which so many men try to achieve.

Denying Others

But *denying other people's pain* is a popular and effective way of denying fear. If someone is in pain, then something fearful has happened. Acknowledging another person's pain can make us frightened. We fear that the disaster which has happened to the other person could happen to us. Even if we can put this fear from us, assuring ourselves that we are safe, acknowledging another person's pain arouses in us the sentiment of pity which is itself a painful emotion. To limit the pain of our pity we rush to help the person in pain – we offer practical help, advice, money – but, if there is nothing effective we can do, we feel helpless, and this, too, is a painful and fearful state. We pride ourselves on being competent, and any situation which shows that we delude ourselves about our competence is indeed fearful and to be avoided.

Acknowledging another person's pain can lead us not just to pity but to empathy, that leap of imagination which allows us to immerse ourselves in another person's experience and to feel their emotions as our own. Thus we can share another person's joy, but also another person's pain and fear, and this can be undesirable. Roy, who was ashamed of the way tears would come suddenly and unbidden to his eyes when he was watching television, said, 'Sometimes I see something, somebody in pain, and I feel their pain, just for a moment.' Lonely as he was, he adamantly refused to join a self-help group for companionship. He could not bear, so Betty told me, to have to listen to people talking about their troubles.

Empathy is a precious human skill which not only prevents us from being cruel but joins us to others. When we experience empathy we are able, if only momentarily, to leave the loneliness of being and enter another person's world.

But to enter another person's world can mean leaving the haven of safety we have built for ourselves and being forced to recognize that life is capricious, unfair and cruel. We have then to recognize that in pain we are jangled, confused, broken. Grief feels like fear, for in grief we find that the loss we have suffered has revealed that the picture of our life which we had was nothing but a picture, a fiction, which the loss we have suffered has shattered. Our security has gone, and we do not know how to reconstruct it. Grief is painful, messy, and the people around us may not wish us to remind them of that. They may prefer, indeed, we may prefer, that the 'acceptable' face of grief be presented.

If people will persist in presenting their pain to us, if they will insist on crying, or looking miserable, or on parading their grief or their emaciated bodies on our television screens, we can protect ourselves from the fear such sights might arouse in us by saying 'they brought it on themselves'. *Blaming the victim* is a popular way of maintaining the delusion that we live in a just world where goodness is rewarded and wickedness punished. The rape victim should have not provoked her attacker, the beaten child should not have aggravated his parents, the starving tribespeople should have known that the drought would last. We are good, and there-fore bad things will not happen to us. But when they do, when we become the victim, we have either to abandon our belief in a just world and see its ways (and God's) as capricious or mysterious beyond our comprehension, or else feel great guilt. If this is a just world, then when we suffer we must feel guilty.

Many people, not wishing to feel guilty and wanting to maintain their self-esteem, refuse to acknowledge another person's anguish because they fear that it will awaken their own anguish and weakness. Rhianon's husband, a soldier with a distinguished war record, came along with Rhianon one day to instruct me to make her better. She was, he said, sick. She had no reason to be miserable and angry, yet there she was, moping around the house and sometimes flying into a violent temper. She had even thrown a plate at him. He could not understand her behaviour. When I asked about his feelings for her he said, 'Of course I love her. She's a fine wife.' When I asked how they organized their domestic

routine he said, 'I help her with the shopping and her housework.'
He had no objection to her interest in music. It was a nice hobby,
but, of course, 'It's natural for a woman to run a home and bring
up children.' She wept, just as at home she wept in loneliness. He
did not move to comfort her, just as at home he would never touch
her. He said to me, 'The sort of chap who puts his arm around his
wife when she's depressed is likely to get dragged down too. He
wouldn't be in charge any more.'

from M. Heath, *Love All, op. cit* p. 10

If being loving and caring is seen as weakness or as a way of
being contaminated by the other person's weakness, then another
person's need to be loved must indeed be denied. In the process of
learning to be manly many boys learn to define the loving, caring
parts of themselves as feminine, weak and despicable, and so they
have to deny that they have such attributes. Such a process of
denial prevents them from understanding themselves, and so when
in later life they sense within themselves the darkness of depression
they are terrified. Rather than face with is inside them, they rush
into some kind of frantic activity. They immerse themselves in
work or sport, they have affairs with younger women, they take to
drink. Anything rather than face their own fear and anguish. Many

men in adult life still rely on a technique learned in boyhood, in Phillip Hodson's words, 'the happy knack of making themselves feel better by making others feel worse',[2] a technique which protects them from the pain and fear of observing another person's pain.

Of course women too can work at denying their own fear by denying other people's anguish, even though it is not a defence which society expects a woman to be seen using. Women are supposed to be sensitive and caring, easily and foolishly distressed by another person's suffering. Many women very effectively reduce the amount of suffering they allow themselves to observe and become frightened about by refusing to read newspapers or to watch the news on television and by concentrating solely on themselves, their family and their friends. Such deliberate ignorance does not always lead to a happy life. Many women still sense the wider world as being chaotic and dangerous, threatening to destroy what they hold dear.

Women, too, do not find it easy to use the denial of fear which *being competitive* allows. Our society considers being competitive to be a masculine attribute. Fortunately there are now many women who reject this nonsense – delight in striving, competing and achieving is natural to all of us – and so both men and women can deal with their fear by putting all their energy and conscious thought into winning and defeating. Some competitive people wisely recognize that the fear is there and that striving, competing and achieving is an effective way of confronting and controlling the fear. But some competitive people do not recognize this. They deny their fear, and then the fear returns in the guise of tension and anger which disrupt whatever non-competitive relationships they may have.

Just as competitive people are often irritable, so are powerful people, or those with aspirations to power. *Becoming powerful* is a much favoured technique for denying one's fear, be it becoming the dictator of a nation or merely the dictator of a family. Power can be described in different ways, such as having the power of wealth or the power to punish those who do not obey, but, in terms of denying fear, power can be thought of as the power to define. The powerful person says, 'The world is the way *I* see it and everyone has to agree with me.' People who do not agree with the powerful person's definition of reality are fought with, punished and, if defeated, silenced. Powerful people might be effective in controlling their own fear but they establish and maintain their power by creating fear in others. We each, naturally, define reality in our own individual way and we give up our definitions only under the threat of rejection, loss, contempt, humiliation and pain. So in the struggle for power, whether in the family or in the state, many of us suffer great fear.

However, becoming powerful does not eradicate the experience of fear. The powerful person has few friends, and so fear returns as loneliness and the fear of abandonment.

One of the oustanding characteristics of the powerful and the would-be powerful is anger and irritability. Anger is our natural response to frustration, and when we seek to impose our own definitions on the world we often find that the world is recalcitrant and will not always conform to our wishes. So the more we try to impose our definitions on the world the more frustration and anger we feel. The discovery that the world does not conform to our expectations can fill us with fear, and, rather than admit that fear, we can turn that fear into anger. Despots are dangerous because they are frightened and will not admit their fear.

The world which refuses to conform to our wishes can be the natural world. The sun will rise, the rain will fall, and the wind will blow, all indifferent to our pleas and threats. Or the world which refuses to conform to our pleas and threats can be the world of people, and here our pleas and threats can have an effect. We can inflict pain on other people to force them to do what we want them to do. But we are people too, and if we hurt other people we can perceive their pain, suffer and feel frightened. One way to protect ourselves from such suffering and fear is to refuse to acknowledge that the people who do not conform to our demands are really people. They are in some way sub-human. They may look like human beings but they don't have feelings like we do. If they are black and we are white, then we know that blacks really don't mind when they are 'resettled'. If we are men, then we know that all a woman wants and needs is to be a sex object, or our mother, or our wife.

M. Heath, *op. cit.*, p. 50

If we are adults, then we know that children soon forget their troubles. After all, childhood is the happiest time of your life, isn't it?

But in denying that other people have feelings we have to deny our own feelings. Objects – stones, mud, cement, machines – don't have feelings. When we deny that other people have feelings we treat them as objects. When we deny that we have feelings we treat ourselves as objects. Thus we become much less of the person that we might have been.

Why do we do this?

How do we do this?

Chapter Three

Learning How to Deny

When we are born we are able to feel the full range of our emotions and we do so totally. A happy baby is happy from top to toe. A hungry baby is possessed by hunger pangs and greed. An angry baby feels total and absolute anger, unrestrained by guilt or the fear of hurting others. A baby's feelings are fully felt and fully experienced.

As the baby enters into his relationship with his mother the baby becomes increasingly aware of his mother's feelings. A baby does not understand causal connections – that exploring the texture of her face by pinching her cheeks causes her pain – but the baby is sensitive to her moods. Her joy or anger or fear are part of her baby's experience.

This experience of emotions and the means by which they are expressed, in smiles and frowns, cries and words, touches and cuddles, create and maintain the relationship which joins the baby to the human race and to life.

Just as we were born with the ability to breathe so we were born with the ability to experience our emotions fully and to be aware of other people's emotions. We can keep our capacity to experience the full range and totality of our feelings and our capacity to empathize with other people. We can use these capacities to know ourselves, to know other people and to let them be themselves. We can do this. But we rarely do. Society, the group we belong to, will not let us.

Babies, like all the newborn of other species, are born with the ability to seek out the conditions necessary for their survival. Just as a hungry baby will search for something to suck for sustenance, so a lonely baby will search for someone to love and will offer this love trustfully and hopefully to the person who offers in return care and protection. Mothers sometimes have difficulty in loving newborn babies, but we, as babies, have no difficulty in loving our mothers, and this hook remains in our hearts for ever, no matter what our mothers do to us.

Mothers start doing things to their babies soon after the baby is born. Babies are very good at being themselves, but this doesn't suit the group they have been born into. Every family has its own rules and expectations, and the baby has to learn to conform.

Long before we have words to define it we are presented with the dilemma 'Shall I be an individual or a member of a group?' We knew, though we felt our knowledge only in our fear and anger and our sense of our existence, that we could not survive alone, yet it was equally dangerous to give up being ourselves. If we are lucky we have parents who understand this, treat us with respect and love us for what we are and not for what we might become, that is, a credit to our parents.

The family, like every group of people who come together for mutual support and benefit, has many rules and standards. Some of these rules and standards are clearly stated (e.g., 'Everyone in this family has a university education') and some are never put into words (e.g., 'Only father is allowed to get angry and no one must comment on this'). The first of the rules and standards which the baby encounters have to do with *greed, defecation and micturation, sex*, and *anger*. These are those parts of ourselves which as babies we felt strongly and which we expressed directly and naturally.

A healthy baby is born *greedy*, and so it needs to be, for only greedy babies will suck. Without greed a baby would not survive. Being greedy, a baby wishes to feed when hungry and sleep when satisfied. Some lucky babies are allowed to do so. But so many are not allowed to do this. Many millions of babies have mothers who are too poorly fed themselves to be able to feed their babies whenever they are hungry. Such babies have to make do with what is offered to them and, if they survive, they are haunted for the rest of their lives by images of hunger and greed.

In affluent countries where no baby need go hungry many do because their mothers, intent on being 'good mothers', obeying the dicta of their own mothers or the child rearing 'experts', feed their babies according to schedules which relate to the adults' needs rather than the child's. Being hungry and being left to cry until the clock reaches a certain hour was for many of us our first lesson in learning that we were of little importance in the scheme of things. We learned that saying 'I want' is greedy, and being greedy is bad. Whenever we feel a desire which we cannot fulfil and perhaps cannot even articulate, and we see other people enjoying the fulfilment of this desire, we feel envy. Envy is a natural response, and a common one, because we can always imagine more than we can ever do, and if it is acknowledged and accepted it can become part of the motivation which urges us on to greater things.

However, if we feel envious and cannot do anything about it, if we feel helpless and frustrated, and the frustration goes on and on, then our envy becomes mixed with rage and a fierce desire to destroy both what we want and the person who has what we want. Babies are helpless, and when their desires are not met they can feel a destructive rage which they express not just in crying and flailing limbs but also in biting the breast which is offering to feed them. Some mothers, pitying their baby's helplessness, accept their baby's greed, envy, frustration and rage, and so patiently hold, soothe, and feed their baby. But other mothers see this violent rage as evidence of the baby's inherent evil. They become frightened of their baby and seek to drive the evil out with stronger rules and punishments. The baby must learn obedience. What the baby learns is that envy is always accompanied by fearful impotence and murderous rage. Such envy is common in our world.

Children who are taught that greed is bad are also taught that envy is bad, and so they are condemned to a life of struggling with their impulses of greed and envy, either sacrificing themselves to others, never daring to ask for anything for themselves, or resorting to devious, dishonest ways of trying to gain more for themselves and to hinder and destroy the people they envy.

All families are clean. All the world over, all families are clean. They each have high standards of what constitutes *cleanliness*. The trouble is there is no universal agreement as to what constitutes cleanliness. For instance, the English deplore the public dirt in

India, while Hindus deplore the unclean habits of the English who lie in their own dirty bathwater. In one family, underclothes are changed every day but there are no rules about teeth-cleaning, while the family next door changes underclothes less frequently but brushes their teeth without fail after every meal. If each family discovers the rules of the other family, then each family regards the other as dirty, or at least as not following the proper rules of cleanliness. Dividing the world into categories of 'clean' and 'dirty' is something all human beings do. We just don't agree on what these categories should be and each of us believes that our categories are right and everyone else's are wrong.

A baby's introduction to his family's rules about cleanliness comes when he discovers that he is no longer allowed to relieve the pressure in his body when and where he pleases but only at certain times and places as his family decrees. Some fortunate infants do not encounter these rules until the sphincter muscles are strong enough to hold back the pressure of urine and faeces. Then the rules of the family are imposed at a time when the infant has a good chance of meeting the rules successfully and so can enjoy the great pleasure of basking in his family's praise and approval. But in our society there are still a great many babies who are sat on pots and ordered to perform long before they can possibly grasp what is expected of them, much less carry it out. Even more there are babies whose performance of their natural functions naturally are treated by the adults around them with great disgust and rejection.

There are sound reasons why the waste products of our body should be kept separate from other objects in our environment. Such waste products can contain elements and processes which can bring about illness and death. But our reactions to these waste substances are more than a sensible response to possible physical danger. There is another danger there, something so terrible that we cannot say its name. Fire is dangerous, but we still just call it 'fire'. Whereas these waste products are never spoken of directly by well brought up people. All kinds of circumlocutions are used. But if one wishes to be extremely vulgar or express great disgust and rejection, then there are a multitude of words and phrases referring to these waste products which can be used. 'Shit' means much more than 'faeces'.

So every infant has to learn far more than the practical procedures of the disposal of one's faeces and urine. All the magical and fantastical meanings which the members of the infant's family hold have to be learned and reacted to. There are meanings which relate to the sense of having within oneself something bad and contaminating which has to be expelled. These meanings link with a sense of being disgusted with oneself and being the object of other people's disgust. There are meanings which relate to the sense of having within oneself something which is powerful and destructive which can be used against other people or retained so that other people are not injured or that such power is not lost. There are meanings which relate to the need for privacy and the danger of intrusions on this privacy. Such intrusions may be in terms of being the butt of other people's humour, as when other people laugh at our discomfiture when we are discovered emptying our bowels and bladder, or in terms of other people's curiosity, as when other people want to inspect what we produce and to assist in its production with enemas and emetics. Such intrusions can take on a sexual quality, so that the anus can become partly or even wholly the location of the person's sexual feeling and interest. It is no wonder that so many of us are incapable of letting our body perform its functions of digestion and elimination but are for ever caught in a painful oscillation between diarrhoea and constipation. For many of us simple cleanliness is a source of great fear.

The exits for our waste products lie in an intimate closeness to our *sexual* organs, and so our sexual organs become entangled in the complex of fearful meanings we give to excretion. But they also have fearful meanings of their own, meanings which we began to acquire when we were tiny babies.

One person who made a major contribution to our understanding of how a baby's experiences can lay the foundation of later mental disturbances was the psychiatrist Harry Stack Sullivan. Although he was writing forty years ago, his observations about a baby's experiences are still relevant. Sex might be more openly discussed now than it was forty years ago, but the existence of the Moral Majority in America and the supporters of Mary Whitehouse and Victoria Gillick in Britain show that Sullivan's description of a baby's experience is still relevant. He wrote:

> [The baby] will have felt of nearly everything, including a great deal of himself, he may have put a good deal of himself in his mouth, or tried to, but in this business of exercising newly elaborated motor systems and gradually clarifying sensory feel, he will almost inevitably, since we make it a 'him', have fallen upon a small protuberance in the groin, and in doing so he will have found it handy. It is suited to manipulation. It is well located geometrically. A slight curve of the elbow puts it well within reach of the already nimble fingers.
>
> So far nothing of any moment has occurred. But we will now have, let us say, the mother . . . encounter this discovery of the infant, and we will make her a person who has been forced to organize the self on the basis of our more rigid puritan tradition.
>
> Under these circumstances, although in ordinary circumstances she is not wholly unaware of this anatomical peculiarity of the male, in her own infant she will feel that Satan is in the very near vicinity, that here is a manifestation of the bestial nature of man in the very act of erupting in her infant, and she will want to do something about it. She will wish to save this infant; Lord knows what awful visions unrolled before her eyes as she witnessed this; but anyway the infant is badly upset by empathy (*i.e., sensing the mother's feelings*), undergoes various somatic disturbances, and experiences what amounts to an acute and severe discomfort.
>
> Infants are not afflicted by long, carefully formulated memories. To the infant whose discrimination of such things is nil, this discomfort does not attach to the manipulation of the little protuberance. Almost anything in the situation may be related to this feeling of discomfort so far as the infant is concerned. He has not learned.
>
> This course of events is discovered again, perhaps the same

day. The stress in the mother is terrific . . . and so the infant has a mitten put on its hand and tied around the wrist.

Thus begins the emphasis in the infant's mind that something about this hand is connected with the recurrent feeling of acute and severe discomfort – an *anlage* of insecurity and later anxiety.

Well, infants, like people, are ingenious. And the immobilization of, let us say, the right hand does not affect the mobilization of the left. As the genital is handy, and as it has a slightly different feel from the thumb, the nose, and so on, the event recurs. Again there is the great discomfort in the presence of the mother. Presently both hands may be tied at the side, and by that time even an infant begins to realize that it has something to do with the genital.

All animals tend to react with rage to immobilization or to thwarting or restraint. To leap over months of struggle between the mother and the infant's natural impulse to explore all his abilities and the limits of himself and the rest of the world; after months of struggle there has been impressed on this infant a type of interest, a mark, if you please – an emotional mark – about the groin area . . . which is primary fear, irrational fear of the genitals.

One does not fear something of no interest to one. Anything invested with fear must by definition, by the inherent character of our contact with the universe, be of interest to us. And, therefore, because of this taboo the child has interest, unusual interest, an utterly useless interest so far as the development of the personality is concerned, attached to the penis.

As a child and as a juvenile he continues to have this interest. Why? Because this thing was precipitated in his personality very early, very firmly. All the red flags of anxiety attach to it. Moreover, mamma is always watching. Where the devil has turned up once, you may confidently expect him to return – quite unlike lightning.

And so we have a person who, long before the puberty changes, has come into considerable conflict of impulse pertaining to genital manipulation, a thing fully meaningful only years later; but a conscious center of interest in the genitals, but a negative one, in that they are to be left alone at all cost.[1]

Sullivan writes here of the little boy baby, but he could have equally written of the little girl baby who, through similar experiences, grows up with an image of her body between her waist and upper thighs as containing something dangerous, dirty and shameful, a source of fear and physical pain. She keeps her knees glued together and, if forced to speak of this part of her body, will say no more than 'down there'. Such a complex of fear and shame makes coping with the discomforts of menstruation very difficult, while all sexual encounters are fraught with fear.

However, there are parents who are pleased when their baby is greedy for food, who do not find their baby's waste products disgusting, and who are not frightened of their baby's sexual potential, so they can ease their baby gently into an acceptance of the family's rules about these matters. But all parents, no matter how kindly and easygoing, have problems about their baby's anger.

Anger is always a problem. It is our natural response to frustration, and without it we, a physically weak species compared to those species which competed with us for food, would not have been able to use our intelligence to establish ourselves as a viable species millions of years ago. Anger can make us creative and brave. Through our anger we express our individuality. But we need to live in groups, and anger within the group is always a threat to the group. In a family, when the father becomes angry, whether he beats his wife and children or merely retires to his room in icy silence, the other members of the family feel frightened. When the baby becomes angry, the parents often feel frightened, for they fear that they will not be able to control this new member of the family. For such parents Winnicott wrote:

We all know what it is to lose our tempers and we all know how anger, when it is intense, sometimes seems to possess us so that we cannot for the time being control ourselves. Your baby knows

89

about being all-out angry. However much you try, you will disappoint him at times, and he will cry in anger; according to my view you have one consolation – that angry crying means that he has some belief in you. He hopes he may change you. A baby who has lost belief does not get angry, he just stops wanting, or else he cries in a miserable, disillusioned way, or else he starts banging his head on the pillow, or on the wall or the floor, or else he exploits the various things he can do with his body.

It is a healthy thing for a baby to get to know the full extent of his rage. You see, he certainly will not feel harmless when he is angry. You know what he looks like. He screams and kicks and, if he is old enough, he stands up and shakes the bars of the cot. He bites and scratches, and he may spit and spew and make a mess. If he is really determined he can hold his breath and go blue in the face, and even have a fit. For a few minutes he really intends to destroy or at least to spoil everyone and everything, and he does not mind if he destroys himself in the process. Don't you see that every time a baby goes through this process he gains something? If a baby cries in a state of rage and feels as if he has destroyed everyone and everything, and yet the people round him remain calm and unhurt, this experience greatly strengthens his ability to see that what he feels to be true is not necessarily real, that fantasy and fact, both important, are nevertheless different from one another. There is absolutely no need for you to try to make him angry, for the simple reason that there are plenty of ways in which you cannot help making him angry whether you like it or not.

Some people go about the world terrified of losing their tempers, afraid of what would have happened if they had experienced rage to the fullest extent when they were infants. For some reason or other this never got properly tested out. Perhaps their mothers were scared. By calm behaviour they might have given confidence, but they muddled things up by acting as if the angry baby was really dangerous.[2]

Unfortunately, there are many parents who do see their baby as dangerous. They perceive this scrap of humanity as being stronger

Guardian, 4 December 1985

and more powerful than they are. The cartoonist Michael Heath has exploited this fear in a series of cartoons called *Baby*.

Babies and children, because they are simply human, can make other people feel exasperated and angry. But there is a tradition in our society that being a nuisance is an essential and permanent characteristic of children. When I was invited to answer readers' letters to do with children in the magazine *Chat*, I was presented with the title of the column as 'The Trouble With Kids'. Kids, you see, are always trouble. I proceeded to interpret 'the trouble with kids' as 'parents who don't understand or accept you'.

By understanding and acceptance I mean the realization that each baby, given the appropriate food and shelter, will, at his or her own pace, grow and blossom, just as a tiny bud will unfold into a flower. Babies are born curious, and so will be busily learning about the world and how they can act upon it. Most of what babies and children learn they teach themselves.

The Perils of Pedagogy

However, what I have said here is not in the ancient tradition of *pedagogy*, a word which comes from the Greek *pais*, a child, and *agein*, to lead.[3] In this tradition the child is seen as needing to be taught everything by parents and teachers. This view reflects an image of the child as being not merely immature and inadequate, but in some way containing a certain badness which will flourish unless parents and teachers take steps to eradicate it. This tradition is alive and well today.

In 1621, Robert Cleaver and John Dod, in their book *A Godly Form of Household Government*, advised parents:

> The young child which lieth in its cradle is both wayward and full of affections; and though his body be but small, yet he hath a reat [wrong-doing] heart, and is altogether inclined to evil . . . If this sparkle be suffered to increase, it will rage over and over and burn down the whole house. For we are changed and become good not by birth but by education . . . Therefore parents must be wary and circumspect . . . they must correct and sharply reprove their children for saying or doing ill.[4]

In 1985 Professor Martin Herbert, in his book *Caring for Your Children*, wrote:

> Parents (and teachers) observe the development of the children in their care with a mixture of pleasure and bewilderment. Development, one is led to believe, is a progressive series of orderly, coherent changes, leading the child towards the goal of maturity. Well, that may be the grand design, but as many long- suffering parents and teachers know to their cost, their children's progress through life is often disorderly and incoherent, and the changes (when change is not being resisted) are not always in the direction of maturity! When this happens, such reactions are quite likely to be labelled as 'problems' and sometimes this is even thought of as abnormal . . .
>
> Many people complain that there are countless books available which suggest ways of understanding children, but they tend not to offer practical advice about what actually to *do*

to remedy, or better still, prevent their problems. Or, if they do provide answers, they are couched in general terms, that precise action is not possible. In an attempt to meet this criticism I have written a pragmatic 'nuts and bolts' sort of book, with suggestions about long-term strategies (guidelines on child-rearing) and also about the kinds of tactics which might change worrying and unsatisfactory situations. The tactics are *not* based (in the main) upon prescriptions or general formulae, but upon the caregiver's own individual analysis of a child's behaviour and his or her particular circumstances. An attempt is made throughout to take account of the child's point of view!

I call this a 'problem-solving' approach, and it is based on social learning theory . . .

I put forward the view that problem behaviour in children (sometimes called abnormal behaviour) is not very different from normal, ordinary behaviour in its development, persistence and the ways in which it can be altered. Many problematic behaviours can be thought of as a consequence of a child's failure to learn successful ways of coping with his or her environment or as a result of applying inappropriate strategies for dealing with life. This is an optimistic book. It suggests that children can unlearn self-defeating behaviours; they can learn new, advantageous ways of going about things; and that in all of this, parents and teachers are generally the best persons to help them achieve the necessary changes.[5]

To underline this approach, the cover illustration on Professor Herbert's book is from the painting '*Eugene Manet et sa fille dans le jardin*' by Berthe Morisot. Here the little girl is sitting respectfully and docilely, at the feet of her father who appears to be instructing her. The Impressionistic style of painting is gentle, appealing, and sentimental.

Professor Herbert is a psychologist, hence his emphasis on learning. He writes within the behaviourist tradition of psychology, which is based on the observation that we tend to repeat doing things which result in us receiving some kind of reward and not repeat doing things which result in us receiving some kind of pain. Psychologists have amassed much research evidence to show that it is much more effective to reward a person for doing what you want that person to do, than to punish the person for doing what you don't want him to do. Thus present-day pedagogues or child-rearing experts, are much more likely to emphasize rewarding a child for good behaviour (now called positive reinforcement) whereas previously the emphasis was on punishing the child for bad behaviour. But behaviourists still advocate in certain circumstances punishment (now called negative reinforcement) and, despite the wise and knowledgeable advice from kindly child-rearing experts, many parents and teachers still beat and abuse the children in their care.

Professor Herbert shows how parents and teachers can arrive at a clearer understanding of their children's behaviour by analysing the situation into *Antecedents* which lead to *Behaviour* which leads to *Consequences*. However, *Consequences*, whether called positive and negative reinforcements or rewards and punishments, lie, like beauty, in the eye of the beholder, or here, in the eye of the receiver. Behavioural methods of training children often go astray because the adult doing the training does not understand how the child perceives what the adult calls the reward or punishment. All of us, children and adults, will often persist in doing something which causes us pain because we perceive in that situation a subtle but more powerful reward, just as we will not do something that would result in pleasure because we perceive in that situation something which will result in a subtle but greater pain. So, too, we may all react as expected to positive and negative reinforcement, but once we perceive, or suspect, that the person providing the reinforcement is insincere and is simply manipulating us, we cease to respond as expected, or else we too become insincere and for our own benefit we manipulate the manipulator.

In reading books about child psychology it is important to understand from what point of view the book is being written. Psychoanalysts and developmental psychologists like Donald Winnicott and Daniel Stern are concerned with trying to understand how the child feels and perceives. They give to the child's perceptions the same importance as those of the parents, because in the relationship between parents and children the child's perception of the parents is as important in determining the outcome as are the parents' perceptions of the child. This way of studying children is relatively new. A much older tradition is to describe the relationship between parents and children from the point of view of the parents.

In this tradition the child's perceptions are irrelevant because they are formed on the basis of immaturity and wickedness. The parents' perceptions are formed by the need of the parents to eradicate the child's inherent wickedness and to guide and mould the child so that he becomes good, compliant, and adapts to society's demands.

Professor Herbert's book is written from the parents' and teachers' point of view. True, he does speak of 'an attempt . . . to take account of the child's point of view', but he ends this sentence with an exclamation mark, suggesting that taking account of the child's point of view is surprising and novel.[6]

As indeed it is. The tradition that the child's point of view is of no importance, that the parents' point of view must prevail, that the parents must teach the child everything of value and that the child must sacrifice himself for the parents is an essential part of our culture, for this is what the Bible teaches. As the psychoanalyst Alice Miller has described it:

It is always the Isaacs whose sacrifice God demands from the Abrahams, never the other way around. It is daughter Eve who is punished for not resisting temptation and not suppressing her curiosity out of obedience to God's will. It is the pious and faithful son Job whom God the Father continues to mistrust until he has proved his faithfulness and subservience by undergoing unspeakable torments. It is Jesus who dies on the Cross to fulfil the words of the Father. The Psalmists never tire of extolling the importance of obedience as a condition of each and every human life. We have all grown up with this cultural heritage, but it could not have survived as long as it has if we had not been taught to accept without question the fact that a loving father has the need to torment his son, that the father cannot sense his son's love and therefore, as in the story of Job, requires it.[7]

This tradition arose out of necessity. When life was 'nasty, brutish and short' a child was of little value. Adults, whose life expectancy was no more than twenty or thirty years, were the tribe members who could maintain the tribe by having the skills to secure the food supply and by producing future generations of the tribe. A dependent child was a burden. The child had to be grateful for being allowed to exist (unsatisfactory babies were left to die) and had to prove his gratitude to his elders. As soon as the child was big enough to carry out some tasks he or she had to begin working, and to work effectively the child had to learn the tribe's rules of conduct. If the child and the tribe were to survive, then the children had to give up their desires to play and to be irresponsible, and had to learn to conform to the rules of the tribe. Physical survival of all, children and adults, depended on obedience.

The lowly status of children and the necessity of children learning obedience in order to survive continues to this day where families live in poverty and near starvation. In the famine in Ethiopia aid workers from the West saw their task as that of feeding the starving children, but for many of the tribal Ethiopians this was not their first priority. For them, the adults should be fed before the children, and this is what they did, even if it meant that the children starved.

If the early generations of the human race had not followed the rule that children should be sacrificed in order to secure the continuation of the tribe, many of us would not be here today, benefiting from a life style which does not demand that a child dies because there is insufficient food or that a child has to begin working as soon as its little hands can carry a burden or its little legs can toddle. We no longer send five-year-olds into the factory to tend the machines, or seven-year-olds down the mine to pull the coal trucks. But we still demand that children be obedient. They must sacrifice themselves for their parents. Pedagogical texts from the Bible to the present day extol this tradition.

A broader application of this tradition is the belief in the virtue of the individual sacrificing himself for the group. Thus obedient little boys grow up to be soldiers and die for their country, and obedient little girls grow up to be mothers who sacrifice themselves for their family. Such individual sacrifices form the essence of the concept of patriotism and the sanctity of family life.

In the world that I grew up in, the tradition of patriotism, '*Dulce et decorum est, pro patria mori*' ('It is sweet and decorous to die for one's country') was extolled and exalted, although the pictures I saw of Australian soldiers battling over the Kokoda trail in New Guinea or of the remains of Russian and German soldiers on the frozen steppes suggested a certain lack of sweetness and decorum. In more recent years the tradition of sacrificing oneself for one's country receded somewhat, though it reappeared as strong as ever in Britain when young soldiers died in the Falklands, and in the USA when seven cosmonauts died in a burning space shuttle, and it can be seen lurking in the background of all those pictures we see of dark-haired young men and women holding machine guns.

But the tradition of sacrificing oneself for one's family remains as strong as ever. Politicians extol it, advertisers brandish it, and soap operas tell us that there is no other way to live. It sets the standards of virtue. Good husbands work hard to support their families; good mothers put their husbands' and children's needs before their own; good children obey their parents. Parents sacrifice themselves for their children, and so children must always be grateful.

The emphasis of this tradition is to protect the parents. Children might be indulged with presents and parties and wonderful excursions, but they must not be spoilt, that is, they must not be allowed to expect that all their needs and demands will be met or even acknowledged. Moreover, children must not criticize their parents, even when they grow up and are parents themselves. There are many British people who are horrified by the outspokenness of the American children they see on television. The reports of drug addiction among young Americans do not surprise them. That teenagers might turn to drugs because the process of becoming obedient had left them with a feeling of weakness and fear which drugs can briefly obliterate does not occur to them.

97

Babies are born all ready to love their parents, and because they love them they want to please them. So in terms of reciprocal love children find obedience easy. But as much as young children want to fulfil their parents' wishes, they do not always know what these wishes are. A baby cannot comprehend that his mother wants him to sleep because she is tired, or frightened because she is alone and deserted. Often the parents make their wishes quite clear, but they are demanding something which the child cannot do. When a little stomach is full it cannot take in more food, no matter how much a father might order that a plate be cleared; when little bowels are empty, nothing can be produced, no matter how much a mother might order that a pot must be sat upon. A little girl cannot turn into a little boy to please parents who wanted a son; a little boy cannot stop the tears coming to his eyes when he is hurt, no matter how much his father tells him not to be a sissy.

Small children cannot always please their parents, and when they fail in this, parents resort to other methods to ensure obedience. These methods may be dramatic and obvious, like hitting the child, or forcing the child to be alone, or refusing to give the child something that the child wanted, or taking from the child something that the child valued, or shouting at the child in terms of anger and contempt, or humiliating the child, or threatening the child with abandonment. Or the methods may be subtle, observable only to the child and parent. A look from a parent covers the child with shame; a sign from a parent can fill the child with guilt. The subtle methods of extracting obedience remain effective for many years, often without the grown child being consciously aware of how potent these methods are. I was in my thirties before I realized what a strong fear reaction I produced whenever my mother began a sentence with 'I don't want to worry you, Dorothy, but . . .' It didn't matter how trivial and easily dismissible was her particular concern (she was a practised pessimist), I always responded with fear to her opening words. Some sin of commission or omission was mine.

All these methods of producing obedience in the child, blatant or subtle, make the child frightened. To the parent the method used may seem nothing much at all, a quick slap, a shout, a small effort on the part of the parent. But to the child, so much smaller than the parent, weak and helpless in a land of giants, the method of producing obedience causes pain and fear, immense fear.

Why don't children rebel? Why don't they say to themselves, 'When I grow up I won't treat my children the way I was treated.' Some of them do. Some parents treat their children very differently from the way they were treated, but most do to their children what was done to them. It is all they know to do. Parenting isn't a skill we learn about at school. When we become parents we have to resort to copying other, older parents, and the parents we knew best were our own parents.

Sometimes we ask ourselves, 'Now what would Dad do in this situation?' but most of the time we draw on our knowledge of what our parents would have done without thinking about it. It seems from the research that the women who know what to do and how to feel when their first baby is put into their arms are those women who had good mothering themselves when they were babies. Those women who feel awkward, confused and inadequate with their new babies have within them few memories of good mothering on which they could draw. Similarly, many men whose only knowledge of how a father behaves is that he shouts, gets angry and impatient, and imposes his will by brute force will think that this is the right and only way that fathers behave and do likewise.

Children endure the pains and humiliations of childhood because they know that as well as the threats there is a promise. If you are disobedient as a child bad things will happen to you, but if you are good you will be rewarded, and the reward is that when you grow up you will have the power and privileges that adults have. One of the privileges of adulthood is that you can not only take your bad feelings out on the children in your charge, but that you can feel virtuous while doing it. 'I'm only beating you for your own good, darling.'

Some parents do not indulge in such hypocrisy, but what we all do as we grow up and encounter life's difficulties is that we try to maintain our self-esteem. We need to think well of ourselves so as to find the courage to face life. If we suspect that we might have been damaged in our upbringing we shall think less well of ourselves, and our courage might fail.

So as to maintain their self-esteem some adults say, 'I had a good childhood and my parents were wonderful', and maintain this view by remembering very little of their childhood. Other people, less successful in forgetting the painful events of their childhood, maintain that what happens to us in childhood has little effect in adult life. I have often heard this view expounded not just by my clients but by psychiatrists who wish to locate the causes of mental illness in the body. Yet all the time these people were hard at work as parents, worrying about their children's education, teaching their children good manners and healthy eating habits, all the things which they believed would help the child in adult life. If I commented, as I often do, that if what parents do has no effect on their children, then a lot of parents have wasted an awful lot of time, they look pained and confused. They had been demonstrating the wonderful ability we all have of holding two opposing beliefs at one and the same time. This is only possible so long as the two beliefs are kept in separate compartments of the person's belief system which is, because these compartments are so separate, split instead of being one continuous whole.

By denying that bad things happened to us in childhood, or by denying that what happens to us in childhood has any significance for our later life we create disjunctions, gaps in what should be the coherent story of our life. This has many serious consequences, but one serious consequence is that because we cannot see the connections between the events of our childhood and our adult self we continue to do to our children what was done to us. Thus do the sins of the fathers continue to be visited upon the children. To recognize that what was done to us in childhood has damaged us and prevented us from fulfilling our potential requires great bravery and an endurance of pain.

Many of us who have come to this realization have done so when our own children are well grown, and so we have to deal with the pain, not only of recognizing what was done to us, but also of what we have done to our own children. I have, to a large extent, come to terms with what was done to me in childhood, or, as Alice

Miller would say, turned guilt into sadness and mourning, but I still cringe in pain at the stupidities and ineptitudes I committed as a mother. I often find in therapy that when my clients and I are talking about some aspect of their childhood they will become pensive, and then say, 'I've just been thinking about what I've done to my kids.' I cannot say, 'Don't worry, your kids will be all right', because we both know that that is not true. All we can do is sit quietly together in shared sadness.

To recognize that what was done to you in childhood has profoundly affected you means that you have not only suffered in childhood but that you can't enjoy the power and privileges of being an adult in charge of children. To change the way we bring up children and so, perhaps, avert the extinction of the human race (as I have argued in my book *Living With the Bomb*[8]), a whole generation of parents would have to miss out on the chance of doing to children what was done to them and so giving vent to the anger and envy left over from their own childhood. The privileges of parenthood are not inconsiderable. I remember how as a child my mother and my sister, six years older than me, used to urge me to obedience by telling me not to be selfish. They would, for instance, tell me to carry out some tasks and save them the trouble of doing the tasks themselves. I would observe that by my acting unselfishly they were enabled to do what they wanted to do, that is, to be selfish. If I pointed this out, as I often would, they would say that I was a difficult, ungrateful child.

The Loss of the Authentic Self

In learning to be obedient, children have to give up a great deal of their vitality and creativity. Much of the punishments which children receive for being active stems from the unacknowledged envy which adults feel for children. They envy children for having something which they have lost, a loss which must not be recognized or acknowledged.

But who is it who is so eager to see that society's norms are observed, who persecutes and crucifies those with the temerity

101

to think differently – if not the ones who have had a 'proper upbringing'? They are the ones who learned as children to accept the death of their souls and not to notice it until they are confronted with the vitality of their young or adolescent children. Then they must try to stamp out this vitality, so they will not be reminded of their own loss.[9]

What we have to lose in the process of becoming obedient is our true, authentic self. We do not become the person we know we could have been. Some of us know this very clearly, but most of us do not. We are all haunted by a sense of loss, but only some of us can name this sense of loss. For most of us, all that we know is an ache and a longing. Because we cannot name it we find it frightening. We try to ignore this pain, or obliterate it with indulgences of food, or drugs, or alcohol, or presents to ourselves, or by prodigious feats of self-denial, or to run away from it into continuous hard work, or frantic, competitive play, or to expel it in our works of art, or bury it in depression, or belittle it in contempt for another's weakness, or destroy it in violent, murderous rage. But it remains, a painful vacancy, there to trouble and frighten us just when we thought we were safe.

Because we gave up our authentic self before we knew what it was, we gave up a *potentiality*, and so in adulthood we have to mourn what might have been as well as what had been. When, as adults, we see children and adults younger than ourselves enjoying what we might have had, we can feel great envy. If our first experience of envy was in conditions where we were helpless and frequently frustrated, and we had no one who would help us deal with these painful emotions, then the envy we feel in adulthood is inextricably mixed with the desire to destroy what we cannot have and to murder those whom we envy. If we consider envy and its accompanying feelings as unacceptable, we can deny that that is what we feel, and instead feel nothing but contempt and disapproval for those we envy. If, however, we have given up expecting much for ourselves we feel envy in terms of wistful sadness.

I have often felt envious of women younger than myself, simply because they were born, as I see it, into an easier age than I was. I envied the young girls of the sixties who did not have to struggle, and fail, as I did, with the inappropriate and sophisticated clothes of the fifties. I envied the choices which the sexual revolution of the sixties and seventies gave to young women. Yet, as I watch what happens to girls and women nowadays, even the educated women who handle work, children, husbands and lovers with such flair and competence, I can see that the same sacrifices are demanded of girls as have always been if they are to join the group called women.

Girl babies aren't all that different from boy babies. True, there are anatomical differences, and some researchers say that boy babies are more active than girl babies, although other researchers say that adults see in babies what they expect to see, but all babies come into the world as themselves, curious about the world, and wanting to act upon the world. But for little girls it is not to be. Neither is it for little boys.

Every society, every family, has very clear ideas about what is masculine and what is feminine. There is considerable overlap in these ideas throughout the world, even though practices vary. Orthodox Jews and Muslims regard women's hair as something dangerous which can snare and incite a man to a sexual fervour, the expression of which he is not responsible for, while in most Christian countries virtuous women no longer have to keep their hair covered. (My mother was one of the last generation of women who felt it a necessary modesty to wear a hat. She and I battled over whether I should wear a hat. I won, but only after considerable humiliation where I was told that it was impossible for me to be properly dressed because my head was so big no hat would fit me.) But the idea that women have to keep themselves covered and/or secluded because their sexuality is a danger to men is common to all cultures. Even in countries where women are allowed to leave their homes unescorted by a man, it is the custom that if a man who is attacking and raping women has not been caught by the police, it is the women who are instructed to stay at home, not the men.

The fear of women's sexuality is not just that the woman may passively, simply by her presence, arouse a man to passion, but that she might use her sexuality in an aggressive, assertive way. A feminine woman is not assertive. Little girls are taught this with great efficiency, for they are taught – and shown – that assertive, aggressive women are not loved. Margaret Thatcher may present an image of attractive femininity, and she may talk of herself as a caring, gentle person, but her toughness and aggression ensure that as much as she is admired, she is not loved.

Giving up anger is as sensible as giving up breathing, and just as easily done. Women may give up the social expression of anger, and they may even deny its existence to such an extent that they never consciously feel angry, but the unexpressed anger is there, and it takes its toll. The preponderance of depressed women has more to do with what they do with their anger than what their hormones do to them. Many men prefer an explanation of a woman's depression in terms of hormones rather than anger, for the second explanation involves a recognition that women have a right to anger, just as a man has. Of course, there are many women who feel, and express, a powerful anger, but as they cannot direct this anger at its true source, the conditions of their lives, they express it against the only objects available to them, their children. Many of us come to adulthood bearing on our soul, if not our body, the scars from the blows our mother's anger dealt us, and many of us, unable to retaliate when we were children, take out our anger with our mother on our own children. Thus do the sins of the mother get visited on the children.

In dealing with her children in this way, a mother treats them simply as objects, something against which she can express her passion, like the door she slams or the plate she hurls at the wall. One way in which children can survive these painful, frightening, unjust events is to turn themselves into objects. 'Sticks and stones may break my bones but names will never hurt me' we might have chanted defiantly to ourselves in order to summon the courage to survive, encasing ourselves in a metal box, on the outside of which the wicked witch's blows and curses rained without effect.

Girls are not so efficient as boys in being able to turn themselves into objects so as to protect themselves from a parent's anger.

Since boys are encouraged from their earliest days to take part in rough and tumble games, while girls are discouraged from climbing, jumping, fighting, boys have more experience in how to develop techniques for avoiding or minimizing physical pain. Since an essential part of femininity is being sensitive to what another person says and does, girls remain vulnerable to their mother's angry abuse and insults, while a boy who is learning how to be a traditional man is learning to devalue such sensitivity. Many boys who receive a great deal of physical punishment learn to take great pride in the amount of physical punishment they can take without showing any pain or fear. Many boys not only make their closest relationships with machines, but they come to think of themselves as a machine, hard, logical, efficient, powerful, unaffected by emotional confusion and doubt.

The processes by which a girl learns to be feminine and a boy masculine require that each gives up vital parts of his or her self. Boys must give up those parts of themselves which might be labelled as feminine and girls those parts of themselves which might be labelled masculine. Having been forced to relinquish parts of ourselves which we valued (we begin our lives by valuing every part of us, and we no more want to give up part of our potentiality than we want to give up an arm or a leg), we envy those people who have what we have lost. Thus men envy women, and women envy men, not their penises, those curious appendages which always make women laugh, but the power and freedom which men have – if they are sensible enough to recognize it. Many men, however, long for what they see as the security and gentleness of a woman's life but are afraid to claim this as their own, clinging instead to women and hoping to share their good fortune with them. The woman may be clinging to him in the hope of sharing his power and freedom. On such misunderstandings are so many marriages made.

Thus so many of us live inauthentic lives. We cannot be ourselves because we do not know who we are. Certainly, we can describe the self which we present to the world, the self which has been created to meet the demands, first, of our family, and second, of our society. But the potential self, the one we came into the world with, this is what we do not know. We may be familiar with our secret self, that part of ourselves which we keep hidden from others, and while this may be our real self, we have never allowed it to act upon the world. We have to keep it hidden, for our real self is, so we have been taught, not good enough. It is unsatisfactory, not up to standard, the source of our inadequacies, our errors and our sins.

We need to keep our real self hidden, too, because if we reveal it, we shall be mocked, humiliated, shown to be a fool, just as we were when we were little. We know, clearly, or sometimes only dimly, that our real self is the source of our creativity and our life, and we may also believe that neither our real self nor our false self has any right to exist. We are there only by the gracious permission of more powerful people, and we must go carefully if we are to survive.

> *the god of my childhood wears black robes, has horns*
> *on his head and carries an axe in his hand. How in the*
> *world was I still able to slip past him?*
> *all my life I have been creeping stealthily through*
> *my landscape, under my arm the little bit of life I keep*
> *thinking I have stolen.*[10]

Who is the god of our childhood? Why, our parents, so wise, so wonderful, so powerful. We were helpless, and we needed their strength. We were helpless and we envied them their power. We looked to them to understand us, to minister to our needs, and they failed (they were merely human, and being so, prone to mistakes, like meaning well and getting it wrong, but we were not to know that; we thought them gods). They did not notice what we were feeling, and we were hurt. They refused to share their power with us, and we were envious. They frustrated us, and we were furious. They punished us, and we were frightened, helpless and in pain. Our helplessness, hurt, frustration, fear, anger and envy merged into a terrible rage which possessed us and drove us to a murderous fury with our gods. They were wicked, wicked gods. Then, suddenly, we were afraid. They were the only gods we had.

If we destroyed them we would be alone. So we buried our rage and said, instead, 'My gods are good. I have perfect parents.'

This process of idealizing our parents is so common that the commandment 'Honour thy father and mother' seems hardly necessary. However, there are some children who find that their parents are so awful that they cannot idealize them, and so save themselves from their own impotent rage and envy. This gives them a lifelong grudge against their parents. Such people cannot come to see their parents as ordinary, fallible human beings, because they cannot recognize the good in them, just as those people who claim to have perfect parents cannot see them as ordinary, fallible human beings because they cannot recognize the bad in them. Each person, the ones with the perfectly good parents and the ones with the perfectly bad parents, wants to live in the secure world of a childhood where everybody is fixed, defined and unchangeable, where black is black and white is white, and there are no messy greys and shifting ambiguities.

But it is the shifting ambiguities which distinguish people from objects. Objects stay as they are. They may decay with the passing of time, but such change can be accounted for in terms of science, the alterations in atoms and molecules. Our bodies change like this, but that part of us which changes most, is in constant change, is that which makes us human, our thoughts and feelings, the reconstruction of our memories, the movement of our passions, our conflicts, our desires, our wishes, our dreams. Science might be able to map the entirety of our body, but science cannot map completely the entirety of our being, for our being is in constant motion, and everything that happens to us changes us. A psychologist may apply his tests to measure our personality and our IQ, and we may comply with his instructions, but as we answer his questions we change, and the being he started out to measure is no longer exactly there. This is what makes human beings so interesting. This is what makes human beings so dangerous.

One way of overcoming this danger is to pretend that people don't change. People aren't like people. They're like objects. My parents are perfect parents. They always have been and always will be. My parents are wicked parents. They always have been and they always will be. I can always predict what they are going to do. (They're rather like clockwork dolls.) Now I can feel a little bit safer.

But you get nothing for nothing in this world. The price for seeing our parents as being in a state of fixity similar to objects is that we have to treat ourselves as objects too. If we see our parents as irredeemably bad, we have to see ourselves as eternally bad, for we have to contain our destructive rage and envy which we know is bad. If we have been able to bury our rage and envy by idealizing our parents, we then have to blame ourselves for all the bad things which happen to us. Our parents punish us because we are wicked; our parents are contemptuous of us because we are contemptible; our parents may abandon us because we do not deserve their love and care. Our sense of badness takes on a terrible fixity, and we become locked into a pattern of trying to overcome our badness by working hard to be good. We can no more just live, and greet each day with joy. We have become a squirrel on a treadmill, running fast and getting nowhere, for we can never outpace the badness which we have fixed inside us.

Moreover, if the process whereby we fixed our parents into their objectified state so as to minimize the damage they could do to us is going to be effective, we have to forget that we have gone through this process. Whatever was the setting for the drama of our first five years of life, whether we were cocooned inside a nuclear family where the Oedipal drama could be played out according to the stage directions Freud uncovered, or whether our father was an infrequent figure on the set, or a mere fantasy figure, or whether the possessors of the sperm and egg from which we grew vanished and other people called us theirs, we had, under the direction of our parental figures, to take those parts of ourselves which did not measure up to the standards of the group which we had joined and hide them, our guilty secret, and then forget the means by which this was done. Memory, for most of us, starts at five.

The process whereby we change from simply being ourselves to experiencing ourselves as bad and having to work hard in order to be good can be characterized as a situation where the parent is inflicting pain on the child and the child reconstrues this situation from 'I am being unjustly punished by my bad parent' to 'I am bad and am being justly punished by my good parent'.

If a child is frequently put in such peril she may take the further step to reduce the pain and fear by deciding that 'When I grow up I shall punish bad people in the same way as my good parent punished me.'

This is the process which first Sandor Ferenzi and then Anna Freud described as the defence of identification with the aggressor. This is the process whereby the human race perpetuates its cruelty and contempt for those seen as different. It is the final step of turning people into objects.

People who as children had to use the defence mechanism of identification with the aggressor in order to survive are very reluctant to become aware of what was done to them, what they did to themselves, and what they are doing to other people, especially their own children.

I was invited to talk to a meeting of the National Childbirth Trust about the subject of depression. My experience of National Childbirth Trust people is that they are well educated, concerned, aware and critical women and men. At this meeting I was talking about the links between childhood experiences and adult depression when I was suddenly interrupted by a young woman, nursing a small baby, who was sitting near me.

She said, 'Can I ask you a question? It's going back to something you said. I didn't want to stop you in full flow.'

I detected a note of hostility.

'It's what you said about not beating children. Don't you think children need to be hit. How else will they learn?'

She went on, passionately, to describe how she disciplined her two older children. (I assumed, hopefully, that she was not talking about the baby as well.) She had a wooden spoon called 'Mr Henry' with which she hit them whenever they misbehaved. 'You can't reason with young children,' she said, and went on to describe how Mr Henry went with them wherever they went. If the children misbehaved in public she would take them to some place where they could not be seen and there Mr Henry would do his work. 'I wouldn't hit them in front of other people. That would embarrass them. Usually I don't have to hit them. They know that if they are naughty Mr Henry will come out.'

I asked her if she had been beaten as a child.

She said, 'I was very unruly as a child, especially when my mother's marriage was breaking up. I wasn't beaten, just hit. I caused my mother a great deal of trouble.'

Some of the people in the room shared my sadness as she gave her detailed account of the punishments her small children received, but others supported her, claiming that all children were too wild and unruly to be brought up without some form of corporal punishment. One woman, who had earlier identified herself as someone who suffered greatly with depression, assured us that *all* the children who misbehaved themselves in the school where she taught came from homes where corporal punishment was never used.

The amount of physical violence used against children is greatly underestimated. I find that many of my clients regard hitting their children as both normal and necessary. If I comment upon this, they usually say that they only hit their children when their children need it and that they don't hit their children as much as they were hit by their parents. I would indeed hope so, for some of the troubled people I see have been brutally treated by their parents. Nevertheless, I suspect that Alice Miller was right when she wrote, 'Parents who beat their children very often see the image of *their* parents in the infant they are beating.'[11] Many people find that one very effective way of getting rid of your own pain is to inflict pain on others. If it were not so, where would dictators find the people to man their concentration camps, death squads and torture chambers?

Many men see as their prerogative the right to beat their wives and children whenever they wish to do so. Sometimes women thrash their children, but mostly it is the woman who stands helplessly by while her husband takes his temper out on the children. In such families the children often regard their mother as a saint, a woman who suffered at her husband's hands for her children's sakes. But,

> The mother watches her child being humiliated, derided, and tormented without coming to his defence, without doing anything to save him. Through her silence she is in complicity with his persecutor; she is abandoning her child. Should we be surprised if his bitterness, although repressed, is also directed at his mother? Perhaps the child will love his mother at a conscious level: later, in his relationships with other people, he will repeatedly have the feeling of being abandoned, sacrificed and betrayed.[12]

There is a truism in psychotherapy that it is not possible to have one good and one bad parent. If the good parent does not protect you from the bad parent, then you have two bad parents.

Parents often justify the violence they do to their children on the incompatible grounds that a) it is necessary in order to make the children good, and b) children don't remember what is done to them.

When the violence which is done to children is sexual abuse the first argument is not used but the second is. Children are so wicked that they have to have their wickedness driven out of them by beating, but they are so innocent that they don't understand the significance of sexual assault and so they don't remember what was done to them, thus suffering no harm. So as not to remind them, we won't talk about it.

Fortunately, incest and the sexual abuse of children is ceasing to be a forbidden topic of conversation, a conspiracy of silence. We are only now beginning to understand how widespread these practices are and what devastating effects such abuse has on generations of families. I shall recount here the story of Jack and his family. This was a tight-knit, loving family, and the events within it, though not the events of Jack's childhood, were not major and shocking as were the events recounted in books like Louise Armstrong's *Kiss Daddy Goodnight*[13] and Sandra Butler's *Conspiracy of Silence*.[14] Yet the effects were devastating to all concerned.

111

Jack and his wife Joy agreed to my recording his story, in the hope that it might be of use to other people in a similar predicament. All that Jack asked was that I should not give the name of the orphanages he lived in as a child. 'Things are different now,' he said, 'or at least I hope they are.'

Jack's Story

They were sitting in the waiting room as I rushed in, late, from a meeting. I recognized them at once even though they were older. Twelve years ago she had been pretty and vivacious, though often anxious. Now the prettiness was still there, but with greyness and sadness. He was hunched up and slow to move. I thought he was ill and that this was what they wanted to talk to me about.

We had met twelve years ago when their son Mark had been in trouble at school. He was a very bright lad, but he stayed away from school a lot and when he was there he wouldn't work. His headmaster wanted to expel him, but before this could be done the Education Department needed a psychologist's advice. Mark and his parents came to see me, and eventually Mark went to a boarding school. His parents, Joy and Jack, came a few more times to discuss their marriage. It had become clear that much of Mark's difficult behaviour stemmed from the strain in their relationship.

We had talked about money, how Jack, a self-employed businessman, worked very hard to give his children all the things he had missed out on as a child, and how he would spend his money as soon as he got it, buying things for the home rather than banking it. Money as figures on a bank statement had little reality for him. This way of dealing with money worried Joy, but she found it hard to criticize him because she knew he was a devoted, caring father. His concern for their children was the one thing which made her overlook her personal unhappiness in their marriage. She wanted to make their relationship better and so she wanted to talk to me about it. Jack was not so keen, but came back with her for several meetings.

After a while they stopped coming, saying that things were

better, and I lost touch with them. Mark came to see me once later, when he had left school and was looking for a job. He had bought himself a huge, powerful motorbike. As he stood beside the bike I feared for his safety. He was a slim, delicately built lad, and the bike was so big.

He pointed out the name of the bike, Yamaha. 'I've been told that in Japanese that means death,' he said.

Mark was interested in Eastern philosophies and we had talked about how Hinduism and Buddhism emphasize the close connection between opposites. I had no idea what 'Yamaha' meant except as the name of a Japanese industry, but I wanted to refute the fatalistic pessimism which seemed to underlie his words. I said, 'If it does mean death then it will also mean life.'

After he had left, a frail figure battling to control the huge machine, I wondered if my words had been enough to deflect him from a suicidal course. Over the years I had often wondered if he were still alive. I was relieved, as we sat down in my office, when Joy said, 'Mark said that we ought to get in touch with you.'

They sat on separate chairs, Jack facing me and Joy looking at both Jack and me. He had his hand up to his face, as if to protect himself from her gaze.

Joy said, 'It's very good of you to see us, and at such short notice too.' She told me that Mark was married with two children and had his own business. Alice, their eldest, was married, their second daughter, Jenny, was working in Edinburgh, Ray was a research scientist, and Louise, the youngest, was at university.

Joy paused and looked at Jack. He looked dreadfully upset. He said, 'I've been very stupid. It's about the children – when they were young – what I did to them. I – interfered – with them – not all of them. I didn't think—'

His voice broke. Joy, gently, took over, and went on talking, taking responsibility for telling me what had happened.

She spoke very simply and directly, explaining carefully and laying no blame, trying to be fair to everyone concerned. She described how their eldest daughter, Alice, had three children and lived a hundred miles away. Joy had noticed how infrequently Alice visited them and how when they visited Alice the atmosphere was very strained. This pained her very much because she wanted to see her grandchildren and because she could not make out what was happening. She worried that she had done something to offend Alice, but try as she might she could not think of anything which she might have done. She knew that Alice and her husband were having difficulties and that Alice was consulting a counsellor about this.

One day Alice phoned to say that she would be calling to see them. She made a special point of arranging to arrive at a time when Jack would be home from work. When she came she asked both of them to sit down so that she could tell them something very important. Joy thought Alice was going to tell them she had left her husband, but was puzzled when Alice said that she was going to leave the problem with them.

Then she told Joy, and reminded her father, how when she was twelve her father had interfered with her sexually. He had asked her to undress for him and he had fondled her breasts. She was very frightened by this. As the years had gone by she had tried to forget what had happened to her. She had begun to wonder whether it had really happened, especially when at college she had confided in a friend, only to be told that Freud had said that girls often had these kinds of fantasies about their fathers. She was sure that this was not a fantasy. When her marriage ran into difficulties she went to a counsellor, and her counsellor had helped her see how what her father had done to her had undermined her trust in men and so had affected her relationship with her husband.

Once she had discussed this with her counsellor she thought that she should ask Mark if anything had happened to him. She did, and Mark had said that it had and that this had gone on for a long time. She wrote to Jenny about it, but not to Louise. Alice had always been very close to her little sister, and she was sure that nothing had happened to Louise. Alice's counsellor had advised her that the problem was not hers but her parents', and that the only way she could rid herself of the effects of this problem was for her to return this problem to her parents. This she was doing, and, having done so, she left.

Joy did not attempt to describe the pain and confusion Alice left behind. Coming to see me was Joy's way of trying to sort out her confusion. It was important to her to see things clearly, no matter how painful they might be. She had always been like that. When my secretary had retrieved Mark's file from our archives I found in the notes I had made twelve years ago that I had written of Joy, 'She would puzzle over the problems our discussions raised, remember them to the next session, and try to find a solution.' I had noted, 'She said that she had a constant, nagging anxiety and a sense of imminent disaster from some unknown quarter.' I had also observed about Jack 'his reluctance to enquire deeply into personal matters'.

Joy spoke of how she could not understand how it was that she had never noticed anything. Alice and Jack were always getting angry with one another, but Alice had always been an angry child, ever since she was little. Later Joy told me how she had been ill in the last stage of her pregnancy with Jenny and had gone into hospital. Without asking Joy, Jack's mother had taken Alice, then three, home with her, and Joy did not see Alice for several weeks. This must have been a terrible blow to Alice which left a legacy of anger and fear.

Joy had spoken to Mark, and he told her how Jack had engaged him in sexual acts for quite some while, stopping only when Jack thought there was a danger that she would find out.

Jack defended himself. 'It was just mutual masturbation, nothing else. Just like boys playing together.'

Joy said, 'What about Ray? He told me there were times with him too.'

Jack shook his head. 'I can't remember.'

Joy said to me, 'This is what's so terrible, he can't remember. If he doesn't remember what he did, what other things has he forgotten? Will he do it again? Can we trust him? You can see why Mark and Alice worry he might – with our grandchildren.'

Jack found it hard to speak. 'I wouldn't, I couldn't. I know Mark and Alice don't trust me. But I wouldn't, not with my grandchildren.'

115

Joy pressed him, reminding him of what he had done to Mark.

Jack said, 'It started when Mark asked me about sex. I never thought much about it. Just two males together. At the orphanage, everyone did it.'

Jack went on to tell me about his life in the orphanage. After his father died his mother felt that she could not cope with him, so eight years old, he was sent to a home for boys. There, he said, every new boy suffered 'virtual rape from the older boys and from the masters. Everybody was involved in it. You learned not to complain because there was no one you could complain to. When you got older you did it to the younger boys. It went on in all the boys' homes. When I got older I was sent to other homes – we were shifted around a lot – and I met up with boys from other homes and they did it.'

Jack said that he had never thought about his time in the orphanage at all. 'I can't remember much about that time. I don't remember anything before I was eight. I know my mother used to have lodgers. One of them used to take me out to the woods. I can remember he used to buy me ice cream. Perhaps something happened then. I don't remember.'

He spoke of the terrible guilt he felt now. Before, 'I didn't think about it. I thought the children would have forgotten it.'

Joy said, 'I knew nothing of what was going on. I remember once, when Alice was about twelve, she was having a bath and Jack came in the kitchen and said he was going up to the bathroom to talk to her. I told him not to. I didn't think anything of it. I just thought he didn't understand how she was at an age where she needed privacy. He often didn't understand the children, but I always thought he was a good father. That's why I stayed with him. I remember talking to Alice about being careful with strangers. When I was about ten my cousin and I went to see my uncle, and while I was there he came into the room and wanted me to touch him – he called it tickling. I knew it wasn't right. When Alice was a child I told her not to let anyone do anything to her that she didn't want and to tell me, even if it was someone close, like an uncle.

Alice reminded me of this. She said, "I couldn't tell you, Mummy, because there was someone, and you were always telling us what a good father we had.'"

Jack spoke of how worried he was that he could not remember touching Ray. What else had he done, or might do? Would he become like one of those old men that molest children and finish up in gaol? He was desperately sorry to have caused Joy so much suffering. 'I see Joy sitting there, not saying anything, just thinking, and I want to comfort her, and I'm the one that caused her this suffering. I want to hold her but I can't.'

Joy told me how over the past ten years Jack had had several sudden, violent illnesses, sometimes necessitating him being admitted to hospital. The doctors had explained these in terms of a virus, but now she wondered if the illnesses were connected with all this. Now these things were being discussed the illnesses had stopped.

I said to Joy, 'You're very brave.' This was a mistake. Tears came into her eyes and her control nearly shattered. I thought then that she would have felt that to have broken down in front of me very shaming, but it was more serious than that. Some weeks later when we were arranging the next appointment she said that in the three weeks between this meeting and the next she had thought that she might go mad. All the structures she had built to form the world she lived in had now been revealed as structures, fictions, which bore little relation to reality, and she was no longer sure of what reality was. In those weeks she felt that she had to hold all her thoughts very carefully in her mind, otherwise everything would fall apart.

Jack threatened every part of her being. She was trying to hold it all together by continuing to be the good, patient, understanding, calm, unaggressive person she had always been and by maintaining her faith that there was something beyond this life which made reparation for her suffering. But Jack threatened even this. He would shrug his shoulders and say flatly, 'This is all there is and when you're gone, you're gone.'

She did not want to be commended for her bravery. Just helped to sort out this mess and to find some clarity. So when I offered another appointment she responded eagerly and overruled Jack's suggestion that there was no rush for us to get together again. She accepted the earliest appointment I could offer.

When we met three weeks later, Jack agreed that he needed people. 'I don't like being on my own,' he said.

He didn't want to talk about what had happened. 'What's happened has happened,' he said, 'and I can't change it. I'm sorry it happened, but I can't do anything about it. If Joy could accept that we could get on with thinking about the future. That's what's important, not the past.'

But Joy couldn't do that. She needed to think about what had happened, to re-interpret so much of what she remembered of the past years, and to understand, no matter how painful that process of understanding was.

'Jack just accepts things without thinking about them,' she said. 'He just takes what someone says or what he reads in the paper without working something out for himself.'

The way Joy would sit quietly, thinking, worried Jack very much. He felt that she had withdrawn from him and that he was in danger. He could not put this feeling into words. Instead he thought of being the one to leave. He said, 'Would it be best if I left? She'd be better on her own, without me.'

I said, 'We can't work out what's best to do until we understand what happened and why it happened.'

So Jack reluctantly agreed to talk some more about his past. He described how he had been conscripted to the Air Force and posted to the Far East where, in the absence of women, many of the men found sexual relief with one another, 'That's all it was, just relief,' he explained.

I asked if he considered himself to be a homosexual, that is, having loving relationships with men as the most important relationships of his life.

'Oh, no,' he said, 'I wouldn't want to live with a man. I like women.'

118

His last sexual experience with another man had been when he came out of the Air Force and was living in Wales. He had later moved to the Midlands where he had met Joy. None of these sexual encounters had been with children.

Joy said, 'Jack's always seen sex as something very surface. When the children were little and he was working very hard, I wouldn't see him until late and we'd no sooner get in the bedroom than he'd want to. I couldn't get him to understand I wasn't like that. I needed time to be with him.'

It was no good if Joy offered simply to oblige him. He wanted every sexual encounter to be passionate and grand where he possessed Joy totally. Instant, total gratification.

We went on to talk about their children. Jack was very proud of them.

All of them, except Mark, had excelled academically, and Mark was now being successful in his own business. 'I couldn't ever believe I could have such bright kids,' said Jack. 'Right from the beginning they seemed older than me.'

He went on to talk about their achievements, and it was only with great difficulty that I could bring him back to what he had said. What did he mean, they'd always been older than him?

Gradually we put together an answer to this question. When the children were tiny he did not see them very much as he was working so hard, but once they went to school he became aware of how bright they were and how much they knew. He could not discipline them, but only, in Joy's words, 'quarrel with them'. He felt inferior to them, and frightened of them. There was only one area of experience where he felt his knowledge was superior to theirs. That was of sex, and so he thought he could teach them about this. All the time he could not see anything wrong in doing this.

Of course, sometimes we teach children something because we feel that it is important that they know it, and other times we teach children something so we can demonstrate our superiority over them. Sometimes we need to demonstrate our superiority because we envy them so.

119

Joy had brought along letters from her daughters Jenny and Alice. Jenny was angry with Alice for speaking about the subject to Joy, causing Joy hurt. Jenny said she had spent years trying to forget 'the experience' and she did not want to discuss the matter now.

Jenny's letter implied that something very unpleasant had happened. Jack said he could remember very little, but he insisted that whatever had happened was nothing more than when he was 'fooling around with her,' playing the childish games Jenny had always enjoyed. He admitted he had touched her breasts. 'I didn't expose myself or ask her to touch me,' he said. 'It was her body I wanted to see.'

He was distraught with remorse. 'I didn't realize how much I had hurt her. I wouldn't want to hurt her ever. I wish I could tell her how sorry I am and ask her to forgive me.'

Jenny had always been extremely good as a child. Alice had been argumentative, and she and Jack had often clashed, but Jenny never argued with him.

Jack was puzzled how Jenny could be so upset now about what had happened; as a teenager she had always been very friendly to him. She had won a scholarship to a boarding school of great repute, and he had often driven her to and from the school, several hundreds of miles away. Moreover, at home she would often go from bathroom to bedroom quite scantily clad. Why would she do this? I guessed that Jenny throughout her teens was trying to prove to herself that these painful events of her childhood had never happened. All the tests she had made supported her hope that she had imagined that her father had done these things to her. Now Alice wanted to shatter this careful construction. I had no opportunity to check my suppositions with Jenny.

As Jenny was coming for Christmas I suggested that Jack write her a letter, saying what he had just told me he wanted to say to her.

He said, 'I never write letters. Joy writes all the letters in our family.'

I said, 'Just put down what you said to me.'

We spent some times discussing this proposed letter. Jack was worried that if he did what I suggested – giving Jenny the letter soon after she arrived home – this might spoil Christmas, and the family's ritual celebrations of Christmas were very important to Jenny (and to Jack). 'She likes everything to be exactly the same every year,' he said. 'I'll give it to her just before she leaves.'

'That won't give her time to discuss it with us if she wants to,' said Joy.

'Give her the chance to talk about it if she wants to and to ignore it if she wants to,' I said. 'It's the risk you'll have to take.'

Joy said, 'We have to show the children that we are able to bear all this, because if we can't bear it, then they'll find it hard to bear what they have to bear.'

When they came back to see me on New Year's Eve they seemed quite at ease, though there was still a look of strain in Joy's eyes. They had had a good Christmas. Jenny, Louise and Ray had come home and there had been a family Christmas.

Jack had written the letter to Jenny, saying how sorry he was and asking for her forgiveness. He had put the letter on her bedside table on Boxing Day morning. Later Joy had looked in and saw that the letter had disappeared. Jenny did not mention it for the rest of her stay.

'Her manner didn't change at all,' said Jack. 'She was just like she's always been, all the time she was with us. Perhaps she'll write to me when she gets back home.'

Mark and Alice, spending Christmas with their own families, had phoned over Christmas. 'They didn't want to talk to me,' said Jack. 'This is my punishment.'

Joy told me how she and Ray had talked together about the sexual approaches Jack had made to Ray and which Jack did not remember. They had not included Jack in this conversation because they both wanted to spare his feelings. Now, in her gentle, precise way, she told me what Ray had told her. Jack sat with his head down.

121

Ray described three events. The first was a simple enquiry from Jack as to whether Ray got erections. Ray had not sensed there was anything wrong with this until Jack, leaving Ray's bedroom, had said, 'Don't tell your mother.' The next time Ray and Jack were playing, just fooling around, Jack put his hand down Ray's trousers and touched his penis. Ray pulled himself away from Jack. The third occasion was no more than a look which Ray, undressed, found hard to distinguish from the close looks which parents give to children when inspecting for unwashed faces and adolescent pimples.

Ray had insisted to Joy that these events had had no effect on him, but he had looked relieved when Joy had said to him that the problem was Jack's and hers, and that he should not trouble himself about it any more.

Jack still could not remember these events.

'Jack doesn't bother to sort things out,' said Joy. 'Something happens and he just covers it up with something else. It's like our attic. When we moved to that house he just piled things up there, just a higgledy-piggledy mess. That attic always reminded me of Jack's mind. I hated to go up there. But now I've got everything in it sorted out. We put up some shelves and changed the glass in the window to let in more light.' She smiled. 'Now we're getting his mind sorted out – getting things clear and in order.'

The reason that the attic, like all the cupboards and shelves in their house, was crammed full of things was because Jack couldn't bear to throw things away. Twelve years ago, when Joy and Jack had discussed with me how they argued over money, Jack had insisted that his habit of buying things instead of saving money was simply his way of doing things. Now he talked of the importance of possessions in terms of his experiences in the orphanage.

'We weren't allowed any possessions there. If you had something you had to carry it with you to keep it or it disappeared. When I went into the orphanage it was just after Christmas and I had all my Christmas presents. They soon disappeared. I had a billiard table and cue. The cue was the first to go. One of the masters took it and used it as a cane. He often belted me with it. I soon learned how you had to get things. You were always on the look-out for something you could exchange for something else. But it always had to be something you could carry with you. It wasn't until you were a workboy that you had a locker, just a small one, about eighteen inches square, and you were allowed to buy a lock to put on it. But even then someone would break the lock and take your things.'

Jack talked about the beatings and indiscriminate cruelty in the orphanage The matron, he said, wore a large ring, and as she walked past a boy she would slap him across the head, often cutting his face with the ring. Even today Jack cannot bear to have his head touched.

'We would get belted for anything and nothing,' he said. 'Every fortnight we had boot inspection. We had to stand holding our boots upside down. The chap who mended our boots would allow us to lose just one stud from the sole. For every other stud missing you'd get a belting. We'd do anything to get studs for our boots. If you found one you treasured it like gold. Sometimes you'd manage to get hold of a new one and then you'd have to scratch it for ages to make it worn like the other ones. If he thought you'd put a new one in, well, you'd had it.'

The boys were beaten and whipped for all kinds of offences and often for nothing at all.

'I wet the bed every night from the time I went into the orphanage until the time I left. There was a group of us that did this, and we were always punished, every time. We'd be beaten, or wrapped up tight in the wet sheets and made to stand out in the cold. All the other boys knew what you'd done. We always had to wash our own sheets. The staff never did anything to help us.'

I commiserated with him, saying how terrible it must have been to have suffered such pain and been so helpless. Jack stressed that there was no one to whom the boys could turn for help. 'No one would have believed us,' he said, 'and my mother, even if she had believed me, which she wouldn't, wouldn't have done anything anyway.'

As Jack described at length the cruelties which had been perpetrated on these helpless boys he smiled and occasionally laughed. I asked him why he did so and he said, 'Well, it's a long time ago, and there's nothing I can do about it.'

I asked him if he had beaten his own children.

'Nothing like the way I was beaten,' he said. 'Only when they needed it.'

'I'd stop him,' said Joy. 'I can't bear violence. It's so – ugly.'

'Alice was the main one,' said Jack. 'She used to wind me up. I wouldn't belt her – just slap her around the face.'

Several times in this conversation Jack remarked with some awe how he was remembering things he had never thought of before, 'not just general things, but specific things. I can remember just what happened and what I felt.'

He went on, 'You know, when I remember being with someone then, I remember it as being pleasant. It was warm. You were accepted, even though it was only for a night. The masters, well, they lived two lives. If one of them said to you "Come to my room at seven o'clock tonight" you knew what it was for. You weren't going to get belted. They were really nice to you then. They gave you sweets and cakes, things you hardly ever got. Then next morning if you stepped out of line they'd belt you. The chap who did the shoes, he was gentle and nice in his room, and the next morning he'd belt you the same as anyone else. If a master chose you, well, it was like being taken out of the pond. We were just like fish in a pond. If one master chose you, then the other masters didn't. They each had their own group of boys. Your master might keep you for a long time, or he might get sick of you and then you'd get thrown back in the pond.'

Jack stressed that the good part was that 'you were always paired off with someone. There wasn't much group sex. Sometimes the boys in the dormitory would have, for want of a better word, a wanking party to see who could come first, and there was one master, a slimy creep, who used to get several boys in his room and make them do it while he watched, but most times, even with the boys in the dorm, even if it was only once, it was just the two of you. It made you feel special.'

Jack was very special for over a year. One master, known as the Major, singled him out. In his room Jack learned more than sex. The Major played records and introduced Jack to classical music. Music became Jack's great love. The Major would also take Jack on excursions out of the school.

'He would take me to Salvation Army meetings. Sometimes they would have concerts, really good music. And they always made a big fuss of me. They'd stuff me full of cakes and buns and give me a big bag of food to take back for my friends. I was really happy there. It was great, getting out and meeting people.'

Then, suddenly, the Major left.

'The staff were moved around the different homes a lot,' he said, 'but we usually had a few weeks' warning. With the Major, he just left in twenty-four hours. I was thrown back in the pond and I was just another boy there for, well, over a year.'

Joy had previously mentioned that one thing that always upset Jack was whenever a married couple they knew split up. I reminded Jack of this and asked if a couple parting reminded him of how he felt when the Major left.

'Perhaps,' he said, still finding my way of linking one event to another all very strange.

I asked Jack if the other boys were envious when one boy was singled out by a master.

'No, they just took it for granted. Everyone did it. If you woke in the morning and saw a boy's bed empty you knew he was with so and so. And the boys who went with masters, they brought back sweets and things, for the other boys. If they didn't hand them out they had them taken off them.'

'Who were you envious of?'

'Everyone who had something I didn't have. Every Christmas the people in the village gave presents to the boys. One Christmas I got a wooden tank and the other boys got air rifles. You can't do much with a wooden tank, can you?'

Despite their continual financial difficulties, Jack and Joy had always found the money to give their children the things they needed to pursue their interests. If one was interested in music, then musical instruments were bought. If another was interested in tennis, then tennis rackets and tennis lessons were bought. Jack was proud of his children's achievements and of his hard-won ability to give them what they needed, but underneath that there must have lurked a small boy's envy of the other kids' possessions.

We had been talking for over two hours and I was beginning to feel tired. The conversation turned to television and Joy remarked that Jack could not stand any programme that revealed emotions. When I enquired, 'What emotions?' it became clear that Jack could not tolerate watching the expression of realistically tender feelings. He enjoyed the violence of Westerns and war films ('Well, it's only on the screen, isn't it?') and in the musicals and old films which he enjoyed tender feelings are packaged as sentimentality. But the expression of real, tender, personal feelings, with all the yearning and the pain, was something he could not bear to witness.

As we were agreeing that it was late and we should go to our respective homes Jack began talking about his time in Malaysia. My question, weeks ago, about whether he considered himself to be a homosexual, had set him thinking. He just didn't know what to think. He began to tell us about one of the chaplains in the RAF who was a homosexual and who would spend time with Jack and his friends. They would drink beer and listen to records and, if there were just three or four of them of like inclination, they would engage in some sexual activity.

Suddenly, in the midst of telling us this, Jack said, 'Ugh, that makes me feel terrible. I'm going home.' Saying so, he stood up and put on his coat.

But he stayed, diary in hand, to arrange our next appointment and to say that he was grateful for the opportunity to talk about things. 'I can talk to you,' he said, 'because I knew you before. I couldn't talk to any of your colleagues, a stranger.'

As they left Joy told me they were going to a New Year's Eve party, the first such party they had been to together for many years. Joy looked quite happy as she told me about the party, but earlier she had said, 'When I got married, I didn't bargain for all this.'

A fortnight later Joy had just returned from a week helping Alice when one of her children was ill. It had been a painful, difficult time for both Joy and Alice. They knew that they should talk, but each did not want to distress the other.

Risking Alice's pain and anger, Joy told her about the discussions she and Jack had had with me and how she now understood him much better.

She said to me, 'Isn't it strange, you can live with a man for thirty-five years and not know him.'

Joy talked to Alice about Alice's childhood when, as the eldest child, Alice had to endure the birth of five siblings. One of these babies had lived only four days, and Jack had ordered Joy, 'You're not to cry.' Forbidden to talk about her grief, for talking brought on tears, Joy withdrew into a depression. She struggled on with performing her duties as wife and mother but, as she told me, 'I can't remember Alice then. She was the schoolgirl in the family. It's no wonder she was argumentative and demanding.'

Alice, as she told her mother later, did not want her mother to talk about those times. 'I thought you were going to criticize me and tell me what a great trouble I was to you.' Joy was not placing the blame on Alice. She was reviewing what she herself had done and was feeling the pain that loving parents feel when they realize that what they have done to their children, often with the best of intentions, has hurt and harmed their children.

Alice told Joy of her encounters with Jack when she was just blossoming into womanhood. 'He said that he wanted to undress me. This made me feel that I was supposed to respond, like the ball was in my court. I had to put up a barrier, but at the same time I felt that because I had refused him he rejected me. I still feel he's rejecting me.'

Joy hastened to reassure her that Jack had not rejected her and that he loved her very much. Alice said, 'I wish he'd write and tell me that.'

Jack felt very discomfited at being faced with writing another letter. But his face lit up with happiness as he told me how, when he had phoned Joy, Alice had answered the phone, and, instead of immediately calling Joy to the phone, had asked him how he was. He was delighted, too, that as Jenny was leaving after Christmas, she had invited them to visit her.

Again his face was alight with pleasure as Joy told me about her visit to Mark and his family and about Mark's little daughter. Jack longed to see his grand-daughter, but, as he told me with great sadness, 'Mark won't talk to me.'

A few weeks later Jack told me that he had written a second letter, this time to Alice. Mark, too, had phoned and taken the time to talk to him.

Jack's story shows how the sexual abuse of children gets handed down from generation to generation, like the family jewels. It seems likely, from Jack's memory of the trip to the woods and the ice cream, and the fact that he retrieved this memory and wondered about its significance, that he had had some sexual encounter when he was small. But the events of his early life (he said he remembered almost nothing of his first eight years) and many of the events of his childhood he hid in the deepest recesses of his memory. When he said that he did not expect his children to remember what he had done to them, he was speaking truthfully, for he did not remember what had been done to him.

This forgetting was not just because he was the kind of person for whom repression is the most favoured form of defence. In those situations where he had been the victim of sexual and physical abuse he was completely helpless. There was no one in the whole wide world to whom he could turn for help, and he was a small child in a world of powerful and dangerous adults. He didn't want to remember what had been done to him, because with those memories would come that feeling of terrible helplessness and abandonment.

Jack's story shows, too, how a child, needing a personal

relationship in the way that he needed food, would, like a starving man will eat anything, accept affection in whatever form it was offered. Children should never be put in a position where they have to accept love at any price but, alas, many of them are.

The price which Jack had to pay did not seem to him at the time all too high. He was in the business of surviving, so learning to laugh at cruelty instead of being shocked by it did not seem much, as did learning to ignore his grief at the loss of the tenderness and love which should have been his by rights. He did not see that learning to laugh at the cruelty which is being done to yourself means that you are no longer shocked at the cruelty done to others, and that you might now be as cruel to others as others were to you. He could not possibly see, as a child, that in not allowing himself to grieve for himself, he would, in later life, not allow his wife to show her grief for the child she had lost, and that this would cause great hurt to the person he loved and needed so much.

Deciding as a child not to allow yourself to grieve over the cruelty which has been done to you can mean that in adult life you cannot assess or appreciate the sufferings of others. This enables you to become the kind of Health Service administrator who says complacently, in connection with the hospital's high suicide rate, 'Well, you can't stop people killing themselves, can you?'

Or you can become the kind of person who sees nothing wrong with persecuting the people whom you dislike. Quentin Crisp, himself no stranger to persecution, was asked on Irish television, 'Are you accepted more now you are successful?'

He replied, 'I think people misunderstand the principle of persecuting homosexuals, or, indeed, of persecution in general. It is not directed at a person, it is directed at anybody who is not likely to find defenders. During the course of your life you pile up a great deal of bitterness – your wife does not love you, there are your children who do not obey you, there is your boss who does not give you any preferment – and one day you see someone whom no one will blame you for attacking, and then all your bitterness pours out. And it doesn't matter who it is, as long as you can lash out at somebody without anyone reproaching you later. This is why people attack the weak, homosexuals, but especially effeminate homosexuals.'[15]

Or you can become the kind of person who is plagued by depression. You have no sympathy for the child that you once were. It is very striking in therapy how people will talk with great sympathy about, say, the starving children of Africa, but when they speak of the child they once were there is not a trace of sympathy or concern for that little, frightened child. 'I was a very bad child,' they will say, 'and deserved to be punished by my parents.'

Among those people who devote their lives to helping others are many people who show enormous sympathy for other people's suffering but are remarkably tough and unpitying towards themselves. They can recognize that as a child they had a difficult time, and they can acknowledge that as a child they suffered a great deal, but they refuse to give to themselves in adult life what, as a child, they lacked. Instead, they lavish this love and concern on others, and draw satisfaction from that. This is the defence mechanism of projective identification, the means by which we can identify with another person, and then give to that person what we would wish was given to us. This is a kind of second-hand self-love, and it is the equivalent of eating thin gruel rather than a decent meal. But those people who have never been loved properly as children find it very difficult to love themselves to the degree which their humanness requires in adulthood.

Unless we can love our self we can never be our self. Unless we can be our own authentic self we cannot live comfortably within our bodies and we can never feel free to explore our potentialities. To deal with fear we may turn ourselves and other people into objects, but once we have done this we have become less than the person we might have been.

Yet, the ability to turn ourselves and others into objects has been a very important factor in the survival of the human race. Without it we would not, as a species, have survived the vicissitudes which have befallen us. Individually we are very weak, but as part of a group we can be quite strong. We are prepared to pay a high price in order to share the group's strengths. If this means turning ourselves into objects, we will do so. If this means turning other people, our group's enemies, into objects, we shall do so. Even if I suffer, even if I do not survive, then my group, my family, my country, my race, my religion, will continue.

Or will they?

Needing Enemies

In describing how we, as babies and children, had to give up being our true selves in order to be accepted into our family, I have also been describing the way in which groups are formed and stay together. Every group has rules and standards which apply, in some way, to every person in that group, and every member of that group, even the leader and the most powerful person in that group, has to give up some part of themselves in order to conform to the rules and standards. Those parts of ourselves which we have to give up for membership of the group we project on to the people outside the group, and these people become the objects of our contempt and hatred, our enemies. (Many people who like to think of themselves as kind, caring, unaggressive people will say that they don't have enemies. What they are actually reporting is that at the moment they are not under threat. Once their security comes under some threat they immediately know who their friends and who their enemies are.)

This way we can restore to ourselves some of the self-esteem which we gave away in order to become obedient. We can say to ourselves, 'I mightn't be much in myself, but I belong to the best family/country/sex/race/religion in the world.' Pride in our group is balm to our wounded soul, and if we feel angry with other members of our group, or if we envy the power and possessions which other people in the group have, but we do not, we can ensure our safety and the cohesion of the group by shifting our anger and envy from them to our group's enemies, and feel the glow of virtue in being loyal to our group. Engaging in a war to take people's attention away from their own grievances is a political device as old as groups and leaders.

Enemies serve a very useful purpose. We can't live without them. But then, it is having enemies which has created our present world, where we have enough nuclear weapons to destroy all of us many times over, and where the resources of our planet are being used at such a rate that the planet will no longer be able to support human life for much longer, perhaps no more than about 150 years. So it seems that while we can't live without enemies, we shall soon not be able to live with them.

Denying fear, in the short term, is an effective survival technique.

But in the long term, denying fear destroys.

Chapter Four

A Bodily Solution?

We turn other people, and ourselves, into objects in order to control our fear.

To turn another person into an object we choose to perceive that person as lacking the needs, desires, and feelings that we have.

To turn ourselves into an object we choose not to perceive the needs, desires and feelings that we have.

One of the simplest ways of turning yourself into an object is to regard yourself as nothing but a body. Everything about you can be explained and understood in terms of your body. If you lash out at other people, it is because you are a man, and men have lots of testosterone which makes them aggressive. If you sink into a deep depression, it is because you are a woman, and female hormones cause depression. If you are anxious, it is because your body is prone to produce too much adrenalin. If you have diarrhoea, it is because you have an irritable bowel. If you have a stomach ulcer, it is because your stomach produces too much acid. If you have migraine, it is because your blood pressure changes. If you get bronchitis, it is because you inherited a weak chest.

These kinds of explanations, whether couched in ordinary language or in the jargon of the medical profession, are 'nothing but' explanations, the aim of which is to enclose, belittle and dismiss, rather than to understand. The circularity of their arguments ('You get a lot of colds because you have a weak chest.' 'How do you know I have a weak chest?' 'Because you get a lot of colds') matches the way in which a part of human experience can be encircled, reduced, and dismissed.

Of course, we can't have rage, depression, anxiety, diarrhoea, ulcers, migraine, bronchitis unless we have a body to have these things in. (I am leaving aside the belief that our soul will continue

133

after our body has disappeared. Presumably in Heaven there are no afflictions, body or soul. Descriptions of Hell seem to imply that we take our bodies with us there.) But to say that these experiences are nothing but events in an object which is a body is to fail to understand what human experience is.

There is a long tradition in Western Europe and in the countries which derive their cultures from Western Europe of explaining human experience in terms of bodily function. Even before Descartes' division of the person into body and soul had been seized on by the intellectuals, the tradition that a human being is basically nothing but a body was well established. The theory of bodily 'humours' described and explained people in terms of their bodies.

This kind of explanation is immensely attractive. A body is *there*. You can see it. It is contained within its skin. Its movements are like those of a machine. It can be taken apart like a machine. To understand a machine you don't have to consider its social situation. A functioning tractor will function just as well on the steppes of Russia as on the plains of the United States. To understand a machine you don't have to understand its feelings, thoughts, needs, desires, because it doesn't have any. A body might produce feelings, thoughts, needs, desires, but you don't have to worry about them because they are nothing but froth and bubble, the trivial foam upon the substance of life.

Moreover, there is nothing to be ashamed of if a machine breaks down. A part can break or wear out. That is the nature of a machine. So, if you are your body, and your body is a machine, then there is nothing to be ashamed of if one of your parts breaks down or wears out. There is no need to be ashamed if you are ill.

But what if the froth goes wrong – all those thoughts and emotions – what if they make you feel confused and frightened? Why, then, remember how machines work. If a machine when it is running properly gives off white smoke as waste, and suddenly it starts giving off black smoke, then you know there is something wrong with your machine. Similarly, when your body is functioning properly, it produces nice white foam, lots of happy, contented thoughts. If something goes wrong with your body it might start producing some nasty black foam, lots of frightening, miserable thoughts. We don't have to worry about what these black thoughts mean. All we need do is discover what is wrong with our body and put it right. If, through the limitations of medical science, we cannot do that, then at least we don't have to feel ashamed if our body isn't functioning properly. It's not our fault if the machine breaks down.

And, of course, since it isn't our fault, then other people will feel sorry for us. What bad luck, they'll say. Never mind, dear. What can we do to help you? Take things easy. Aren't you brave! I don't know how you put up with it. I do admire you.

Jacky, stricken with osteoarthritis and a thyroid disease for some twelve years, wrote to me to say that she found my book, *Depression: the Way Out of Your Prison*,[1] helpful. She said, 'I am not arguing that chronically sick people become depressed. Indeed, I have met many who seem to take a pride in being ill and have found that their illness brings them attention and consideration which had previously been denied them. The fact that their disease is physical, chronic, and recognized as such, seems to give them a sense of wellbeing and security which they can expect to be lifelong. They have, in fact, become much happier people.'[2]

But not all people welcome an explanation in bodily terms of their pain and confusion. A senior nursing sister, writing of her experience of depression, described how she became depressed while she was a patient in hospital following an accident which badly damaged her leg. She wrote:

I know all about the importance of significant life events in the aetiology of depression, but I cannot accept other people's explanation of my depression in terms of my orthopaedic history. I found it helpful to have sympathy for my accident, but infuriating to be told time and time again that I had ample reason to be depressed. Perhaps there are patients who find it more acceptable to be depressed because of a physical ailment. For me this kind of attempted reassurance merely confirmed me in my view that people have a total lack of understanding of how much worse it was to be depressed than to have a broken leg. I found it devastating to be forced to have a physical reason for the way I felt and a belittling of my very real and over-whelming personal and emotional problems.'[3]

When you recognize that you do have 'very real and over-whelming personal and emotional problems', it is very painful when other people treat your problems as being nonexistent, or as being much less than their problems, or as being no more than everyday troubles which anyone can deal with just by being sensible or pulling themselves together. But this is indeed what many people will do, for the sight of other people's personal and emotional problems might remind them of their own.

If, as a child, you have been taught that it is not permissible for you to reveal all your needs, desires and feelings, if you have slotted yourself into the role which your family and your society has decreed is yours, those of your needs, feelings and desires which you are forbidden don't evaporate away. They are still there, and you have to find some way of dealing with them, even if you don't consciously acknowledge their existence.

How can you solve this problem?

Why not try a bodily solution?

If having a lot of frightening thoughts is a sign that there is some-thing wrong with your body, then perhaps if you are able to make your body very healthy all these frightening, miserable thoughts will go away. So many of us develop *an obsession with health*.

There we all are, jogging ten miles each day, pedalling away on our stationary bikes, going for the burn or through the pain barrier, all in the belief that if we make ourselves stronger and healthier we shall never be frightened, or overtaken by old age and death. Perhaps it is not just coincidence that over recent years, when there has been an increasing understanding of how in a nuclear war no one will be safe, so many people, men and women of all ages, have taken up the pursuit of physical fitness. It is a forlorn hope that you can run fast enough to outpace the waves of a nuclear warhead's destruction, or that a lean and muscled body can withstand radiation, but it is a way of feeling a fraction less helpless in the face of such immense peril.

So, too, in recent years, there has been an increasing interest in choosing food to promote health and not merely to sustain life or indulge a fancy. This interest reflects a distrust and a turning away from the vast, complex food industry which is part of the even vaster industries which dominate our world. If we eat food that we know and trust, we shall be safe. Underneath this may be the hope that if we could get back to a simpler life and live close to nature, then we shall be safer. The problem is that when people do, or did, live close to nature, life is both dangerous and short.

When I was a child in Australia it would have been quite unthinkable for a woman (except a *masculine* woman) to take a serious interest in sport. Feminine women walked and never ran. In hot weather feminine women could don a swimsuit and bob up and down at the edge of the ocean, but they did not swim. My mother forbade my father to teach me how to run (he had been a champion runner) but, fortunately for me, she didn't supervise my swimming, and so I spent many magnificent hours surfing out beyond the first line of breakers. This is one part of Australian life that I miss and long for, although I no longer have the confidence that I had then that no hungry shark would come swimming by. I still benefit from the physical strength that swimming developed in me, just as I still suffer from the effects of the form of the obsession with health which my parents had in common with many other people.

This was the belief that it was absolutely imperative that your bowels should be emptied every day. The fear that life was full of hidden dangers and that people might have within themselves dangerous and destructive powers was transferred into bodily terms, namely, that the waste products of the body are dangerous and must be flushed out daily, else something terrible will happen. In my childhood home the kitchen cupboard always contained a packet of Epsom salts which my mother took ritually every morning. Many of my battles for autonomy and independence were around Epsom salts and a metal container and rubber hose which my mother regarded as absolutely essential for good health. The number of packets of laxatives which I see on chemists' shelves suggests to me that the belief that danger can be averted by a daily bowel movement is still powerful.

Of course, a successful evacuation of your bowels can leave you with a sense of completion and achievement. The behaviourist child experts who advise parents to give regular praise to children who pee and crap in the appropriate receptacles are themselves reinforcing this idea. The importance of this feeling of being able to act effectively on the world should not be underestimated. It is the means whereby we knit together our inner reality with our outer reality, and feel a sense of power, despite the immensity and power of the world we live in. Such experiences are not merely pleasurable. They give us the hope and courage which we need to carry our lives forward. We can prove ourselves by acting on the world.

Such acting upon the world and proving oneself can be conceived of solely in bodily terms. Many boys, going through the process of rejecting those aspects of themselves which might be labelled 'feminine', attempt to prove themselves by carrying out feats, like gargantuan eating, or ingesting unusual objects (like live frogs) or leaping out of high windows, or climbing the tallest trees, or being the one who can pee the highest up the wall. Many men, feeling but not understanding their loss of part of themselves in the process of fulfilling their society's concept of what it is to be a man, will try to prove themselves by developing a body which is exceptionally strong, or capable of swift movement, or by carrying out some feat of bravery and peril. The desire to prove yourself by bodily means has provided leaders with an easy means of persuading men to die in battle.

To put yourself through tests of strength and endurance, or to devote much thought and effort to making yourself healthy, you have to have some notion of yourself as being of value. Of course, you are not good enough, but there is something there which you can regard as good. You are worthy of preserving.

If this sense of self-worth diminishes or has never been established, then a bodily solution to fear by making yourself healthier and stronger will not be appropriate. Instead, the bodily solution is to use your body to blot out your fear. Instead of becoming healthy, you become *addicted*.

A Bodily Solution?

Nicotine Addiction

Some years ago my friend and colleague Miller Mair grew tired of trying to treat with behavioural methods smokers who said they wanted to give up smoking, because he found that his results were no better than what would be expected in the general population when people decide to give up smoking. Some succeed; some do not. He decided to concentrate on finding out what meaning the cigarettes have for each person. He would say to his client, 'If your cigarette was a person, what kind of person would it be?' He got some very revealing answers. One man saw his cigarette as the perfect woman, beautiful and compliant. Another man always smoked one particular brand, no matter how difficult they were to obtain. They were his mates, and he was always loyal to his mates.

I often use Miller's question when someone complains to me about not being able to give up smoking or insists that no matter how smoking affects health he (or, so often, she) will not stop. At a workshop on depression that I was running, one of the participants, a young psychologist whom I knew to be most able and aware, smoked heavily throughout. He also revealed himself to be no stranger to depression. The topic of smoking came up, and I asked him to imagine that his cigarette was a person and to describe that person to us. He described a person who gave him confidence, enthusiasm and the power to achieve. Could he not give these things to himself? I asked. He said no, he could not. Without his cigarettes he was empty and frightened.

In their book *Smoking: Psychology and Pharmocology*[4] Heather Ashton and Rob Stepney describe nicotine as having a biphasic or two-stage nature. It acts as a stimulant, making you feel more active, and as a tranquillizer, making you feel calmer under stress. So people who find their work both boring and stressful find smoking attractive. Perhaps this explains why so many women smoke and why women find giving up smoking more difficult than men do.

I asked a woman psychologist, someone I knew to be tremendously capable and skilled at her job, how she came to take up smoking. She said, 'I was fourteen and I went to my first grown-up party. I was scared to death. I was sitting there, not talking to anyone, and this boy came over and spoke to me. He asked me if I had any cigarettes and when I said I didn't he went away. So I thought, "That's how you get boys to talk to you, smoke." When I went home I stole some of my mother's cigarettes – both my parents smoke heavily – and practised in secret. At first it was horrible, but I persisted because when I went to parties after that I didn't feel so nervous if I was smoking a cigarette.'

Many people talk of 'deserving' a cigarette after all the difficulties and hard work they have to endure. Sometimes a cigarette stands for that aspect of one's life which one is not allowed to express. Helen, who from earliest childhood had to be neat, clean and tidy and who maintains this in her adult life as wife and mother, sees her cigarette as someone who is dirty and disgusting, yet someone to whom she has an immense loyalty.

To give up smoking, the person can simply resolve to do so, providing smoking has ceased to have a meaning the aim of which is to protect you from fear. When such willpower fails, the next step is to make conscious the important meaning which the cigarette carries and to ask, 'Is this meaning something so important that I cannot give it up or change it?'

Alcohol Addiction

Margaret did not tell me that she drank a good deal and often, but after she had phoned me at home late at night I began to suspect that the distress and incoherence she showed during those late-night calls was a common pattern and not a chance occurrence. So I asked her about her drinking. She was very defensive.

She said, 'I'm not going to stop drinking.'

To justify this she told me something she had never told anyone before.

'I can't stand the pain.'

'What pain?' I asked.

'In my chest, under there.'

A Bodily Solution?

I recognized the place and the pain. I remembered when I had made the discovery that the phrases 'a broken heart' and 'heartache' were not simply empty metaphors but referred to a real physical experience. When we lose somebody or something very important to us our hearts do ache and break. That special muscle which pumps our blood might keep on working normally, but somehow, perhaps because our anguish alters the way we breathe, a pain, sometimes dull and aching, sometimes sharp and piercing, develops behind the lower end of the breast bone, in the region of the heart.

I told Margaret about this. She was amazed to find that this pain was a common phenomenon. She had always thought that the pain was peculiar to her, further evidence of her essential badness. Drinking, to some extent, eased the pain.

I was quite stern with Margaret. I was not going to continue to see her unless she consulted a doctor about how her drinking was affecting her health. There was no point in my trying to help her sort out her emotional problems if meanwhile her liver was solidifying into cirrhosis.

We argued about this for some time, and eventually she agreed to have one of those complete overhauls which a private medical scheme offers as the last word in medical care. Margaret's liver proved to be all right, but her blood pressure was up, quite worryingly so. This made her realize that something potentially serious was amiss and she made a determined effort to cut down on her drinking. (When Margaret read the first draft of this chapter she pointed out to me that she was still drinking, though not as much. Her social life was with people who drank a good deal. But she was now following a daily exercise routine which involved regular running, something she found immensely satisfying and peaceful. This seems to have solved the problem of her high blood pressure.)

In my experience with people who drink heavily and often, Margaret's reaction was unusual. So many heavy drinkers cling to their drinking because without it they would stand revealed as weak and frightened. A consultant psychiatrist whose heavy drinking was a way of life called it 'a sinister but effective peacemaker, a means of securing for however short a time some way out of the prisonhouse of reality to the Golden Age'.[5] Heavy drinkers use their drinking not only as a way of avoiding their own pain but as a way of bamboozling those people who want them to stop drinking. Discussions about how much you drink or what appalling things you did when you were drunk prevent your would-be helpers from perceiving how depressed and lonely you are.

Alcohol does more than just hide pain and fear. It provides some marvellous excuses. Snyder, Higgins and Stucky, in their book *Excuses: Masquerades in Search of Grace*,[6] devote six large, tightly packed pages to all the research studies which show how useful drinking alcohol can be. For instance, people who believed that they had drunk alcohol when in fact they had not (some research psychologists have no compunction about lying to their subjects) and who also believed that you were allowed to be aggressive when you were drunk, or that alcohol made you feel less nervous in company, became aggressive when aggravated, or more relaxed (as measured by heart rate) in meeting someone new.

A number of studies where the hapless male subjects were wired up to a machine which measures penile tumescence (for so many men, sexual desire is considered to reside solely in the penis) showed that

men whose normal sexual response is inhibited by sexual guilt or social restraints will show the greatest disinhibition effect when they believe they are drinking alcohol. There is an important payoff in this process, since the men can absolve themselves of responsibility for their actions by blaming alcohol for their disinhibited behaviour.[7]

One study[8]

found that those child molesters who claimed to have been intoxicated at the time of their offence expressed significantly more derogatory attitudes toward other child molesters than those who did not claim to have been intoxicated. We would suggest that those subjects who claimed intoxication may have held more derogatory attitudes because, *having the excuse of intoxication, they could deny their personal membership of the reviled fellowship of child molesters*. In effect, they could disparage child molesters without disparaging themselves. By admitting a relatively minor problem (alcohol abuse), they were enabled to simultaneously admit their crime and deny personal responsibility for it.[9]

Drinking alcohol is something which we can choose to do. It is an *activity*. Nevertheless, an increasingly popular way of referring to this activity is to say, 'I have a drink problem.'

Social workers and volunteer counsellors often speak in this way of their clients. 'He has a drink problem' sounds more polite and understanding than 'He's a drunk'. Whenever I hear about 'a drink problem' I always get a vision of some ordinary person carrying a briefcase. The briefcase is the problem which the person has. I always want to ask the person to show me his problem in the same way as he could show me his new, shiny briefcase.

I sometimes do this when the person who declares himself to have a drink problem is actually presenting himself to my scrutiny. My request 'Show me your problem' is like a Zen koan, aiming to show that so many of the confusions and conflicts we get ourselves into come not from what *is* but from the language we use.

English, like the other Indo-European languages, prefers nouns to verbs, that is, words which refer to objects rather than words which refer to actions. Some languages, like that which the Hopi Indians speak, are not like this. They can talk about activity without having to create an object doing the activity. A Hopi Indian might observe an event which he calls 'sudden brightening' but which we, using English, have to refer to as 'the lightning flashed'. Now we have created an object, lightning, which does something, like flashing.

We might say, 'I was swimming', but often we say, 'I had a swim.'

Where is the lightning when it isn't flashing?

Where is the swim before I had it?
Where is your drink problem?
Why don't you throw it away?
Why can't you throw it away?

The only answer is that you can't throw your drink problem away because it isn't a thing which you have. It is what you do. Your problem *is* you.

(This same language trap is present when people talk about *having a personality*, or *having depression*, or *having schizophrenia*. More of this later.)

By claiming that you have a drink problem you are, in fact, by your choice of language, distancing yourself, splitting yourself off from part of your experience. Here you are; there is your problem.

While you split yourself in this way you cannot deal with the problems which your drinking creates, much less the pain and fear which underlies your drinking. You have to own every part of yourself. Your language has to be not 'I have a drink problem', but 'I drink a lot'.

Alcoholics Anonymous demand that the first step to cure is to acknowledge that you are an alcoholic, and this recognition, with the support of AA members, has allowed a large number of people to find the courage to change their way of life. However, the statement 'I am an alcoholic' which the AA requires its members to make contains another kind of 'distancing'. Drinking alcohol to excess, according to Alcoholics Anonymous, is not something you choose to do, but something you can't help doing because you have a disease called alcoholism.

The idea that there is a disease called alcoholism is widely held. Nick Heather and Ian Robertson, two psychologists who have made a special study of people who drink a lot, have written:

> The main assumptions of the disease perspective, as presented by AA, are that alcoholics possess an inborn, constitutional abnormality which prevents them from ever drinking normally; that this abnormality results in a 'loss of control' over intake, and an insatiable 'craving' for more which is triggered off by the smallest quantity of alcohol; that these processes are

irreversible, so that the only way to arrest the disease is by lifelong and total abstention; and that, if drinking is continued, it leads invariably to further deterioration, insanity and death. Slogans such as 'once an alcoholic, always an alcoholic', and 'one drink, one drunk', embody this disease model. Although originally proposed by a lay fellowship, it has been enormously influential in shaping the medical response to problem drinking.[10]

They point out that regarding alcoholism as a disease has many disadvantages

The only implication here from the disease standpoint is that, until the elusive 'biochemical abnormality' (on the hunt for which millions of pounds of research funds have been fruitlessly spent) is eventually discovered, all we can do is to provide more and better treatment services. Yet the epidemiological evidence clearly shows that the number of alcohol problems is closely related to *per capita* alcohol consumption, and this in turn is related to the availability of alcohol, mainly its retail price.[11]

Put simply, if there is no alcohol available, or if you can't afford what is available, you can't have the disease of alcoholism. Neither can you have a drink problem. What you do depends very largely on the society you live in.

Heather and Robertson explain drinking alcohol to excess in terms of *social learning theory*, that is:

Problem drinking is learned habitual behaviour, in the same category as compulsive gambling, some forms of over-eating, heroin or tobacco use. Indeed, some of the common features of these phenomena may be observed in a wide range of normal activities carried to excess: compulsive physical exercising, some forms of sexual behaviour, and certain types of compulsive over-working, are just three examples . . . Social learning theory is an umbrella term for a range of well-established psychological processes, ranging from classical conditioning to self-concept.[12]

So, you drink a lot because certain things remind you to drink ('All my friends at work have a drink at lunch time'), because the advantages (positive reinforcement) of drinking occur sooner than the disadvantages ('The first drink always makes me feel better. It's not until I get home and the wife starts nagging that I feel worse'), and because drinking has something to do with your vanity ('A man who doesn't like his pint isn't a real man').

Alcoholism isn't a disease. Alcoholism is a word we use to refer to something we choose to do in order to make ourselves feel better and to try to blot out pain and fear.

The same can be said about drug addiction.

Drug Addiction

Many people try drugs and give them up or indulge occasionally, using them in much the same way as many people use alcohol. Those who use drugs persistently, irrespective of the damage the drugs cause, do so because the drugs offer a means of overcoming a terrible deficit. For extraverts it is a sense of emptiness and a chance to belong to a group which will not reject you as all other groups, or so it seems, have rejected you. For introverts it is the chance to withdraw into an inner world and to give up trying to relate to or make sense of the outer world.

Terry wrote to me to say he was back in Lincoln for a short time and would like to call to say hello. I hadn't seen him for nearly a year as he had been living in London. He had been referred to me three years before, and I had not expected that there would be anything I could do for him. The referral letter spoke of a twenty-year history of drug and alcohol addiction, with many admissions to the local psychiatric hospital and just as many periods in prison on charges of fighting and violence. I doubted if coming to talk to me would make any difference to Terry, so I decided to offer him an appointment once a month and in that time just to converse without any particular therapeutic purpose in mind. I was surprised when, after a few months, Terry would say on leaving my room how helpful he found our meetings.

I enjoyed our discussions. Terry was a gentle, reflective man, who, when his brain was not clouded with alcohol and drugs, saw things and people very clearly. He was an artist, but he rarely put his talents to use. He told me how the first time he was admitted to the psychiatric hospital he was just sixteen. Eighty men of all ages were crowded together in one of the old wards which had changed little since the hospital was built a hundred years before. He was terrified, but gradually he got to know the other men and he began to learn the rules of how to survive in a psychiatric hospital and how to use the system to his benefit. Whenever he came to see me he would visit his friends who were sojourning in hospital. He would try to time his visit to the wards so as to coincide with meals being served. Whenever he came to see me he was always neat and clean and quite lucid (just two cans of Special Brew on the way were enough to give him the necessary courage to meet me), but from the way he dressed (he traded, amongst other things, in old clothes) he always looked as if he needed a meal, and this the nurses would often provide.

Over the years I knew him Terry was often depressed and despairing, seeing no future ahead of him. He was greatly liked by his many friends, and there were many who loved him, but he could not tolerate prolonged closeness. He showed me nothing of the violence which he showed to others when he felt frightened or attacked, but he showed me much of his inner loneliness and his need to withdraw. There were many times when I was saying goodbye to him I would wonder if I would ever see him again.

Along with these self-destructive characteristics went a superb ability to make an honest, or mildly dishonest, penny. He was not greedy, but he had all the practical skills necessary for survival in our society. He told me that the books which had influenced him most when he was young were Jack Kerouac's books and W.H. Davies's *Diary of a Supertramp*.

Terry bought and sold this and that, and towards the end of the time when he came to see me regularly he had begun making visits to London. There he could supplement his income by casual labouring work, which was easier to obtain in London than Lincoln, and he found adequate accommodation without difficulty by joining those people who squatted in empty houses and flats.

He wrote to me to say that he would be staying in London, but would keep in touch.

When he came to see me he looked healthier and happier than I had ever seen him. He was no longer doing labouring work but had managed to resurrect some building skills which he had acquired when he was young and was now doing some casual work which paid good money. He was in love with a girl who could not live permanently in England, and so he had found a balance between closeness and distance which seemed to suit him. He had acquired, if squatters can ever acquire, a huge flat in London, where he provided rooms and mattresses for his itinerant friends and any of the waifs and strays that he discovered down on their luck. Many of these people were writers whose work had not been published, and musicians whose music had never been recorded. Many, often the same people, were drug addicts and alcoholics.

Terry told me that he had given up drinking, but added, 'I've done that often before.' He was having more trouble giving up cannabis.

'The cannabis they're selling me, it's not so strong. They mix it with henna oil and wax, but it costs just as much.'

He spoke of how on this visit to his home town he found himself creating all sorts of spurious reasons why he should go to a particular place, knowing that these places were close to homes of drug dealers whom he knew. A certain drug dealer had died and Terry had gone to his funeral. 'Everyone there was smoking after the funeral, and I had to say I wasn't smoking that week. I couldn't say I had stopped smoking. They wouldn't accept that.'

He went on to talk about the attractions of drug taking. 'All these campaigns to warn kids off drugs, they're just a waste of time. The kids on drugs, they just look at the posters, you know, the pictures of that lad all curled up, or the girl with spots on her face, and they think, 'That's me', and feel real proud. It makes them feel important. When I was starting on drugs, I was the only heroin user in Lincoln. If anyone broke into a chemist's shop, they'd just gather up all the drugs they could find. They'd use or sell the amphetamines and the barbiturates, but they'd bring the heroin to me because I was the king, the only one brave enough to take heroin.'

This was the man who all his life had been painfully, cripplingly shy. At sixteen, taking heroin did wonders for his self-esteem.

'It's the same with drink. The person who can drink the most, well, he's the most famous. Same as when you come into hospital and the doctor tells you you're lucky you're in hospital because your liver wouldn't have lasted another week with what you were drinking. Then you go on the ward and start to talk to a chap there, and you tell him what the doctor said and he says, "He told me I only had three days to go." Then you know he's better than you are.'

He told me about 'Flora, the glue sniffer', as he called her, who had a room in his flat. 'She just stays in her room all the time and watches television. That's all that matters to her, her television. She's terrified someone will steal it. She never goes out, except on Thursdays when she has to sign on. She gets me to stay in then, so no one'll steal her TV. Her social worker comes to see her, but she won't go out. She's frightened of other people, so what she does is make them frightened of her. If she has to meet anyone, like the people who come to my flat, she'll take a big sniff of glue, just before she comes into the room, and she comes in holding the bag, and that frightens people. She's twenty-three and she's been glue sniffing since she was sixteen. She makes out she's a lesbian. She dresses like a boy, she's real thin, and looks like a boy. She frightens people off by pretending to be a lesbian, she goes up to women and squeezes their breasts, but it really doesn't mean anything. She just does it to frighten them before they frighten her. She's not a lesbian. She's just a glue sniffer. That's all she is.'

'You mean if she stopped glue sniffing she wouldn't be anything?'

'That's right. And she's the queen of the glue sniffers. All the other glue sniffers come around to see her. She's been doing it for longer than any of them, and they all look up to her.'

Terry said that he had tried glue sniffing just to see what it's like. I asked him how it felt.

'It's hard to tell. I was drunk at the time. It was just a buzzing in the head. But that's what drugs are, a buzzing in the head. They stop you thinking.'

If you don't want to stop thinking but you do want to control your thoughts, you can try using food to do this.

Food – Too Much or Too Little

Food is the first object we learn to use in negotiations with the outer world and in reducing our own feelings of discomfort. This learning takes place in the context where we are learning about love, anger, guilt, reparation, power and control.

Food is never just food but always carries a great weight of meanings.

Eating Too Much

This can be a way of comforting oneself, or warding off fear, or setting up a barrier of fat to protect yourself from outside dangers. Many women have recognized the truth of Susie Orbach's work, *Fat Is a Feminist Issue*,[13] which shows how being fat can be a way of avoiding sexual intimacy. Being fat is also a way of preserving oneself and avoiding annihilation.

I was an ordinary-sized small child until, at four years old, I went into hospital with suspected diphtheria. Brief though this stay was (it seemed like an eternity to me) it disrupted my already shaky relationship with my mother. I was afraid of her and would do anything to avoid her unpredictable, fierce, destructive bad temper. I would also do anything to please my father who was my only security. So to please them both I would eat, and the food came with messages of both love and danger. In both my mother's and father's family there was a tradition of showing love and affection through the preparing, giving and eating of food. There was also an implied sense of danger. Both families took great pride in 'having a good table', and this came from the experience of my parents' parents and grandparents, and further back in family memory when there was not enough money for food and starvation was a real and imminent threat. I was well and truly grown up before I realized that behind my parents' insistence that I, as a schoolchild, should have a proper breakfast, biscuits for 'playlunch' at 11 a.m. and a substantial pile of sandwiches and cake for lunch, followed by a snack after school and meat and three veg plus dessert for tea was the shame of not being able to feed your child and the spectre of starvation. As a child I didn't know the history of this attitude. The message I picked up from my parents' actions and unspoken attitudes was, 'If you don't eat something every two hours you die.'

The only way to cease feeling compelled to eat is to make explicit in words, not actions, what eating means to you, and to recognize the fear against which the eating and the fat is a defence.

Eating Too Little
The majority of the world's population eats too little, but only out of necessity. Yet, in Western countries where there is an embarrassing surplus of food there are many people, mainly women, and mainly young women, who choose to eat so little that their lives become in danger. When this happens the woman is diagnosed as suffering from the disease of anorexia nervosa. The second half of this century has seen a tremendous increase in the number of women who choose to limit their eating to such a drastic extent, and the treatment of anorexia nervosa has become, in Susie Orbach's words, 'a growth industry. Eating disorders in general are a hot topic in psychology, and the number of journal articles and dissertations on the subject is soaring. Similarly, clinics and training programmes in eating disorders are proliferating to serve the medical and mental health practitioners confronting the growing number of cases of anorexia.'[14]

For Susie Orbach anorexia is not a disease but something that a woman does to preserve a sense of self which she experiences as weak, helpless, and fragile.

On the one hand, anorexia is about being thin – very, very thin.

It is an expression of a woman's confusion about how much space she may take up in the world. On the other hand, her food denial is driven by her need to control her body which is, for her, a symbol of emotional needs. If she can get control over her body, then perhaps she can similarly control her emotional neediness. Submitting her body to rigorous discipline is part of her attempt to deny an emotional life. The anorexic cannot tolerate feelings. She experiences her emotional life as an attack on herself, and she attempts to control it so that she will not be devoured by her emotions. She tries to gain control over her body and her mind by creating an altogether new person out of herself. In other words, she negates who she is – needy, hungry, angry, yearning – and through the adoption of strenuous diet and exercise rituals turns herself into someone she finds more acceptable. In turn her submission to the rituals creates a boundary between herself and her needs. She gathers strength from the knowledge that she can ignore her needs and appetites.[15]

Women, feminine, acceptable, attractive women, are, in our society, not supposed to have needs or appetites, or, if they do, they should deny and conceal them. They should not be aggressive and demanding: they should serve the needs of others. Since all women, being simply human, do have needs and appetites, every woman, to some greater or lesser extent, has a conflict between being herself and meeting the standards which society sets about being an acceptable, feminine woman. An individual who is in conflict with his or her society is, in one sense at least, involved in a political contest. Thus choosing not to eat is itself a political act. Thomas Szasz, who describes 'mental illness' not as a disease but a language, wrote, 'Addiction, obesity, starvation (anorexia nervosa) are political problems, not psychiatric; each condenses and expresses a contest between the individual and some other person or persons in his environment over the control of the individual's body.'[16]

Sheila MacLeod, writing of her own experience of anorexia, said that Szasz's observation struck her 'with the force of a revelation . . . What was happening to my body – not only the changes brought about by puberty, but the fact that the clothes it wore and the food it consumed were chosen by someone else – was a metaphor for what was happening to me as a whole person.'

She went on:

I think I seized upon that metaphor in order to turn it to my own advantage. I had nothing; I was nothing. More positively, I was being given what I did not want (which amounted to being given nothing) and being classified as what I was not (which amounted to being classified as nothing). My only weapon in my bid for autonomy was to go on strike. Withdrawal of labour, in the literal sense, would have been impractical and, more importantly, would have caused more destruction to my self-esteem in that without work (schoolwork) I should have had less and have been less than the nothing I already felt myself to have and to be. So I 'chose' a form of passive resistance. Just as the worker's ultimate weapon in his negotiation with management is his labour and the threat of withdrawal, so my body was my ultimate and, to me, only weapon in my bid for autonomy. It was the only thing I owned, the only thing that could not be taken away from me. My motivations were not as clear-cut as those of any contemporary workforce, but there is no doubt in my mind that I was going on strike the only way I knew how to, and that in this sense Szasz is right to describe anorexia nervosa as a political problem.[17]

The anorexic woman chooses her body as the grounds of her political stance. In industry, workers who go on strike choose their workplace as the grounds of their political stance. They leave their workplace and prevent, or try to prevent, work being carried out there, even though such action penalizes them as much, if not more, than their employers, for the workplace is both the object and the symbol of their political grievance. They can choose whether to work or not to work. Women, being usually economically dependent on others and not having labour to withdraw, have to choose a place where they do labour. Looking after one's body is a labour, and so one's body can be chosen as the place for a strike.

But to do this a woman has to observe a split between her self and her body. The workplace is an object, and so the body must be an object before it can be used in such a strike. The anorexic woman regards her body as an object, and a useless, demanding, degraded object at that. Susie Orbach wrote, 'There is no notion or sense of the body as an integrated aspect of the self, rather it represents in physical form the internal struggles to control needs and unsatisfactory object relations (*i.e., internal representation of people in the external world*), an attempt to dress oneself with an acceptable self-image. The body is something one puts on and off, not the place where one lives.'[18]

This is easily possible in a consumer society, where pictures of women's bodies are used to sell every commodity. 'For women themselves, the body has become a commodity in the marketplace or their own commodity, the object with which they negotiate the world.'[19] Anorexic women use their bodies 'as a vehicle for self-expression'[20] but, unlike those successful actors, dancers and sportsmen and women, who regard their bodies as their finest attribute, anorexic women do not regard their bodies with pride and satisfaction. They seek approval and acceptance, but they observe their bodies with contempt. Bodies are objects which can go out of control. Bodies demand food and rest; they grow fat; they excrete faeces, urine and blood. Other people's bodies may be satisfactory, provided they are not fat, but to the anorexic woman her body is an object of profound disgust. In no way can the anorexic woman accept the humanness of her body. She has grown up in a family which has impressed on her that she is unsatisfactory and that the body she was born with is unsatisfactory. Sheila MacLeod dated the first step on her path to anorexia when she heard her aunt's remark about her to her father.

'She's going to be stout – just like Dolly.' (Dolly was my mother.) All the light and colour seemed to be drained from my surroundings. I was blazingly angry with her and wanted to shout, 'No, I'm not! Why the hell should I be? And who are you to say so?' But of course I said nothing – to retaliate would have been considered insufferably rude – and walked on, pretending not to have heard . . . it is clear that she had no idea what effect her remark could have had on me . . . she was following the family pattern of talking about children in their own presence in the third person instead of addressing them directly. This pattern implies that children have no thoughts or feelings of their own and are incapable of understanding the wider meanings of the simplest observations.[21]

Whatever the particulars of an anorexic woman's upbringing, she develops a sense of her body as, in Susie Orbach's words, 'a false body'. 'Where the developing child has not had a chance to experience physicality as good, wholesome and all right, it has little chance to live in an authentically experienced body.'[22]

Most women from their earliest childhood are taught not to enjoy their own physicality, that is, not to explore to the limits the functions of their body and not to enjoy what their body can do. Boys can take part in rough and tumble games, they can run and climb and swim, but girls do not do these things, or, if they do, they have to perform them according to certain rules and to aim for perfection. At a swimming pool boys may enjoy themselves by hurling themselves and one another into the water in every which way they please, while the girls there are learning to dive correctly and neatly. Boys may climb and swing, but girls, if they want to explore the relationship of their bodies to space, have to take up gymnastics and follow the strict rules of that sport. A friend once told me that she took up gymnastics as a girl because she wanted to prove that even in movement through the air she was perfectly controlled all the time. When she was too old for gymnastics she took up depression, another occupation which aims at being perfectly controlled all the time.

Boys, too, are allowed to explore the functions of their bodies. They can take great interest in how they pee, shit and fart. They can compare erections and the speed with which they can ejaculate. Girls are taught that curiosity about excretory functions is not permissible and that jokes about such functions are extremely vulgar. Excreting something as simple as perspiration is most indelicate. The old adage, 'Horses sweat; men perspire; ladies *glow*' may no longer be fashionable, but the plethora of anti-perspirants show that horses may have disappeared from our roads but the sentiments about sweat have not changed. I remember when I was in labour and the nurse mopped my face I realized that for the first time in my life I was actually being encouraged to sweat.

So the one thing which girls excrete and boys do not, menstrual blood, becomes for many girls something of horror and secrecy. It is not a badge of womanhood to be worn with pride. Sheila MacLeod said that in her teenage years,

> I was horrified and disgusted by menstruation rather than by sexuality. I felt that some dreadful punishment had been visited upon me, punishment for a crime which I had never committed. But I think I knew unconsciously that the crime was twofold: I was being punished for being female and for having grown up. At the same time I didn't *feel* female, in the sexual sense. Neither did I feel male, but rather neuter. And I certainly didn't feel grown-up. The crimes in question had been committed by my body, not by me.[23]

To treat our bodies in this way, to see them as contemptible and dangerous objects which have to be controlled, hidden, and forced into a shape which they would not naturally assume (my mother's generation of women wore corsets; present generations wear the invisible corsets of exercise and diet) is to do terrible damage to how we experience our existence. Our body is the only part of our existence which occupies both our internal and our external reality. It is the bridge between our two realities. To live comfortably and bravely in our two realities we need to live comfortably and bravely within our bodies. We should not feel ashamed and frightened of our bodies, nor should we be ignorant of them.

This is what yoga teaches, how to be intimately aware of how our body moves and feels and simply is. Yoga is contemplative, and the aim of such contemplation is to discover that there is a form of annihilation of the self which is not to be feared but to be sought as the greatest peace we can ever know, an annihilation which is union, not separation.

But the anorexic woman is very far from such peace. She is trapped in the belief that her fragile self is in danger of being wiped out. To protect her fragile sense of self she structures the defence of anorexia.

Since, as Susie Orbach said, 'psychological symptoms express the ideas a culture has at any time about itself'[24] and since so much of our present culture is concerned with women's bodies and food, women nowadays choose anorexia as a defence rather than other defences which introverts and extraverts have available.

Writing about one woman whose efforts to protect her fragile sense of self focused on a rigid programme and set of rules about eating, exercising, and ordering her environment, Susie Orbach said:

Thirty years ago the very same environment at home creating a similar psychology might have found a solution not in anorexia but in a cluster of obsessive symptoms. (Such symptoms might have bound up the anxiety she experienced as effectively as did the anorexia.) She might have instituted a series of rituals, not related to diet or weight but to washing or counting or locking doors and so on – acts that in themselves would have been as understandable and psychologically opaque as the anorexic stance.[25]

For another woman who experienced herself

to be chaotic inside and a mess . . . while it predisposed her to develop a psychological symptom which could bind the feelings of messiness and chaos inside, would not in a different historical period have led so directly to taking up anorexia nervosa. Her psychology would have had much in common with the cases in the literature of pre-orgasmic women or 'frigid' women found two or three decades ago. Typically, such women were unable to experience sexual pleasure personally, but in an attempt to get satisfaction they were for the norm of their day often considered promiscuous or nymphomaniacs. The frigidity expressed, like the anorexia, a withdrawn attitude, involuntary closeness, and inability to open up and let go psychologically and physically. The fear, when analysed, was that the letting down of false boundaries that frigidity symbolized, would lead to feelings of disintegration; the chaos that lived locked up inside would gush forth, rendering the woman vulnerable and shattering her to (psychic) pieces. The involuntary frigidity (which could be more or less extreme ranging from inorgasmic to vaginismic) was the somatized solution such a psychic structure sought as a means of defence. For today's women, where the sexual taboos are considered, though they may not be a thing of the past, the test of acceptance is deemed to come through the attainment of a perfect body-image.[26]

Many other women (and men) who experience their internal reality as a frighteningly mysterious, chaotic mess or as a terrifying emptiness choose panic attacks and the restrictions and rituals to avoid panic attacks as their defence against the fear of annihilation.

Both Susie Orbach and Sheila MacLeod are scathing in their criticism of those methods of treatment of the anorexic woman which rely on control and force-feeding. This is just another form of the way in which men (most psychiatrists are male) try to control women. Force-feeding will make anyone fat, but it will not give anyone 'the ability to *experience* the body as the place where one lives',[27] nor will it encourage the discovery that we each have the right to exist as ourselves. Knowing that we have the right to exist and to be ourselves, we can then enter openly into negotiations with society as to what our role in that society should be. Realizing this, a woman can give up the defence of anorexia.

All this is much easier said than done by the woman who chooses anorexia as her defence. Fortunately, the insights developed by the Women's Liberation Movement have led to the creation of women's therapy centres,[28] and the growth of the self-help movement has led to the creation of groups,[29] all of which are concerned with the way in which women can seek to defend against the fear of the annihilation of the self by choosing not to eat and how they can find the courage to relinquish this perilous defence.

Anorexia is not an illness. But many people in their battle against fear do experience themselves as ill. Pain is their truth.

Not Frightened, Just Ill

As psychologists are wont to say, only behaviour which is rewarded is repeated. Anything which causes us nothing but pain we do once and once only. When I say this to my clients who see themselves as the passive victims of phobias, panic attacks, depressions, obsessions, compulsions and various physical complaints they look at me in disbelief and anger. Why would anyone willingly inflict pain upon themselves? Yet we do.

To explain this I usually give the example of what each of us decided the day we first discovered what happens when you put your hand in the fire or touch something extremely hot. For most of us this was a totally unpleasant experience, one which we decided to avoid for the rest of our lives. But some of us drew different conclusions. Some of us when we were small children had parents who ignored us, or who noticed us only to punish us. Then one day, when we burned our hand, we discovered that we were neither ignored nor punished but loved and cosseted and given the attention we craved so much. We drew the conclusion that the pain or injury or illness was a price worth paying for love and security, and so we entered into a lifetime of being ill.

People who believe that they are not sufficiently good and valuable *in themselves* to be the centre of other people's concern can use illness as a way of gaining the kind of attention which is almost as good as being loved and wanted. When such people have been using this device from childhood as a way of dealing with fear, they do not develop a language in which to talk about emotions. If as a child you discover that when you say to your mother, 'Mummy, I'm frightened', you are ignored, punished, or humiliated, but if you say, 'Mummy, I'm sick', you are comforted and loved, then you do not develop a language which distinguishes degrees and kinds of fear, anger, envy, greed and love, but you do develop a language which distinguishes different kinds of bodily sensations. These names for bodily sensations come to stand for different emotions, but as the language of the emotions is never developed the person cannot translate bodily sensations into emotions. It is like having a French/English dictionary where all the English words have been removed. The person cannot translate a pain in the neck into the tension and fear we feel when we are under attack from others and cannot retaliate, or a headache into the rush of blood to the head which accompanies sudden and unexpressed anger.

Having only a language of bodily sensations to explore oneself and one's relationships through life means that all questions and answers that arise have to be framed in this language. 'Why am I afraid?' becomes 'Why does the sweat pour off me whenever I tackle a new job?' and 'Why am I lonely?' becomes 'Why do I have this terrible pain?'

Having only a language of bodily sensations in which to frame questions about experience, a person has to consult other people who know this language. These are doctors, and if the doctor knows only the language of bodily sensations and does not have a language of the emotions, then the answers to his patient's questions can only be in bodily terms. Some doctors do have a language of the emotions and can translate bodily sensations into emotional experience, but many doctors are as limited in their range of languages as their patient, and so the doctor and patient join together in looking for solutions in pills, potions and operations. When the X-rays and the pathology tests fail to reveal a physical cause and the pills, potions and operations fail to remove the symptoms, the doctor may grow weary of the patient, label him hypochondriacal, and may end his relationship with the patient.

Walter once had the opportunity to read his own medical notes and had seen himself described a hypochondriac. This had hurt him deeply, for the pain he felt in his shoulder and arm were as real and strong as any other pain he had ever felt. The fact that the doctors he had consulted could not find a cause for the pain was not his fault. He tried to be patient with them and to believe them when they said that the pain had nothing to do with his heart. When his old GP retired, a young man came in his place. He asked about his family (he had none) and his friends (he had two) and suggested that he join a social club where he could meet people, Walter tried not to be offended when this young doctor said he would like him to go and talk to a psychologist. He agreed to go, just as he had agreed to years of tests, examinations and medications.

Walter's face showed all the lines of unhappiness and worry and his eyes were filled with pain. He told me about his life. He had always worked hard and so had done well. Money was no problem. He could afford to travel and there was hardly an exotic or interesting place which he had not visited. His marriage had been brief and painful, and now he lived alone in considerable comfort with a daily housekeeper who kept his house immaculate, just as he wished. His hobby was buying and repairing antique clocks which he did with consummate care and precision. Many a man would envy him his life.

That is, a man who had little need for other people and who wished to pursue his own interests would envy him. But Walter had an immense need for other people, and what he had done was to construct the way of life which extraverts dread, a life of nearly complete isolation. The pain of that was terrible.

Most extraverts develop in childhood the social skills which assure them of a steady supply of friends and acquaintances throughout their lives. They may not be greatly interested in the hidden depths of the people they meet, but they are interested in their superficial characteristics, their names, the names of their children, the football team they support, the hairdresser they recommend, the food they are allergic to, and so on, and they flatter and please their friends and acquaintances by remembering these details and enquiring about them. Many an introvert, deficient in these skills because so much time has been spent in learning the skills of keeping things in order and in trying to understand their own hidden depths, has had cause to bless the extravert who eases social interaction and makes us all feel warm, comforted and loved.

But not all extraverts learn these skills. Perhaps they grew up in a family which kept itself to itself and visitors were not encouraged. Perhaps in their childhood they were made to feel so frightened and insecure that all their attention was on themselves and they had no time to get to know other people, especially since all the people around them frightened them so. Perhaps the people around them demanded such high standards and achievements from them that they were so busy being good they had no time just to play and so get to know other people.

Whatever had happened to Walter in his childhood, he had certainly not learned the life-saving skills which every extravert needs. He had no social skills whereby he could get to know other people. He had never learned the art of small talk – how to discuss the weather, or the best route from A to B. If a person asked him a question about something he knew a good deal about he would answer at length, perhaps at greater length than his questioner wanted, but he could not initiate a conversation unless he felt certain that what he wanted to say and to hear was of considerable importance and practical value. The delights of gossip were totally lost on him. But this was not surprising. He did not find people interesting, and so the foibles of our fellows which amuse so many of us amused him not at all. He longed for companions but had no talent for companionship.

I asked him about his childhood. Just an ordinary one, he said, and went on to describe an extraordinary one. His father had died when he was little and his mother married again. His stepfather, he said, was a very fine person. He took a great interest in Walter and in everything he did. He believed in the precept 'If a job's worth doing, it's worth doing well', only in his case it wasn't just 'well' that he demanded. It was 'perfectly'. He was a fine craftsman and he taught Walter his skills. Walter tried hard and did well, but no matter how well he did he never earned his stepfather's praise.

'He never praised me, not once,' said Walter. 'It was always "You could have done better". He never accepted my excuses.'

So Walter tried harder. He didn't get angry with his stepfather. That wouldn't be right, and besides, Walter didn't like any kind of anger or aggression. That always made him feel very uncomfortable. He hated it at school when the boys started fighting. He always tried to avoid fights. He didn't like school much.

'I wasn't any good at sport. I had a lot of sickness, missed a bit of school.'

I didn't know whether Walter's shoulder pain was caused by some physical disability or not. I have seen too many physical symptoms being dismissed by doctors as 'hysterical' or 'neurotic' in people unfortunate enough to have a history as a psychiatric patient only to be shown at a later date to have a basis in a menstrual disorder, or high blood pressure, or to be a symptom of the psychiatric drugs themselves for me to feel with confidence that the pain of which a person complains has no physiological basis at all. However, it is possible to see in Walter's account of his childhood a pattern whereby he had learned to escape from the pressures of home and school by being ill. His mother, he said, always looked after him well when he was ill. Perhaps when he was ill she was allowed to show him the affection which at other times his stepfather would regard as unsuitable for a boy to receive. In his adult life he certainly got on better with women than with men, and it was to women that he looked for love and friendship.

Walter was extremely puzzled when I said that he would feel a lot better if he made the effort to meet more people and actually be interested in them. He could see no connection between his loneliness and his pain. I did not try to describe to him the real physical ache we all feel when we long to be held and there is no one there to hold us. I have never had any success in teaching the language of the emotions to people who failed to learn it in their childhood. Like all languages, it is something we can pick up with the greatest of ease when we are small and learning to speak, but to learn it later in life requires great effort and desire. Like all languages, it can only be learned and practised in relationships with other people, so perhaps if Walter concentrated on some basic social skills he might, in passing, acquire the elements of a language of emotions. He might then be able to distinguish between the pain of loneliness and the pain of a malfunctioning body.

Walter came to see me for several months, and then one day he announced that he would not be coming any more. He was starting to depend on me, and that would never do.

Some of us, when we were making the discovery that fire burns, and burnt flesh is painful, discovered something else, and this discovery made us seek out pain for the rest of our lives. Some children discover that their pain produces not love and comfort but pity, and this is welcome and acceptable, for at other times what they receive is contempt. Biographers of T.E. Lawrence have described how he was fascinated by pain and how he would punish and degrade himself in an attempt to evoke pity rather than contempt. As a child he was frequently thrashed by his mother who was both powerful and puritanical. People like Lawrence prefer pity to love, because pity is something which comes to us from a distance, whereas love is something up close and therefore dangerous.

Sometimes the pain of real physical injury takes away another more terrible pain. This is the pain of the tension that can build up when we are expecting to be punished for some wicked deed. Some people burdened with the guilt of their sheer existence find that by inflicting wounds upon themselves the physical tension of this guilt disappears, at least for a little while. Dave described to me how on the ward one evening he felt the tension building up and up until he could stand it no longer. He found a pair of nail scissors and dragged the points with as much force as he could muster over his wrists. As the blood gushed from the wounds he felt a wonderful sense of peace.

'The funny thing was,' he said, 'that a few weeks later when I had to get the stitches out it hurt like hell. But I wasn't so tense then.'

Many people who believe that they are bad and useless and who are frightened of the chaos and emptiness inside them experience their fear of annihilation as many unpleasant physical symptoms.

A Bodily Solution?

Some of these are not just the sequelae of a prolonged physical state of fear but the breakdown of bodily functions which occur when we are under continued stress.

From Fear to Illness

Sarah described how the trouble had started two years ago. She had been riding her moped and a lorry had pulled out suddenly, knocking her down. She wasn't badly hurt, just bruised, but her moped was destroyed. Next day she felt ill. She developed a high temperature with vomiting and diarrhoea. This illness persisted for a week and then reappeared. Her general practitioner diagnosed 'a virus'. She appeared to get well but the diarrhoea and nausea .persisted. She could not eat and lost a great deal of weight. Her GP sent her to a specialist who diagnosed 'an irritable bowel' and prescribed some medication. She put on the weight she had lost but the diarrhoea and nausea remained. Her GP sent her to me.

She came, she said, because having to rush to the toilet was spoiling her life. She would feel herself getting tense, and then she would have to dash for the toilet. She would wake up in the morning feeling fine, but then she would start to worry about whether she was going to feel tense, and so the tension and churning would start. 'It's the fear of fear,' she said.

She hadn't told anyone that she was coming to see me. Both her husband and her father had no time for people who were mentally ill. Her father thought that getting upset was 'a weakness'. It was all right to get angry. Her father always hit his children when they annoyed him and that was often. 'He used to hit me around the head. Couldn't be bothered bending down, I suppose.'

I was struck by how often in her conversation she used words and metaphors to do with the stomach and bowels. In speaking of her father she said, 'I hate his guts.' To explain to me how she felt that her mother-in-law who kept her house so perfect looked down on her she said, 'In that house nobody farts.'

Sarah was a good talker, and in her torrent of words she scattered the significant pieces of her life with prodigal abandon. But she could not pause and put the pieces together. She could see no connection between the nausea and diarrhoea and the conditions of her life, not even the obvious one that terror can loosen our sphincter muscles. She had always had, so she said, 'weak bowels', 'spent a lot of my time in the loo', but she did not connect this with the fear she had of other people. She said, 'A lot of people don't like me. I talk too much. I always get picked on. If my sister and I were fighting my father would blame me for starting it. If my brother was beating me I would be blamed for provoking him.' She denied that her married life was tense, even though she said, 'The children and I feel much better when he's out.'

Again and again Sarah spoke of fights in her family, and most of the fights involved her father. His way of imposing his will on his family was to hit his wife and children.

When we are in a prolonged situation involving fighting, either as a participant or as an observer, whether the fighting is in a war or in a family, we have to deny that we are frightened. Soldiers learn to deny their fear by deadening it with alcohol or, as in Vietnam, drugs, or by boredom, obscenities and cruelty to others. In families fear can be ever present, and no more remarked on than the air the family breathes. Every action taken can be aimed at avoiding violence, or defending oneself, or getting one's blow in first. Soldiers may remember witnessing their first battle and the fear they felt then, but children born into a violent family may not consciously remember the first battle they witnessed. Nevertheless, the effect on small children is profound.

When Sarah was small she saw her father strike her mother. She heard shouting and her mother crying. From a child's perspective such events are terrifying and inexplicable.

From our earliest days we are in the business of explaining our world to ourselves. In every moment of our experience we are explaining our world to ourselves. Most of the time our explanations are split-second activities, because everything around us and everything happening to us are familiar and already explained, but when something new happens we immediately have to find an explanation. This way we *master* our experience.

The explanations we create can come only from our past. We

166

interpret every new situation in terms of our past experience. We hear a loud noise, and immediately explain it to ourselves. 'It's the back door slamming.' 'It's grandad falling downstairs.' But if we say to ourselves, 'What's that?' and can't find an answer, we have to rush outside to look, or ask somebody, 'What was that?' Until we can explain the event to ourselves in some satisfactory way we feel uncomfortable, somehow not at one with our world. The explanation we give ourselves need not be true. When I was a small child and through the sultry evening air would come a deep rumbling sound, my father would say, 'There's Jim McMahon rolling his stones.' I found the line of distant hills beautiful and mysterious, so the picture of Jim McMahon rolling big boulders above and beyond them was to me a thoroughly satisfactory explanation. To me it was true. After all, my father said so. I was never afraid of thunder. Dad's explanation allowed me to master that situation.

But all too often we come across a situation we cannot master because we cannot explain it in any satisfactory way. It may be that the event is completely novel to us and there is nothing in our past experience which would prepare us for it. When our house disappears in an earthquake, or foreign troops take over our country, or our good and obedient child is revealed as a drug addict, we find that we cannot explain these events in terms of our past experience, and so we cannot master these events. They remain in our minds as inexplicable horrors over which we had no control and over which we have to puzzle endlessly.

Sometimes something happens for which we do have explanations available from our past experience, but none of these explanations produces satisfaction and contentment, and so mastery is not possible. We are left puzzling and fretting. We might have been told, as children, that if we were good and worked hard at school, when we grew up we would get a good job and live happily and securely ever after. So we were good and worked hard, and we did get a good job and counted ourselves happy. Then, suddenly, the job disappeared. We were without work. How can we explain this? Was it because we did not work hard enough? Were we not good enough? Or had our parents and teachers lied to us? Do we live in a world where goodness is not always rewarded? To master this event we have either to denigrate ourselves or change the way we see our world and remember our past. Thus mastery can be very difficult to achieve.

A small child has very little past experience to bring to new events. So many events in an infant's life are new, and wise parents try to restrict the number of new events an infant has to encounter each day. They try, too, to make these new events something which the child can enjoy and so master. If the event isn't enjoyable, then wise parents help the child master it by lots of comforting and cuddling and explanations which the child can understand and accept.

But when a small child is presented with events which he cannot master because there are no explanations which he can understand or accept, and because the parents neither recognize that the child is distressed nor seek to comfort and reassure him, then the child is in peril of being overwhelmed and his fragile sense of self annihilated. In this situation one desperate defence the child can use is to take the whole experience inside him. He cannot distance himself from it, for it is too vast and all encompassing, and too important, for it involves the people most important to him. It becomes part of himself, part of his fantasies and nightmares, part of his very *self*.

This is the process by which many of us 'inherited' depression. We took in our mother's depression, and carry within us images of darkness, despair and murderous rage – not our own but our mother's. It is the process whereby many of us first acquired the notion that we were bad. We could explain all that darkness and violence and hate inside us only by seeing it as part of us and knowing it to be bad.

Sometimes this darkness filled with violence, rage and fear is felt as something more compact than a generalized sense of badness. It is felt as an evil *thing* inside, and as a thing in our body it could, perhaps, be got rid of. If we locate this evil *thing* in our digestive system we have ways of getting rid of it. We can vomit it up, or we can void it through our bowels. Persistent diarrhoea often has this meaning.

A Bodily Solution?

To discover these meanings and make them conscious the person has to return to those events which gave rise to the meanings, and that involves returning to the original fear and helplessness. This is often too perilous a journey to make, even in the company of a friendly therapist, and so many people prefer to explain much of their experience in terms of 'weak bowels'. If your powerful, terrifying and fascinating father has defined fear as weakness, then you will not risk an even more frightening situation.

If fear is a weakness then Sarah dare not admit that she is afraid. Afraid of being ill, yes, but of a deeper, more pervasive fear, no. When I spoke of how a close brush with death, as she had had in the accident, can make us all too aware of our mortality she said, 'I remember when I was twelve, lying awake at night and worrying about dying.'

It seemed that the conclusion she had drawn from this experience was that she had to be in control of every aspect of her life. She said, 'I make all the decisions in our house – where we'll live, what we'll spend our money on,' and 'I want everything to be perfect.' She seemed to have planned every part of her future. 'My children aren't perfect. I wanted my daughter to look like me and she looks like my mother-in-law.'

Our children's looks are something we can't control, just like death. Our bowels can be the battle ground where we can fight to control fear and death, just as our bowels were the first battle ground between our desire to do what we wanted and the greater powers of our family to control and punish and threaten to annihilate us. The problem about making our bowels the place and the metaphor for this struggle is that they are no more than weak flesh and when they are expected to do more than cope with the results of our digestion they soon suffer damage. 'Irritable bowels' can lead to very painful and unpleasant disabilities.

When we do not ask for help with our fear but carry it within us for a long time our body reaches a stage where it can no longer stand the strain. Perhaps the part which shows the damage the fear has done in some way represents our predicament or is a wordless language to express what we have suffered. Perhaps when Rhianon decided that she would stay with her husband, no matter

169

how many affairs he had or how many times he told her he didn't fancy her once she was no longer a young woman, her heart indeed did break. In middle age she developed angina and now her poor cracked heart operates not very well at all.

Until recently such notions would have been regarded as entirely fanciful by medical science. But over the past few years the link between mind and body has been found and its functions are being uncovered. It seems that the physiological changes which accompany fear can have profound effects on the body which lead to a breakdown of the immune system, the system which enables us to throw off noxious substances and viruses. Once this system ceases to function efficiently we are laid open to the ravages of all kinds of diseases.

There does seem to be some link between the kind of person we are and the kind of illness we develop, although the relationship is far from clear. Studies of the ways that people habitually live their lives has led to the description of two types of people. Type A people are those who are competitive, aggressive and very active and who view life with hostility and cynical mistrust, while Type B people are quiet, non-aggressive, non-competitive people who repress their anger. It seems that Type A people are more likely to have heart attacks, while Type B people are more likely to develop cancer.

Professor Cary Cooper, head of Organizational Psychology at the University of Manchester Institute of Science and Technology studied 2,163 women who were screened for breast cancer and found that the women who developed breast cancer were less competitive, more withdrawn, and when they cried, they cried alone. He concluded that women who tried not to show their feelings were more likely to develop breast cancer because the extra effort of coping with stress lowered the effectiveness of the body's immune system.

I remember back in 1961 my friend Noelene said to me bitterly, pointing to the empty space where her breast had been, 'My husband did this to me.' There was no point in her saying this to her doctors. They would have dismissed her connection between this faithless, brutal husband and her breast cancer as the ravings of a foolish, sick woman. So she kept her knowledge to herself, and struggled on. Later, the cancer spread, and she died.

Professor Cooper advised women who are under stress, 'If you cry, don't cry alone. Do it when other people are around so that someone will see you are upset and will listen to you. If that is too difficult, seek other help – counselling will do much more good than Valium.'[30]

Just how the immune function is affected by stress and distress is now being demonstrated by a research team of a psychologist, Janice Kiecolt-Glaser, and a physiologist, Ronald Glaser. They have shown that loneliness is associated with poorer immune function, that unhappiness in marriage is associated with depression and a poor response on three measures of immune function, and, among separated and divorced women, the shorter the separation and the greater the attachment to the ex-husband, the poorer the immune function and the greater the depression.

Fortunately, such suppression of the immune function need not be irreversible. The Glasers report that 'distress-reducing interventions like relaxation may enhance some aspects of the immune function'.[31]

Such studies are difficult to carry out, for we do not have 'an attitude' in the same way as we have a sore or a growth. 'An attitude' is something that we feel, think, and do, and in so feeling, thinking and doing we can lie to others and to ourselves. If God did send a thunderbolt to strike us dead whenever we lied, my office would be littered with the corpses of my clients who are for ever declaring, 'I never get angry.'

Attitudes always determine the outcome of any physical illness. Only if you value yourself will you seek (and demand when necessary) medical help and then treat yourself kindly by taking care of yourself. I never fail to be amazed at the degree of physical suffering my clients endure, all because 'I don't want to bother the doctor', or, 'They can't manage at work without me', or, 'A chap doesn't give in to little things like this', or, 'My family needs me'.

We do not always frame and express our attitudes in simple statements like 'I mustn't let people know I am angry with them because then they will reject me and I shall be alone and abandoned', or, 'I must not acknowledge that I am frightened because I am helpless'. Instead we create, experience and express them in symbols, images and metaphors which haunt our dreams, underlie our thoughts, and creep into our language. Over recent years a great many people have found relief for their physical suffering by identifying some substances to which their bodies are allergic and then avoiding such substances. It is perhaps not surprising that the substances which occur most frequently in accounts of such successful cures are milk, wheat flour and household dust. These are real things in themselves which can no doubt affect our body's functioning, and they are also symbols of family relationships and obligations.

To find a bodily solution to our fear we have to separate ourselves from our body and treat it as an object. Doing this, we try to control our body in the way we might control an object like a car or a vacuum cleaner, but our body is not such an object. Cars and vacuum cleaners, by themselves, do not act on their own. They just stand about. Live bodies are always busy being themselves, throbbing, pulsing, acting, and if we see our body as merely an object which we control, we soon find that our body defies us. It goes out of our control and starts controlling us.

Bodily solutions to fear are no solutions. All we have done is changed languages. Instead of saying 'I am afraid' in words, we have translated this into the language of the body, a primitive, obscure language which admits of no solutions other than medical ones, and these are not always effective. Changing our language from words to pains and bodily discomforts is, in dealing with danger, as effective as closing our eyes and putting our fingers in our ears.

Turning Fear into Madness

Chapter Five

The Alternatives

Many of us in early childhood suffered those kinds of experiences which led us to be enveloped and overwhelmed by annihilating fear. The adults in whose care we were did not protect us, and their reassurances, such as they were, were ineffective. We recovered, but never completely. The memory of those devastating events became our dark secret. We struggled on, trying to survive, trying to prevent such terrible experiences ever occurring again.

For years – into our teens, our twenties, thirties, for many of us into our forties and fifties – we were successful, but then the demands of the world we lived in, or bad fortune, or physical illness and ageing threatened to bring our efforts to naught. Greater effort did not reduce the danger. So we had to resort to a more desperate defence. It was an expensive, debilitating defence, like that of a country which acquires a large, well-equipped army while its people starve, but, like such a country, we saw this as the only way to survive. It was not an army we bought for our defence, but what the world calls madness.

We began to behave in ways which seemed strange to other people and, indeed, were strange to us. In the way that a soldier in the midst of a battle asks himself, 'What am I doing here?' but feels compelled to go on fighting, for if he doesn't he will be killed, either by the enemy or by his own comrades, so a person behaving in strange ways will ask of himself, 'Why am I doing this?' but feel compelled to go on behaving in this way, else he will be overcome and destroyed by some powerful force from outside or within.

When madness is called mental illness, these strange ways of behaving are called the symptoms of mental illness. They are named as *panics, phobias, obsessions*, and *compulsions, depression, mania, hallucinations* and *delusions*. But a 'phobia' is not the same as a 'red spot' in measles. Red spots are things which we have; phobias are actions, ways of behaving, something that we do. We may feel compelled to behave in a particular way, but, in the last analysis, it is our choice as to whether we act in the way we feel compelled to act.

Thus do we choose our defence against fear. When our choice is madness, we choose a particular set of defences according to whether we are an introvert or an extravert, and according to how strong or weak we perceive our self to be. The weaker our self, the more desperate our defence. Depression is a defence that we all can choose, extraverts and introverts of all degrees of personal strength, and everyone can enjoy a measure of paranoia, but extraverts prefer panic attacks and phobias, and, in great weakness, mania, while introverts prefer obsessions and compulsions, and, in the extremes of danger the delusions and hallucinations of schizophrenia.

Having made our choice of which defence to use, we are always reluctant to give it up. Other people may use all sorts of means of persuading us to relinquish our defence, but we cannot do this while we still perceive the danger there. Our defence becomes an old friend, often bothersome, often embarrassing and painful, but someone reliable, someone we can trust. Even when the defence seems like the very devil, we still hang on to it, for it's always better the devil you know than the devil you don't know.

But this way of seeing madness is not the way chosen by those people who, for their own reasons, prefer to see madness as something of no purpose and value and who wish to dispose of the 'symptoms of mental illness' in the same way as the symptoms of physical illness are removed.

Theories about Madness

Scientific theories, be they about people or protons, do not arise and exist in some pure space, unsullied by the human and the commonplace. Instead, they are always part of the society in which they were created, and when that society changes, so do the theories. Theories about why people behave as they do relate to the institutions of the society and to the people who hold power in that society.

It is not simply a coincidence that in an era when not only have the means of communication vastly increased, but such means of communication are greatly valued, theories about why people behave as they do frequently stress the importance of communication.

In our society today *communicators* are powerful, and the means by which they communicate are highly valued. One word, *media*, covers them both.

So, many of the current theories about why people behave as they do relate to the way people perceive and communicate. Good communication and good communicators are highly valued. Madness is seen as a result of poor communication.

As I, like everyone else, am a child of my time, so I explain human behaviour in terms of perception and communication. What power and influence I have comes not from what I do in the privacy of my consulting room, but through my books and magazine articles and my appearances on radio and television.

Madness has not always been seen in terms of communication. When the most powerful people in society were the priests (they could excommunicate even the king, that is, they could prevent the king from communicating with God) madness was seen as their province. Theories of madness were concerned with possession by the Devil and damnation by God, and the mad were cared for by the most powerful institution, the Church.

The Church, however, did not lay claim to all the people who might be considered mad. Up to the eighteenth century 'mad people for the most part were not treated even as a separate category or type of deviant. Rather, they were assimilated into the much larger, more amorphous class of the morally disreputable, the poor, and the impotent, a group which also included vagrants, minor criminals, and the physically handicapped'[1]

So wrote Andrew Scull, who, in his study of the history of lunatic asylums, showed how in the late eighteenth century certain members of the medical profession had realized that money could be made out of providing accommodation, asylums, for those whom the doctors could diagnose as insane. There were already existing a number of such institutions operated by kindly, and not so kindly, people, not members of the medical profession, who offered, according to their advertisements, a protected and health-giving environment, sometimes with 'moral therapy'. Such a service could be provided at a profit to the landlord.

To justify their taking over the care of the insane, doctors needed to show that they had some special expertise. So they set about showing that insanity was a physical illness and that they were the only people with the necessary expertise to cure such an illness. Such a claim to the territory of insanity might not have been accepted by the rest of society had not other major changes in society been taking place.

During the eighteenth century the population of Britain, like other industrialized countries, had increased. The enclosure of the shared public lands by the powerful landowners forced many people to leave their villages. The British government dealt with the large numbers of people who broke the laws by transporting them, first to the American colonies, and then, after the American Revolution, to Australia. By 1840, however, the Australian states were refusing to take any more convicts.

The idea of collecting all the people who could not or would not work and putting them in one secure place was appealing to a government which felt more securely in place when most of the population were law-abiding, obedient and hard-working. The Protestant work ethic, flourishing in the success of nineteenth-century British industry, defined the inability or refusal to work as bad or mad. So those who couldn't or wouldn't work were tidied away into the asylums for the lunatic poor which the Lunatics Act of 1845 required to be built in every county and borough. There was an immediate rise in the number of insane people, as good citizens disposed of those people who were an embarrassment or an annoyance.

The practice of confining those people who were considered to be insane in asylums in the care of doctors became the preferred method of dealing with those who couldn't or wouldn't work and was adopted by all industrialized countries. Labour was needed for industry, and those who refused to be part of the work force were a nuisance which had to be confined and controlled.

Fulbourn Hospital in Cambridge was opened as the Cambridgeshire and Isle of Ely Pauper Lunatic Asylum in 1858. Its history was not dissimilar from the other pauper lunatic asylums in England. When Dr David Clark was appointed as superintendent there in 1953 he found that the back wards were

> overcrowded with people, with scrubbed floors, bare wooden tables, benches screwed to the floor, people milling around in shapeless clothing. There was a smell of urine, paraldehyde, floor polish, boiled cabbage and carbolic soap – the asylum smell . . . The women were in 'strong clothes', shapeless garments made of reinforced cotton that couldn't be torn. Many of them were in 'locked boots' which couldn't be taken off and thrown. There was nothing movable. There were no knives. Spoons were taken in and counted every meal. The women all had their hair chopped off short giving them identical grey mops. At the back of the ward were padded cells, in which would be one or two naked women smeared with faeces, shouting obscenities at anyone who came near. Then there were the airing courts. Grey, big courts, paved with tarmac, surrounded by a wall twelve feet high and a hundred men milling around. A few of them walking, some running, others standing on one leg, posturing, with the urine running out of their trouser leg, some sitting in a corner masturbating. A couple of bored young male nurses standing on 'point duty', looking at them, ready to hit anybody who got out of line, but otherwise not doing anything. A scene of human degradation.[2]

A hundred years after 1845 the industrialized countries no longer needed such amounts of labour, so to lock away the non-workers was no longer necessary and was, indeed, absurd. This change of political and economic attitude coincided with much criticism of the psychiatric hospital as an institution. So in the last few years it has become government policy to close the large psychiatric hospitals and to provide care for the inmates in the community. Now long-term patients are being discharged to live in the community. The theory is that they will then receive care which would be as good as, if not better, than the care they received in hospital. But in practice in many places they are being 'assimilated into the much larger, more amorphous class of the morally disreputable, the poor and the impotent'. History has come full circle.

When we contemplate some great cruelty in the past it is usual to express horror that such terrible things should happen and imply by the expression of horror that nothing like that could happen today. 'They', those unnamed people who allowed such cruelty to exist or who caused such cruelty, are quite different from *us* who are so wise, compassionate and caring.

Yet, if we do enquire who 'they' were, and the records are there for us to see, 'they' turn out to be not some strange breed of evil men and women, but just ordinary people, not unlike us, going about their business and trying to be good. They were husbands, wives, parents, responsible employers and employees. The doctors, nurses, administrators, and members of the hospital boards in the nineteenth century were virtuous men and women, just like the doctors, nurses, administrators, and members of the health authorities are today.

The trouble is that the processes whereby children learn to be good can also be the processes whereby they learn to be blind to the suffering of other people. When the extremes of pain force a child to change his perception of the situation from 'I am being unjustly punished by my bad parent' to 'I am bad and am being justly punished by my good parent' the child not only sacrifices himself to preserve his parent as good, but he damages or even destroys his ability to perceive evil in the here and now. He is no longer able to view with a clear, perceptive, steady gaze the pain, cruelty and injustice which people suffer in this world. He may be able to see it in far-off lands, in places unconnected with his personal life, but when the evil is close by, part of the world where he has responsibilities, he has to turn away, to hide his eyes, pretend that nothing has happened, or wrap up all that he sees in all kinds of sentimentalities, pretences, moralities and lies. The people who crammed thousands of helpless, disturbed men and women into the bare, locked wards of a pauper lunatic asylum were no different from those who now put helpless, disturbed

180

people into small, miserable rooms or let them wander the streets, homeless, cold, and hungry, and call this cruelty 'community care'. When we lose part of our spirit in learning to be good we usually have no compunction then in trying to destroy the spirit of other people.

Psychiatric hospitals are monuments to the destruction of the human spirit. There is always the imposing façade, built to impress the worthy, sane citizens and to intimidate the mad and those who fear that within them the seeds of madness lie. Behind the façade are the long, echoing corridors in a pattern where corridor mirrors corridor and turns inward, a maze without an exit rather than a path with a goal. Along the corridors are little, sly doors whose secrets are known only to the staff, and large, heavy doors, fitted with big locks, and which open into rooms not built to any human scale, but simply storage space, cold and dead. In more recent years these vast spaces where people were once herded have been 'cubicalized', furnished with single beds with matching small dressing table and wardrobe, each given the illusion of privacy by a curtain or a thin partition, while other rooms have been given an illusion of homeliness with a carpet and easy chairs and a television. The bare cells where once recalcitrant and dangerous patients would be imprisoned are now 'side-rooms', containing a bed and wardrobe, but the narrow window and the slit in the door, through which the nurses can cast a watching eye, prevent any sense of personal space and belonging. The attempts to turn these hospitals into places where people can feel comfortable and at home are as successful as turning the Pyramids into bungalows by putting a white picket fence round them would be.

I had visited psychiatric hospitals in Sydney, Australia, but it was not until I came to England that I had to work in them. Eighteen years of knowing such places has not reduced my horror at the inhumanity they represent.

The people who become inmates of psychiatric hospitals differ in the kinds of problems they have and in the way they behave, but the one thing they all have in common is that they have a very low opinion of themselves. The psychiatric hospital does nothing to change this, but rather serves to decrease the patients' self-confidence even further. The buildings stress the patients' insignificance and unworthiness. The procedures and practices of the staff, despite their care and concern for the patients, prevent the resurgence of the spirit and the recovery of self-confidence which is necessary if the person is to find the courage necessary to return to ordinary life.

Goffman, in his description of life within a psychiatric hospital,[3] called the case conference 'the degradation ceremony'. I have witnessed many of these ceremonies, and the greatest horror I felt was at the way so many of the doctors and nurses did not see anything questionable in what they were doing. Recently, in a television programme about long-stay patients going into the community, a case conference was shown where the consultant psychiatrist and the nurses were seated in a circle in the consultant's office. A woman patient, carelessly dressed and hair unbrushed, was brought in and seated in the centre of the circle. The consultant questioned her about her weekend outside the hospital, when she had quarrelled with her lover. The woman began to cry, huge, wrenching cries.

I was not surprised that no one moved to comfort her. The doctor and nurses just sat, stony faced. This is what would have happened in most case conferences. The doctors and nurses would have let her cry until she stopped, or the consultant, discomfited or irritated, would have asked one of the nurses to take her out of the room. What did surprise me was that they did not move to comfort her when the camera was watching. Many of us, under the eye of a television camera, 'fake good' in order to win the approval of our unseen audience. But it did not occur to these people that amongst their unseen audience might be someone who would consider their inaction to be cruel and insensitive.

Within the psychiatric hospitals where I have worked my criticisms of the case conference have been treated as, at best, irrelevant, and, at worst, dangerously revolutionary. My critics have been those nurses and doctors who hold and practise the medical theory of mental illness. This theory, while making passing reference to social and psychological factors, states that there are mental illnesses which parallel phsyical illnesses. They have a physical cause and a physical cure.

Theories are Made by People

We all like to talk about our favourite theories as if they are objects which somehow exist in their own right, separate from the people who know about them and use them. By regarding our theories as objects in their own right, we can then regard them as embodying the Absolute Truth, and there is nothing more comforting than an Absolute Truth.

Where do these Absolute Truths reside? In the Bible, and the Koran, of course, and the Bhagavata Gita, and *Das Kapital*, depending on which Absolute Truth you prefer. They also reside in scientific textbooks, and literary texts, and on microfiche and video and audio tapes, and on computer disks. Some people say they reside in paintings and sculpture and in music.

One problem with Absolute Truths is that there are so many of them, and few of them agree with one another. The other problem about Absolute Truths is that books, films, tapes, disks, paintings, recordings of all kinds, are *in themselves* as communicative and alive as rocks and rivers. It is only because there are human beings to read and interpret certain of their attributes that these objects take on a special significance. Such objects are nothing but the repository for our thoughts. Our thoughts create these Absolute, and not-so-absolute, Truths, and if we become just another extinct species, then our Absolute Truths, along with all our other truths and lies, will disappear with us.

Theories don't exist separate from us. We create them and are affected by them.

Because we like to think of theories as existing separate from us, it becomes possible for us to make up theories with little reference to what actually goes on in our world. Pure mathematicians work in the realm of pure ideas, and despise those of their colleagues who apply their mathematical knowledge to real issues. Economists create theories based on unexamined assumptions about the ways people buy and sell. Psychologists and psychiatrists have developed their theories with only a minimal questioning of the people whose behaviour the theories are supposed to explain. Psychologists, especially research psychologists, have always been very prone to spending no more time than absolutely necessary with their subjects to gather some figures and then scampering off to the safety of their computers. Psychiatrists, trained to regard patients as inferior beings and in some way contaminated and contaminating, try to spend as little time as possible with patients. The more senior the psychiatrist, and therefore the more likely to have his theories accepted by others, the less time he spends with patients.

Because we like to think of theories existing separate from us, we often neglect to ask, 'What kind of people made up these theories?'

The theory that madness comprises several kinds of mental illnesses which have physical causes is a theory which has been made up by *men*. These men have been middle-class Europeans – chiefly Germans, British and French. Most of their patients have been women. (Women make up two-thirds of psychiatric patients.) I have sat in case conferences over the years and listened to middle-class Englishmen theorize about their women patients, and I have read innumerable letters written by such middle-class Englishmen about their women patients, and I can say that these men would have been better employed applying their theory-making skills to the behaviour of Martians, for they have a much more intimate knowledge of Martians than they have of women.

One middle-class Englishman who had a profound influence on the thinking and practice of psychiatrists was Henry Maudsley, whose memory is revered in the name of the most prestigious of psychiatric institutions, the Maudsley Hospital in London.

Writing about Maudsley's book, *Body and Will*, published in 1883, Dr W. Ll. Parry-Jones quoted 'Maudsley's forthright conclusions':

'Mind and all its products are a function of matter, an outcome of interacting and combined atomic forces not essentially different in kind from the effervescence that follows a chemical combination or the explosion of a fulminate.' By 1885 Maudsley's writing, disparaging psychological approaches to mental disorder and their replacement by somaticist views, had far reaching effects on Victorian psychological medicine.

A decade earlier he had made it explicit that: 'It is not our business, as it is not in our power, to explain psychologically the origin and nature of any of these depraved instincts; it is sufficient to establish their existence as facts of observation, and to set forth the pathological conditions under which they are produced; they are facts of pathology, which should be observed, and classified like other phenomena of disease.'[4] Mental disorders, therefore, were simply nervous disorders, like epilepsy, in which mental symptoms were prominent.[5]

Dr Parry-Jones went on to comment that 'the therapeutic barrenness of such views, however, was soon apparent'. While this may be apparent to Dr Parry-Jones, it is certainly not apparent to many of his colleagues. The spirit of Maudsley is alive and well through psychiatry worldwide. There are still a great many psychiatrists who believe that everything that human beings do, feel, think and create can be fully explained in terms of chemical changes. Great despair, great joy and great love are nothing more than a few electrons.

The belief that human behaviour can be understood and explained scientifically and completely solely in terms of physiological or chemical changes is a belief which can be held only by those people whose own experience of their humanness – their full range of feelings, needs, desires and fantasies – has been neglected and repressed.

It is men, rather than women, who hold such views. Women, on the whole, choose explanations of why people behave as they do which try to appreciate the full range of human experience and capability. 'Scientific' men dismiss such an approach as 'unscientific'; 'feminist' women praise such an approach as evidence of women's superior, innate wisdom. But the capacity to understand that to be human is more than being a body is a capacity we all have when we are born; it is a capacity, however, which can be easily lost or under-developed. Through their upbringing it is boys, rather than girls, who are likely to suffer this loss. The capacity to be aware of other people as human beings and not as objects is a kind of vision, and where this kind of vision is concerned, so many men are blind. This blindness, however, does not prevent them from taking positions where they are responsible for the care of other people. On the contrary, they regard their blindness as a virtue, as proof of their manliness, courage, and common sense. They are usually good, well-meaning men, but they do not see the pain and injury they inflict on those in their care.

Whenever such men assume positions of authority as doctors and administrators within the mental health care system they exhibit blindness, particularly in their relationships with people whose backgrounds are different from their own. Such doctors and administrators tend to come from the middle class, while the majority of psychiatric patients are working class who then find themselves on the receiving end of the prejudice that middle-class people can hold about the working class (that is, working-class people are stupid, uneducated and uncouth). When doctors and administrators are of a different nationality from the patients, the patients find themselves on the receiving end of racial prejudice, which may range from the most blatant denigration to simply not appreciating that there is no common language between them. Roland Littlewood and Maurice Lipsedge, who describe them-selves as 'white, male, middle-class doctors', have found that many West Indian patients are labelled as unintelligent or schizophrenic because their white, middle-class doctor does not recognize that the form of English which a West Indian speaks can be very different from his own.[6] Similarly, many patients born and brought up in Britain have great difficulty in understanding those doctors for whom English is not simply a second language but one which they learned from teachers for whom English was also a second language. English may be the world's most common language, but the way it is now being learned and spoken in Delhi and Cairo makes it incomprehensible to people who learned their English in Britain.

Perhaps the greatest incomprehension exists over sexuality. The common, traditional upbringing of boys means that they have to split off and hide their tender feelings and to acknowledge and seek to express sexual feelings only in terms of aggression and power. This prevents them from understanding themselves and prevents them from understanding that women are not objects but human beings like themselves. Within the traditional upbringing of a boy, especially for those middle- and upper-class boys who are educated at boarding school, there are homosexual, erotic experiences which can range from true, loving friendships, through sexual curiosity and exploration to the kinds of homosexual activities which Jack described in his orphanage. Their own childhood sexual experiences have prevented many psychiatrists from acknowledging the prevalence of sexual assaults on children. Instead of seeing that the distress of so many women patients is a result of childhood sexual trauma, they disparage these women as 'hysterical', 'neurotic', 'inadequate', favourite terms in psychiatric diagnosis, and recommend to one another the appropriate cure for such women – 'a good fuck'. For this reason many women patients seek a woman doctor. Women as consultant psychiatrists can be as imperious and power-mad as their male counterparts, but they do not recommend 'penis therapy', as it is known in the trade, for their patients.

There are, fortunately, many men psychiatrists who would never be guilty of such crass, cruel behaviour towards women. But their upbringing has left many of them unable to relate to women as friends, fellow human beings. Women are to them what they were to Freud, a mystery. Freud had the upbringing typical of a middle-class boy. Later he wrote to his friend Fliess:

> I do not share your contempt for friendship between men, probably because I am to a high degree party to it. In my life, as you know, woman has never replaced the comrade, the friend.[7]

Many men psychiatrists, I have found, have never realized that they do not understand women, much less have attempted to develop their understanding. There is no tradition in the training of doctors in Britain that they should review their upbringing and come to understand how they were affected by it. Rather, the tradition is not to enquire. This tradition continues in psychiatry. Of recent years some psychiatrists have become interested in psychotherapy but the Royal College of Psychiatrists does not make knowledge and experience of psychotherapy an essential requirement for entry to the College. Some of the psychiatrists who become psychotherapists are extremely skilled, sensitive and aware, but others interpret their training in psychotherapy in the same rigid, authoritarian way that they learned in becoming doctors. They cannot tolerate the uncertainty and freedom which is the essence of psychotherapy.

In the United States an acceptance of the importance of psychotherapy seems to be more widespread. Advertisements for psychotropic drugs in the *British Journal of Psychiatry* carry the message 'Give this to your patient and she will get better', whereas advertisements in the *American Journal of Psychiatry* for the same drugs carry the message 'Give your patient this drug and she'll be in a better frame of mind for psychotherapy'. However, there are still plenty of American psychiatrists who would applaud the Professor of Psychiatry at the University of Iowa, George Winokur, when he said:

> I do not believe I understand the mind any better than I did before going into psychiatry. What's more I do not believe that my colleagues in psychiatry, no matter what they say, really understand motivation or what makes a person behave or think as he does. Many of them say they do but I do not believe them . . . I decided that psychiatric illnesses and particularly the mood illnesses (depressions and mania) were best studied under the imprimatur of the medical model. It seemed that most psychiatric illnesses had a familial and probably genetic basis; at least this was true of most serious psychiatric illnesses. This was certainly so in the mood illnesses. This meant that there was some underlying biological background. Also, these illnesses could be defined in the same way as any ordinary medical illness could be defined.[8]

It is no wonder that many men, not just psychiatrists, have to resort to explaining human behaviour in terms of physiology. Their upbringing has prevented them from learning a language to talk about their feelings.

Medical training prevents many doctors from coming to understand how we live in our language world like a fish lives in water and that everything we know and do is mediated by language. On many occasions I have tried to explain this to psychiatrists and to psychiatrists in training, and each time I failed. Lawyers, I find, have no difficulty in understanding that 'language creates reality, and not reality language', but then, of course, language is their business.

I have often tried, and failed, to explain to doctors the process of 'reification', whereby we turn a verb into a noun, and then think that because we have a name there must in reality be a *thing* which possesses that name. For instance, a person is observed to be behaving strangely, and this 'behaving', a verbal form, is turned into a noun. 'This person has schizophrenia.' 'Schizophrenia' becomes a *thing* which some people have and on the search for which millions of pounds and dollars have been fruitlessly spent.

The idea that mental illnesses are things which actually exist and which exert influences is quite popular. Thus, the *Guardian* carried the headline 'Depression forced mother to jump from window'[9] as if depression crept up behind her and pushed her out of the window.

Traditional psychiatry places great emphasis on finding the correct diagnosis. The idea is that if somehow you can isolate from the continually changing spectacle of life a particular portion and give that portion a name, you have, in some way, taken control of the passing spectacle, or at least a part of it. This is, of course, an illusion, as Hindus would say, or a fiction, as Buddhists would say, but we all do it all the time in the attempt to make sense of our experience. Wise people don't take their isolating and naming activities too seriously, but less secure people hang on to their vocabulary of names like a drowning man holds on to a lifebelt. Psychiatry is full of drowning men.

One woman I knew came into the hospital in a very distressed state. She couldn't, she said, cope with looking after her home and husband and children any longer. She was greatly troubled by headaches and by strange sensations in her head. She had been examined by a consultant physician and a neurologist, and numerous tests had been made, but no physical cause for her symptoms could be found. So she was sent to a psychiatrist, and he had brought her into hospital.

I met her and her husband after the junior doctor had asked me to see them. The husband was a tall, powerfully built man with a fierce temper. He had been reduced to working as a truck driver because the business venture into which they had put all their money had failed. She dared not complain that she had lost her home and her security, because she was afraid of him. It was safer to blame herself and to make her complaint against him a physical complaint which he had to take seriously and treat with concern.

That was my analysis of the situation. It was not difficult to see what was going on, as the couple were very ready to talk. The difficult part would be to get them to pay attention to what they were doing and to consider changing it. The senior nurses on the ward had come to the same conclusion about the couple and together we tried to work out a treatment plan.

The consultant psychiatrist took no notice of our efforts. He was the clinical tutor who arranged and led the training case conferences. He instructed his junior doctor to present the woman at the case conference as an interesting case for diagnosis.

So the junior doctor interviewed her and prepared a case history. The woman was taken to the case conference where she found herself in a room with fourteen men, only two of whom she had met before. They asked her a lot of questions and she grew more and more confused.

When there were no more questions, the clinical tutor told her to leave the room. Then the doctors set to work to decide upon the correct diagnosis. 'Schizophrenia' and 'manic depression' were discussed and dismissed. 'Endogenous depression' and 'anxiety state' seemed likely, but there was no agreement. The reports of the physician and the neurologist were examined, but an organic cause could not be revealed. The clinical tutor urged his doctors to arrive at a diagnosis. The other consultants grew weary of the discussion and the junior doctors became more and more puzzled.

Finally, the clinical tutor produced the answer. The correct diagnosis was 'hypochondriasis in an inadequate personality'. The junior doctor recorded it obediently in the case notes.

Next day the student nurse on the ward showed it to me.

'What does it mean?' she asked.

'It means that the woman says she's ill when she isn't and that she can't cope with her responsibilities.'

Any hope the nurse had that some advance had been made in helping the woman vanished.

Patients can find being labelled quite helpful. David, writing of his years of being depressed, said:

> I experienced a year long period of depression and withdrawal, the first time that I had been aware of feeling 'mad' for more than three or four weeks at a time. A GP diagnosed 'endogenous depression'. I quite liked that label and enjoyed rolling it around on my tongue. It sounded vastly more impressive than mere 'depression', and less degrading than 'anxiety neurosis' or 'nervous exhaustion'. That new label helped when explaining my problems to friends or business colleagues. 'From within,' I said with an air of superiority and confidence I never felt. 'It means that I suffer from a chemical deficiency which causes the depression.' They didn't understand what I was talking about; neither did I. To clarify the explanation, I often copied on a piece of paper an illustration of what it meant. I drew a horizontal line across the centre of the sheet and a large 'U'-shaped curve starting at the top of the paper, dipping to the bottom and returning to the top. 'The straight line represents the "normal level of activity,"' I explained. 'The curve is my particular level. When I'm above the line, I use up too much chemical, and so, to make up for the excessive energy, the body dips below the "norm", that's what it means.' I felt that even if I wasn't cured, I had a respectable answer.[10]

There is a tradition in psychiatry that the psychiatric patient is an inferior being, born inferior or becoming so by developing a mental illness. There are very few psychiatrists who eat with their patients, wear the same clothes as their patients, and allow their patients to call them by their first names, although they will use the patient's first name with the jolly familiarity of a superior addressing an inferior. Problems arise when someone who should not be inferior develops the symptoms of a mental illness. This is an embarrassment in any hierarchical organization, such as the Royal Air Force. An advertisement for the Ex-Services Mental Welfare Society in *The Royal Air Force News* told the story of 'Perhaps the bravest man I ever knew':

> Six-foot-four Sergeant 'Tiny' G*t*r*e, DCM, was perhaps the bravest man his Colonel ever knew.
>
> But now, after seeing service in Aden, after being booby-trapped and ambushed in Northern Ireland, Sergeant 'Tiny' cannot bear to turn a corner. For fear of what is on the other side.
>
> It is the bravest men and women from the Services that suffer most from mental breakdown. For they have tried, each one of them, to give more, much more, than they could in service of our country. We look after these brave men and women. We help them at home, and in hospital . . . These men and women have given their minds to their country.[11]

Madness being a sign of extraordinary courage and virtue has a certain face-saving charm, and is an explanation which many psychiatrists use when one of their colleagues first shows the symptoms of mental illness.

Pat Wakeling, writing of his experience of being depressed, said:

> God, how I longed for my depression to be magically changed into a decent, straightforward physical ailment! The psychiatric hospital is intolerant of weakness in its staff. Compassion is for patients; for 'them' not 'us'. When the dreaded plague strikes a doctor's house, the rest put up their shutters and circulate the comforting notion that the victim's illness is the direct con-

sequence of the sterling qualities possessed by every member of the caring professions: an excess of virtue, if you like, turning upon its owner like a two-edged sword. But in their secret thoughts the survivors are saying to themselves, 'Always knew there was something rum about him. Not surprised, really.' I knew there was no recognized way of getting help. Perhaps some could have braved it out, but disclosures do not always make for 'good' professional relationships, and there are very few junior doctors who would risk endangering their prospects by coming clean to those consultants whose work is built upon the ever-pressing need to defend themselves against precisely the same fate.

He discovered that:

The psychiatrist's family needs special attention. I have witnessed enormous suffering – compounded of anguish, insecurity, embarrassment, and downright humiliation – in a colleague's family subjected to brutally insensitive attentions, and arrangements, of attendant consultants who were, in fact, acting out their own neuroses.

He concluded that:

What mattered most to the patient is what mattered most to me: namely, the personal 'accessibility' of the psychiatrist – those subtle qualities of personality rendering him non-judgemental and a fully paid-up member of the human race. Someone who listens to more than the mere words one falteringly utters. Above all, he must be able to distinguish his problems from those of the client. To be a good psychiatrist requires the same honesty and courage expected of the good patient.[12]

Pat Wakeling, my colleague and friend, is certainly the good psychiatrist that he describes.

What Many Psychiatrists and Psychotherapists Ignore

The theory that mental illnesses are the result of some biochemical imbalance and/or faulty genes implies that what happens to a person in childhood is of no significance in the later development of a mental illness. While psychoanalysis emphasizes the importance of childhood experience, much of this experience is subsumed under the heading of fantasy. When a patient recounted some event involving a sexual involvement with an adult in the patient's childhood, psychoanalysts, following Freud, defined this as a fantasy created as a compensation for a wish. Freud had discovered that many of his patients gave a history of sexual abuse as small children, and at first he considered that such events accounted for the later development of a neurosis. But then he decided that so many sexual assaults of children could not possibly have taken place in these middle-class Viennese families, and so he developed his theory of the Oedipus complex. His patients had simply imagined that they had been abused.

Quite recently, some people in the United States, and Germany (notably the psychoanalyst Alice Miller) and in Britain began to point out that many more children were sexually abused than was admitted in our society. Women's groups found that many of their members had endured such experiences. Psychotherapists who were not slavishly attached to Freudian theory accepted their clients' accounts of their childhoods as real and not fantasy, and found that they were increasingly being told of horrific events of sexual and physical abuse, once their clients felt secure enough in the therapeutic relationship to risk being disloyal to their parents. Like wildfire, the idea that it was permissible to talk about incest in public caught on, and soon there were incest victims' groups, and magazine articles, and books, and television programmes, as if some new craze had taken hold. But it was not a new craze, a new family hobby. It was just that people were talking about it now, and because they were talking about it, more cases of incest and sexual abuse of children came to light.

In 1986 the National Society for the Prevention of Cruelty to Children found that reported cases of child sexual abuse had risen by an estimated 90 per cent. David Hencke, writing in the *Guardian*, said:

> The charity estimates that more than 2,850 children were placed on local authority registers last year compared with 1,500 in 1984.
>
> The society believes the increase, the largest recorded, shows a growing awareness of the problem rather than a great increase in the number of children being abused. Twenty-nine per cent of young boys reported assaulted were under the age of four, compared with 11 per cent of girls. The majority of reported sexual assaults are of young girls aged 10 to 14.
>
> Most of the people who sexually assault children are fathers, close male relatives or stepfathers . . .
>
> There are more reports of sexual assaults on children among those on low incomes and living in bad conditions but this may be because middle class people tend not to be monitored as closely by social workers or health visitors . . .
>
> The initial analysis of the first 200 who sought refuge in Britain's first 'safe house' for runaway adolescents, run by the Church of England Children's Society, shows that one in six who have run away from their parents has been sexually abused.
>
> One in seven of the children – nearly all under the age of 16 – has been referred to the centre by the police after being caught soliciting in London.
>
> Each case has been confirmed by staff at the centre, who found that many complaints to teachers and social workers had been dismissed earlier as fantasy.[13]

Working in the United States, Sandra Butler examined the incidence and the effects of incestuous assault on children and reported her findings in her book *The Conspiracy of Silence: the Trauma of Incest*. She wrote:

> I felt sure that I would find incestuous assault occurring primarily in ingrown mountain communities and fragmented inner-city

families, but I was wrong. What I found was a cross-section of American families who are suffering from the traumas of incestuous assault – families from all socio-economic classes, families like those I had known all my life, families that subscribe to the work ethic and whose members are upstanding pillars of their communities, civic leaders and church members . . . Among the affluent, incestuous assault is simply a better-kept secret . . . In the vast majority of incestuous assault cases, the offender is an adult male and the child victim a female . . . Seventy-five per cent of all reported sexual abuse is committed by someone the victim knows and trusts. And all too frequently that someone is a member of the victim's immediate family.

Of the aggressors, she wrote:

When all else in their lives fails, they have been led to believe that the exercise of the power of the genitals will assure them of their ultimate competence and power . . .

In nearly all the studies of adult male sexual offenders that have been done to date, well over half, and in some cases nearly three-quarters, of the men studied who are serving time in prison were found to have been sexually abused as young boys without any intervention.

Where could there have been any intervention?

It was in the professional community that I found the silence I had anticipated finding among those who had been victimized. Again and again as I sought out men and women with the training and experience that should have equipped them with the foundation upon which to develop alternatives in treatment and counselling, I heard the same phrase: 'We don't see much of that here.'[14]

The reports on the long-term effects of sexual assaults on children show that Constance's story is not unusual.

Constance is a silent woman. She had been coming to the psychology department to see one or other of the psychologists or to be a member of our groups for some four years. I knew her from one of the groups I ran, from the conversations I had had with the psychologist who saw her for individual therapy, and from the brief greetings we might exchange when she came to the department. Sometimes we met when we were shopping, and sometimes I took her phone messages when she called about her appointments. In all, I suppose I knew her quite well, yet I could summarize what I knew about her quite briefly.

Constance was in her late thirties, was divorced and lived alone. She had once been a nurse. She married, had four miscarriages, and entered a psychiatric hospital in a severely depressed state. Her marriage broke up, she was unable to work, and she went in and out of hospital, often depressed and suicidal. When she found there were psychologists she could consult, even though these psychologists came and went as they changed their jobs, she clung tenaciously to this opportunity to work out what was happening to her. Yet, once in the psychologist's room she was silent, or she talked only about trivial worries or of her sense of helplessness and despair.

As time went by some progress was made. She began studying and passed her A levels. I had heard of her success and how she was planning to do some college courses when my secretary passed me a phone message to say that Constance wanted to talk to someone urgently. Her own psychologist, Roger, was on holiday, and it seemed clear that Constance wanted to see me. So I phoned her and arranged to see her the morning of the day she was to enrol in her new classes. Only she wasn't going to enrol. Something had happened in Cleethorpes which meant that she could not go on with her study.

'Something had happened in Cleethorpes', that fabled resort on the North Sea Coast, conjured up for me a fantasy of some tragic or ridiculous sexual encounter, but this was not what Constance spoke of. She had gone to Cleethorpes to consult a faith healer, and this faith healer had told her that the Devil had possessed her. All her depression and suicidal impulses were the work of the Devil who inhabited her.

'People know that you are possessed by evil spirits,' the faith healer told her. 'That's why people back away from you.'

Constance, who had spent her life backing away from other people, was rather bemused by this. But the faith healer was insistent, and Constance was left with a large doubt. Perhaps she was possessed.

I asked Constance whether she believed in a vast and powerful God whom we can trust but never understand (the explanation of evil which does not require a Devil) or whether she believed in God and the Devil, locked in combat. She favoured the God and the Devil conception. Trusting an unknowable God is a feat quite beyond those people who are unable to trust even one human being. So the Devil was a reality to her. Part of her knew that the faith healer was mistakenly using the concepts of the medieval explanation of madness, but another part of her felt that perhaps the faith healer was right. How else could she explain the strange, alien feelings which came upon her? And was not suicide a sin?

I spoke of how the Devil was without a conscience and how a person possessed by the Devil, someone who was evil, would act without guilt.

Constance smiled. 'I was born feeling guilty.'

Constance had spent four days with the faith healer who encouraged her to talk. Under the faith healer's influence she found memories coming back, things that she had blotted out. Now she said to me, 'I can't talk to Roger about these things. Not to a man.'

Then she said, 'I was sexually assaulted as a child – by a relative. It must have happened several times, but I remember it only once. He said that if I told anyone he'd go to prison and I'd be taken away and put in prison.'

I said, 'The terrible thing is that the child doesn't know that this isn't true. You couldn't ask anyone, could you? The terrifying part is that this is done to you by someone who should love you and look after you. And then, when other relatives don't protect you, it means they haven't noticed, in which case they're not looking after you, or they have noticed and aren't doing anything to protect you.'

'It was my father.'

I had guessed as much, but was still surprised. Constance's father had died four years ago and Constance had nursed him through a long illness.

She said, 'When I was a child I just pushed the thoughts away, and then it would come back in dreams. I told myself that I'd imagined it – it hadn't happened. I forgot it. Later, when he was ill, he came to live with me. I nursed him. I used to sit on his bed. I didn't remember what had happened. What would have happened if I had?' Dare she recognize and contemplate her murderous hate?

She went on, 'Father left home when I was a teenager. I didn't see him for three years and then I met him accidentally. I asked him why he hadn't been to see me, and he said that my mother told him that I didn't want to see him. That wasn't true.' Now she had to contemplate her love for her father.

'The man I looked after was quite different from my father when I was a child. Quite different. My parents used to argue. I'd go to sleep at night with the pillow over my head so I wouldn't hear them. My name always came into it. He'd say he wouldn't still be there if it wasn't for me. She'd say it was his fault I was there. So I knew it was my fault they were fighting. I thought that if I went away they'd be all right. Later I found out that my mother was three months pregnant with me when they married. So it was my fault. I've always been guilty. Now it's all coming back, I don't want to remember.'

But the memories were there, and Constance knew that the only way to deal with them was to talk about them. She said, 'I watched that television programme on incest and I wrote down the address of that organization for incest victims, but later I thought I couldn't talk about it to anyone and I threw the bit of paper away.'

I gave her the phone number of a local group. She put it in her handbag and took out a copy of her college's timetable. We talked about the subjects she wanted to do for her A levels and then she went off to enrol in classes for sociology and psychology. Those subjects have a devilment all of their own.

199

Sexual abuse in childhood has long-term effects. Alice Miller has written of these:

> The consequences of sexual abuse are not restricted to problems in one's sexual life; they impair the development of the self and of an autonomous personality. There are several reasons for this.
>
> 1. To have one's helplessness and total dependency taken advantage of by the person one loves, by one's mother or father, at a very early age soon produces an interlinking of love and hate.
>
> 2. Because anger toward the loved person cannot be expressed for fear of losing that person and therefore cannot be lived out, ambivalence, the linking of love and hate, remains an important characteristic of later object relationships. Many people, for instance, cannot imagine that love is possible without suffering and sacrifice, without fear of being abused, without being hurt and humiliated.
>
> 3. Since the fact of abuse must be repressed for the sake of survival, all knowledge that would threaten to undo this repression must be warded off by every possible means, which ultimately results in an impoverishment of the personality and a loss of vital roots, manifested, for example, in depression.
>
> 4. The consequences of a trauma are not eliminated by repression but are actually reinforced. The inability to remember the trauma, to articulate it (i.e., to be able to communicate it to a person who believes you) creates the need to articulate it in the repetition compulsion.
>
> 5. The plight of being at someone else's mercy and being abused by a loved object is perpetuated either in a passive or active role, or alternatively in each.
>
> 6. One of the simplest and completely unnoticed forms of perpetuation of the active role is abuse of one's children for one's own needs, which are all the more urgent and uncontrollable the more deeply repressed the original trauma.[15]

When a child is the victim of physical violence the child suffers great pain and a sense of helplessness which can haunt the child for as long as he or she lives. Sexually abused, the child may be equally helpless and the sense of helplessness just as overwhelming and pervasive. But sometimes the events surrounding the sexual abuse are not all bad, and then the child is left trying to come to terms with this mixture of pleasure and pain. The outcome of this can be repetitious behaviour which might be labelled perverse.

Joy had suggested that Jack might like to come to see me on his own. I thought it unlikely that he would take up this suggestion. However, I was wrong. Joy went to visit her mother who was not well. I had finished writing the first two chapters of this book and wanted Jack and Joy to read them so we could check my account of Jack's story. I called in at Jack's place and left the manuscript, and just as I was leaving Jack asked if we could arrange an appointment for him. So we did, and a few days later he came to see me.

He spoke again of his sexual experiences at the orphanage. He described how he had been at the orphanage only a few hours when a boy came to him and said he was wanted. He was taken down to the basement where the boiler was, and there was a group of the older boys.

'They grabbed me, spread me on the table, and each of them raped me. If I struggled they hit me. They were big boys, fully developed, big enough for it (anal rape) to be very painful.'

A day or so later he was taken again, this time by just two boys. 'It wasn't as bad as the first time. I got used to it.'

With most of the masters 'it was just down with the trousers and, bang, in. All you got out of it was a sore bottom.'

He told me how one master would beat the boy on the bottom with a cane until the boy's flesh was red and sore. Then the master would smooth cream over the boy's buttocks very gently. Then 'bang, in. It was pain, pleasure, pain. Funny thing, I really like smoothing cream on. I like smoothing cream over Joy's back.'

He said, 'I was a skinny little kid, and I always was the passive partner, but after, when I got older, I did it to the younger kids. I wonder now what happened to them.'

Jack spoke fondly of the Major. He said, 'The Major had a great influence on me. With him, well, sometimes we just sat in front of the fire and made toast – you know, bread on toasting forks – and listened to music. Other times, well, he wasn't in a hurry. There'd be mutual masturbation, and after, well, I know I was the passive partner, but I'd got something out of it.'

He described how the Major would dress up in a woman's suspender belt and stockings and would dress Jack as a schoolgirl.

'I got something out of it – being loved and wanted, if only for one thing.'

Jack spoke of 'men's sex and women's sex'. Men's sex, as he wanted it, was chiefly arousal and excitement, not orgasm. 'I don't put much importance on that,' he said. If when they are making love Joy had an orgasm first, Jack would lose interest immediately.

Making love to Joy was very important to him, but so was masturbation. He also valued his collection of pornography. Reading pornography was, he said, very stimulating. He found it immensely pleasurable to spend an afternoon in his bedroom where he would dress up, as the Major had done, in suspender belt and stockings and read what he called 'my books', his collection of pornography.

Joy accepted these activities, although she refused to watch his blue films and hated to look at his pornography. This was part of his life which was separate from her, and, as she explained to me later, when she first discovered what Jack did, she didn't know any other men and had supposed that all men were like that. She now knew that they weren't – Mark's abhorrence of Jack's collection of books made that quite clear – but she thought that she should accept this quirk of Jack's character because she loved him. 'I'm very good at loving,' she said.

Jack defended his activities to me. 'Why should I stop doing it? I'm not hurting anyone.'

It seemed to me that Jack's dressing up and masturbating was the repetition compulsion which follows when the child cannot master such traumatic events because he lacks at that stage of development the capacity to do so. For, as Ferenczi said, 'the erotic life of the child . . . remains at the level of foreplay, or knows satisfaction only in the sense of 'satiety' but not the feeling of annihilation that accompanies orgasm'.[16]

The 'conspiracy of silence' which has existed for so long about the sexual abuse of children is part of society's way of putting the parents' interests before the children's. Alice Miller calls this the unchallengeable rule 'Thou Shalt Not Be Aware'. You must not be aware of what your parents have done to you.

Jane described herself as being once very friendly, confident and outgoing, but now she was terribly nervous. From time to time she would be swept by panics. She was a beautician, and when the panic came she would go quiet and rigid to control her shaking. This made working very difficult.

She had noticed the change in herself when, three years ago, she had gone to work in a salon where the manager was a woman much older than her. Jane found this woman hard to get along with. She was very changeable. One minute she would be urging Jane to take responsibility for a certain task, and the next minute she would be castigating her for not asking permission to carry out the very same task.

'I don't know what to do to please her,' she said, and wept in despair.

Pleasing people was very important to Jane. She needed to be liked. But the roots of her despair went deeper than this. It was not just that she wanted the manager to like her. It was that the situation with the manager was a repetition of another, much more painful situation.

When Jane was talking to me about the manager I asked how old this woman was, and established that she was old enough to be Jane's mother. It was a while in our conversation before Jane mentioned her mother, and then with great reluctance. Her mother, she said, had had a series of nervous breakdowns. Jane's childhood had been marked by strange, frightening events, and life in her home had been dominated by the rule 'don't upset mother'. Even now she would never know as she went to visit her mother, or picked up the phone to speak to her, what sort of mood her mother would be in. She might greet Jane lovingly, or she might be harsh, hurtful and rejecting. She had always expected Jane to fend for herself, while at the same time she criticized Jane in the way that people who are prone to depression criticize their nearest and dearest. Jane could never rest secure in her mother's love, and so she could never rest secure in the belief that people would find her charming and beautiful (which she was) and so like her.

Until I drew the parallel between the manager and her mother Jane had not seen it.

The rule 'Thou Shalt Not Be Aware' leaves the small child inside each of us uncared for, unless we can be sufficiently aware and selfish enough to care for ourselves. David came to realize this when he was a resident in a therapeutic community.

Residents arrived at the unit at a time in their lives when momentous and destructive behaviour made some form of help inevitable. What none of us realized in our first days and weeks was that our latest 'crisis' was a mere scratch compared with the deep scars which had been inflicted at a time when we were too young to understand, but old enough to be affected by what had happened to us. Jim, the unit's 'baby', verbally expressed our real bond most accurately: 'Oh, God,' he said when feeling helpless, 'I wish I was two years old and somebody would look after me!' Whether or not we could admit it, his cry was for us all.

Later he wrote:

There was one fundamental lesson I could not learn. It led me into tortuous battles during these months; the same battles that all the residents had to fight, and which many refused to do so. It never occurred to me that I was one of the refusniks. We all came to recognize our stranger, whatever we called him, and showered him with descriptive feelings – hate, fear, sadness, and many more; but, because we were constantly under attack, we became battle weary. We needed time to recover. When our feelings were at their most raw, and our memories their most vivid, we collapsed, not from today's or yesterday's battle, but from the earliest childhood battles we could remember. When Jim's plaintive plea to be a two-year-old made me exasperated, I was denying what I later admitted; that my emotions, the ones which have proved and continue to prove most destructive, are those of a helpless child, wounded and isolated, screaming for attention.[17]

Alice Miller observed that:

Many parents . . . desperately try to behave correctly toward their child, and in their child's behaviour they seek reassurance that they are good parents. The attempt to be an ideal parent, that is, to behave correctly toward the child, to raise her correctly, not to give too little or too much, is in essence an attempt to be the ideal child – well behaved and dutiful – of one's own parents.[18]

'Thou Shalt Not Be Aware' is not just a rule for protection for our parents. In psychiatry and psychotherapy it can be a protection for the therapist's parents. The therapist, whether a psychotherapist who believes that the client's memories of sexual abuse are fantasies, or a behaviourist or cognitive therapist who believes that it is 'unscientific' to enquire into the client's deepest beliefs, fantasies and fears, or a psychiatrist who believes that all madness can be adequately explained in terms of chemical changes, is in the business of protecting the patient's parents in order to protect his own.

On the surface, everything possible is being done to spare the patient, but in reality it is the therapist's feared, internalized parents who are being spared at the cost of the patient's failure to discover his own truth.[19]

By refusing to acknowledge what a person has suffered in childhood the therapist actively prevents that person from retrieving, recognizing, working through the pain and anguish, and so finding acceptance and peace. Even when the therapist and client want to do this together, the journey is long and hard.

The child who is beaten and/or sexually abused feels hate for the aggressor. This hate has to be discharged, but the child cannot, dare not, vent this hate against the aggressor. So the child must resort to fantasy.

In developing our fantasies we have only our experience to use. When we are the victims of aggression we are given ready-made material for fantasies in which we feel and express our aggression. We know what it is to be the victim of aggression. We know what the aggressor does. So we can in our imagination switch sides and become the aggressor. If we have been beaten we can imagine what it is like to beat someone. If we have been shamed and humiliated, we can imagine what it is like to inflict shame and humiliation. If we have experienced our body being invaded and torn, if we have felt great, searing pain, we can imagine what it is to invade and tear another person's body and to inflict great pain. We can, in our imagination, make our aggressor our victim.

If the degree of pain and humiliation we have suffered is not too great and there have been only one or two incidents, it may be possible through such fantasies to vent and so master our hate, so that we can get on with our life, wiser and sadder, but unhampered by unresolved pain, hate and fear.

But if the pain and humiliation have been great and frequent, then it becomes impossible for us to resolve our hate through fantasy. We keep trying to do so, and the fantasies then keep coming back, each with a content more vile and horrendous.

Extraverts repress the original event and the fantasy created in an attempt to master it. But the emotions from the event and the fantasies keep coming back, forcing the person to seek some explanation in outer reality to bind the fear into manageable phobias. If the emotions are too powerful to be bound into phobias, the only defence left is that of mania, tremendous activity and denial of the fear.

Introverts isolate and repress the emotions aroused, but the content of the fantasy remains constant. They feel great guilt at harbouring such obscenely murderous thoughts. They try to control their thoughts, but the fantasies keep recurring, like some intrusion by an alien being, and no amount of obsessional propitiation and reparation can prevent them. If the fantasies become extremely powerful, and the introvert lacks a sufficiently cohesive sense of self to maintain the distinction between fantasy and external reality, the fantasies themselves take on a reality which psychiatrists label as hallucinations and delusions. A few such people may act within their fantasy and commit upon some innocent bystanders some version of the cruelty and destruction which had once been wrought upon them.

Many people give their fantasies of hate another kind of reality. They identify with the aggressor and feel hatred and contempt for the weak and helpless person they once were. They may not be diagnosed as mad, but they cause many of the people with whom they come in contact to earn this label.

The Alternatives

When a healthy baby is born that baby is immediately in the business of communicating with the world around it. A baby looks at the world with great interest, and when part of the world looks at it and responds to it, the baby is delighted, just as it is delighted when the world feeds it.

Communication between ourselves and others is as essential as breathing. When communication breaks down or does not develop we get peculiar ideas. We create fantasies to cope with the failure of communication. A favourite fantasy is that people who are not communicating are really sending hostile communications.

Isolating yourself means that you reduce your opportunities to test reality.

One day Mary, very distressed, told me about the disaster of her uncle's visit to her home. Actually, the visit had gone much better than she had expected, despite her considerable anxiety beforehand, and when he left she allowed herself to feel a small glow of pride that she had managed a dinner and breakfast for her family and her uncle without anything going wrong. Or so she thought, until her uncle's thank you letter arrived. In it he said all the usual things about enjoying his visit and how delightful the dinner had been. Then he wrote, 'You really ought to have a hook for dressing gowns on the bathroom door.'

With this Mary fell apart. 'That's just what my family always do to me. They come and visit and they say everything's nice, and then they go away and criticize me. It's always me. I'm always the one that's stupid, that's got it wrong, and they're going to put me right. It's always me.'

I had a sneaking sympathy for her uncle. On my travels I'm always finding myself in strange bathrooms with nowhere to hang my clothes. But I would never dare mention this to my hostess, and Mary was terribly hurt. So we spent a long time discussing the affair of the missing hook on the bathroom door.

Months later Mary arrived looking happier than I had ever seen her. She had been on holiday, 'a marvellous holiday. I've really been spoilt', and she had met a cousin, someone she was fond of and hadn't seen for a long time.

'It was lovely to meet Joan again. We went sailing, just the two of us, like we did when we were girls, and we anchored for lunch, and just talked. I haven't talked like that for years and years. When we were talking, she said uncle came to visit them – do you remember, when he came to visit me—'

'The hook on the bathroom door,' I said.

'Yes. You do have a good memory. Well, he came to visit Joan, and when he left he wrote and criticized the kind of notepaper she uses. Joan says he always does that when he stays with anyone in the family. It's because he sees himself as head of the family and he thinks it's his job to keep us all up to the mark. I'd have never known that if I hadn't gone sailing with Joan.'

When I told Mary that I had written about the bathroom hook incident as an illustration of the importance of testing one's construction of reality, she said, 'Yes, but if every time you check you get told that you're wrong and it's your fault, you give up checking, don't you? If you don't get anything right, you have to withdraw.'

Fortunately, now Mary is being told by at least some people that she has got her constructions right. More importantly, she now has the self-confidence not to be devastated when her loved ones tell her she is wrong.

Living is the process whereby we create the structures we call meaning. To live securely and comfortably, our world of meaning must have an internal consistency, and the meaning must lead to a reduction rather than an increase in our fear. For this to be, we must not have any secrets from ourselves – not lying to ourselves, even though we might not choose to be so open and truthful to others. Perhaps, though, we can never know all the secrets of our unconscious, but we can at least accept that these secrets exist and not be frightened. Having such confidence in ourselves we can feel reasonably sure that if disaster did overtake us we could cope. Living thus, we can count ourselves happy.

But when we do lie to ourselves, and when we lack self-confidence, then our world of meaning is not consistent and we feel that we are unable to meet danger with courage and mastery. Then we have to choose a defence against fear.

What are called mental illnesses are simply different kinds of forts which we build to preserve a sense of self and to create some kind of permanent structure in the face of change.

Winnicott pointed out that 'Clinical fear of breakdown is the *fear of a breakdown that has already been experienced*. It is a fear of the original agony which caused the defence organization which the patient displays as an illness syndrome.'[20]

Whichever 'illness syndrome' we choose depends on the mechanism of defence which we prefer. Extraverts prefer repression, the forgetting of the events which gave rise to painful emotions, and introverts prefer isolation, the separation of emotion and thought.

To survive without too much pain we have to be able to fulfil our basic need – extraverts to be a member of a group and introverts to find some measure of personal achievement. We are dependent upon society to provide us with the necessary conditions to fulfil this need.

Many women introverts find that society demands that they be no more than wives or mothers, always fulfilling other people's needs before their own. Unless they then make their family their own personal achievement, becoming the dominant and powerful leader of the family, they feel themselves to be without achievement and suffer greatly. This was the source of much of Mary's suffering. All her attempts to achieve something for herself had come to naught. Once she did achieve something which she could call her own, life ceased to be a torment.

Extraverts need to be part of a group, so they need to develop ways of always keeping a group around them.

Betsy lies awake at night listening to her husband's breathing. She listens carefully, fearful in case the breathing stops. He is a healthy man, so there is no reason why he should stop breathing. But every pause in his breathing makes her heart flutter.

When she was a child she used to listen to her parents' breathing, fearful that it would stop and she would be left alone. Often in the living room after dinner they would doze in front of the fire, and she, instead of reading or playing a quiet game, would sit and listen.

Betsy cannot bear to be alone. She complains about having to look after her daughter's dogs, but they make being alone in the house during the day bearable. 'I can talk to them,' she said, 'and if I hit them they come back for a cuddle. They won't go away and stay away.' (As her teenage children might if she chastizes them. So she suffers their outrageous behaviour.)

Betsy knew as a child that to exist she needed to be part of a group. But she did not solve the problem of how always to be part of a group by identifying with her mother and determining to become a wife and mother. Instead, she was drawn to her father, preferred roller skates to dolls, and developed a passionate interest in cricket and football. Boys who discover that they need to be part of a group can solve this problem by becoming proficient at team games but such a solution is rarely possible for girls. Not many football teams would have a place for a middle-aged woman.

Psychologists who are interested in the physiological mechanisms which underlie our behaviour have found marked differences between introverts and extraverts in terms of the *arousal* properties of the nervous system.[21] Various measures show that introverts have high arousal and extraverts low. Each, then, has to seek an equilibrium. This would account for the fact that introverts need a considerable degree of tranquillity, but extraverts prefer excitement to peace. As Stephanie wrote to me after she had been re-reading my book *Depression: the Way Out of Your Prison*:

I was particularly taken with the description, from your own upbringing, of attempts by adults to break the child's spirit through falling over backwards not to spoil her. I recall in my teens constantly talking about myself and being crushingly told what a bore I was (true) and it seems to me now a feeble way of asserting myself, of saying things aloud to prove I was real. This boring talking about self recurs now when I am low or agitated. Hard to realize I no longer need this sorry ploy to be real. The trouble with realizing it is nonsense to cart a load of childhood junk around is that you begin to realize that as soon as you've unstuck one bit and thrown it away, another bit rises up out of nowhere and sticks to you. It's like wading through disgusting chewing gum.

A book I read as a result of reading Prison was that journal by P. Toynbee.[22] Half the time, I think, OK. The rest of the time I find him maudlin and scratching about to make his religion work by all sorts of weird and shaky arguments. However, I did come on one interesting question. He yearned for tranquillity, and yet felt that if he achieved it it would remove the edge from his writing. I must say I feel the same, not just about writing (and I do strive for edge, often through being scathing) but about being me. Calm, tranquil, joyful me would not, I feel, be me. Yet agitated, anxious, stressed and prickly me is a pain.[23]

By contrast, Roy, when I asked him what he did with his day, would say, 'I sat in the lounge room.' He refused to join a group. 'Too much chatter,' he would say. There were times when, sitting

211

alone, he did not even think. Quite a few introverts, I find, have this ability to suspend the chatter of thought and to enter a quiet place, all without recourse to the techniques of meditation. When they are experiencing no particular difficulties in their lives they value this peaceful space, but when depressed the space becomes the black centre of depression, and when under the great stress which loosens their hold on reality this capacity becomes the 'thought stopping' of schizophrenia.

Fear into Madness

In describing how those ways of behaving which are regarded as symptoms of mental illness are the defences we can choose to use against fear, I shall not attempt to discuss all the multitude of diagnostic labels which are used by the medical profession to cover all kinds of unusual or socially unacceptable behaviour. I regard diagnostic categories such as 'pre-menstrual tension', 'paraphilic coercive disorder' (rape), and 'self-defeating personality disorder', as proposed for the American Diagnostic and Statistical Manual, simply as a means whereby psychiatrists and psychologists can stake out more territory to support their claims for money and power. Similarly, the inclusion of homosexuality as a category of mental illness is another attempt by those who regard themselves as experts in mental illness to increase their wealth and power. In the way that we can both love and need someone, our sexual orientation is both an expression of ourselves and a defence against fear, in the same way that all our behaviour is an expression and a defence. The same can be said of those strange, compulsive behaviours called sexual perversions. I find it impossible to consider transvestites and transexuals as perverted, just peculiar in the way that every individual is peculiar. I suspect that transvestites are extraverts and transexuals are introverts, but as most of my work with them was done before I became aware of the importance of distinguishing the construct systems of introverts and extraverts I cannot make any definite statement about this.

Psychopathy is frequently called a mental illness and many people who have broken the law and are diagnosed as psychopaths go to hospital instead of prison. This is just another gambit by psychiatrists to extend their power and influence, for there is no effective therapy for psychopaths, other than very intensive, very skilled mileau therapy, such as has been used in prisons like Barlinnie in Scotland. Such therapeutic measures which are based on understanding the person rather than punishing him are not favoured by those who feel that punishment for crimes is more important than rehabilitation. The drugs which are used on psychopaths in hospitals, the major tranquillizers and the anti-epileptics, are effective only as keeping the person under control. They have no curative effect.

Paranoia, the belief that you are the object of another person's ill will, is extremely common, and is, in some greater or lesser form, always present in the way groups are formed. I have written about this at great length in my book *Living With the Bomb: Can We Live Without Enemies?* Both extraverts and introverts are capable of developing a delusional paranoid system of belief to explain everything which happens to them. Lonely, isolated extraverts can give themselves the illusion of being part of a group by deciding that they are the focus of attention by important people, albeit their hostile attention, while introverts who have failed to achieve their personal goals can comfort themselves with the thought that they were prevented from revealing their superior talent and worth to the world by the destructive envy of powerful people. Thus they can defend themselves from the fear of annihilation which comes with the recognition of being completely alone or without achievement. Some element of paranoia can be found within all the defences against fear which are called the symptoms of mental illness.

What Defences Can We Use against the Fear of Annihilation?

1. We can turn fear into panics and phobias. Extraverts are very good at doing this. Fear is more manageable when you can give it a name.

2. We can turn fear into obsessions and compulsions. Introverts are very good at doing this. An organized world, they believe, should have no room for fear.

3. We can turn fear into depression. Both extraverts and introverts are good at this. A prison is a safe place.

4. We can turn fear into mania. Extraverts do this by denying that they are afraid.

5. We can turn fear into schizophrenia. Introverts are extremely good at doing this. They escape into their private world.

However, no matter which form of madness we choose, fear, like the Hound of Heaven, still pursues us.

Chapter Six

Turning Fear into Anxiety, Panic and Phobias

Helen was a very sensible woman. She was practical, down-to-earth, full of common sense. She ran her home, brought up her children, taught part time, and organized the household to fit in with the demands of her husband's business, all with great efficiency and success. She could not understand why one evening, as she was standing beside the kitchen table, serving the children their supper, she was suddenly swept by terrible fear.

The feeling began in her stomach, a sense of falling away. She tried to stop it, but it rose, enveloping, shaking, drenching. There was a thundering in her ears, a pounding in her chest, a tightening in her throat. She thought it was death.

No one was there to call. Her husband was away. Her next door neighbours were on holiday. She was amazed to see that the children went on eating and noticed nothing.

Gradually the terrible feeling ebbed away. She stood beside the sink watching the children eating, then sent them off to change for bed, having reminded them that she was going out and they should behave themselves when the baby-sitter was there. Then she tidied herself and was collecting her books when the baby-sitter arrived. Helen gave her the usual precise instructions and set off to take her class in Children's Books.

The class went well. She was, as usual, well prepared, and her students responded with their usual curiosity and enthusiasm. But all the time she was in dread that that terrible feeling of panic would return.

And it did. Three days later, as she was transferring her husband's supper to plastic containers for freezing (Gordon had just phoned to say he wouldn't be home until late and would eat out) and thinking about what shopping she needed to do for the weekend when her mother was visiting, the terrible panic came again.

She was alone. Afterwards, as she thought about it, she was sure that anyone watching would have seen a peculiar sight. She must have looked as if she was going mad.

She became afraid to go out. What if someone saw her like that? She tried to reassure herself that the panics had occurred only at home. Perhaps there was something there she was allergic to. Then, one day, just as she had finished arranging the flowers in the church, she overheard the vicar's wife saying to the vicar that the summer flowers were really beautiful, but didn't he think that the vase of red and yellow roses near the altar was a little, well, *gaudy*. Helen felt her hands shake, and then the full panic was upon her.

She wanted never to set foot in that church again. But to do that she would have to explain to her husband why, and that meant telling him about the panics. He listened sympathetically and said, 'It's probably got something to do with your hormones. Why don't you see Dr Trent?'

So she went down to the clinic and talked to Dr Trent. She was surprised that he was so matter-of-fact. He didn't seem to think that what was happening to her was anything special or unusual. What surprised her even more was that he suggested that she talk to a psychologist. She didn't understand that at all. He did give her some pills, but with so many warnings about not taking them too often that she daren't take any at all. She left his surgery feeling very puzzled.

Gordon listened to her account of the visit and said, 'Well, you'd better do what he suggested. Go and see this psychologist.'

Helen decided that she would. Not that she wanted to, but because she didn't want to upset Dr Trent and Gordon by not doing what they said.

So a few weeks later she was sitting very nervously in my office.

She told me how it had started and how by now the fear of having a panic attack was almost as bad as the panic attack itself. She didn't want to give up doing things, but it was getting harder and harder to leave home. She dreaded going to places where she'd had an attack, and she just had to force herself to go. Being with other people worried her most, especially people she didn't know very well. Yet she hated to be alone. Every day was a struggle.

She told me how helpful her husband was. He didn't really understand what she felt like, but he was sympathetic and kind. Whenever he could he went with her to places – she couldn't manage the supermarket on her own – but of course he couldn't be with her all the time. Anyway, that was no way to live.

I asked her if she had talked about it to anyone else.

'No, no one.'

'Why not?'

'Well, people wouldn't understand.'

'What about your mother? Would you tell her?'

'Oh, no, never.'

'Why not?'

'She would say it was weakness. She always expects me to cope.'

'With everything?'

'Yes. My housework, the children, teaching. She expects me to do everything perfectly every time. Even the clothes I wear. She's always been very particular about the way I dress.'

She went on to describe how, when she was a little girl, she was not allowed to get dirty. 'She'd put me in a white starched frock and heaven help me if I got it dirty. I could only play in the back garden. Not in the front garden, and never outside in the street. I wasn't allowed to play at all on Sunday. When I went to school she always checked on my friends. She was – she still is – a . . . I suppose you could call her a snob. I'm lucky I married someone she approved of. She approves of anyone with a university degree. That is, if they're white. Not if they're black, or Indian, or anything like that. When she comes to stay, Gordon and I just try to keep off any subject that might have anything to do with racial matters. And television. There's so much on that she disapproves

217

of that when she's staying with us we just don't put the TV on. She thinks the world of the children, but she's always telling them what a hard life she had as a child and how they have to be grateful for all the things they've got. She doesn't think I'm grateful enough for all she did for me. I am grateful to her. I know things weren't easy for her. Dad was a teacher, and teachers weren't paid much. But she felt she had a position to keep up. So she expected me to be perfect all the time.'

'What happened to you when you weren't?'

'I'd get a telling off, or if I'd done something really bad I'd be sent to my room. She didn't hit me much. I'd have to stay in my room until she said I could come out. Or she wouldn't speak. If she was annoyed with Dad she wouldn't speak to him for weeks.'

'How did you feel about being sent to your room and not spoken to?'

'Terrible. I hated it. I'd rather have a slap or a telling off and get it over with.'

'If you hurt yourself or felt upset, what would your mother do? Would she give you a cuddle?'

'Oh, good heavens no. She never cuddled me or sat me on her knee. Don't get me wrong – if I was ill she'd look after me very well, but I was never allowed to cry. She didn't approve of tears.'

'Would she allow you to get angry with her?'

'Angry? Absolutely not. That's unthinkable. I still wouldn't dream of getting angry with her. I often get annoyed with her – she still talks to me as if I'm three years old – but I wouldn't dream of saying anything to her. I know she loves me and I wouldn't want to upset her.'

I asked her what she meant by 'upset'. She thought that what she had said was a self-evident truth, but as we unravelled her meaning for 'upset' we found that it meant for her making the other person feel angry, worried or guilty.

'Why,' I asked, 'is it important not to upset people?'

Again, a self-evident truth, but one which could be unravelled to reveal that she needed to be needed. She needed to be part of a group.

'So when you were naughty and your mother locked you in your room, that must have been the very worst thing that could happen to you. You were all alone. The fear you felt then must have been like the fear you feel now.'

'Yes, I suppose it was.' Helen sat silently thoughtful, and then said, 'I guess I've always felt insecure. I hadn't really thought about it. Are you saying that what happens to us in childhood affects us in our adult life?'

She was genuinely amazed at this idea. As a teacher and mother who had spent much time and energy in trying to influence children, she was surprised to find that I thought that children had experiences which influnced them all their lives.

However, in our subsequent conversations Helen came to see that there is indeed a connection between our experiences in childhood and in adulthood. As we went painstakingly through the events of the night of the first panic, not just the external events, what she was doing, but the internal events, what she was thinking and feeling, we found that she had been feeling increasingly alone. Gordon was becoming more and more wrapped up in his business. All her children were now at school and seemed to need her less and less. Gordon was talking of moving house to somewhere more convenient for him, and she didn't like to tell him how much she felt attached to their house. She didn't like being in strange surroundings. She hated change.

On that particular evening she was worried about whether she had prepared enough material for her students. They were all mature students and inclined to be critical, especially one woman who was older than her.

'Old enough to be your mother?' I asked.

'Not quite. But she can be critical like my mother. I try to make sure that she doesn't criticize me.'

'What's so bad about being criticized?'

'I can't take criticism. I just flare up.' It was dangerous 'to flare up' because if you get angry with people they will reject you, and being rejected – cast out of the group – means that you are annihilated for ever and ever.

So she tried to be perfect in everything she did to avoid criticism and thus survive. But there was one person whose criticism she could not avoid.

'My mother criticizes me all the time. I just have to switch off. You can't get angry with a 75-year-old woman.'

There was no way she could talk to her mother about how, all those years ago, she had been so frightened and her mother had not comforted her. Any readjustments she might make to her feeling about her childhood had to be done without her mother's help.

Rosa

Rosa's husband had died suddenly several years ago and her sons had grown up and left home. Even before she was widowed Rosa took Valium to help her cope with her family problems – money worries and the responsibility of caring for two sick old women, her mother and mother-in-law. Now she was alone, always anxious and often swept by waves of panic.

As she told me about herself it was clear that she was a 'people person', someone who is happiest and most secure when part of a group. She told me that what she had enjoyed most was amateur dramatics and singing. 'We used to go as a concert party to hospitals like this one,' she said. 'I loved that.'

So she could understand what her panics meant, I described to her how 'people people' need other people around them and suffer dreadfully when they feel they have been abandoned or rejected.

Rosa nodded. 'When I was a child my sister died. It affected my mother terribly. She got very depressed and suicidal. She used to say that she was going to take me with her – she was going to kill me and then kill herself. She had some photos of my sister and me, standing side by side. One day, when I was a child, I found them amongst my mother's things. She'd blotted me out. I wasn't in the photos any more. There was just my sister and a black smudge where I had been.'

I said, 'Would I be right in thinking that the terror you feel now is just like the terror you felt then, when your mother said she'd kill you and when you found yourself blotted out in the photos?'

'Yes,' said Rosa, 'yes, it is.'

Megan

Assaults upon a child's sense of self come in many ways. Megan as a teenager had always enjoyed company, and when she met Tim, a young naval officer, the social life of a navy officer's wife appealed to her. But as she got older she found the round of social engagements more and more difficult. She was so frightened of panicking and having everyone looking at her that she kept making excuses not to go. Tim tried to understand and to help her with her anxiety in a logical, sensible way, but, somehow, his suggestions never seemed to work.

Megan knew that her childhood had something to do with her problems. She told me first about how her parents had led busy lives with little time for their daughter. Her mother never even took the time to see that her daughter had enough clothes.

Megan described to me how at thirteen her breasts were so well developed that she needed a bra. For once her mother noticed Megan's need, but she met it by taking her to a shop which sold old-fashioned, matronly underwear and buying her an ungainly cotton brassiere, 'two huge cotton circles', as Megan called it.

While Megan's mother was showing her that she regarded Megan's body as unattractive and of no value, Megan's father was creeping into Megan's bedroom at night when he thought Megan was asleep and fondling her breasts.

I asked Megan why she had not protested to her parents about their treatment of her – why had she pretended to be asleep when

221

her father came into her, why hadn't she demanded decent clothes? – and she said that she loved her parents and didn't want to hurt them. They were splendid people, especially her father, and she was broken-hearted when he died.

Megan could remember and talk about the events which had brought her such pain, helplessness and total fear, but the conclusion she drew from these events was not 'How dare my parents treat me in this way' but 'I must have deserved their bad treatment'. She had already learned to construe herself as bad and her parents as good. To construe them as bad would have meant that she was entirely alone, and that too would have meant annihilation.

Lucy

Lucy remembered the event which made her realize that her parents were not pillars of wisdom and goodness who held up the sky so she could play safely beneath. At the most terrifying moment of her young life they failed her.

She remembered the event, but she did not want to talk about it. One day, when I had said something about how young children suffer sexual assaults and how these experiences, though they might not be remembered consciously, have long-term effects. Lucy said, 'That's happened to me.'

She would not tell me what happened, except to say that she was four when it happened and that she had run home crying and told her father what had happened. He was standing there shaving, and when she finished telling him he went on shaving. Her mother said to him, 'Don't you think you ought to do something?' and he did not reply. Nothing further was said or done.

Many months later Lucy told me the rest of the story, and then only in the briefest, baldest terms. I shall add one detail, something which Lucy would not have said. At forty Lucy was very pretty. At four she must have been breathtakingly beautiful.

All she told me was that she had been playing in the park and a man had come by and picked her up and sat her on a ledge. Then he urinated into her mouth.

I commented on how devastated she must have been by this, not just by the ugly act perpetrated upon her which must have rendered her helpless and frightened, but by her parents' failure to find and punish her traducer, to protect her from further assaults, to comfort her and to reassure her that no matter what filth had been flung upon her body, it was nothing that could not be washed away, and she was, as ever, their dearest, sweetest, much beloved daughter. Instead, they had shown her that they did not think she was worth any special effort or concern. They might be prepared to give her food and a roof over her head, but where her survival was concerned she was on her own. And if they didn't value her, how could she value herself?

There were many other events in her childhood and adolescence which proved to her, time and time again, that she was of little value. Her father was a domineering man who demanded, and got, obedience from his wife and children. The household was run for his benefit and no one else's. Her mother would not dare stand up for herself or protect the children from him. Lucy tried to help her mother, but often found her efforts unappreciated. Moreover, she was regarded as the stupid one of the family. At school her anxiety about not being able to do her schoolwork prevented her from doing it, so school was a misery, and she left as soon as she could. It was not until years later, when she and her husband had started their own business that she came to realize that she was not stupid at all.

Whenever Lucy talked about her childhood and her family she always interspersed her narrative with comments like 'Don't get me wrong, Dorothy. Dad thinks the world of me', and 'Mum's a wonderful person. She'd do anything for anybody'. Thus must the child protect the parents.

But at what price? The price Lucy paid was panic attacks and the fear that the constrictions in her throat and chest and the dizzy, muzzy feelings in her head were the symptoms of a serious illness. But she would prefer that she did have a physical illness, for if she didn't, if all these strange feelings were the result of 'tension' and 'nerves', then she was mad, and mad people end up in psychiatric hospitals, despised and rejected by everyone, and being rejected and alone was the fate she feared most of all.

So coming to see me in my office in a psychiatric hospital was a very risky business. She dared not let anyone know she came. She often said to me that she'd love to meet someone else who had panic attacks, and I could have granted her wish and arranged such a meeting – with some difficulty, though, since so many of her fellow sufferers also feared being found out – but her curiosity could not overcome her fear.

The only way she could risk coming to see me was to come with her husband Gavin. Our sessions, which were usually of at least two hours, always began with a discussion of Lucy's symptoms, out of which I would try to develop some further mutual understanding of how Lucy experienced herself and her world, and from that would come some revelations of how Lucy and Gavin got on together.

All the physical things that Lucy complained of were always vague, shifting, confused and confusing unpleasantnesses, difficult to describe and define. She never complained of sharply delineated pain. Indeed, whenever she did feel sharp physical pain, like when she fell over her son's bike left standing in a dark hallway, thus banging and scraping her shins quite severely, she would say, in passing, 'The pain, that was nothing.'

One day I asked her about this. She said, 'I don't mind pain', and when I questioned her further, I found that she valued physical pain, for it showed her that she was alive and existing. Sometimes, she said, when the muzziness and her sense of unreality were at their strongest, she would pinch herself to produce a sharp, distinct pain.

When she said that, I valued Gavin's presence even more. So many women like Lucy, bereft of someone to love them, find themselves in psychiatric hospitals where they are no more than just another patient to the nurses and doctors. Nothing in the monotonous, impersonal hospital routine has any personal significance for them, and they feel their fragile sense of self dissolving, emptying into a nothingness. In desperate terror they seize a razor blade to slit open their arms, or matches to set fire to their clothes, and in the ensuing pain they feel once more the basis of a human being's existence, the sense of I AM. Many hospital staff call such behaviour 'attention seeking' and punish it severely.

There were times when Lucy hated herself so much that she felt that everyone – Gavin, her children, her parents, me, even her dog – were tired of her and wanted to be rid of her, and with this feeling the black tide of depression would rise and envelop her. When that happened she found it even harder to follow the rule she had set herself of getting out of the house and doing something. She was determined not to give in completely and hide herself away. She took the dog for a walk every day, even though she always had to follow the same route each time, clinging close to the houses at the edge of the playing fields and never venturing into the vast open space of the fields, and never going so far from home that she couldn't get back there in a few minutes. She had become a very efficient shopper, knowing what she wanted, no browsing, in and out in minutes. She had given up going to most social events, but she could manage church or a visit to the cinema with Gavin, so long as she sat right beside the aisle. She could travel in the car with Gavin driving or driving herself over short, familiar distances, but she was always terrified of being caught in a traffic jam. She could not travel with another driver and she would not even think of travelling by bus, train or plane.

'Why not?' I would ask, and each time the answer was the same.

'I might faint.'

What was so terrible about fainting?
Shame. That terrible, draining, annihilating fear. All those hostile, uncaring, rejecting eyes on her, and she alone, small, weak and disgusting.

It was no use pointing out to Lucy that in all the places she feared, people are usually very sympathetic and helpful when someone there becomes ill or faints. Lucy knew this, but she felt that the kindness of strangers was reserved for others, not for her. She was not worthy of their concern.

She knew this was so because she had had one terrifying experience of breathlessness and fainting, so bad that at the time she was sure she was dying, and this had ended with what felt to her as rejection. One summer day, when she and Gavin were on holiday, they had been driving along, and suddenly Lucy found that she could not breathe. Her throat had constricted tightly. She fought to get her breath and couldn't. She collapsed. Gavin rushed her to hospital where she was admitted. Three hours later the doctor came and told her that the problem was hyperventilation and there was nothing to worry about. She was discharged from hospital.

She felt rejected. The doctor obviously thought she was mad, getting herself into such a state that she could not breathe. He couldn't be bothered with her, so much so that he didn't examine her properly, and so, she worried, missed discovering what was really wrong with her. That inability to breathe was, perhaps, a sign that there was something seriously wrong with her heart and lungs.

She didn't think a great deal about dying, not like she did earlier in her life. She told me, 'I used to worry a lot about dying. It's funny, since I've had these panic attacks I've stopped worrying about dying.'

Not that dying itself promised a relief from panics. When I asked her what she wanted when she died, to be buried or cremated, she answered immediately, 'Cremated. I couldn't bear to be shut in a coffin under the ground. That would be terrible.'

Dying is the ultimate in being alone. If panic attacks stop you thinking about it, then panic attacks are useful.

On the first occasion when they came to see me Lucy told me how she had been upset recently because they were having problems with one of the small firms which supplied their business. Gavin said that he thought she was worrying unnecessarily. Businesses always had problems like this. It was just one of the challenges which running a business always presented. He said that he liked challenges.

I asked him why a challenge was important, and he said that that was what life was about – meeting a challenge and winning. This was the reply of an introvert, committed to extending and developing himself.

But Gavin set some very real limits on what he responded to as a challenge. He never entered a contest or responded to a challenge unless he was sure of winning. He never spoke out or argued unless he was sure that some positive achievement would follow.

He saw no point in arguing with their suppliers. He could call them selfish and crooked, and all they would do, so he said, would be to agree with him that they were and then challenge him to do something about it. There was nothing he could do about it. The sums of money involved were too small for it to be worthwhile for them to take the suppliers to court. Lucy thought that he should speak out. She believed in plain speaking. He did not.

Then, after nearly two hours' discussion, the reason for Lucy's terrible panic in the car on holiday became clear. It had occurred while they were in the car driving away from her cousin Martin's home. While they were there they had witnessed Martin treating his daughter in a vile and despicable way. Lucy was horrified. She hated cruelty. She wanted Gavin to say something to Martin, but Gavin would not let her say anything and he would not speak out himself. After all, he didn't know the full facts. He didn't know what the girl had done. It was best not to interfere.

I pointed out the similarity of that situation with the situation in Lucy's childhood, when she had been the victim of cruelty and how no one had come to her defence. Lucy seemed unconvinced by what I said. Six months later Lucy still said she didn't know why she had had such a terrible panic while on holiday. We had by then talked of how authoritarian her father had always been and how frightened she was of him. I reminded her how the scene she witnessed must have awakened her memories of harsh treatment at the hands of her father. She brushed this aside. Her niece, she said, was very badly behaved.

There was one challenge which Gavin often wondered about whether he should accept. One day, when we were talking about how meaningless and empty Lucy found her life to be, she turned to Gavin and said, 'Sometimes I think, if only you'd make me do something. If you'd just say to me, "We're going for a drive, I've booked a table for dinner. Get your coat on." I think I might be able to manage that.'

Gavin asked me if I thought this would work. 'If you say so, I'll do it.'

I demurred. 'I'm not going to be responsible for your most monumental row.' I could just imagine the scene, but I knew it wouldn't take place.

Gavin knew that if he confronted her with such a challenge she would refuse to accept it. She would make some excuse, like she hadn't washed her hair, and she couldn't go out with unwashed hair.

But it wasn't just because Lucy would produce excuses as to why she couldn't go out. Gavin was scared even to try to push Lucy into anything which would lead to a row because he was frightened she would leave him.

'That's silly,' she said. 'You know I wouldn't leave you.'

He reminded her that when they do have a row she would often say that she would leave him.

'But I don't mean it,' she protested. 'I just say that because I'm angry.'

Gavin looked stricken. She patted his hand (they always sat side by side) and said to him, 'I know you get worried you'll be left again, like you were when you were a child. But I won't leave you. You know that.'

Gavin saw very clearly that Lucy's panics and depression were not just inside her, but linked to her family, past and present, and to him. He not only searched for and found these links, but appreciated them in the context of the ridiculousness of human endeavour, something we often laughed about together.

One day when Gavin was talking about the severe migraine attacks he had had, he said, 'I don't get them now. I always used to get them when we had to go to some social do. It's only lately I realized that that was when I got them.'

I asked, 'If Lucy gives up having panic attacks does that mean that you'll have to go back to having migraines?'

He laughed and said that he would have to give that some considered thought.

Spouses

So many husbands, I find, are not like Gavin. They see their wife's panic attacks, and her fear of all situations where a panic attack could occur, as nothing but her own weakness and stupidity. They would not dream of going along with her to talk to a therapist. It's her problem, and she has to solve it alone.

But being alone is the one thing that she can't bear.

Marjorie told me how 'We used to do things as a family' but now her children have withdrawn from her into the self-absorption of adolescence and her husband into his work. Night-time was very difficult for her. She said, 'I was upset and crying and he turned over and went to sleep.'

Even concerned and caring husbands do not always see what is happening between themselves and their wives, especially over how anger is expressed and received. It is not just that the phobic person (male or female) is afraid to express anger because that might lead to rejection but that within the family the phobic person's anger may not be accepted by the spouse, the 'sensible' one.

One day when Gordon came with Helen to see me we got on to the subject of arguments between them, and what became clear was that even if Helen felt secure enough with Gordon to express her anger with him, he did not accept her anger as real and legitimate. She was just being silly.

Helen said, 'I get angry and you go quiet and just walk away.'

'I'm just waiting for you to get over it,' he said.

Helen felt strong enough to ignore this put-down and continued, 'I have supper ready and then you phone and say you're going to be two hours late. You know earlier than that that you're going to be late. You could let me know.'

'You know I'm not always near a phone,' said Gordon, sweet reason himself. But he did admit, as we talked about it, that in the home he grew up in and the school he went to, expressions of anger were severely punished. It was not so much that he was being reasonable in refusing to accept the reality and legitimacy of Helen's anger, but that her anger frightened him.

Lorna's husband had his own way of invalidating Lorna's anger. If she overcame all her inhibitions about expressing her anger and actually did give vent to it in an outburst, he would say, 'Do you feel better after that?'

If another person will not accept our anger then it means that that person will not accept us. We are belittled and humiliated, and we can lose confidence in ourselves. This is why so many women lose confidence in themselves. They have been taught that anger is unfeminine, and if you're unfeminine you will not be loved. We all need love, whether we are men or women, extraverts or introverts.

Anger may be frightening to an extravert who fears that the expression of it will result in rejection, but it can be equally frightening to an introvert, who sees in the expression of anger a dangerous, uncontrollable emotion which threatens chaos. Since extraverts so often marry introverts, this means that so many of their misunderstandings and arguments are not so much about the couple's anger as about their fear of anger.

Sometimes it is not just the problem of anger and the fear of anger between the partners of marriage which has to be resolved if the spouse who has panic attacks is to be able to give up the panic attacks. Sometimes it is the problem of love and the fear of love.

Bill, whose panic attacks were destroying his life, was desperate for love. He knew that he needed to be loved. But he shut himself off from his wife and parents.

'Your mother would love you to kiss her and give her a hug,' his wife Felicity said, 'but you never do.'

'I can't help it,' he said to us both, 'I always put up a shield. It's a defence mechanism.'

I put to him the alternatives he was facing. 'If you keep the shield then you will always be frightened and lonely. If you drop the shield and open yourself to other people, you run the risk of being hurt, but you have the possibility of the closeness you desire.'

Bill didn't seem ready to make the choice which meant no longer going on being frightened and lonely. I asked him how long he had had this shield, and he said for as long as he could remember. He didn't know why. His parents had always been kind and loving to him.

'His mother's told me that Bill was always a good child. Never any trouble. Not like his sister,' said Felicity.

'She's seven years older than me,' said Bill, 'and she's always been spoilt. She'd have a terrible temper tantrum when she couldn't get her own way. My parents never hit me, but I can remember my father taking the dog lead to her.'

It was not until much later in our conversation that Bill gave the reason for the barrier he kept up against his wife. 'It's so I can keep her in control. If I dropped it, she'd just go crazy, spending money, doing what she wants.'

'Don't be silly,' said Felicity. 'I'm not like that.'

'You feel that she's just like your sister,' I said.

'I never thought of that,' said Bill, 'her being like my sister.'

We are always in the business of creating meaning, of linking one part of our past experience with our present experience, but we are not always aware that this is what we are doing, simply because we have always done it and no one has ever pointed out to us that this is what we all do and, because it is something that we have done from our earliest days and never questioned, we take our construction of our reality as the One and Absolute Truth. The way we see reality is the way reality is and everyone else in their right minds sees reality just as we do. Unaware and un-questioning, we do not see the bars of the cage we have built for ourselves.

Don

Don's GP asked me if I could help Don out of the terrible tangle he had got himself into. He had started having panic attacks some two years before. He'd lost his job, and now here he was, a family man, with little chance of getting another job in a town where there were a lot of unemployed people, and he was still panicking.

Don described the panic attacks as a complete mystery to him. He had always been an anxious sort of person – 'highly strung,' he

231

said – but he'd been a good worker, learned a trade, and had a reasonably well-paid job, with overtime, in a large factory. He earned enough to support his wife and two children, he was buying his own home, he had a car and they could afford a decent holiday each year. Then things started changing. He wasn't quite sure how, but there wasn't as much overtime and he found that they couldn't afford a holiday that year. This disappointed him a lot. He always looked forward to a fortnight away with friends whom he wasn't otherwise able to see for the rest of the year because they lived a long way away. There were other treats that disappeared – days at the seaside for the children, a meal out for his wife and him. When he found that it would be a struggle to buy the children the Christmas presents they wanted, it felt like the last straw. Then he found that he was getting more and more anxious, especially so in the mornings on weekdays. He'd wake up with a feeling of dread, and he'd have to force himself to get out of bed and get ready for work. He rode a bike to work, and sometimes on the way there he would suddenly be completely overwhelmed with panic. He would have to get off his bike and stand on the side of the road until the shaking stopped and his heart stopped pounding. Sometimes it was so bad he had to go back home and take the day off work. Even if he did force himself to go on, it meant he was late for work and soon he was in trouble for poor time-keeping. He couldn't explain what was happening, and so, after a lot of unpleasantness with his foreman and others at work, he was dismissed.

He wasn't too keen to tell me the next part of the story. From what he said it sounded like he had gone into a sort of manic, defiant state, where he ceased to be the good responsible person he had always been and instead indulged himself in some riotous living. But neither his family nor his conscience could cope with this for long, and the realization that he had wasted what little money he had saved brought him to the stage where he knew he had to do something to get himself out of this mess. But how, especially as his anxiety was ever present and ready to turn into a full-blown panic?

We talked about the changing economic conditions in the town and he showed himself to be like so many good people, caught up in the shifting and diminishing of industry, who blame themselves rather than the political and economic circumstances. Many good people prefer to blame themselves and so feel guilty because that way they preserve an illusion of control ('If I had behaved differently, then the world would be different') rather than see themselves as a helpless victim of huge forces totally beyond their control. Many such people take good care not to inform themselves about economic and political matters because that way they have no knowledge which might challenge their belief that had they been a better person, wiser, more hard-working, with greater foresight, they could have avoided the disaster which was upon them. Don had carefully avoided informing himself of the vast economic and political forces which were changing the lives of most people in Britain. He gave himself the excuse that he wasn't bright enough to learn about these things.

His belief that he wasn't bright came out when we were discussing how he felt about work. He had always worked hard. His father had owned a village shop and post office, and he had expected Don to work ever since Don had been old enough to do anything useful. He didn't know what it was like to go out playing after school. He always had to help in the shop, or run messages, or look after the vegetable garden. His whole life had been one of hard work.

This had not given him the feeling that he was good at doing things. Whenever he had to do a job he worried about whether he would be able to do it. This was the problem about getting another job. Even if he was offered a job, his problems would not be solved. He would feel he was under stress, and under stress he would not cope.

I asked, 'What do you mean, "under stress"?'

'There'll be something new, something I don't know about, and I'll feel I ought to know about it. I ought to know these things.'

'That sounds like your father or one of your teachers talking.'

He went on to tell me how nervous he got if he has to do mental arithmetic in public, like when he's playing darts. He always tried not to be the one who kept the score. 'I ought to be able to do it,' he repeated, 'and I can't. I don't want the others to know I can't do it.'

He didn't realize that so many people can't do mental arithmetic. I pointed out the immense popularity of pocket calculators to support my argument. I told him I was one of those people who never do mental arithmetic in public. When I was in primary school my teacher, Miss Gellatally, would put a column of figures on the blackboard, then point with her long, thin cane to a child to stand up and add up the figures aloud. If the child faltered or made an error, the cane would be brought down sharply on the child's hand. My hands often felt that cane, for when I was ordered to stand and perform, my mind would go into a complete blankness, a response which I still produce whenever something has to be done with numbers in public. Mental arithmetic has to be for me a completely private act.

All this came as a great surprise to Don. He was equally surprised to find that millions of people share his inability to fill in forms. He had no idea that it is a major function of government departments to produce forms which are totally incomprehensible to everyone but the initiated. That way the form makers feel more powerful and elite and the form fillers-in feel more powerless and inadequate, and thus more easily governed.

This kind of political analysis was right outside his experience. He still thought, 'I ought to be able to do these things.'

Where had this belief come from? His childhood. His father had expected him to do things straight off. If Don couldn't – after all, nobody is born knowing how to do every possible thing, although there are plenty of people who would lead you to believe that they were born in this omniscient state – his father wouldn't take the time to show him what to do but, with a 'Here, give that to me', he would impatiently take the task away from Don and do it himself.

Don never had the chance to make mistakes and so learn. He had grown up pretending he could do things and fearing that he couldn't. When he worked in a factory where everything was laid out for him he could pretend that he could do things.

'Now I feel I've been found out.'

When I asked him why it was important for him to appear to be able to do everything he said that it made him feel popular. He thought people would reject him, as his father had done, if he couldn't do things. It had not occurred to him that people who claim to know everything aren't always popular. In fact, people who admit to ignorance and inadequacy are often regarded as charming and are very much liked.

The trap which Don had built for himself concerned rules which he had never questioned but which he could, when questioned, make explicit fairly easily. Sometimes the meanings which create the trap are more difficult to find because they have never been put into words but reside in images and feelings. Such meanings are often associated with the specific but ordinary places where a person may panic or be frightened of panicking.

Cherie

Cherie is so pretty and so charming that it seems inconceivable that she would have any problems in meeting people and going places. If you met her you would think that to give herself confidence all she needed to do was to look in the mirror. But if I said anything like that to her, as I sometimes did, she would look at me as if I was crazy. I suspected that she thought that I said such things, not because I meant them, but because it was my job to make her feel better. She was too kind a person to put such ungracious thoughts into words.

She told me of terrible panics and of her fear of such panics. She could not possibly travel by bus, so she bought a car and learned to drive. This solved some of her practical problems, but even if she could drive into town she still found it well-nigh impossible to get out of the car and go into the shops. Also, she was running out of excuses as to why she couldn't visit and meet for the first time her boyfriend's collection of family and friends. She could manage visiting people she knew very well, but visits to acquaintances and strangers were a torture she could no longer inflict upon herself. It was getting into these places which was so difficult. If she got in and didn't make a fool of herself by shaking or going red, then she might manage. But more and more those first few minutes of shopping and visiting became like some high unscalable wall. The social things she could actually manage to do were becoming fewer and fewer.

There were other things she couldn't do as well. Like standing up for herself. When the electricity bill for the flat she shared with two other girls was extra large because one of the girls had insisted on keeping the radiator on in her bedroom all night that winter Cherie dared not argue that a three-way split of the bill was not fair. She paid more than she thought she should have, and despised herself for doing so. She despised herself too because she was so pitifully grateful that her boyfriend had come back to her after they had split up and he had started going out with someone else. But along with her gratitude to him was the belief that when he said he loved her he was lying and that one day he would leave her for good. Sometimes she found herself wishing that he would go now and the agony of waiting for his defection would be over.

She told me these things about herself simply because of the relief of being able to talk about them to someone. She didn't think her fear of getting angry and her belief that anyone who said he loved and admired her was either a fool or a liar had anything to do with her panics. She rather liked the psychiatrist's definition of the panics as an illness, something which had come upon her like a bad attack of flu and which, if she was lucky, would, like flu, go away. She didn't know whether or not to be grateful when I pointed out to her something which the psychiatrist had failed to tell her, that the Frisium he had prescribed for her was addictive and that she should use it sparingly.

She was surprised when I asked her about her childhood. Surely I didn't think things that had happened all that long ago (when you're twenty, childhood is a long time ago) had any effect on her now.

She said that she remembered very little of her childhood and supposed it to have been quite ordinary. She then went on and told me of a childhood far from ordinary, of one fraught with pain and suffering and great uncertainty. It was only over many months that the story of her childhood emerged. She told me of her father's painful death from cancer when she was fourteen, and how, in what proved to be his last day, she was rude to him, and he died, without her having the chance to say goodbye and ask for his forgiveness. Neither did he ask for her forgiveness. Not that she would have dared to ask, or even think, consciously that is, that he owed her this, but he did, for he and her mother had inflicted on her, as a tiny girl, the most terrible of pain.

Her parents may have loved one another, but any sign of their affection was blotted out by their fights. It would begin with her mother starting to nag and criticize her father and he becoming silent. Quick to recognize the beginning of a fight, Cherie would try to stop them, to deflect their attention to something else. Sometimes she was successful, sometimes not. Then she would hide under the table while the fight raged over her head. Her mother would goad and goad her father, until he in violent anger would turn on her and hit her. Her mother would fight back, until he would leave, slamming out of the house, declaring that he would not return.

Even when he had not left the house in a rage her father was often away because of his work. Alone with her daughter, Cherie's mother would often vent her frustration and anger and her disappointment with her life onto her small daughter. It was not her mother's blows which frightened Cherie so much as her mother's oft repeated words, 'If it wasn't for you I wouldn't be here.' Cherie felt that she had no right to be in her parents' house. Indeed, she had no right to exist at all.

When Cherie and I had a look at the practical dimensions of her panic problem, where she couldn't go and what she couldn't do, it became apparent, at least to me, that the territory which she saw as dangerous was territory which belonged to other people, especially people whom she didn't know very well. She was all right in her own home, in her mother's home (she and Cherie got along very well together now), in the small office where she worked where she knew everybody, in her own car and in what might be called common property like a street. Where she felt in danger was in territory which belonged to other people who could tell her that she had no right to be there and who could throw her out. It didn't matter if the shop assistants and her boyfriend's relatives and friends were pleasant to her. She knew that pleasantness could hide an uncontrolled rage and that the most loving of people could become violently rejecting. When she went into territory which she knew was dangerous, she didn't need, or want, to bring to mind the reasons why she knew it was dangerous. All she felt was the fear and the need to escape. When she couldn't escape, she panicked.

Cherie listened to my description of the meaning of her fear with great interest. I don't know whether it made any great difference to her. There was something else I said which she remembered and reminded me of the next time she came to see me. There was a gap of more than six months between these two visits. Cherie hadn't found it necessary to make another appointment in that time. We worked on the understanding that as it was hard for her to get time off work she would phone and make an appointment whenever she felt the need and could fit it in with the demands of her job.

On this occasion she looked more relaxed and free than I had ever seen her. She said, 'Do you remember, you said to me that if I changed I might find that my boyfriend wasn't as important to me as I thought? Well, I didn't believe you at the time, but you were right.'

Then she told me how she had decided to take an evening job working in the local sports centre as a receptionist. There she had met this wonderful man. She was still very fond of her boyfriend, but this man, well, he was different. And he thought she was wonderful too. The problem was not just that she had to decide between her boyfriend and this wonderful man, but that he was working here for just a few months. His home was in London. She'd never been to London.

Cherie had already decided what she was going to do. All she wanted from me was support, and some advice about driving to London. She had worked out that the horrors of driving on the motorway to London were as nothing compared to the horror of letting your life slip away and doing nothing of significance and meaning with it.

To retrieve the devastating childhood experiences which laid the foundations for anxiety and panic attacks in later life, and to reassess them in the light of adult knowledge and experiences, it is very helpful if some of the adults who played a part in the childhood experiences also take part in the retrieval and reconstructing of the past, sometimes simply in supplying more information and sometimes sharing in mutual reconciliation and forgiveness. Unfortunately, this is not always possible.

Sometimes our parents have died before we reach the stage of reassessment. Sometimes our parents are not prepared to help us reassess, for it involves a reappraisal of their own past actions. A friend told me how, having reached a point in her therapy where she could understand and accept her mother's actions towards her which had caused her great pain, she went to her mother and said, 'Mother, I forgive you.' Whereupon her mother flew into a rage and said, 'How dare you forgive me! I've never done anything which requires forgiveness.'

Sometimes we can be lucky. Our parents are alive and they are prepared to help us reassess.

Bill

Bill had such good fortune, although it took him many months to realize that it was necessary to talk to his mother.

When Bill first came to see me all he could talk about was the terrifying physical symptoms of a major panic attack. He had had several, the worst being when one day, far from home, he had collapsed on the grass verge beside the road where he had been driving. Everything he had ever dreaded, a heart attack, total helplessness, death, seemed to him to be happening there. Friends got him home, and after that he dared not go very far away from his house. He could no longer tolerate crowded rooms without an easy exit. He gave up playing squash, running, and going for a drink at his local, all things which he used to enjoy very much. He had always been convinced that he would die of a heart attack, and now he feared that a panic attack would bring on such a fatal attack. So he tried to avoid all the situations which might provoke one, but he was not always successful, and even when he went for days without an attack, he was waiting anxiously for the next one to occur.

At first Bill thought my interest in his life was quite pointless. All he wanted me to do was to produce the magic word, or wave the magic wand, and all his panics would disappear. He got somewhat irritated with me for not doing this, but, on the other hand, I did sit and listen to him, and this was more than his wife and parents would do. Felicity found his complaining very wearisome, especially when he was also so bad-tempered and unapproachable. He didn't like to talk to his parents about his problems, because he did not want to worry his mother (she had high blood pressure) and he did not want to let his father know just how weak he was. 'He's twice the man I am,' he would say, as he told me of how active and determined his father was, even though he was well into his seventies.

Bill admired his father tremendously and would never dream of criticizing him, even when he told me of one vivid memory he had of his childhood, when his elder sister was very angry and disobedient and his father thrashed her with the dog lead. He remembered her afterwards lying on the floor and crying, but he felt no sympathy for her. His father had done the right thing. It was at that time that Bill resolved never to get angry or to disobey his father. Bill never linked this episode with his belief that he was weaker than his father. Yet, as his father had never let him win an argument, Bill could only grow up with the belief that he could never measure up to his father, a truly wonderful man.

Bill found his mother to be equally wonderful. She was always loving, always kind. 'I was spoilt,' he said, as a way of explaining how such perfect parents could have such a weak man as a son. They had loved him too much. He wished his marriage was idyllically happy as his parents' marriage had always been.

He spoke of his childhood as extremely happy, yet, when I asked him about it, there was remarkably little that he could remember. He was uncertain about which schools he went to and when he went to them. This forgetting of childhood, which I come across so often in my work, never fails to amaze me. I can run the memories I have of my childhood through my mind like a film, I can remember the names of people from fifty years ago more easily than the names of people I met fifty minutes ago, and if I want to remember when some event took place all I have to do is to bring a picture of it to mind, judge where I was and how tall I was within that picture, and I can arrive at a date and a place and a memory of what went on and how I felt. These are certainly not all happy memories, but they are important to me, and if I woke up one morning and found that they had gone I would be bereft. Yet so many of the people who report that they do not remember their childhood seem indifferent to this situation. But then they are usually extraverts, and I am an introvert, and introverts tend to remember the events of their life story.

Bill and I went on talking over a number of months. Then Bill's mother took ill and went into hospital. Bill was ashamed that he could not overcome his fear of hospitals to go and visit her, but as soon as she was home again he could return to his usual habit of calling in to see her every day. One day he decided to ask her about his early childhood. He had started to feel curious about the events he could not remember. He began by telling her a little bit more about his 'nerves' and about his visits to see me.

Bill's mother shocked and amazed him by saying that when she was pregnant with him she had suffered with her nerves just like him. Further, she said that her marriage then had been far from happy.

Bill came to see me soon after this conversation and told me about it with a mixture of surprise and pleasure. As we were talking he started to remember scenes from his childhood. They came into his mind like new events, yet he recognized them with all the joy and amazement we feel as we find some long lost treasure hidden in a trunk.

First, he remembered walking down the garden, looking over the fields and feeling the strange feelings, which he now knows as panic, and wondering what these feelings were. He must have been only about eight, for when he was nine they had moved to another house.

Then he remembered walking home from school and feeling everything he saw becoming unreal. He knows that feeling only too well now, but had never thought that he could have known it all that long ago.

He remembered, when he was about six, seeing a man on the bus on the way to school each day and wanting this man to be his father. He described a kindly, gentle, fatherly man. This memory puzzled him. He could not yet see that when he was six he knew his own father to be harsh, dangerous and powerful and would have longed for a father who was loving and kind.

Having retrieved these memories and more, Bill was then able to tell me what it was that really terrified him about death. Up till then, in many conversations about his panic attacks and his belief that he would die of a heart attack, the one form of death which terrified him the most, he had never been able to answer my question, 'What's so terrible about dying?' Now he could speak of 'a sense of impending doom' and the panics as being a reaction to this. He had always sensed 'a force of evil' which was much more effective than 'the force for good'. He feared death because he felt that beyond death lay 'hellfire and damnation'.

That conversation with his mother was the turning point for Bill. It freed him to get on with his life. He could distinguish between the parents of his childhood and the parents he had now, and see that while they had not been the wisest and kindest of parents then, they had gained in wisdom and kindness. He did not have to see them as bad, just human. He had no need to protect their reputation at the expense of his own. It was all right to feel good about himself.

Often, in the negotiations which go on at the beginning of therapy, a client will ask, 'How long is this course of therapy going to last? How long will it take for me to get better?' Different therapists have different answers. My truthful answer is that I just don't know, and that is because I don't know what part luck will play in it. It was none of my doing that Bill's mother had the courage to confront what must have been a very painful part of her life and talk about it with Bill. Also, a client's strengths are not apparent in a first interview, when the client is busy talking of all his deficits and weaknesses. I did not know that Bill, for all his uncertainty about himself, never felt that his panic attacks were something so shameful that he could not talk about them with other people whom he met in the course of his work. Over the time he was coming to see me he met a large number of people who proved to be suffering from some form of anxiety and depression. He would enter into conversations with them, recommend my book on depression to them (something I approved of enormously) and discuss ways and means of coping and becoming more confident. He seemed to be running a continuous therapy group across the town.

Clearly all of this helped him to change. At our last meeting he told me that Felicity had said that he was now like a stranger to her. She would have to get to know him all over again. Fortunately, or so it seemed from what he told me about the change in their relationship (they no longer lay without touching side by side in bed), he had become the kind of stranger she approved of very much.

Panic attacks produce the fear of panic attacks, and to defend against this fear a person will develop all kinds of patterns of avoidance of problem situations. Sometimes as well the person can find himself involved in anxious ruminations that go on and on and on. Such ruminations can be very wearing, producing all the signs of physical exhaustion, which, of course, the person can then interpret as symptoms of a fatal disease.

Ken

Ken (first mentioned in Chapter 1) had such ruminations, and all the symptoms of anxiety and tiredness to go with them, though, fortunately, they occupied so much of his thought he didn't have time to worry too much about a fatal illness. He talked of the terrible anxiety he felt over whether he had carried out his work correctly or whether he had made a mistake and left the technical work for which he had been responsible in some dangerous state. He worried about jobs which he had done many years before and in places where, if there had been any fault, that fact would by now have been discovered. The jobs he worried about most were those where, if there were an electrical fault, people's lives would have been put at risk.

The first few times we met he was grey and drawn and totally serious, but as the months passed he became more relaxed. One day he arrived looking happier than I had seen him before and during our conversation he frequently smiled and laughed. But he still had great difficulties. He was waking at 5 a.m. and was unable to get back to sleep. The lack of sleep made his head ache in a most unpleasant way. When he was tired he found it much harder to resist the questions from the Judge.

On previous occasions when he had described how he would worry about whether he had carried out some electrical work correctly, he had talked in terms of asking himself questions like, 'Did you set that switch correctly?' Now he spoke of these questions coming not from himself, but from the Judge.

'I see this Judge sitting up high, and he's asking me these questions, and I'm down here and I'm responsible. I've got to answer these questions. He picks on one thing I did and if I answer that question then he asks another question and on and on. If I can't answer, or if I got it wrong, I'll be responsible. I'll have hurt someone and everyone will know.'

'You'll be shamed in front of everyone?'

'Yes. I'll be blamed for everything. It's the sort of thing, suppose I had two balls, a black one and a white one, and I put the black ball in a drawer and locked it and went out of the room and locked the door. The Judge would say to me, "Which ball did you put in the drawer?" and if I say, "The black one," he'd say, "Are you sure? Are you sure you didn't put the white one in the drawer?" I'd have to go back and unlock the door and the drawer and look. He'd go on and on, and at last I'd get to a point where I couldn't answer his questions. It's amazing how much I remember about jobs I did years ago, but even with how much I remember there comes a point where it's impossible to answer, and then it's just terrible. Now I try to stop the Judge. I won't answer his first question, because if I do he'll go on and on. If I ignore him he'll be quiet for a bit, and then he'll start again on something else. He's always up there, looking down on me.'

Ken's mother had always dominated him and everyone else. Her family was her whole life. She wanted the best for them and she would do everything she could to make sure that they got the best and that they did their best. So shop girls would hide when she came into the shop and greengrocers would submit to her critical inspection of their fruit and vegetables. Her son submitted to her demands and tried to please her. If he did not she would shame him.

'That's the way it was. I didn't know any different. That was the way things always were,' he said. But later he said, 'I let my sons please themselves. I don't tell them what to do.'

'So you did know, and you wouldn't do to your sons what your mother did to you.'

'I must have, I suppose.'

It had not occurred to him that the Judge might be his mother, demanding that he justify his existence, and measure up to her standards and achieve what she wanted him to achieve. The parent of our childhood becomes our conscience, the eye that is always upon us, making us aware that we are ourselves and filling us with shame that we are as we are, the judge that sees everything we do and finds us guilty of our actions.

But shame, painful though it is, is a means by which we affirm our existence and withstand the threat of annihilation. To be ashamed of ourselves we have to be our self.

The next time Ken came to see me he said, 'I've realized that in my life I've made only two decisions – who I'd marry and what car I'd buy. Everything else my mother has decided for me.'

Three months later Ken returned after a holiday. It had been a good holiday, but often, as he stretched out in the sun, the Judge would start his questioning. Ken said, 'I get very careful in what I say to people. For instance, I might notice that you had a bald tyre on your car. I might say to you, "You ought to get that changed." Then later I'd think, "She'd better make sure she's tightened the nuts properly", and then this would start on me. I'd be worrying about whether you'd tightened the wheel nuts. Next time I saw you I'd have to ask you about the tyre, and I'd say, "Did you tighten the wheel nuts?" I'd make a joke of it, mind, but I'd have to say it.'

He told me how some time ago he had given an old car to the local technical college for their Youth Training Scheme and then spent months worrying that the students might have an accident and that he would be blamed. He said, 'It didn't matter that their teachers are trained. If something went wrong, it would be my fault.'

We talked about his sense of responsibility which went far beyond what would ordinarily be expected. He took upon himself responsibility for others, and then punished himself for failing, or perhaps failing, to meet his responsibilities. He could not leave others to be responsible for themselves but had to take all responsibility on himself.

'It's like I'm God,' he said, 'responsible for everybody.'

Even though shame is a defensive measure to preserve the self, it contains within it a sense of helplessness. We are powerless in the eye of the beholder. To overcome the powerlessness and passivity of shame we can totally deny that we are so, and claim complete power and activity. However, the advantage of being powerless is that we are not responsible for what happens. The disadvantage of being completely powerful is that we are totally responsible. Poor Ken. He had tried to overcome his sense of powerlessness, and, without ever once enjoying the heady delights of complete power (as an extravert using the defence of mania will do), he went straight to the great disadvantage of power, total responsibility.

Now he had to find a point somewhere between a sense of complete helplessness and a sense of complete power, and from that begin the task which is presented to all human beings, 'What in life are my responsibilities and what responsibilities belong to other people?' People who had parents who dominated them as children always have difficulty in understanding what responsibility is and in defining the limits of their responsibility. As children they often heard their parents telling them to be responsible, and they did not realize that what their parents called responsibility was really obedience. The only way parents can give their children a sense of responsibility is to give them the freedom to make choices, and, with those choices, mistakes. Parents who need to be dominant are people who are so frightened of themselves and their world that they cannot give their children the freedom to learn courage.

Summary

It can be said that a person develops anxiety and panic attacks in a position of extreme danger when a situation arises which is reminiscent of a situation in that person's childhood when that person suffered the greatest threat to the self which an extravert can suffer, the threat of complete abandonment and isolation. The same overwhelming fear which was felt then arises now. It can be experienced as the shame and the humiliating rejection which the person sees as would follow some disgraceful behaviour such as fainting or vomiting in public. Or it can be experienced as disappearing into a vast nothingness, as is felt by the person who fears to go into an open space or even face an open window for fear of being swallowed up by the sky.

Because the first situation was so painful, the memory of it has been forgotten, although the effects of it, which are a loss of self-confidence and a persistent anxiety, continue into adult life.

Because the memory of the original situation has been repressed, the person has not developed the ability to link all the past and present events of his life into one continuous, meaningful story and to see the significance of present events in the context of his whole life and thus gain mastery over them. Instead, when a situation arises which is reminiscent of the earlier, self-annihilating one, he cannot see the significance of the present one and so master it by the recognition that he is now an adult, not a child, and that he is no longer helplessly dependent on powerful and dangerous adults whom he is not allowed to see as bad.

Because he cannot name the fear he feels in the context of his personal life, he experiences it as alien, which makes it all the more frightening. The fear has to be named and explained, so he looks for a name and an explanation where extraverts always look, in external reality, that is, in his body and in the place where the fear arose. So he interprets the physical concomitants of fear as the symptoms of a fatal illness, and he avoids the places where the fear arose. The careful monitoring of bodily sensations, the anxious thoughts about the physical sensations which are observed, and the avoidance rituals which are developed all act as a defence against overwhelming fear.

This form of defence can rapidly lead the person into living a severely circumscribed life, as more and more places are identified as 'no-go' areas. To gain the courage to leave this defensive position, the person needs to do two things simultaneously.

One is to retrieve the hidden memories, so as to construct the continuous story of his life, to see his childhood from two perspectives, that of himself as a child and himself as an adult, and thus to understand the meaning of the great fear which he sees as threatening to overwhelm him.

At the same time he needs to integrate this new experience with his experiences in his outer reality by entering the 'no-go' areas of his territory. He can do this gradually (a slightly longer journey each day) or all at once (doing what he feared most to do), but whichever, by acting differently in his outer reality he changes his inner reality by coming to perceive himself as stronger and more capable.

But to achieve all this he needs his loved ones to change. They have to be prepared to see him differently and to support his efforts to find increased autonomy and independence. They have also to inspect their own attitudes to anger and to recognize their own anxieties about its expression.

The changes in his inner reality which will allow him to

relinquish his rigid defences altogether is the realization that '*Just because I am alone it doesn't mean that I shall die.*'

Isolation might feel like annihilation but it isn't. We go on existing.

Chapter Seven

Turning Fear into Obsessions and Compulsions

At one point in my life I was living in a house which had a large kitchen whose floor was covered with green linoleum which showed every footmark. There were plenty of footmarks as my five-year-old son and his friends ran in from the garden and the beach. If I had been sensible I would have ignored the floor. But I could not do that. Every day I washed and polished it. As soon as a mark appeared I hurried to remove it. I was very busy. I was working full time and studying for my clinical diploma, as well as looking after a husband, a child and a large house. Yet the floor had to be kept clean and spotless.

At the time I couldn't see why this floor was so important, but later I understood. In the years I lived in that house the pattern which I called my life, present and future, slowly disintegrated. As I began to feel it slipping from my control I looked for some part which I could hold on to and keep ordered, clean and perfect. Only the kitchen floor was willing to meet my requirements.

I was an introvert doing what all introverts do, perceiving the threat to self as coming from my outer reality and trying to deal with the chaos there by establishing order and control in that outer reality. Like an army under attack, I retreated to an area which I thought I could defend, and, like an army close to defeat, I pitched my standard which is the symbol for the meaning and purpose of that army, and prepared to defend it against all onslaughts as the world I once governed dissolved into chaos.

Fortunately for me, I did not have to defend my standard (the kitchen floor) to the death. I did not have to go on cleaning it day after day for it did not become an obsession, a defence against the threat of the annihilation of myself from within. Instead, it was a *transitional object*, something I could hold on to like a comfort blanket, while I made the transition from one way of life to another. For, while I dreaded the chaos of change and was angry at losing many of the things I valued, I could see the possibility that through this chaotic change something better would emerge, as it did.

One thing I did gain was a better understanding of myself. Of course, for an introvert, understanding is *all*. If introverts can understand, that is, see some clear pattern as to why things happen as they do, they feel much better, even though the pattern they see and the events they study can be quite horrific. Three years ago I grew tired of feeling worried and confused about the threat to our species by nuclear war and pollution and decided to sort out these issues in my mind (writing a book is a way of sorting things out). I created an understanding which is in itself a statement of an implacable and unacceptable truth, that human beings need enemies in the way that they need air, food and water, and unless we are able to change our fundamental nature, we are as a species doomed to extinction.[1] Appalled though I was at my conclusions, I felt the kind of satisfaction which introverts feel when they get something straight in their minds, and the even greater satisfaction that introverts feel when the people they value give their approval. My fellow psychologists agreed with my theory. So I can go to my doom knowing that I know why!

Extraverts think introverts are crazy, always wanting to know why, and coming up with all kinds of ludicrous explanations which change nothing. Extraverts prefer to get on and *do* something without waiting for an explanation. So long as they get their feelings right – plenty of excitement and enthusiasm, warmth and closeness – they feel fine. Introverts like to keep their heads in order; extraverts their hearts.

For introverts, keeping your head in order, that is, thinking clearly and logically, is the only way of keeping your external reality in order, which you must do, since an excess of stimulation is very painful and, if carried to extremes, threatens the very self.

There are three things which create chaos in external reality – objects, people and feelings.

Introverts are very good at keeping objects in order, whether it is keeping the kitchen clean or developing a management system for a multinational company. Objects can be put in perfect order, but then along come human beings, and they ruin the system. So introverts try to deal with human beings by controlling them. Extraverts are keen on controlling others too, but the aim of their control is different. Extraverts want to control others so as to keep them in the extravert's group. Introverts want to control others so as to keep everything orderly. But, as every extravert parent desperate to keep the children from leaving home finds, and every introvert dictator committed to creating the perfect society has found, human beings are very adept at slipping out of another person's control.

The reason that human beings are so difficult to control is that they have feelings, and feelings, even though we are prone to deny this, are spontaneous. They happen. We might try to deny that certain feelings have happened, but that is like trying to deny that the rain falls and the sun shines.

Feelings make external reality very difficult to control, and that is why introverts are always very wary of feelings. They are all very skilled at separating feelings from thought, and then minimizing their experience of their feelings, or denying their feelings altogether. If you let go of your feelings you will stir up trouble for yourself in your external reality.

Hate

All emotions cause trouble for us in the world we live in, but the one emotion which can cause the greatest trouble is hate. The expression of hate is destruction, and the objects of our personal hate are usually the people and objects which matter most to us.

The other evening I had finished peeling the potatoes and was wrapping up the peelings in newspaper when I thought, 'I never wrap up the sharp knife with the rubbish.'

This was a memory from my childhood. In our house we had one sharp knife which did all the jobs that sharp knives have to do. But frequently it would go missing. Someone, usually Mother, could not find it – it was not in the cutlery drawer, or on the draining board, or on the kitchen table – and there would be a great hue and cry. Then, perhaps, Mother would ask herself the question she always asked us when we couldn't find anything, 'Where did you have it last?' and she would hurry down the back stairs to the space under the verandah where the garbage can was kept. There she would unwrap the neatly rolled newspaper packages of rubbish and in one of them, along with the peelings, would be the knife.

I took this to be one of those regular events in family life which had no particular significance. After all, it is easy to lay a knife down among the peelings and not notice it later when you clear away the peelings. But now, forty years later, I saw the significance of this.

. I still remember vividly the occasions – not many, but enough to frighten and anger me then – when my mother would beat me and shout that she was going to kill me and then kill herself. Now I could see why the sharp knife had to be wrapped up and disappear – to protect me, and my sister and father. She hated us so much that she wanted to kill us, but she loved us and had to protect us. She hated herself so much that she wanted to kill herself, but she had too much pride to show such weakness to the world. It was better to hide herself, and the knife, right away.

Hate is an emotion which comes to us very early in our life, as soon as we have some notion of our self and of objects which we want. When these objects frustrate us we feel anger and hate. The baby who is still at the stage of different 'mother' objects, like mother-playing-with-me and mother-bathing-me, knows a mother-satisfying-me and a mother-not-satisfying-me, that is, a good mother and a bad mother, a mother who evokes love and a mother who evokes hate. As the images of all these mothers start to fuse into one, the baby has to deal with the realization that the mother on whom he depends and whom he loves is also the mother who frustrates him and whom he hates. He now has to deal with the co-existence of love and hate.

This is another of the problems in life for which there is no ultimate solution, other than death or an acceptance that the people we love the most can provoke in us the greatest hate, simply because they can possess and refuse to give us that which we need the most. We can, as small children, arrive at this acceptance provided the people we love and need do not present us with too many occasions to hate them and, when we do hate them, they tolerate our hate because they are able to tolerate their own.

If we are fortunate we are born into such a family. But if we are not fortunate, then hate remains a problem and a threat for the rest of our lives. All those ways of behaving which psychiatrists call the symptoms of mental illness can be understood as ways of running away from hate and of expressing hate in devious and symbolic forms. The people who have to defend their self from annihilation in these ways had in their first years of life a multitude of experiences which provoked their hate and adults around them who refused to accept their hate.

Hate is not a totally bad emotion. No emotion is. Hate serves some very useful purposes. Hating, we strengthen our sense of individuality, be we an infant needing to develop a separate identity from our mother or an adult needing to rediscover a separate identity as a relationship like a marriage comes to an end.

Hate sensitizes us to danger. Instead of going blithely on and running the risk of allowing ourselves to be harmed, hate warns us to beware and points out the dangers which can lie behind the most innocent of facades. Hate makes us aware, too, of those things in our environment which we can use to defend ourselves from attack. Hate helps us to survive.

Even though we deny that we feel hate we can still enjoy its benefits. We can turn our denied hate into a strong sense of justice, or into national, racial or religious pride, or into humanitarian zeal, and allow ourselves to feel outrage with those who are unjust, or who denigrate our nation, race or creed, or who are cruel and uncaring.

Denying our hate, we can still be made aware by it of the dangers which lurk nearby and the opportunities there for hate and destruction to be expressed.

However, if we deny our hate, we do so because we believe that it is wrong to hate. If we catch a glimpse within the darkness of our self of the hate which hides there, we can feel great shame and guilt.

Intimations of the hate within can make an extravert flee into external reality and deny the hate with an excess of activity. (This is described in Chapter 10 on mania.) Such intimations can provoke in an introvert a sense of guilt which, in the chaos such fear brings, threatens to annihilate the self. An introvert thus threatened becomes an expert on guilt and in ways of atoning for such guilt.

When the threat to the self becomes very strong, the introvert creates many ways of dealing with the guilt. These are the traditional ways of sacrifice, propitiation, atonement and reparation. Freud noted the similarity between the defences of obsessions and compulsions and the rituals of religion. 'If I sacrifice something which is important to me, or if I sacrifice myself, then I shall atone for my sin and be protected from harm.' 'If I carry out this ritual then I shall propitiate the gods and I won't be punished.' 'If I cleanse myself of sin (dirt) then I shall be safe.' 'If I make good or undo the harm I have done, then I shall be safe.'

Seeing oneself as guilty and so seeking forgiveness is a fruitless task, for unacknowledged hate can never be confronted, experienced and assessed, understood and brought to a conclusion. Thus the guilt grows, and the rituals aimed at moderating and controlling it become more elaborate, and the demand for their repeated performance becomes more and more pressing.

Thus, what was just a cleansing ritual to prove to God (mother) that you are a good boy who would not even *think* of hurting her by being dirty becomes a ritual washing of hands performed over and over again, until the skin is cracked and bleeding, and the tasks and responsibilities, and pleasures, of life are left ignored outside the bathroom door.

Thought and Doubt

Painfully repetitious though the various actions the obsessions and compulsions may be, the actually performed actions are only a small part of the obsessions and compulsions. The major part of obsessions and compulsions is *thought*.

This is thought without emotion, other than the emotion of fear. An introvert in the grip of an obsession can think in emotionless clarity, 'There is a knife. I could pick that knife up and plunge it into my child's heart', and only afterwards, when the possibility of this action has been clearly and calmly acknowledged, comes the realization that the action could have been carried out and the person most dear and valuable would be lying bleeding and dead. Then comes the fear. The whole process may take no more than a second, but it is always emotionless thought followed by fear.

So now sharp knives must be wrapped up and put away. No reparation is possible. Only a turning against yourself. You are wicked even to have thought the thought. You might have acted upon the thought, spontaneous, so easy, so dangerous. So, you must not act until you have thought and thought again. Spontaneity is dangerous. Spontaneity is forbidden. Observe, consider, plan, think and think again before you act. Only when you have thought everything through and controlled for every possibility can you act.

In thinking such thoughts the obsessional introvert may not use much visual imagery. He may not actually see himself, say, seizing the knife and plunging it into his child (whom he loves/hates because the child reminds him of himself). The thought is in words. This is very much in contrast to the extravert whose daydreams are dramatically visualized. The obsessional introvert's thoughts come in the clarity of the language of the child's first use of words and the simple, uncomplicated attitudes of that time – 'Knife – strike – kill.'

'No,' says the obsessional introvert. 'No, I didn't do it.' And then, doubt. 'I didn't do it, did I?'

The trouble is that if we rely on thought alone, stripped of emotion, we are always prey to doubt, for without emotion part of the equation is always missing. It is like one of those equations with x, y, and z, where we can find values for x and y but not for z. We can think of alternative values for z, but there is always a doubt. It may be this, or it may be that.

So, no matter how much an obsessional introvert plans, organizes, considers, reviews, the doubt will appear. *Did I do what I ought not to have done, or fail to do what I ought to have done?*

To deal with doubt he checks. Over and over again. He may wash his hands. (No one will die from my filth.) He may check the locks, the gas taps and the power points. (No one will murder my loved ones or destroy their possessions. My loved ones will not die from gassing, electric shocks or fire.) He may retrace again and again his path from office to home. (No motorist, cyclist or pedestrian will die at my hands.) But such actions performed over and over again do not erase doubt.

The television advertisement *Wipe away doubt with Dettox* is an advertisement made by an introvert for an introvert.

By stripping away emotion and using only thought the obsessional introvert gives to thought a power far beyond its actual capacity. Thought becomes magical. By thought alone the introvert can influence the world.

One of the tasks of infancy is to discover the difference between internal and external reality and to realize that our thoughts are private. This task can take a long time, for there can be many events in a child's life which suggest that thoughts are not private, and that thought alone can influence the environment. An infant does not know that his mother is not actually reading his thoughts when she responds to what he is thinking, but simply observing the expression on his face, or using her knowledge of children generally to interpret his needs and wishes. Hate often arises in an infant when his mother fails to read his thoughts – 'She ought to know what I want without my telling her' – and it is not until the infant comes to understand and to appreciate the privacy of thought that the infant can forgive his mother for her failures.

The realization that thought alone does not affect the environment may be delayed because sometimes our wishes are fulfilled without us having to act. We can feel hungry and fantasize food, and, lo, food appears. Or we can fantasize murder, and the mother who failed to meet our needs disappears. It may take the child a long while to realize that while the first event was a result of his mother's empathy, the second had no causal connection. His thought did not cause her to take ill and go to hospital, or to leave her family, or to die.

The understanding that our thoughts are private and their power limited has a benefit and a deficit. The benefit relates to how we can then, freely and securely, use the privacy of our thoughts to express and master our most selfish and dangerous wishes. We can expend our hate in fantasized murder, and, when the hate vanishes with the fantasy, continue to enjoy the company of the person we had just in our thoughts killed. The deficit is that we can think all kinds of marvellous thoughts, but such thoughts have no effect upon the real world until we put our thoughts into action. We have to find some way of linking our inner reality with our external reality.

The obsessional introvert cannot appreciate the privacy and limited power of thought. He has been taught that he can sin by thought alone. Thinking murder is as evil as doing murder.

Such a teaching gives to thought an immense power, and an introvert will accept that, for we like to have power within our preferred reality. Moreover, if the child has suffered many traumas and indignities, he will try to shore up his confidence and to comfort himself by vowing to inflict similar punishments on those who have harmed him. The frightened, weak child dreams of becoming the most powerful and dangerous person in the world by thought alone. The adult obsessional introvert still believes that thought is magic.

Of course, thought is magic in one way. Through thought we can experience many more things than we could ever perform in our external world. These can be wonderful things; these can be terrible things.

George was a parson, just like his father. He told me, 'I can say that I'm very much a person that likes tidiness. . . . If you want to hear about obsessions I could keep you here till teatime. They're all concerned with am I doing any harm to anybody else. I don't think this is a virtuous thing. It has to do with guilt in me. There's a whole range of hygiene ones. When I go to the toilet, I wash my hands for hours, and when I've finished I'm under a terrific compulsion to do it again. This is particularly strong if I'm going to church to take communion service where I'm handling bread. There are all sorts of ramifications of this. If I pick up the bowl with the cat's meat, I have to wash my hands after that. If I'm out on the road and I pull something out of my pocket and I drop a ten pence piece on the pavement, now I'll pick it up and I'll have an absolute horror that it's dropped into some dog dirt. There's nothing on the pavement, but I've got to walk back to make sure there's nothing there, and this coin feels almost deadly to anybody else. If I put it in my pocket I wonder if I've got something infectious in my pocket. I might pick up my briefcase to take to church and because the gate's padlocked I might put the case down to open it, and I'll wonder if I've put it in some dog dirt again. Then there's a whole range to do with money. If I go to the post office and pay for something, when I come out I wonder, "Did I give that chap the right amount?" I wonder if I've done him. And this happens many, many times. There's a whole range of other ones. If I'm driving a car – it's not as bad as it used to be – I overtake a cyclist and I wonder if I've touched him or not. This was awful one time, when I, many times on a journey, had to stop and turn round and go back. Until the psychiatrist I was under said whatever you do you mustn't go back. Generally speaking now, if I don't check up it goes. It could happen even as a pedestrian. I cross the road and I might be thinking of something else and when I get to the other side I think, I wonder if I looked. Has a car, in order to avoid me, crashed into the side or something? I'll go back and look and see if the road's clear. As a rule, it's to do with money – have I cheated someone? Or on the road or as a pedestrian – have I caused an accident? Or hygiene things – am I passing on to someone some infection? Another one is glass. If I'm washing some glasses and I tap the glass and it goes ping, I've got to make sure it isn't chipped, but if it's chipped, where's that bit of glass gone – if someone were to drink it and harm themselves. Perhaps the chip has bounced into some food. Those are the main things. You mentioned panic. I'm not aware of panic, although if I give way to checking I'll go on and on and on, and that feels almost like panic. But, if I can stop myself, after a bit it will disappear. Some of these obsessions, like the road ones, they'll last for a week. Once I rang the police and asked if there'd been an accident there . . . I would always rather work to clear a backlog than have the feeling "I haven't done it, I haven't done it." It worries me if things aren't done in time. It worries me if . . . I like planning ahead and know that I've got things organized before I get there . . . I'm concerned to keep the bit that's my responsibility under control, and then when someone takes over from me that's his fault, not mine . . . I'm always frightened that I haven't got everything right – that I'm not going to be there on time, or when I'm in church, something'll go wrong . . . I always feel guilty in case I've harmed somebody.'

George's obsessions concerned keeping chaos at bay and at proving that he was good. He would not wish harm on anyone anywhere at any time. The harm which he wished not to inflict was death. When we hate we fantasize murder, and then in fear of punishment for our evil thoughts, we see ourselves threatened with death. As I described in my book *The Construction of Life and Death*, we can construe death in many different ways, and our personal constructions of death have profound effects on the way we live our life. In this book I wrote about Jill who came to see me hoping that I could cure her 'of her obsessional habits of excessive washing of clothes, hair and hands, and of refusing to touch certain objects or to go into certain parts of her house. She involved her young son in these rituals which now occupied so much of her day that a normal family life was no longer possible. Jill was a beautiful, well-educated, intelligent young woman brought up in a family where, she told me, "My father expected us to do what he said and I always did" and mother was "a worrier". When she was first married she worked in the office of a chemical firm. One day when she was walking through the laboratory a small quantity of a chemical compound was accidentally squirted on her skirt. She went to the First Aid room where, she said, "They looked it up in a book and said, oh, well, there's nothing we can do. There's no antidote. If you're still alive by nine o'clock tonight you'll be all right." "I was very worried. Someone since told me they were joking because they thought it wasn't very serious, but I didn't realize this at the time. I went home and took the skirt off and put it aside because I was a bit scared to wash it and I didn't want to throw it away because it was brand new. I don't know how it got into the back of the cupboard where it was when we moved."

'The skirt became the source of the contagion. As Jill saw it, the contagion spread to all the objects in the cupboard where the skirt was. When Jill and her husband and child moved house the contents of the cupboard were shifted and the contagion spread to every object and person that touched them or even just came in close proximity to them. The only way the contagion could be removed was by washing. Some things, like books, could not be washed, and while Jill was washing what she could the contagion spread to her hair and clothes. She drew lines of demarcation in the house and made rules for her husband and child to follow, and when they transgressed the lines and rules she panicked and washed everything again. Even when all the rules and rituals were kept she would look at something and doubt. "I opened a cupboard door and saw a cup which I hadn't used for ages. I suddenly didn't want to touch it. Anything that hasn't been in circulation or is unusual, I get worried. There seems to be no end to it."

'I asked Jill if she saw this contagion as being able to harm her. She said, "I don't really know what I think will happen if I touch them. If they're small things I lick them if they're suitable to be licked to prove to myself that nothing will happen. I get this feeling that I don't want to touch them. If I do touch them I have to wash my hands or my hair as well. I washed it four times yesterday. I don't know why I have to do it, but I can't relax until I've washed my hands and my hair." . . .

'Jill would come and sit nervously on the edge of her chair, her scaly, overwashed hands clasped tightly in her lap, and look at me, waiting for me to produce a practical solution which she could then show me by words or deeds was no solution. She would talk about her obsession, but questions about other topics – childhood, relationships with husband and parents – received guarded and conventional replies. She could see no reason to discuss her childhood – it was quite ordinary – and when I explained how we carry the image and metaphor of our childhood into our adult life she said that this could not apply to her since "I'm not an imaginative person". Nevertheless, I thought I would try and get her to imagine the contagion as being a person and then to describe the attributes of that person.'

Not without difficulty Jill described the contagion as minute particles of a grey and deadly dust which spread by touch or drifting. She could imagine it as a person, 'a bit like a ghost that doesn't want to be seen or touched. I think it wants to be left alone.' However, if she did not keep a close eye on the shape it might come after her, surround her and annihilate her. Proving to her that one object did not have the grey dust on it only led her to the thought that the dust had moved on to something else. In one conversation 'Jill and I worked out that in all areas of her life except one she deferred to her husband and her mother. Only in her relationship to the contagious shape did she make her own decisions. If she gave up her obsession she would be doing what her husband and mother wanted her to do. It is sad that when all we can see ourselves as owning is our death.'[2]

Steve's wife Madeline phoned me. 'I'm sorry to trouble you,' she said in a voice breathless and shaky, 'Our GP told me he's written to you about my husband – to ask you to see him.'

I explained that I didn't have a vacancy until early February, some eight weeks ahead. She said, 'That's all right. Just to know that something's going to be done. Such a comfort.'

So I sent him an appointment, and duly the day and Steve arrived. He was very composed. He explained that he had had no difficulty in getting time off work for the appointment because he was already off work with a bout of flu.

The flu had more significance than I first realized. Later in our conversation he told me about his interest in running. He had been impressed with one well-known runner who said that he trained every day. So, said Steve, he had made a New Year resolution to train every day. He had kept his resolution for five years. Irrespective of the weather or how he felt, he had run a mile or two, or more, every day. But when he got this flu and was very ill, and went to the doctor and the doctor said, 'Go home, go to bed and stay there', he thought about going for a run before going to bed, and then decided against it. He went home, went to bed, and hadn't trained for five days.

'I was surprised how well I took it,' he said. 'I thought I would have a bad time but I didn't.'

What he meant by 'a bad time' was what he did to himself when he failed to meet one of the challenges he set himself. 'I have a guilt complex,' he said, and meant that cruel, persecuting self which drove him on relentlessly.

'Why is it so important to set yourself challenges?' I asked.

'It's important to achieve. People are like that. It's an instinct.'

His existence was a striving for clarity and perfection. The threat of chaos came with any falling away from this striving.

He spoke of how sometimes when he woke in the morning just for a moment everything was 'clean, empty, peaceful'. Then suddenly the guilt would come crowding in and he was in misery.

I followed the word 'clean'. 'Is cleanliness important to you?'

'Yes. Very. I wash my hands too much. When I was in my teens, when I was doing my O levels and working very hard, I used to be always washing my hands. I was washing away germs. I think it's crazy now, but then I thought I had something on the back of my shoulder and I'd always be rubbing it on something.' He demonstrated this on the back of the chair. 'I was working very hard. I'd do a paper round first thing in the morning, then some study, then school, homework when I got home, and then to evening college for more study.'

We talked about his family. He had been adopted. His adoptive parents, well into their thirties when they took him, were Methodists. When he was three they had a child of their own, a boy who, so Steve said, was able to have an easy and full social life and still do well at school, not like him for whom everything was a hard slog.

Sex was never mentioned in his home. He remembered being scolded by his mother for walking from his bedroom to the bathroom with no clothes on. His parents had told him he was adopted when he was about nine, but they told him nothing about his real parents except, he said, that they were a very young couple who couldn't marry and raise a family.

Anger was expressed in his family home, but only as the anger of parents expressed against the child. He was beaten for certain misdemeanours. He remembered his mother beating him with a poker. He and his brother would fight, but at school he avoided fights as much as possible. 'I was a coward,' he said.

But now anger and sex had come together in terrible, frightening impulses. He was a school teacher, teaching mathematics and physics, but often called upon to help in training the children in athletics and swimming. He described, in very general terms, the impulse to thrust his hips towards a child in an act of sexual aggression, and the terrible guilt which followed. He spent much time going over and over these matters in his head, trying, and failing, to prove to himself that he had not given vent to this impulse.

I spoke of how some people find driving a car difficult because they can fear that they have knocked someone down and not noticed it at the time. He nodded, understanding the pain of this, and said that he too suffers in this way.

Steve found it very hard to talk about feelings or anything which is not simple and practical. He did not reminisce. Often when he spoke of something which anyone might imagine would result in a great deal of emotion he would say, 'I never thought anything of it.'

One time when he did talk directly about feeling was when one of their cats was killed on the road outside their house. This distressed him greatly.

'Our cats are like our family,' he said, 'It's hit me more than when my grandfather died.'

I spoke of the strange sense of emptiness a loss brings, an emptiness as real and palpable as a presence.

He agreed that this was so. Afterwards, when he began again to talk about his obsessional thoughts he talked more about his feelings, how he felt no desire to act sexually to a child, but how the thought without the emotion would come, followed by the doubt about whether or not he had done something, and that accompanied by an enormous sense of guilt. 'It happens quickly, but I think about it in slow motion.'

He often spoke of guilt. I asked him how far back in his life he could remember this sense of guilt.

He said that he couldn't, and then he suddenly remembered when 'I was seven or eight, I was given a watch – for birthday or Christmas – I looked at this watch,' he set the thumb and fingers of his right hand carefully round the watch on his left wrist, 'and I thought, "I mustn't scratch it, I must keep it perfect." Then I suddenly got this urge to scratch it. And I did, and then I felt terribly guilty.'

I wondered whether as a child Steve had had a man expose himself to him. 'Children often have this experience,' I said.

'No,' he said immediately, without reflection.

On another occasion, when Steve was telling me about his recent obsessive ruminations whether he had splashed some orange juice on a little girl, a highly unlikely event which had a sexual connotation for Steve, I asked him how a child who was sexually assaulted would feel. He could not answer this, but when gently pressed, said that children didn't remember such things.

Yet in his obsessional ruminations is the voice of a little child.

He said, 'My arm turned just a fraction. That's natural, isn't it? I thought, if it did turn, the drink I was holding, it could have splashed. But I wasn't that close to the girl, was I?' and there was the little child saying to himself, 'Did that really happen, or didn't it?'

He said, 'When I'm walking up the street and I see children coming towards me I turn away. I know I wouldn't do anything, but still . . .', and, 'I think I didn't flick any stones up, but there were some at the edge of the road and I did drive the car a bit fast across the intersection. So I went back to look. There was an old man getting off the bus. I couldn't see him when I went back. He might have got on the bus. I don't think the stones would have hurt him', and there was the voice of the little child saying, 'It wasn't my fault, was it?'

Aggression

Those introverts who are forced to defend themselves with obsessions and compulsions go to extreme lengths not to be aggressive. George stressed to me how conventional and obedient he was, but he was prepared to defy convention and risk the disapproval of many of his parishioners and clergy colleagues by promoting the cause of the Campaign for Nuclear Disarmament and denying the necessity for a nation to defend itself with weapons of total destruction. Except for her persisting in her obsessions, Jill would not defend herself against the demands of her family. Steve called himself 'a coward'. One obsessional young man, Russell, abhorred all kinds of fighting and argument. He had attended a secondary school where fighting among the boys was taken as a way of life, but he had in six years there avoided all fights except one, and he still felt guilty about this. Some evenings it would take Russell three hours to complete a journey of four miles, for whether he drove a car, rode a bicycle, or walked, he would become convinced that he had injured someone on his journey, and he would have to keep going back to check and check and check again. But all his efforts to be completely unaggressive and to undo any harm he might have inadvertently inflicted on another person could not prevent grotesquely cruel fantasies of injury and death to others, especially children, coming again and again into his mind. There was nothing I could say which would assuage his guilt at thinking such thoughts, and nothing could persuade him that these thoughts were not evidence of his inherent wickedness but rather the outcome of childhood traumas. He had had, he insisted, a perfectly happy childhood.

If hate has to be denied, then the events which gave rise to that hate must be forgotten, or, if remembered, their significance must be denied.

George said, 'I accept the fact that there's a massive amount of anger buried in me, but I'm not aware of feeling any anger, so obviously there's a lot of repression there. Occasionally I get angry with my wife Heather, and on rare occasions I explode but not very often.'

I asked, 'Do you remember as a child being angry?'

'No, I can't actually. I was sent away to a boarding school when I was not quite eight. I don't think I can remember – I've got a rotten memory anyhow. I remember calling my aunt an old so and so, but I don't think this was really anger. It was because she was just so blooming bossy. I went straight from boarding school to the Services. It was a great relief to go into the army.'

I asked, 'What were the rules in your family about anger?'

'What do you mean? Could you be more explicit?'

I explained that every family has its rules, and there are always rules about anger. These rules might never be put into words, but children always knew that in their families there were rules like, 'No one gets angry ever', or, 'Only father is allowed to get angry'.

George said, 'My sister's description of my father would be entirely different from mine. We used to call him the vicarage policeman, but father was father. I'm not aware when I was at home that it was anything but a fairly relaxed atmosphere.'

Heather explained, 'His sister describes him as fairly authoritarian, but George has no memories of this.'

George said, 'If I thought I was going to be late for lunch I would come back like hell for leather. You weren't allowed to be late for meals, though if you were you'd get a disapproving stare. I think as a youngster I would always stick to the rules. I always had an exaggerated respect for anybody older than me, which was reinforced by the public schools, until it was shattered when I got in the army and saw that older people weren't so wise after all. I don't think, perhaps it's my nature, not to be rebellious. I don't think I felt rebellious. My main impression of childhood is of happiness. I was much more of a loner than my brother, but I think I was happy.'

I explained that for children to have a happy childhood they have to learn to follow the family's rules. 'If we have parents who expect obedience, we have a happy childhood if we are obedient.

267

If we have parents who expect cleanliness, we have a happy childhood if we learn to be clean. You learned your family's rules very well. You were good at being good.'

George said, 'On the other hand, I had a great deal of freedom. I could get on my bike and disappear. I quite liked my own company.'

'Both you and your sister are most uncritical of other people,' said Heather.

'Underneath is the feeling of anything for a peaceful life,' said George wryly.

I commented that as a child he could protect himself by escaping from his home, away and free on his bikes but as an adult he had no such freedom. A vicar is always being observed by his parishioners.

'We've taken life much too seriously. All we've done is work, work, work,' said Heather.

George said, 'I know that we all put on a front to the outside world, but, no, I don't know who I am . . . I think certainly in my teenage years to some extent, when I was thirteen and went on to public school, I didn't enjoy life as I should have done because of what I saw as the constraints of conscience. I was a very priggish Christian. Before communion on a Sunday morning I'd go through a long list of things and check that I'd obeyed every one – they were all written down – things like masturbation and thinking wrong thoughts. Looking back now I can see how ridiculous it was – but it turned you in on yourself. As long as I hadn't done any of these, to hell with anybody else, but, as long as I hadn't, that was fine and therefore I suppose I worried more about trivial things . . .'

He went on, 'I was brought up in the tradition of making a confession before major festivals. Now, I used to do that to my father, and I think, looking back, some of the things which disturbed me most, like masturbation, those sort of things . . . there must have been lots of other petty little things . . . I have learned now that that is the kind of religion which cripples a person. It's not the sort of thing which enriches but sort of cripples. Now to what extent that affected me I don't know. I suppose it was the kind of thing one did. I would think, once this is behind me I can enjoy Christmas. Almost a ritual in a sense, almost a connection between that and my obsession about hygiene. It does show how much a conformist I was. My conscience would demand that I told my father everything. So there can't have been anything very important to tell him. I must have been a one for the rules . . . When I went to the Services I began to grow up and I almost dropped out of Christianity altogether. Then when I became a parson I started this confession business again, but then I stopped because I found it wasn't doing me the slightest bit of good. It was a negative thing.'

'Had it helped you as a child?' I asked.

'I don't think so. I thought of it as one of the hurdles you had to get over if you're a Christian.'

'It gave your father tremendous power.'

'I don't think so. To me it was one of the things you had to do.'
Making a ritual confession to your father, a priest who is invested with God's power to punish and to absolve you of your sin, takes from the child the privacy of thought and action which is a necessary part of being and becoming your true self. Melanie Klein psychoanalysed her three children when they were small, and at least one of them, Melitta Schmideberg, as she once told me, never forgave her. Melitta, like most psychoanalysts today, felt this to be a terrible misuse of a parent's power. But at least Melitta felt she was allowed to be angry with her mother. George dared not criticize the man who had demanded to know the secrets of his soul.

'I remember before I was eight I was away at school two-thirds of the year. In this British stiff upper lip tradition you didn't tell your parents not because you were frightened to tell them but because you were taught to keep your trouble to yourself. There were lots of things I just didn't tell them. You had to keep yourself to yourself.'

George and Heather told me about George's grandmother, how her son had been killed in the First World War and how she had said, 'I've now got nothing to live for', thus leaving her daughter, George's mother, to cope by herself.

George's mother had not coped very well. She had periods of deep depression and, finally, when George's children were small and Heather ill, she committed suicide.

George said, 'It wasn't just my mother who had a breakdown. When I came out of the Services at the end of the war, my father had a breakdown. I thought it was because he'd had so much worry with mother he'd just folded up. Eventually I persuaded him to retire. He was depressed, and then he eventually slipped into senility.'

'It's one of the things which is worrying George. That he'll go the same way,' said Heather.

George said, 'I've always felt because I was sent away to school I had great attachment to my home county Cornwall, but my attachments are very much more to the place than to people. I'm ashamed to say I didn't grieve particularly when my parents died. When I came home from overseas, if I could have got off that plane and got on another and gone straight back I'd have done so gladly. The war ended when I was still overseas. I was offered an early release to go to university, and then my brother wrote to me and said, "Look, you've been enjoying yourself for long enough. Time you came home and took up your responsibilities." So very reluctantly I accepted the opportunity to come home. If I hadn't I'd have stayed out in East Africa.'

'You knew that going back home wasn't good for you,' I said.

'I don't know why particularly.'

I told George how, when I was in India, I met Ashishda whose ashram was high in the Himalayas. Ashishda was an Englishman who, so he told me, had been sent to India during the war. At the end of the war he decided not to return home because, if he did, his sister and widowed mother would have expected him to allow them to depend on him for support and care. This, Ashishda said, would have destroyed him. So he stayed in India to seek his own enlightenment, and this had led him to the ashram of which he is now the much loved and respected leader.

George said, 'I would have been finished by that kind of decision. I wouldn't have got over it. I would have had it on my conscience all the time.'

Whenever Steve came to see me I became aware, yet again, of his lack of experiencing his emotions. It was not that he did not have emotions. His passions were strong, but they were not felt, acknowledged and named. They resided in a darkness which was part of him, like a carapace which was joined to him and which inhibited and frightened him.

Slowly, though, it seemed that we were getting to know one another. One day we were discussing how he could not talk to his mother, a topic where he would make a statement like 'I can't talk to my mother' and not elaborate it. When I asked him what attitude his mother had to men in general he, as usual, could not answer this question. He had no idea what she thought about men. I ran through some of the attitudes women have to men. Some women like men and think them wonderful; some women are frightened of men, especially of their sexual power; some women are very envious of men and seek to bring them down; some women hate men and want to destroy them. Of course, men have a range of generalized attitudes to women. He nodded when I mentioned the way some men divide women into the Madonna and the Whore, the asexual, idealized woman and the sexual, bad woman, a splitting which many men make within themselves.

I asked him how I saw men. He turned to me, his face alive with interest. He had plenty of ideas about this. He spoke of me expecting men 'to do their whack', not waiting on them, but expecting them to do their share. At the same time, I liked men. 'But you'd have to, wouldn't you, to do this job?'

Steve went on to talk about his mother and said more than he had said in all the months we had been meeting.

His mother had always been a powerful woman. Now, at sixty-five, she was mellowing, but always she had been an obsessional, religious woman who dominated her husband and sons. Her husband would always go along with what she wanted, and her natural son might be rebellious in her absence but was always obedient in her presence. Only Steve dared to argue with her and disobey her.

But he never won an argument with her. If he did disobey her and insist on doing what she forbade him to do she would 'whinge and whine' so much that his victory became a defeat. He spoke with passion of the petty restrictions and rules which she imposed.

'We weren't allowed to play football on the lawn. We'd wear the grass out. We used to wait until they went to church and then we'd go and kick a ball around. Sunday was the most boring day of the week. I hated Sundays. You weren't supposed to do anything except go to church. I stopped going as soon as I could.'

He spoke with scorn of the obsession his mother had with keeping the house clean and tidy. 'On Sunday afternoon she'd be complaining about how tired she was and how much she had to do. I'd tell her she didn't have to do it. They used to go to church in the evening, and sometimes they'd invite people back for coffee. If I was at home – this was when I was at university – I'd go for a run then, but when I got back she wouldn't let me have a bath. She said it steamed up the bathroom. I'd tell her that when visitors came they didn't go in the bathroom and give you a mark out of ten for neatness.' She never appreciated his humour.

He spoke, too, of how inhibited his mother was about sexual matters. 'Her generation didn't know about these things.'

As he spoke he was revealing the picture of a boy who was often isolated in his family, rejected by his mother and deserted by his father. He had been rejected and deserted by his natural mother whom he never knew. If he fought to defend himself he was defeated. His parents never allowed him to win a battle. It was no wonder that in his darkness there was a great deal of rage and hate.

But, even so, he could feel some sympathy for his mother. 'My father handled all the money. He didn't say much, but in the end he made all the decisions. She couldn't do anything without him. She never learned how to look after the bills. She never learned how to drive a car.'

His mother had shown none of the contentment which a happy woman would reveal. Instead, her behaviour suggested that she was in the grip of helpless rage, just like her son.

In early summer Steve and Madeline visited his parents. Later he told me, 'Except for one thing that happened, it wasn't too bad a time.'

He described the 'one thing'. They had gone on a day's outing to Scarborough. 'My parents and Madeline and me were walking along the front, the four of us. I saw this family up ahead of us – the parents and two girls – small girls. Just as we came up near them, one of them – she wasn't very tall, just up to here,' he indicated his waist, 'ran across in front of us and leaned on the rail. In a flash, you know how you can think these things in a millisecond, I thought, "She's going to turn round and run back just in front of me", and I thought if I thrust – but I didn't. Afterwards, Madeline said it was nothing, I didn't do anything wrong. I mean, we were just walking by. I didn't look at the girl, but you know how you can know there's someone there. But I didn't do anything wrong, did I?'

He looked agonized. All that had happened on that seafront had gone on in his mind. Anyone surveying the scene would have seen four people strolling down the front and passing a little girl who was looking over the rail. Madeline, with her arm through Steve's, saw or felt nothing untoward, and knew nothing of what Steve saw and felt until later that evening he told her what had happened and asked her, repeatedly, to reassure him that nothing he had done was wrong.

I tried to understand what had happened. Steve described how everything seems to happen very slowly. It sounded like the way action can seem very slow in a situation of great danger. He did not have a visual image of what he might do, but just the thought of what he might do, followed by the terror that he might have carried out the impulse. Here he had seen that the little girl's head was the same height as his pelvis, and he had thought of pushing his penis into her mouth. .

As soon as the thought had entered his mind he had been filled with terror and guilt, and immediately began the endless questioning of himself, 'Did I move my hip? Did I do anything wrong?'

It took us some time to talk about this. Steve had difficulty in putting these matters into words, and I had difficulty in coming to feel sure that I understood what he was telling me.

'Did I do anything wrong?' he asked.

'That's the wrong question,' I said. 'Of course you didn't do anything wrong. The question is why do these thoughts come into your mind.'

Until Steve had come to talk to me he had not considered that his childhood had been in any way different from other children's.

'Well, you don't know, do you?' he said. 'You think your family's just like that.'

Now he was beginning to see that perhaps his childhood had not been the easiest. Now he was puzzling over why his mother could laugh at jokes about sexual innuendoes on television, but she still would not accept anything but the most correct behaviour from him.

I was saying something about the way a small child can be punished for doing things that are quite natural when he interrupted me to say that he had just remembered something. When he was about ten his mother had washed out his mouth with carbolic soap because he had been swearing.

I suggested that there was a connection between his thought

about the little girl and the resurgence of this memory of having his mother wash out his mouth.

Such an action by his mother suggested that what he had in his mouth – his words – was filthy and dangerous. In helpless rage and hate at such injustice, a small boy could give vent to his feelings only by fantasizing a terrible revenge upon his mother. What could he imagine pushing into his mother's mouth that was as filthy as that which she had washed out of his?

Throughout this chapter I have spoken of 'obsessional introverts' meaning those introverts whose obsessions (all introverts have obsessions) have come to dominate their lives. There are many extraverts who do certain things over and over again in such a way that these actions can be called obsessional. For instance, there are millions of introverts and extraverts who devote a large part of their time cleaning and tidying their homes and getting furious with their children and spouses for making a mess. However, while the extraverts' and introverts' actions may appéar to be the same, the reasons which lie behind the obsessional cleanliness and tidiness are different. Extraverts keep their homes clean and tidy to avoid shame and rejection. They need to be an accepted member of the group. Introverts need to keep their home clean and tidy to avoid guilt and chaos.

Shame and Guilt

Both introverts and extraverts assess themselves as good or bad in terms of what other people will think of them and in terms of what they think of themselves. But when they perceive themselves as failing to be good enough, extraverts are more likely to react with *shame* and introverts with *guilt*. Shame for the extravert is 'Everyone will know and they will reject me'. Guilt for the introvert is 'I know that I am failing to achieve clarity and to keep chaos at bay'. In the extraverts' panic attack is shame at being exposed to the rejecting gaze of others. In the introverts' obsessions and compulsions is guilt at having transgressed the Law, a Law which may reside in the introvert's superego and nowhere else.

Shame is about the whole self or the sense of identity. In shame we think, 'How could *I* have done that?' Guilt is about specific actions and involves remorse about what we have done. In guilt we think, 'How could I have done *that*?'[3]

The ancient Greeks saw shame as *fate*, something which comes upon us and which we can do nothing to avert, and guilt as *hubris*, the sin of challenging the gods. Feelings of shame are associated with helplessness, impotence and weakness. Feelings of guilt are associated with a sense of having overstepped some limit, to have transgressed, to have acted as an individual out of pride and selfishness.[4]

Ken's battle with the Judge (Chapter 6) concerns the avoidance of shame. The Judge constantly tried to shame him in the way that his mother had shamed him, and all his obsessional thoughts and checking were aimed at proving that he had *acted rightly* and that he had no reason to feel ashamed. Whereas the obsessions and compulsions which people like George, Steve, Jill and Russell carry out are concerned with guilt. They fear that they have *acted wrongly* and must atone for their guilt.

Ken, feeling helpless in the eyes of his Judge/mother, tried to overcome this weakness and terror which threatened to destroy his sense of self by moving from the position which his mother forced him as a child to adopt, 'I have no responsibility for my life. Other people make my decisions', to 'I have total responsibility for everyone'. Such a move strengthened his sense of self by giving him a sense of power, but it also meant that in addition to striving to avoid shame he had to feel considerable guilt. If we are responsible, then when we fail we must feel guilty.

The great attraction of guilt is that it supports our pride. Guilt helps us preserve the illusion that we can actually control our environment, ourselves and others. What immense personal pride is present in the belief that we can live within the continuity of our physical world and not collect and pass on noxious substances, or not inadvertently cause objects to move in ways dangerous to other people. What immense personal pride is present in the beliefs that we can control the natural spontaneity of thought, or that we have more knowledge and power than other people and so must be responsible for them. Guilt is impossible without pride. It always contains the belief 'I could have acted otherwise'. Terrible though guilt may be, many people find it better to hang on to guilt than to look behind it for those early childhood experiences of shame where the young child, helpless, weak, humiliated and friendless, felt the terror of the annihilation of the self.

This is one of the reasons why obsessional introverts resist therapy. Guilt and the obsessional rituals to atone for the guilt may be terrible, but they are preferable to complete vulnerability.

Moreover, if your conscience will not allow you to attack your loved ones directly, you can inflict pain and discomfort on them by demanding that they conform to your rituals, answer your endless questions, and by not rewarding them by giving up your obsessions.

The obsessional introvert takes great pride in his awareness of the importance of morality. But the moral rules which he has created for himself are harsh and the punishments for their infringement very severe. 'An eye for an eye, and a tooth for a tooth.' Or, as in the Spanish proverb, 'Take what you like, says God, and pay for it.' There is little room in his moral world for understanding and forgiveness. Some obsessional introverts can be understanding and forgiving of others, making allowances and bending the rules in ways which they would never do for themselves, but others apply their rules strictly to all, and so place themselves in a dangerous isolation from which it is easy to fall into depression.

As a therapist working with an obsessional introvert it is very easy to see why Freud created the concepts of id, ego and superego. These three aspects of the person are clearly delineated in the client's behaviour. The id is present by default, so to speak, by always being denied. The ego and superego are there so clearly that the therapist gets the impression of talking to two people at once. This makes for a very difficult conversation, for there is very little the therapist can say which will please the introvert's ego and superego simultaneously. The introvert's ego will be on the look-out for anything the therapist might say which could be interpreted as criticism and a siding with the punitive superego. The ego will have nothing to do with the superego's allies. But if the therapist tries to argue that the introvert should be kinder to himself, the superego will be shocked at the immorality of the therapist and refuse to join an alliance with the therapist. I try not to get caught in this trap by bringing it out into the open and pointing out what an impossible situation my client has placed me in, but as an introvert myself I know that, no matter how much I want to believe the wonderful things someone might be telling me, my sceptical superego whom I wouldn't part with for the world is standing at my shoulder saying, 'You're not going to believe that rubbish, are you?' and I don't.

Where a sceptical superego is so valuable is that it helps me sort out within my inner reality what is valuable and what is just the tinsel of vanity. This is a very necessary exercise for introverts, for there is always the temptation to give to thought too much power, just as for extraverts there is always the temptation to give too much importance to action. To live wisely we have to knit together our inner and outer realities. A flight into either is a flight into madness. When an introvert fails to check his thoughts against his experience of outer reality, or refuses to accept the consensus of what external reality is (for instance, most of us would think that if you do knock a chap off his bike as you drive by, it is highly likely that the police will tell you about it) he is letting his vanity override his common sense. He does this because he is still trying to comfort the frightened child within, but as he will not acknowledge why the child is frightened he cannot understand why he does what he does, much less choose to change it.

To live peacefully within ourselves we have to be able to accept and love and feel sorrow for the child we once were, and to regard our conscience not as an adversary but as a good friend, someone who is on our side and telling us we're doing well and, if we make a mistake, next time we'll do better. If you feel that it will take a long time for you to develop such a relationship with your conscience, you might draw comfort and strength, as one of my friends does, from the words of Gerard Manley Hopkins:

> *My own heart let me more have pity on: let*
> *Me live to my sad self hereafter kind,*
> *Charitable; not live this tormented mind*
> *With this tormented mind tormenting yet.*[5]

To make our conscience our friend we have to come to realize that we cannot control our thoughts. We have to accept that thought is spontaneous. To make our conscience our friend we have to be able to accept our anger and to realize that we don't have to feel frightened and guilty when we think angry thoughts. But to accept our thoughts as being spontaneous we have to be able to experience helplessness, not as something potentially annihilating, but as the way we float in and are part of the ever-changing cosmos. It is possible to be helpless, not in control, but still safe and strong.

However, if you cannot face this kind of helplessness, the ultimate in uncertainty, you can choose the most secure and unchanging of all defences, depression.

Chapter Eight

Turning Fear into Depression

Given the choice between immense physical pain and depression, anyone who has been depressed would choose physical pain. Depression is far worse than physical pain. In physical pain, no matter how ferocious it might be, it is possible, at least from time to time, to separate yourself somehow from it, to rise above it, to share a joke and to feel close to others, loved and loving. But in depression you are utterly and completely enclosed, shut in a prison, bereft of all contact with others, without humour, peace or love.

How could this appalling state be a defence, something which we choose to do?

If it is a defence, some people use it just once or twice and others for most of their lives. People of all ages can get depressed, and people of all races and cultures, and references to it are found right through recorded history. It has not always been called depression. In Elizabethan England it was called *melancholy*, and in medieval times it was called *accidie*, the falling into despair and despondency.

The word 'depression' is a modern term, used first by doctors to describe what they saw as an illness. Now the word has entered common parlance, so that in everyday conversation we talk of being depressed when we may mean feeling merely bored or dispirited. This leads to much confusion as to what depression *is*.

The confusion about what depression is is not confined to the general public. Among the various health professionals, doctors, nurses, social workers, psychologists, occupational therapists and physiotherapists, there is, I find, considerable confusion as to what depression is and how to distinguish it from unhappiness. Psychiatric textbooks give the *symptoms* of depression – lowered mood, loss of libido, sleep disturbance, irrational guilt, and so on –

but somehow they never describe what depression is. *How is being depressed different from being unhappy?*

If you ask someone who is depressed, or has been depressed, that person can describe an experience very different from being unhappy.

Images of Depression

If you say to someone who is depressed, 'If you could paint a picture of what you are feeling, what sort of picture would you paint?' you will get some remarkable answers.

Some people will answer very simply. They'll say, 'I'm at the bottom of a black pit', or 'I'm in a thick fog', or 'I'm walking along an endless dark tunnel'. Other people will give much more elaborate, idiosyncratic images.

One man told me, 'I'm under a transparent dome and I can't get out. There's a sort of white paint running down the outside of the dome, and the people outside the dome sort of loom over me and look vague and ghostly.'

One woman, a mother of three small children, said, 'I'm in my kitchen standing at the sink. There's piles and piles of washing up. I'm looking out the window and outside it's raining and cold and horrible, and I can't get out of the kitchen until all the washing up is done, and the more I do, the more there is to be done.'

Jackie said, 'A black square – it's just blackness, and I feel as though I am in the middle of a horror movie and there is no way out. There is just dense darkness, nothing there but blackness. You feel as though you're going deeper and deeper into it, and there's no opening.'[1]

All the images are different, but they have one common meaning. The person is alone and in some sort of prison.[2] Images of unhappiness are grey and miserable, but they do not contain this sense of enclosure, and other people are present, or easily available, in them. Also, images of unhappiness are often described in 'as if' terms, 'I feel as if I'm walking along a rainswept street'. A depressed person will say that it is not 'as if' but 'is'. The essence of being depressed is experiencing a sense of isolation, of being utterly and completely alone.

Reactive and Endogenous Depression

This sense of isolation is not mentioned in psychiatric textbooks. This is not surprising, because, to discover this isolation and to understand its significance, you have to listen to what the depressed person says and understand it in terms of that person's value system, and not just in terms of your own. This, however, is not what psychiatrists are trained to do. In that most influential of psychiatric textbooks, *Clinical Psychiatry* by Eliot Slater and Martin Roth, the authors advise their psychiatrist readers that, 'It is the objective world in which we live and to which the subjective world must pay deference. It is even more important to know what the facts are than what the patient makes of them.'[3]

According to this belief, there are FACTS which the psychiatrist can perceive and assess, which are objective, exist in the real world, and are valuable, unlike the opinions, attitudes and feelings of patients which do not exist in the real world, are subjective and therefore not valuable. A curious anomaly underlies this, that in assessing FACTS the psychiatrist has to use his own opinions, attitudes and feelings. If all opinions, attitudes and feelings are subjective and bad, then surely the psychiatrists' opinions, attitudes and feelings are as reprehensible as the patients'? However, if someone questions this, the answer will be given that psychiatrists are trained to be objective and not to let their personal feelings intrude upon their clinical judgement.

'Clinical judgement' – what crimes have been committed in your name!

Using such clinical judgement a psychiatrist will decide whether a person is suffering from reactive or endogenous depression. The theory behind these two classifications is that *reactive depression* arises when a person has a personal reason in his life to be depressed. *Endogenous depression* arises when there is no such reason. It is a physical illness which arises from within the person who, so the theory goes, usually has a 'previously normal personality'.

These two classifications have what psychologists call 'face validity'. They fit in with what can easily be observed. Some people suffer such terrible reverses in their lives that it is not surprising that they become depressed in response to them. Hence reactive depression. But other people appear to be living successful, contented lives when they become depressed. They will say to themselves, 'I don't know why I'm depressed. I have every reason to be happy.'

But appearances can mislead, and no one who wants to know the truth should be content with them. Quite often we will say that we don't know why we do something – why we get headaches, or drink too much, or stay in a job we don't like, or get depressed – when in fact we do know, but we are not going to tell the person who is asking us. Many of us were brought up not to discuss family matters with strangers, and we won't do this, even if the person asking us is a doctor. We might think we could tell the doctor, but of course he makes notes, and you never know who else might read them. If you've lived in a community for a few years it is almost certain that there will be someone on the staff of the local health centre or the psychiatric hospital who knows you and your family, so it's best to be careful. Sometimes we know what the problem is, but it makes us feel so ashamed and embarrassed that we don't want to talk about it to someone who might not understand. When you're depressed you can't cope with any more criticism and rejection. Even the littlest thing hurts. And then there are the things that we don't want to admit even to ourselves. So we can be very happy to collude with the doctor and say, 'There's no reason in my life why I should be depressed.'

Even if we overcome our anxiety about people knowing our secrets and our shame, we might tell the doctor about what in our lives we find very troubling, only to find that he rejects our assessment of our own lives. We might think that our marriage, or our job, or what our children do are matters which cause us so much pain that we react with depression, but those are just our personal, subjective opinions, attitudes and feelings. The doctor in the process of arriving at a diagnosis may dismiss them as unimportant, or simply label us as 'inadequate' or 'hysterical'. (Many psychiatrists use the term 'inadequate personality' in their formulation of the patient's disabilities. I have yet to see a definition of an 'adequate personality'. In case conferences I have often been tempted to ask the consultant for such a definition, but suspected that in doing so I would reveal myself as a fool. After all, a definition of an adequate personality was right there before my eyes, in the person of the consultant himself.)

It is the doctor, not the patient, who decides whether there is anything in the patient's life which would make that person feel depressed. From my extensive observations of psychiatrists over twenty years I can say that many of them make very subjective and uninformed judgements about what in a person's life could be a cause of sadness, despair and depression.

There are, I regret to say, a great many psychiatrists who hold the belief that all a woman needs to feel happy and fulfilled is a home, a husband and children. Thus, when a woman who has these things presents herself in a depressed state to such a psychiatrist he draws the conclusion that she has no reason to be depressed. Therefore the correct diagnosis is endogenous depression. This is a more serious matter than just a choice of words. Psychiatric textbooks teach that the appropriate treatment for endogenous depression is electroconvulsive therapy (ECT). Since the majority of adults who are diagnosed as depressed are married women, many more women than men receive this treatment.

But it is not just women who are given such a diagnosis. Many good, hard-working men are so diagnosed when they become depressed in later middle age. Sometimes the diagnosis seems to have been arrived at with the psychiatrist and patient in collusion. Neither wishes to let the side down and acknowledge and reveal the pain and weakness which the depressed man is feeling. An explanation is given by the psychiatrist and accepted by the patient where the sterling virtues of being hard-working, conscientious, responsible are seen as creating a physical debility which allows the physical illness of depression to take hold. No mention is made of the desperate pain of feeling unloved and unwanted, as younger men rise past you to more senior positions, or as your job disappears when the firm is organized to greater efficiency, or when your children become too grown-up to take any notice of their father, or your wife treats you as a piece of old, useless furniture in the home and finds her interests elsewhere.

To uncover these hurts, to find out not just what has happened in a person's life but how that person feels about what has happened takes a very long time. It cannot be done in a ten-minute consultation, or even in half an hour. And it requires careful listening with the attitude that what the patient has to say is of the greatest importance. This is hard work. It is much easier to ascertain the FACTS, decide whether to call the depression endogenous or reactive, and to write a prescription while reassuring the patient that his is a common problem, something which will clear up in a week or two and not to worry. The diagnosis of endogenous depression is a great labour-saving device.

I am not alone in my dislike of the diagnosis of endogenous depression. Anthony Storr, writing in the *British Journal of Psychiatry*, said:

Years ago, when I was in training at the Maudsley Hospital, we were taught that there are two kinds of depression, reactive and endogenous. I am glad to say that I have never accepted the validity of this distinction. All it seemed to mean was that, in cases labelled reactive, the doctor would define an obvious external cause for depression, like bereavement or bankruptcy, which he could see might cause depression in himself. Where no such obvious circumstance could be discerned, the doctor concealed his ignorance by calling the patient's condition 'endogenous'. The word 'endogenous' ought to be forbidden in psychiatry. Its implication that the condition so described is rooted in the patient's genetic structure discourages research. Much the same structures apply to the use of the phrase 'depressive illness', or 'affective disorder'. The assumptions underlying this use of language have prevented us understanding depression. Depression is not an illness which one catches, like influenza, but a psychobiological reaction which can be provoked in any of us, given appropriate circumstances, and which may have some positive uses. Today, one encounters patients who refer to 'my affective disorder' as if it was as unrelated to their personality as measles, which seems to me quite ridiculous. Every time I encounter George Brown's work on *Social Origins of Depression*,[4] I blush for my profession. We have allowed a sociologist to discover what psychiatrists ought to have found out years ago, but failed to do so because of their pseudo medical assumptions.[5]

Another term popular with doctors is 'clinical depression'. These words can be used with great sympathy and concern. The doctor can be saying that the person is so depressed that he should not try to continue with his ordinary life but should withdraw from the fray and take care of himself. The doctor is saying, 'This is serious and we must treat it seriously.'

Unfortunately, some doctors use the words 'clinical depression' not simply to help the patient but to stake out an area for themselves and to claim that they and they alone have expertise there. Thus used, the words are in the service of mystifying the patient and the public. They are often used in connection with some impressive sounding words which apparently relate to physiological processes which only a doctor could understand and which prove that depression, or certainly 'clinical depression', is caused by some physiological or chemical change. This has to be said in a mystifying way, for if the doctor explained what he was saying clearly and accurately, it would become apparent even to the non-medical listener that the physiological changes of which he speaks have been identified as occurring while a person is depressed. They have not been found to precede depression and, since we believe that a cause precedes an effect, cannot be the cause of depression but simply a concomitant. Removing the physical concomitants of depression, as certain drugs do, can make a person feel better, but this does not prove that the complex human experience which we call depression can be fully understood and explained solely in physiological and chemical terms.

There are many depressed people who prefer to see their

depression as a physical illness and to live with it in the way that people live with epilepsy or diabetes. It is a nuisance, demanding regular pill-taking, and periods of good health can be ended abruptly, but, like epilepsy or diabetes, it is something you are born with and it is not your fault.

Whether or not depression is something which comes upon us or something we create for ourselves is a question which has been around for a long time. In the early days of Christianity, when monks would go into the desert and live in solitude, contemplating and worshipping God, they would sometimes find that their religious passion and enthusiasm drained away, and they were left feeling empty and despairing. This feeling they called *accidie*. Since this would often happen when the sun was high in the sky, accidie was explained as resulting from an attack by the Noonday Demon.

Being attacked by a demon wasn't your fault. Obviously you would have to fight the demon off, but it wasn't your fault the demon attacked you. So you felt ill and miserable, but you didn't have to feel responsible. Then along came the theologians of the Church and they said, 'Accidie isn't caused by a demon. You do it to yourself and it's a sin.'

So these poor monks had to acknowledge their responsibility for their accidie, feel guilt for their sin, and resolve to sin no more.

History is full of action replays. Now we have the psychiatrists, like the monks in the desert, saying, 'Beware of the noonday demon (your genes and your chemical changes)', and the psychologists, like the theologians, saying, 'There are no demons. It's you. Acknowledge your responsibility.'

Many depressed people are not concerned with this argument about who or what is responsible for their depression. All they know is that they feel very guilty because they are depressed. 'The depression,' they will say, 'is bad enough. But the guilt is worse.'

Such guilt serves to strengthen the walls of the prison of depression.

Inside the Prison of Depression

Guilt is fear, and this fear compounds the fear that one's self is going to be annihilated.

Jackie said, 'I used to get fast heartbeats. I used to go to the doctors and they said that it was tea, coffee, cigarettes that stimulate you and one doctor did send me to the hospital. I had those things plugged into me to see if I'd got a dicky heart or something to do with it. But it wasn't. It was part of the depression. That heartbeat is terrifying. Takes your breath away. You feel as though you're gasping for air and it's the last breath you'll take. Night-time used to be the worst. I used to get into bed and all I could hear was my heart going twenty to the dozen and it used to get louder and louder. The more I tried to go to sleep, the louder the heartbeat got. I eventually went to sleep, not as a normal person would know it. I wasn't fully asleep because my mind was never at rest. You're not at peace with yourself, therefore you don't sleep. You go off to sleep but it's an exhausted sleep. Many a night I would wake up and my nightclothes were absolutely wet through. I used to panic on going to sleep and panic on waking up. You're frightened of what the next day would hold, you've had no sleep the night before, you got up feeling totally exhausted from what you've gone through in the night, so you were never physically at your best at any time. You had no energy to do anything with.'

A doctor, writing of her experience of depression, said:

The most devastating experience was early morning waking. I experience a stomach lurch when people tell me about it in the surgery today. It is, of course, a useful symptom of physiological depression to 'elicit' from a patient, but experientially it is soul destroying. It felt like my own private torture chamber, devised to undermine every ounce of strength, and drive me under completely. Night after night, month after month, I woke up at two or three and felt lonely and hopeless, hour after hour, wishing someone else was awake to be alive and human, getting up quietly in the night to cry in the other room so as not to disturb my friend, and, worst, knowing that neither he nor anyone else could help, that I was cut off, removed from the world.[6]

Being frightened is exhausting. So is not sleeping. So is trying to fight the depression.

Val said, 'When the depression was at its worst, I felt as though I would fall into a bottomless black pit, and somehow I had to keep out of it. By my own efforts I had to pull myself out of it, but the effort of doing this day after day is a bit like trying to ride a bicycle uphill with the brakes applied, and you don't seem to get anywhere but neither do you fall backwards down the hill. But it's completely exhausting and there comes a time when you wake up and look at the day ahead and you just haven't the energy or strength to get on the bicycle, and those are the days when you just lie in bed and put the covers over your head and do nothing.'

With all the fear and exhaustion there is anger.

Peter said, 'People in the family were aware that something was wrong. I suppose it goes back thirty or forty years before it became a crisis situation. When it got to that point I really ceased functioning externally. I couldn't go out and go to places and so on. The other side of it which was extraordinary was that if somebody came to the house, I mean, an outsider, a friend, a visitor, then I had lots of sparkle and was joking, and nobody, I'm sure, would have had the least idea that there was anything wrong at all, and when they left, down one went and became almost incommunicado with the rest of the family.'

He went on, 'It was very frightening. I imagine that the fear fed the anger, because one got very angry. Never over really important things, always over trivial things like there wasn't any marmalade. That could lead to quite appalling rages. Rage where one became, not one, *I*, became abusive, aggressive, obscene, violent, very violent indeed, which was very frightening, and it felt wrong. One sort of felt out of kilter. I used to have the most terrible sort of post-rage senses of shame and guilt and lack of understanding. Really, quite acute misery. I mean real, you know, real tears. I mean, it's not easy, I suppose, for most men, it's not easy for me certainly to say that one used to cry, and cry and cry on occasions, and I think that because one is a man, and because these expectations are put on men, certainly in my generation, that made it even worse. Where it should have been a release, a safety valve, it didn't work like that, and you felt less than a man, you felt almost castrated in a way. It was quite a dreadful feeling.'

He explained further, 'I was very violent and aggressive and blacked eyes and broke things, I mean pots and plates and chairs and furniture, I mean I just destroyed things completely. It wasn't a question of throwing a teacup at a wall but stamping on the bits afterwards and shattering the furniture and things like that, and this was something which had been going on for years. These rages gradually became more frequent, very gradually, but they went back for a very long time when they were very, very destructive. I find it very difficult to talk about it. I don't really want to talk about it, yet I feel I should because I think this sort of thing must be happening to other people and they don't know why. I'm sure that there are things like murders that must come out of depression. It's not in any way excusing them, but if you know the cause you can sort of help stop things, can't you? Awful. Quite awful. And very destructive.'

How does the prison, and the terrible feelings within the prison, come about?

Building the Prison

Depressed people are often reluctant to talk about the strange isolation they are living in because they feel that if they tell anyone about it that person will think that they are mad. That feeling of isolation is strange because when we are coping with our lives we feel that we are connected to the rest of the world. When this feeling of being connected to our environment and to other people is present all the time we forget that it is there. It is only when it stops, when we feel disconnected, that we become aware of the missing feeling of connectedness. The feeling of being disconnected can appear when we go to some place which we find very unfamiliar. Refugees feel this disconnectedness and, having no home to go back to, suffer greatly. Other people avoid this feeling of disconnectedness by never venturing into unfamiliar territory. They usually refuse to acknowledge the sense of disconnectedness and say instead, 'We never go abroad. It's full of foreigners, you know', or 'Why go away when I've got everything I need at home?'

Similarly, if we manage to stay within a circle of relatives and friends who accept and love us we may avoid that feeling of disconnectedness which we all have when we are among strangers. If we are among strangers, we seek someone with whom we can establish some sense of connectedness. When I was travelling in India I often felt that I had come there, not from England, but from another planet. It was amusing to observe myself and other travellers looking out for someone who resembled the people we felt connected to back home. I greeted total strangers as if they were the oldest of friends, simply because we, as Australians, Americans, Britons, Dutch, Germans, shared something, had some established connections. I found myself being welcomed by people who, back in Europe, would have passed me in the street without acknowledging my existence. What we were all trying to do, though we would not have admitted it, was to banish the pain and uncertainty which arises in us when we feel that we have no connection with the world we are in.

Because the sense of connectedness is usually omnipresent and because the sense of disconnectedness is so painful, we have very few words for it. With regard to our feeling of connectedness to our environment, we talk of 'feeling at home', or, more pretentiously, 'being at one with nature'. But the Western tradition is to separate ourselves from nature and see nature as something which needs to be fought and conquered. Feeling connected to nature is not valued, as it is by the Japanese, the American Indians and the Australian Aborigines. (The Japanese feel that their capacity to be at one with nature is one of the signs of their inherent superiority over all other races.[7])

291

If we want to talk about our connectedness to other people we are restricted to talking about 'relationships' and 'communications'. To describe the actual experience of feeling connected to other people we have to talk about a sense of something inside us going out and connecting with other people, and this something we can refer to only as a 'spirit' or as a 'feeling'. 'Spirit' has all sorts of religious and magical connotations, which makes its use here unsatisfactory, while 'feelings' is a very overworked word with all sorts of meanings, and often with the connotation of vagueness and weakness.

Yet, all the time in our relationships with other people, ourselves and our world we are making statements which serve either to connect us to these or to cut ourselves off from them. A statement like 'Isn't it a glorious day!' links us to our environment, while 'I can't stand the cold' cuts us off from it. Saying of someone, 'He really pisses me off' means that we have cut ourselves off from that person, while saying to a baby, 'Aren't you just gorgeous' reflects our connection, however fleeting, to that child. Saying of yourself when you've made a mistake, 'I'm a fool' cuts you off, however temporarily, from yourself, and saying, 'But I'll do better next time' re-establishes the connection.

No one goes through life feeling totally connected all the time. We all know that there are dangers in our environment. We might begin our life trusting everybody, but we soon learn that every person has limitations and that total trust in everything should not be given to other people, no matter how good they are. We learn, too, that we are not infallible and omniscient. So we all have some disconnections.

Those of us who cope with life have put up some barriers, have made some disconnections but maintain many connections. Those people who become depressed have disconnected themselves completely, and the barriers they have built are the walls of the prison of depression.

All of us have the capacity to be depressed because all of us in our childhood laid the foundation stone of depression when we learned that as we were we were not acceptable. We had to become good. The foundation of the prison of depression is the unquestioned belief that '*No matter how good I appear to be, I am bad, evil, unacceptable to myself and to other people.*'

If you define your unacceptability as nothing very much, and if you believe that you don't have to achieve very much to come up to scratch, then you don't feel too bad about yourself, you don't keep after yourself to do better, and you don't feel frightened that people will reject you because you are not good enough. So when you make mistakes, or fail to achieve, or suffer loss and disappointment, you feel unhappy but you don't get depressed.

But if you believe that you are basically very bad and that you have to achieve a great deal in order to feel comfortable with yourself, when you make mistakes, or fail to achieve, or suffer loss and disappointment you feel enormous pain and fear. If you hold the other five major beliefs that serve to cut you off, then, instead of finding a way out of your pain through the love and wisdom of other people, you retreat into the defence of depression.

If you experience yourself as bad, then, no matter how hard you work at being good, you are always worried that other people will discover just how bad you are, and they will reject you. This makes you frightened of other people, but what frightens you further is that they might be like you, really bad but pretending to be good, and this means that you can't trust them. If we are frightened of anyone for long enough we come to hate that person. When we are frightened of another person we never get close enough to them to see what difficulties they themselves are struggling with, and so we see them having an easy life and we envy them. So, all of this can be expressed in the second belief, '*Other people are such that I fear, hate and envy them, and never trust them.*'

All of us have a set of religious or philosophical beliefs which explain to us the nature of death and the purpose of life. If we believe ourselves to be bad, and if we believe that other people are bad, either intrinsically like ourselves or simply because they have or will reject us, then when we think about life and death, we come to the conclusion that '*Life is terrible and death is worse.*'

If you see yourself as bad, if you are estranged from other people and you fear life and death, you then believe that '*Only bad things have happened to me in the past and only bad things will happen to me in the future.*'

You learned of your badness when you were a child when you learned that so many of the things you did were bad. One of the very bad things you did was to get angry, and so you grew up believing that '*Anger is evil.*'

When you were learning just how bad you were and how frightening other people were, you had to do something to protect yourself. The one protection always available to people who find themselves in a weak position is to vow never to forgive those people who have hurt them. So you grew up with the belief that you must '*Never forgive.*'

Not forgiving other people means that you are cut off from them. Believing that it is morally wrong to forgive, you never forgive yourself, and, if you believe in God, you believe that He will never forgive you.

These six beliefs can be felt and expressed in a multitude of different ways. They are not strange beliefs. There is strong support for each of them in our culture. Many people live with them unquestioned all their lives and do not become profoundly depressed because they are able to balance their sense of badness with the standards they set themselves in meeting their obligations and in achieving their goals. But if they feel themselves failing, then their sense of badness increases until they feel overwhelmed by it.

Feeling Bad about Yourself

Feeling bad about yourself is something that we choose to do. We can choose to feel good about ourselves. But it is very difficult to feel good about yourself if the people around you keep showing you by their actions, if not their words, that they do not think very highly of you. As Jan Morris set about changing from being a man, James Morris, the journalist whose adventures in getting the news of the first ascent of Everest back to England in time for the Queen's coronation were almost as exciting as those of Hilary and Tensing themselves, to Jan Morris, the travel writer, she found that how people perceived her changed her perception of herself. This change of perception affected her actions. In her autobiography, *Conundrum*, she wrote:

We are told that the social gap between the sexes is narrowing, but I can only report that having, in the second half of the twentieth century, experienced life in both roles, there seems to me no aspect of existence, no moment of the day, no contact, no arrangement, no response, which is not different for men and for women. The very tone of voice in which I was now addressed, the very posture of the person next in the queue, the very feel in the air when I entered a room or sat at a restaurant table, constantly emphasized my change of status.

And if others' responses shifted, so did my own. The more I was treated as a woman, the more woman I became. I adapted willy-nilly. If I was assumed to be incompetent at reversing cars, or opening bottles, oddly incompetent I found myself becoming. If a case was thought to be too heavy for me, inexplicably I found it so myself . . . Men treated me more and more as their junior . . . my lawyer, in an unguarded moment one morning, even called me 'my child'; and so, addressed every day of my life as an inferior, involuntarily, month by month, I accepted the condition. I discovered that even now men prefer women to be less informed, less able, less talkative, and certainly less self-centred than they are themselves: so I generally obliged them.[8]

In depression the sense of being bad intensifies to excruciating proportions.

Jackie said, 'I felt I'd probably end up in the psychiatric hospital because I felt as though I was going mad. Nothing seemed to fit together. I couldn't concentrate on anything. I had no interest in anything. No interest in living. No interest in the house, my job, and least of all myself. You tend to put yourself last on the list in everything. You just drain yourself from everything around you.'

She went on, 'I feel as though I'm two people. One's telling me to do the good things in life and the other side's bad. And the bad always wins over the good. I feel a weak person, so I suppose character does come into it. But I feel it's not so much character, it's personality with me. I feel that along life's way I've had it all knocked out of me, which doesn't help a depressed person at all. It doesn't matter what stage of depression you're in. Lack of confidence in oneself can destroy you anyway.'

Peter said, 'I didn't like myself. I think that my self-image was very, very bad. I used to wonder why I was such an awful person. My attitude to people who appeared to like me was "If they really knew me they wouldn't like me. They wouldn't have any time for me at all."'

We all make mistakes. We all get rejected. The only way to cope with these reversals is to be kind to yourself. But if you feel that you are bad and don't deserve any comfort then you won't do anything to meet your own needs. Even if you might consider doing something for yourself, you haven't time to do anything for you are far too busy.

Meeting Other People's Needs and Blaming Yourself

Posy Simmonds, who chronicles the lives of the English in her marvellous cartoons, has a keen eye for the ways in which we experience ourselves as bad and have to work hard to be good.

Wendy Weber is a practised worrier who works hard at being good. She knows that to be good she mustn't meet her needs, not even simply worrying about them.

The resentment which a depressed person feels is very much the resentment of having given so much to others and received so little in return. Jackie said, 'I've had fifteen years of marriage and two daughters and I feel I've missed out along the way. But to say what I've missed out on, I don't know. People say that life is what you make it, but I honestly can't see that. I feel as though I've given that much of my life away to different people along the

296

Guardian 3 March 1986

line and I don't feel I've got anything in return. And I still feel angry about that. That gets me depressed.'

Jackie often got angry with her family but the first time she could actually talk about her resentment was when she came into therapy. For Elizabeth it was only in the safety of my room that she could explain how she felt to her husband.

Bernard could not understand why Elizabeth was depressed. He was a very caring, loving husband, but what gradually emerged in our discussions was that he could not admit that he made mistakes and he put the responsibility for all mistakes onto his wife. She accepted the responsibility, blamed herself and thought even more badly of herself.

Elizabeth said, 'If something goes wrong, it's always my fault. If I write him a list of things that have to be done and he forgets one of them he says, "It's your fault. If it was important you should have underlined it." Then I think, "Yes, I should have thought of that – but all the things on the list are important. I shouldn't have asked him to do so much." So then I say to him, "Well, don't you bother, I'll do it", and I do. If we have a row and he storms out of the house, I spend the rest of the day going over and over it in my mind, trying to work out what I'd done wrong and what I can do to put it right.'

This was one of those marriages where the wife has to appear to be weak so that she can support him in his role as the strong, unchanging, infallible hero.

I asked Elizabeth, 'Do you feel that Bernard depends on you a great deal?'

'Yes,' she said, 'but he makes out that he doesn't.'

Bernard looked puzzled as Elizabeth and I talked. Then he said, 'We're talking at two different levels. When you said about me depending on Elizabeth, I thought that you meant I needed her, relied on her, to look after me, cooking, that sort of thing, but you're both talking about something else.'

'Yes,' said Elizabeth, 'of course I wash your shirts. That goes without saying. But that's not the kind of depending on I mean. You depend on me to take responsibility for your mistakes.'

Arthur came to see me because he had heard me on a local radio phone-in, where several callers had described their fear and depression.

'That's what happens to me,' he said.

He was a very successful man, at the top in his profession.

'I always set goals and I see that my staff achieve them.'

I asked, 'Why is it important to set goals and achieve them?'

'I don't like coming second.'

'Why set goals?'

'That's the best way to hold everything together and to move things forward.' He illustrated this by making a circle of his arms and moving slightly forward.

'Why is it important to hold things together?'

'Well, security.'

'Why is it important to have security?'

'That's hard to put into words.'

'What would happen to you if you didn't have any security, if you couldn't control things and everything fell into chaos?'

'That's what's happening to me now.'

We talked about the fear that came with early-morning waking and how this was the fear of annihilation. I said, 'I expect as a small child you were often nearly annihilated by your father. He would just about wipe you out as a person and you had to find some way of defending yourself.'

'That's where I learned to achieve. It was the only way I could please – well, nothing pleased him. By coming first, second or third, I could protect myself. Coming last, that was unthinkable.'

He would have liked to have played rugby, but his father wouldn't let him. He had to go home straight after school and do his chores on the farm. He couldn't stay at school and play rugby. Yet his father would talk with great pride and interest about his schoolmate who was a good rugby player. 'He was always telling me about Bob's achievements, yet he wouldn't let me play. I couldn't understand that. I played rugby when I went to university, but that was too late to be any good.'

It was not until Arthur had talked about these things that he could recognize how all of his achievements had been for his father, not for himself. He had lived his life meeting his father's needs.

Those people who spend their lives meeting other people's needs become very skilled in blaming themselves when they feel they have failed in doing this. Because women are supposed to spend much of their lives meeting other people's needs, they are usually well trained in blaming themselves.

Recently I met a group of trainee midwives to discuss any of the psychological problems they might come across in their work. They immediately raised the problem of stillbirth. What could a nurse say to a woman whose baby had just died?

Two of the nurses talked about one woman they had nursed who had given birth to a beautiful eight-pound dead baby. The cause of death was a separated placenta. Some weeks previously the woman had gone to a GP with a complaint of pain in her pelvic girdle. He treated her for a urinary infection. It must have been at that point the placenta had become detached, but the uterus was blocked, so there was no sign of bleeding. Thus the baby died.

One of the nurses was with the woman when, in hospital, the obstetrician and midwife tried to locate the baby's heartbeat. The nurse told us how no one spoke to the woman, but left her alone while they prodded her stomach or huddled in corners and talked in whispers. Only the student midwife sat with her and held her hand. 'What could I say to her?' she asked me.

We talked about what the woman would have been feeling then and later, when she would be trying to work out why this terrible thing had happened. Was it better to see it as a random accident or as something with an identifiable cause? We came to the conclusion that it would be better to see the death as having an identifiable cause because that made for greater safety. If we can identify the cause of that death then perhaps we could act differently in future and so avoid a similar death.

We then looked at the question of whom the woman should blame. The nurses quickly absolved the GP of blame. 'He wasn't her usual doctor,' they said.

Of course she would not blame the obstetrician, they said. She would blame herself. 'She would say to herself that she should have rested more or shouldn't have lifted something heavy.'

'Women are conditioned to blame themselves,' one of them said, 'Men always blame them, and women accept this and blame themselves.'

All the nurses present agreed with this. They all seemed quite adept at self-blame. Of course, by taking the blame upon yourself you may not be happy but you do feel virtuous.

If we are born into a family who accepts us as we are, with all our human attributes, we grow up knowing that everything in the world is a mixture of good and bad, and that the bad bits can be good and the good bits bad, and that things are changing all the time. But if we are born into a family which shows us that we are not good enough and that we have to learn to measure up to some high standard of goodness, we come to believe that no one and nothing is acceptable unless they are perfect. Since change means imperfection (you can't go from perfection to greater perfection, but only from perfection to imperfection) all change is dangerous. So we grow up wanting perfection and security.

Wanting Perfection and Security

Jackie said, 'My world is a fantasy world where everything stays the same. Clean and bright and white, and you just stare; it's just like happiness, I suppose, within a white world. I don't like a lot of change. We all, as human beings, have to accept change through our lives, but I don't like a lot of change, quick change, not that involves me anyway . . . It's very hard to lower your standards; well, I find it is anyway. Because if I don't keep the standards I've already got, then I feel more depressed. So when the strength is draining, you've got no energy, you've still got to keep up those standards. Well, I have anyway, to prove to myself that I'm still around.'

Val said, 'I've always been taught that if a job's worth doing it's worth doing well, and I took that to the extreme of having to do everything perfectly, which is of course impossible, and you always fall short so that you feel you've failed, and it becomes a sort of treadmill, the more you feel you've failed the harder you've got to try to be perfect. But it's an impossible goal. You never achieve perfection . . . I simply felt guilty because I couldn't achieve perfection. I constantly punished myself for not being perfect. The perfect me never made mistakes, did everything perfectly. I was completely self-sufficient. I didn't intrude on other people, kept my needs to myself, denied my own needs and thought I was doing the best thing.'

Being depressed is an attempt to be secure and to prevent change. It can give a sense of complete changelessness, but it never achieves the other goal of perfection, no matter how much you drive yourself to be perfect. When your failure to be perfect makes you totally despair, you can always seek perfection and security in death.

Suicide

Everyone at some times thinks of suicide. Most of us reject it, but very often it is the thought that we can choose to leave life that gives us the strength to stay.

If we are able to accept ourselves we are able to accept our death. If we believe that our life ends in death, accepting ourselves means that we see ourselves making the best use of our lives. If we believe that our death will be a doorway to another life, we see ourselves as going to an even better life.

302

But if we don't accept ourselves we are not able to accept our death. If we believe that our life ends in death, not accepting ourselves means that we see ourselves as wasting our lives. If we believe that our death will be a doorway to another life, we see ourelves as going to further punishment.

The thought of the horrors of death keeps many a depressed person from suicide. But, as the pain of depression increases, death starts to look more attractive. When the world outside your prison looks totally unacceptable, the only escape that seems possible from the prison is into death.

Jackie said, 'I think that every person that goes through a depression does think of committing suicide. It is the easiest way to get out of the fright that they are living in. There isn't another world outside the fright and the fear and the pain that one lives in, when you are depressed.'

Human beings have a wonderful capacity, as they approach death, to reconstrue it. Most people, as they get older, find that the thought of their death gets less and less frightening, until in old age it becomes a friend whose arrival is anticipated with contentment. A similar reconstruing of death can be done by the depressed person who looks at death as the only possible release. The person may change from thinking, 'I wouldn't commit suicide because I wouldn't want to upset my family' to 'I would be helping my family by dying'. Or the person may change from seeing death as a terrifying annihilation of the self to a welcome merging into the wholeness of everything.

Val said, 'When you reach a point of black despair and there seems no way out and you're threatened to be swallowed up in this black nothingness, then death is very appealing, and I believe that whatever lies beyond death has got to be better than this life that I was leading, and it seemed very attractive . . . I hadn't really decided on one particular method. I mean, one toys with all sorts of ideas. The most attractive one was to throw myself off a cliff into the sea. I love the sea, and there's something very magnetic about standing on a cliff top and watching the waves swilling, and to be sucked into that sort of spiral, I'd be part of the mass. There's something very appealing about that.'

Sometimes when we shut ourselves in depression we don't want to come out because we don't want to discover that the things which made us lock ourselves away were really not all that important and that if we acknowledge this people will say, 'I told you so!' When you are a child and you get so upset that you have to rush to your bedroom and slam the door, it is horrible, when you come out àgain, if the adults laugh at you, or tell you how naughty you were to get angry, or belittle your major injuries by offering you a sweetie to make you better, or telling you to realize just how lucky you are compared with the starving children of Africa. If you feel that all you have is your hurts, then you have to hang on to them, even if this means dying.

A doctor wrote, 'I cannot see why one should not have the right to end a life of intolerable mental pain. Promises that the pain will vanish, one's suicidal wishes evaporate, and the rest of one's life be perfect euphoria, are irrelevant. It would still not be enough to compensate for the agony of the present.'[9] Not long after writing this, this young doctor took her life.

The Uses of Depression

When we were children we created our life story, not just the story of our family and our life so far, but also what our life would be. Our stories were not just 'When I grow up I'm going to be a doctor', or 'When I grow up I'm going to travel all around the world', but also contained plans for compensating us for the hurts and disappointments in childhood. A boy, left lonely and ignored by his parents, may make an important part of his story getting married and having a large family. A girl may plan to become famous and so receive from her father the recognition and admiration which he denied her in childhood.

When we reach adulthood we may not be as consciously aware of our compensatory fantasies of our childhood as when we were a child, but such fantasies still operate in forming our decisions and in creating a sense of dissatisfaction and disappointment whenever life threatens not to fulfil them. When life threatens never to fulfil them, or to destroy what we have created in their fulfilment, we know that we are in the greatest of danger. The whole structure of our being is revealed to us as something of no substance. It will be swept away like matchsticks in a flood and we shall be annihilated. To stem the flood and to create something which will hold us together we become depressed.

Sometimes the defence of depression is needed for only a short time. Within a few days or weeks a person may, from within the safety of the depression, review himself and his life, and make some adjustments to his perceptions of these so as to be able to create anew a continuing sense of self and to live his life with hope.

This kind of experience is very common. I recall how one day when I was talking about depression to a group of women who work for the charity Home Start, one woman told of her experience. She had gone into hospital to await the birth of her second child, confident that she and her husband shared a close, loving relationship and that their children were an important part of this relationship. The next twenty-four hours proved her wrong. She gave birth to a Down's syndrome baby and her husband totally rejected the child. She described how, as she discovered this, she felt herself falling downwards in a spiral of panic. Then, somehow, the falling stopped, and she was held safely (here she held out her hands to show us how) within the walls of depression. Within this safety, over the following months, she was able to review her situation and to recognize that she had to deal with the reality of her marriage. There were practical things to be done, and she did them.

But sometimes there are no practical things which can be done. There are no remedies other than the relinquishing of those fantasies and wishes which sustained us in our childhood.

Milton had received the usual diagnosis of endogenous depression from a psychiatrist and had had the usual treatment. But the depression did not go away. Taking Imiprimine made him feel a bit better and he could get back to work, but every day was a misery and a struggle. His wife phoned me and arranged an appointment, and Milton, somewhat reluctantly, came along with her.

There was no reason why he should be depressed. He had a good job, a nice home, a loving wife and family. The depression came out of the blue.

Well, not quite. His depression started soon after his son, who was doing his A levels preparatory to going to university, announced that he was leaving school and getting a job. Nowadays this is not an unusual thing to do. No longer is having a university degree a guarantee of getting a job, and many young people, when they see the opportunity to get a job, abandon their studies and take the job. But this was irrelevant to Milton. It was tremendously important to him that his son should stay at school. He should get qualifications.

Milton made 'qualifications' sound like the Holy Grail. I asked him why qualifications were important to him, and he said, 'Because I haven't got any.' Because he didn't have any qualifications he had been a disappointment to his father.

Milton's wife protested, 'Your father was proud of you and the work you do.'

Milton brushed this aside and explained to me, 'My father was a wonderful man. I'm not half the man he was. I've always looked up to him.'

One of Sheldon Kopp's Eternal Truths is *If you have a hero, look again; you have diminished yourself in some way.*[10] This indeed was what was happening here.

Milton, as a small boy, had looked up to his father as small boys have to do. After all, fathers are taller and bigger than them. His father was an important man in their local community. He was on the Council and the committees of different clubs and sporting bodies, so he was not at home most evenings. This meant that he was not there to protect Milton from his mother. Milton's parents did not get on, and his mother often took her frustration out on Milton. Milton dared not tell his father how angry and disappointed he was with him. His father would not accept his son's anger. He never let Milton win an argument, so Milton never had the joyous experience of feeling that he was the equal of his dad. Instead, Milton grew up never getting angry, but prone, as his wife said, to sulking.

The only way to bury his anger with his father was to concentrate on his admiration for his father. But the only way he could maintain this uncritical, sentimental admiration of his father was to see himself as his father's inferior. (Milton seemed surprised when I suggested to him that it is possible to admire someone without feeling inferior to that person.) Inferiors always feel obliged to give their superiors gifts, in the hope of receiving love and approval in return, and so Milton wanted to give to his father the gift of gaining his qualifications, something which his father had not done for himself.

However, National Service and other problems prevented Milton from gaining those precious pieces of paper with his name on them. So he comforted himself with the promise that his son's gaining of qualifications would be the gift he would give to his father. But his son insisted on doing something which would mean that he would not gain any qualifications. So when his son left school, Milton's world was in ruins. Being depressed was the only way he could stave off the recognition of this, but it meant going on feeling inferior, 'not half the man my father was'.

Being depressed is a state of great security. Jackie said, 'I go very quiet. I don't want to know anybody. Very angry. I get very hurtful, not intentional hurt, but that's the only way I can get through to people, so they don't get any closer. If I hurt them, they'll stay away and therefore I can be on my own in this depression, and hide behind the mask and just solely by hurting people, being quiet, feeling angry inside and putting the barrier up, that's how I can keep people away, which I feel helps me in the state of depression . . . I used to feel safe within the blackness. A fear of being with people. Being really frightened of everything and everybody around you. It's just so painful. You feel drained of everything . . . Hiding behind the mask is putting yourself away from the outside world, the world you were frightened of stepping into, but people still seeing you with that smile, the joking, the laughing, and that is where the mask comes on. Behind that mask I am suffering hurt, pain, rejection, helplessness, but behind the mask and shutting myself within four walls I feel secure, because none of the outside world can come in unless I let them hurt me.'

Because depression gives a feeling of security, the depressed person can feel very much in control. (We are always capable of being two contrary things at once. Depression is always a state of complete helplessness and complete control.) A depressed person can take great pride in being in control.

Val said, 'I certainly felt a certain pride in carrying this depression and coping with it, living with it, not letting anyone else see that I was depressed and I felt, from a religious point of view, that this was my cross and I would bear it, and there was a certain pride in doing that . . . and I've always wanted to be in control of things so that I would know exactly what would happen and I could control what would happen and avoid situations that might cause some spontaneous action on my part. It's very difficult to act spontaneously because you don't know where it's going to take you and it might lead you into some risky positions. You might get hurt. Depression is a sort of security. As I've taken some steps on the path out of depression it's been very tempting to slip back, and I can see that over the years I've used depression as security to avoid taking responsibility for myself. It's a way of avoiding making decisions.'

Changing: First- and Second-order Changes

A lot of people become depressed and go and see their GP who prescribes a course of anti-depressants, and after a few weeks they are their old selves again. Other people see their GP and are sent to a psychiatrist who brings them into hospital. There, away from their responsibilities, and finding life in the wards comfortable and restful, they take their medication and in a few weeks they feel much better and go home. Some people, perhaps while they are in hospital, or perhaps just following the advice of their GP or a friend, find a counsellor, perhaps a Marriage Guidance counsellor, or a Samaritan, or a psychiatric nurse, or a social worker, and spend some time talking things over with that person. They don't go deeply into things, but they do express a lot of the feelings that they have kept bottled up and they sort out some confusions in their thinking, just by having to explain things to another person. After a few sessions, or perhaps just one session, they feel much better and can get on with their lives.

Most depressed people who do one of these things cease to be depressed, and, of these, most do not get depressed again. Some depressed people do not cease to be depressed because these methods do not reveal and confront the underlying feelings and attitudes for which depression is a necessary defence. Those people who cease to be depressed but who later become depressed again have been pushed back into this defence by some event which threatens their existence.

We can understand these changes if we think of them in terms of first-order change or second-order change.

All the ideas we have are in terms of pairs of contrasts. We think of up/down, in/out, here/there, good/bad, perfect/imperfect, top/bottom. We can picture these pairs of ideas as being the ends of a line or dimension, and we can give things a place on that line. For instance:

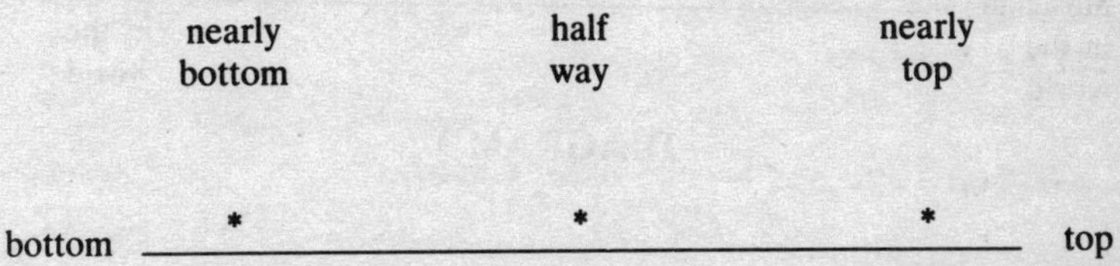

	nearly		half		nearly	
	bottom		way		top	

bottom —————— * —————— * —————— * —————— top

DIAGRAM 1

The ideas and attitudes we have about ourselves we can think of as a line and we can place ourselves on that line. If we think of ourselves as, say, an athlete, we could position ourselves on a line like this.

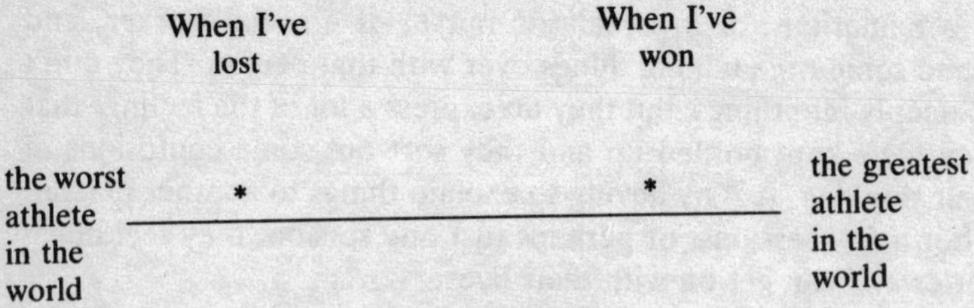

When I've
lost

When I've
won

the worst
athlete
in the
world

      *

      *

the greatest
athlete
in the
world

DIAGRAM 2

Our position changes as we win or lose.

A first-order change is when we change our position on the dimension on which we assess ourselves.

Suppose you decide to give up thinking of yourself as an athlete and decide to think of yourself as a musician instead. You have abandoned your greatest athlete/worst athlete dimension and acquired a new one.

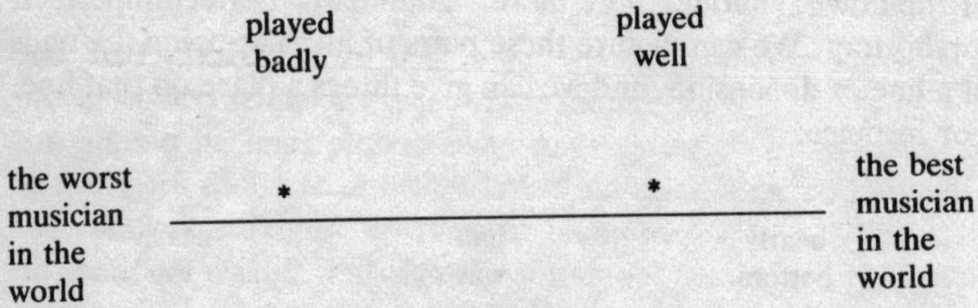

played
badly

played
well

the worst
musician
in the
world

      *

      *

the best
musician
in the
world

DIAGRAM 3

Now you have made a second-order change.

A second-order change is where we give up one way of assessing ourselves and acquire another one.

It seems that the changes which take place when depressed people take a course of anti-depressants, or have a few weeks in hospital, or some counselling are first-order changes.

Turning Fear into Depression

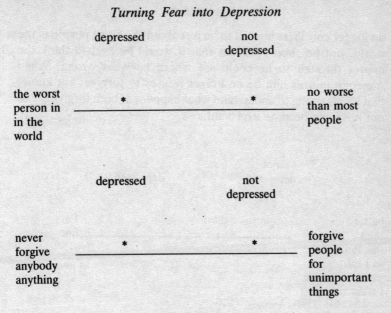

DIAGRAM 4

Here the person holds the belief that he is basically bad, but feels that this is a continuum from being the worst person in the world to being no worse than most people (and all people are basically bad). He holds the belief that it is wrong to forgive, but feels that this is a continuum from never forgiving anybody for anything to forgiving people for unimportant things. At times he experiences himself as close to being the worst person in the world and close to being totally unforgiving, and then he has shut himself off from himself and everyone else, and he is depressed. He can make a first-order change by feeling better about himself and by forgiving some people. Thus he brings himself in better contact with himself and others, so can leave the state of depression. But he still uses these same dimensions and he can always shift on them back into depression.

To give up the defence of depression forever the person has to make a second-order change. Thus, when he makes a mistake he no longer considers himself to be just about the worst person in the world, but he simply decides that it would be best to think the matter through so he could see where he went wrong. When someone injures him he no longer refuses to forgive, but knows that by his trying to understand what happened, both forgiving and not forgiving become irrelevant.

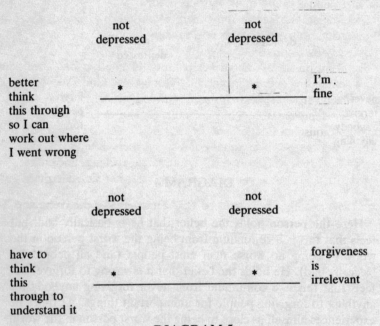

DIAGRAM 5

Such beliefs render the defence of depression unnecessary.

Some people make these second-order changes by themselves. This is the ordinary human process of growing older and wiser. Some people need a therapist to help them on the journey of self-understanding.

Leaving the Prison of Depression

Whenever Lucy came to see me she would talk of her panic attacks and her physical sickness, but only sometimes, right at the end of the session, she would say something which revealed her depression. If I inquired, she did not want to talk about it. Like so many depressed people, she feared that if she talked about what she was feeling, people would think she was mad.

So I loaned her a copy of my *Depression: the Way Out of Your Prison*. She returned it at our next session, saying, 'Yes, I'm going to buy my own copy.'

She went on to talk about her parents. Her father had always been demanding and authoritarian. ('But he is so kind,' she would say, whenever what was being said sounded critical.) Her mother had been depressed for all of Lucy's life. At twelve Lucy had taken on many household duties and, as she said, 'I worried about her.'

Now her mother likes to visit and spend the whole day. Gavin, Lucy's husband, has to drive her home in the evening. She comes, not as a friend, but as a mother to look after her sick daughter.

'I think mother likes me to be sick. That way she can come and spend the day with me.'

Gavin smiled in relief. This is what had always been clear to him, but he had to wait for Lucy to see it. 'I'd get a hammering if I said it,' he laughed.

Lucy didn't find her mother's visits a help, quite the reverse. But she dared not ask her not to come, and she dared not get better.

Quite often a person may see what needs to be done to leave the prison of depression but is prevented from carrying it out by another person, usually the spouse. One of the reasons that so many married women stay depressed is because their husbands will not allow them to seek interests outside the home which would build up their confidence and give them a sense of being a person in their own right. I have met many a husband who cannot tolerate his wife ceasing to be depressed because then she becomes argumentative and wants her own way. Similarly, a depressed husband may feel that he cannot develop those aspects of himself which he had given up in the process of becoming a good, responsible person, because if he does he would have to confront his wife whom he sees as being much stronger than himself. Moreover, developing himself could mean becoming less of a husband and father. He may not need to go to the South Seas to paint, but it might mean taking up rock climbing and giving up painting the house.

One of the striking things in talking to people about the events leading up to their depression is the way in which they had, over a period of a year or so, given up doing those things which gave them a sense of personal value, not just by doing the things which made them feel virtuous, but which strengthened their sense of I AM. Depressed men describe things like giving up the sport which they enjoyed, or leaving their smallholding for a suburban garden, or changing their sports car for a family saloon. The protective value against depression of a job outside the home for a woman is well documented in the research literature. It is not that the work itself necessarily boosts the woman's self-confidence – so much of women's work is menial – but that in the workplace people speak to her as the person she is, and not, as at home, in one of her roles of wife, mother, daughter, daughter-in-law, sister, aunt, granddaughter, grandmother. Morover, working means that a woman has some money of her own. It may not be much, but it is her own.

If a married woman wishes to avoid being depressed there are two things which she must make sure she possesses. Her own bank account and a driving licence. These, combined with a sense of her own worth, such that she will always take the time to recognize and to meet her own needs, will ensure that the shades of the prisonhouse of depression will never descend upon her. If she should lose her sense of self-worth, then these two possessions will help her overcome the practical problems she faces when she decides to leave the prison.

Therapists always hope that something will happen in the lives of their depressed clients which will help them gain confidence in themselves. When Jackie first came to see me she had completely lost confidence in herself and was deeply depressed. When, two months later, the producer of the BBC TV programme *The Mind Box*, Angela Tilby, asked me if Jackie would take part in the programme, I thought this most unlikely. I didn't even want to put Angela's request to Jackie because I felt that this would have been yet another burden for her. But Angela was insistent, so I complied with her request. Jackie shocked me by saying immediately, 'Yes, I'll do it', and then put me in my place by explaining that 'I get so frightened when I come to see you that having a film crew in the room at the same time wouldn't make any difference.'

Jackie had a lot of work to do in this programme. When the filming was complete it was clear that all had gone well. Jackie came to see me, and she was no longer depressed, and has not been depressed since. The making of the programme in which she was a key figure gave her the opportunity to make a statement about herself and to achieve something in her own right.

In one of her interviews with Angela, Jackie said, 'I find it very hard to forgive. I can forget but I never forgive anybody . . . I think that forgiving is getting closer to people and I don't want to get that close.'

But she was already in the process of making a second-order change. Now she thinks that forgiving is a good idea, and that when you accept yourself there is no danger in getting close to people.

Peter made a similar second-order change. He said, 'I've learned that I don't mind being emotional. I mean I can cope with being emotional, whereas at one time I used to feel guilty about it.'

When Val was reviewing the changes she had made she said to me, 'The one thing you said which I hadn't heard before was that we can change. I never thought that I could change and no one had ever suggested to me before that I could change. People sort of pulled me to pieces and said, "Well, you feel guilty, you feel as though you're not worth anything", but they never suggested that I could change the way I felt.'

She said to Angela, 'In my experience of depression I feel as

315

though I'm falling into a bottomless pit and if I let go I shall just disappear into the bottom of this pit. But I felt a love reaching out to me like a pair of hands. I've wanted to let go and disappear into the black hole but somehow the hands won't let me go. I used to think that I would find nothing inside me, but I've come to realize as my depression lifted, that if you let go, you don't fall into a bottomless pit, and that the hands that I thought were beyond and outside me reaching out to me in love are actually within me and supporting me from within and if I let go I fall into these hands that hold me in love.'

She went on, 'I have changed from feeling that I have to suffer by trying to be perfect to earn God's love to a feeling that I only have to be still and be myself and reach within me to the . . . I suppose the soul centre you might call it, and find God there. Ever present. Loving, giving Himself and creating a sort of peace and drawing strength and confidence from that. I suppose the biggest shift is that I don't carry a burden of guilt any more in the same way. I've learned to forgive myself. I think that's the biggest shift. I used to go and pray for forgiveness, but I never really experienced forgiveness because I never forgave myself for not being what I thought I ought to be. Once you can do that and be yourself, then you live comfortably with yourself and I think that's the biggest change . . . If you start opening yourself out to relationships with other people, this is life-giving. In depression you cut yourself off, and it's death. You know, thinking of the garden, a flower opens out and can be crushed in the same way as a person. If you open yourself out you can be hurt and crushed but you've got to let this life blossom forth somehow . . . When I was depressed I sought to prove that I was good enough to be loved, and this really kept the depression going because I had to be perfect. But as I've grown spiritually and learned more about my depression I've realized that I am loved just as I am. I don't have to prove I'm lovable, and that has been an immense relief. I can stop the struggle, let go, and rest within the love I've found within me. It's nothing new. It's just something that's always been an intellectual fact to me but now has become part of my experience. Thousands of people must have discovered it in the past.'

Angela asked Jackie and Val about me. What they said about me is what any client who has found a therapist helpful would say about that therapist. As therapists go, I am very run-of-the-mill. Good therapists are usually too busy doing good therapy to spend much time writing about it. I have quoted Jackie and Val here because they give a good explanation of what therapy and therapists are about.

Angela asked Jackie, 'What does Dorothy do to help you confront the dark things you're feeling?'

Jackie said, 'She makes you see them in a different light. A depressed person sees it from one angle, but there are that many different ways of looking at it, and Dorothy goes through all those and somewhere along the line you attach yourself to one you can relate to and see it in the way she's telling you to see it. But whether you accept it, that's a different thing.'

'Tell me how she's surprised you.'

'She surprises me in the quickness of weighing a person up. On the first occasion she met me, I felt she had known me all my life.'

'What does it feel like when she shows you the things that you've said?'

'It brings back to you what you had once forgotten and you think to yourself I didn't think like that and I didn't say that, but you did, but you're seeing it differently through talking . . . You don't need sympathy and kindness – you need understanding.'

Val said, 'I feel as comfortable talking to Dorothy as you can be sharing things that you'd rather people didn't know about. But Dorothy has no vested interest in what you tell her . . . No axe to grind. She's completely neutral. I think it's important to have someone that you can talk to quite freely and openly, even if it's only to help you sort out your own ideas, and Dorothy helps you make sense of what you're saying . . . I don't suppose she's always happy. I think she's an optimist. I think she has an inner strength with which she can cope, which is the sort of strength that most depressed people don't have. She doesn't just listen. She makes you look at yourself honestly. She can make you laugh at yourself. When Dorothy takes you to pieces you can see how ridiculous it was really and you can smile about it.'

She went on, 'When things get tough, and they do still get tough, and I think it's going to be a lifetime's hard work, there are times when I think "I can't cope with this" and I want to rush and talk to Dorothy but I don't. I sit down and I think about the things I've learned from Dorothy and try and apply it to the situation I'm in and sort it out for myself. I have felt angry with Dorothy as I came out of depression and started getting more involved in more things. I felt it was getting out of hand because I'm so used to having everything under control and I wanted to slip back into depression for security but I've learned to cope with that one now.'[11]

In his account of his experience of depression Pat Wakeling wrote, 'It seems to me that from depression itself one learns nothing. Rather it is from what one makes of depression that benefit derives. Depression is depression. It lays waste and may prove, too, a total waste of time unless one uses the experience, and all its consequences, to build anew. In that sense, it is an experience like any other; yet simultaneously unique in the opportunities it affords . . . Perhaps the most precious outcome of this personal development – of which depression was a vital part – has been the certain knowledge that, for me, depression is a sign that I am not dealing honestly with my problems.'[12]

It is the truth which will set you free.

Chapter Nine

Turning Fear into Mania

In the psychiatric lexicon there are many words to do with depression. Quite popular are the terms *bipolar* and *unipolar* depression, and, even more popular, *mania and depression*. Unipolar depression is simply depression; bipolar depression is where the person becomes manic as well as depressed. Gordon Claridge described the manic person as being

> restless, quick, and impulsive to act, and his rapid talk expresses frequently changing trains of thought that are sometimes difficult to follow. In this case delusional ideas will reflect the manic individual's supreme optimism and grandiose beliefs about himself, beliefs that may lead him to undertake wildly improbable schemes that are far beyond his capacity or financial resources and which, if thwarted by others, may cause him to become irritated and paranoid.[1]

This restlessness and quickness might be no more than an exaggeration of the person's ordinary life style, with more tasks being undertaken, more work done, more talking and less sleep. In this case the person would be labelled as *hypomanic*. When the activity goes beyond simply a heightened level of activity, when the person undertakes a great many activities and few of them wisely, the person would be labelled *manic*. When there is no sign of wisdom and forethought, when the person acts without regard to the realities of the situation, and becomes unable to rest or to listen to what others have to say, he is diagnosed as having a *manic-depressive psychosis*.

At one time in my life I spent a great deal of time with people who fitted one of these categories. I was working in a psychiatric department where the head of the department, Professor F.A.

Jenner, was researching into the metabolic basis of mood change. So these delightful people came, for short visits or for long, to the clinic or the research unit where they patiently and co-operatively allowed their blood and urine to be sampled and most aspects of their physical functioning to be observed and recorded, along with a record of their moods, whether they were 'up' or 'down'.

According to the theory, periods of mania, followed by depression, followed again by mania and so on were the result of cyclical changes in the functioning of the body. That certain cycles do exist was well documented. All that needed to be done was to find the cyclical physiological changes which produced the cycles of mania and depression. I wasn't a doctor, nor a physiologist, nor biologist nor chemist, so there was no part I could play in this research. Except, perhaps, elaborate the descriptions we already had of the behaviour of these people when they were manic or depressed. So this meant that instead of wearing a white coat and doing important things in the laboratory, or recording data on the report sheets in the office (this was before the invasion of computers) I sat on the sidelines, usually in my office or in the garden or in the patients' day room where I talked to the patients and observed the goings-on in the ward.

At this stage, at the end of the sixties, I knew very little about depression and mania except what I read in textbooks, so I was quite ready to accept the theory of the metabolic basis of these extremes of mood change. However, through my observations and conversations, I began to wonder.

One of the people who visited the unit every few months was a man called Jimmy who, in his youth, had wreaked havoc on himself and his family through the wild excesses of his behaviour when he was in a manic state. He had ended up in a hospital where Professor Jenner was beginning his researches, and Jimmy came to play a major part in this work. His mood changes lasted twenty-four hours each. For twenty-four hours he was in the depths of depression; and then, suddenly, like Cinderella turning into a princess, he became manic. But when the clock struck twelve, or thereabouts, like Cinderella he was stripped of all his finery and he plunged down into a depression again. So he and Professor

Jenner, himself no mean worker when he was in an expansive mood, entered upon a series of investigations which included, at one time, being shut up together in a large box in which each day was no longer twenty-four hours but varied according to the experimental design. Professor Jenner would often talk of the importance in science of 'dotting the i's and crossing the t's', and this work dotted a lot of i's and crossed a lot of t's.

Jimmy was still having quite large mood swings which made it difficult for him to plan a life outside the hospital. Professor Jenner became interested in the research on the use of lithium carbonate in manic-depression and decided to see if lithium would help Jimmy. It did, most remarkably. When I met Jimmy he had been living outside the hospital for some time and to all intents and purposes was an ordinary man. However, those people who knew him had no difficulty identifying whether today was an up day or a down day for Jimmy. There was a difference, and each change came every twenty-four hours. On one day there was a liveliness and on the next a stillness. Proof, if proof were needed, that these mood changes were the result of physiological changes and that these changes could be controlled by lithium.

And yet. My 'and yet' came one day when I was sitting in the garden with Jimmy and he was telling me about his life. He expressed regret for the hurt and damage he had done to different members of his family, and then he said, 'When I think about my family and what I've done to them, and about all the chances I've had and I've thrown away, I could feel that I've wasted my life altogether. The only thing that stops me and that makes me feel that it hasn't been entirely wasted, is that I've been a good research subject for Professor Jenner. He's a wonderful man.'

I shared (and still share) Jimmy's admiration for Professor Jenner, so I could understand how Jimmy could endure all the indignities, unpleasantness and boredom that can be part of being a research subject, but I could not help wondering if a desire to please and to make recompense on the part of the subject might confound some of the research results.

My misgivings were increased when I sat with Geraldine in the day room. The nurses' office was next to the day room, and I could often hear the nurses' conversation there and in the corridor quite clearly. Perhaps, though, I could hear them because I wasn't a patient, and all good patients (hospital patients must aspire to a higher level of goodness than people outside hospital) do not hear the conversations between their betters, the nurses and doctors. I didn't know what Geraldine heard or didn't hear, but I would often hear the nurses discussing which of the patients was, by the charts kept in the office, due to have a mood change. 'Geraldine', I might hear them say, 'should go up later this week', meaning that she should change from her near immobile depressed state to an active manic state. Meanwhile, Geraldine might be saying to me, 'Do you think Professor Jenner will let me go home this weekend? Do you think, if I'm good, he'll let me go home?' I didn't tell her what I thought, except to say that she should ask him. What I did wonder was whether she was being good by being deaf, or being good by dutifully going 'up' before the end of the week.

When a piece of behaviour has entered our repertoire, whether it was caused by a physiological change, as in epilepsy, or by something in our environment, like going to an acting class and learning how to fall, we can always produce it again. We may not do it so well – we might not still be able to swim a hundred metres flat out – but we don't forget how to do it. This is often one of the issues I have to tackle at the end of therapy, where the person asks me, 'Will I get depressed again?' The answer is, 'If you choose to do so', for once you have learned how to be depressed, you can always choose to do it again, if you want to, just like you can always choose to do the foxtrot if you have ever learned how.

Once you have learned the behaviours of mania and depression (and all the other defensive manoeuvres) you can always use them again to your advantage. The manic phases of one of the patients at the clinic, Christopher, included wild spending sprees, often involving Professor Jenner and the other staff at the clinic. I remember Christopher going to Professor Jenner and telling him that he had bought him, as a birthday present, a large organ which would be delivered that afternoon. This was just a tease, and Christopher was delighted with the way Professor Jenner's face went white. Momentarily he believed that Christopher was manic and that he had again been involved in one of Christopher's disastrous escapades. Then he saw Christopher grinning and realized that it was a joke and laughed with him. However, there were some staff there who considered that teasing the professor was itself an example of manic behaviour. But there were no staff there then who would have wondered what lay behind this joke, not merely a desire to make people laugh, but also a desire to hurt. In those days at that clinic no such questions were ever given serious consideration.

As well as talking to the patients in the research unit, I would sometimes go over to the main psychiatric hospital to see patients who seemed to get depressed at regular intervals. The first of these that I saw was Maude, a gentle, unassuming woman in her sixties who was a patient on one of the women's wards. She had begun her career as a psychiatric patient in a clinic situated in a very beautiful part of the city, but as her depressions returned year after year, longer and slower in responding to the anti-depressant drugs and ECT, she was transferred to the big psychiatric hospital. I was horrified to see her, to see any woman, on such a ward which could have been designed and built only by men (I don't imagine there were too many women architects in the 1930s in England) who regarded psychiatric patients as no more than sheep to be herded, fed and watered. For any woman who was concerned both about personal cleanliness and privacy, this ward must have been a nightmare. There was Maude, enduring it, feeling that she deserved it, because she was such a wicked person. Wicked because she felt feelings like anger and jealousy which she should not feel, and wicked because she was a shame and a grief to her family because she was depressed.

Maude was thought to be a victim of her cyclical body rhythms because she got depressed every August. By now her depressions were much longer than the month of August. They stretched over much of the year. But that was her history. Every August she had got depressed. ·

I suppose she talked to me because she didn't have many visitors, and I suppose she told me about her marriage because I told her about mine, how I had come to England after my husband

and I had separated and he had remarried. She told me something which she had never told her consultant. She explained why. When she was first depressed she had gone with her husband to the clinic to see the consultant psychiatrist. Her husband had gone in first to talk to the consultant, and she had been left sitting outside in the hallway, while these two men talked about her. Then her husband came out and said to her, 'He wants to see you now. I have told him that we are happily married.'

So she went into the consultant's office, and when he asked her, 'Has anything happened recently which has upset you?' she said, 'No, nothing', and when he said, 'How do you and your husband get on?' she said, 'We get along very well.' He said, 'What about in bed?' and she said, 'I'm happily married.' She didn't say, 'My husband had an affair with one of his colleagues at work and it broke my heart.'

There were other tragedies in her life, and many burdens, and sometimes these were associated with autumn. So it was in autumn that she became depressed. What had looked like a cyclical event in her physiology was an anniversay reaction.

So I lost faith in the idea that some special cyclical physiological rhythm can explain the periods of depression and mania which some people experience. Nowadays, when a person tells me that she has been diagnosed as hypomanic, as a woman did the other day, I am more interested in exploring her statement that when she is depressed 'I feel that I am not worth the air I breathe' than in looking for a calendar to plot her mood changes.

Of course we live in our bodies and so are bound by the limitations of them. It does seem, too, that we divide into two groups, introverts and extraverts, and that this division reflects a difference in the functioning of our nervous system. Extraverts seem to need much more stimulation from the environment than do introverts, and so much of their behaviour has as one of its purposes the search for and the acquisition of the optimum amount of stimulation. But whether our search for and acquisition of what we feel is the right amount of stimulation *per se* fills us with fear or happiness depends on what we make of what our environment has to offer. This division of human beings into extraverts and introverts merely sets the stage. We are born with a great many capabilities, but what we do with these capabilities depends on what our environment elicits from us. We are not born with a fixed amount of extraversion, any more than we are born with a fixed amount of intelligence. To the question 'Heredity or environment?' the answer is 'Both'.

When we are born into consciousness we have the task of making sense of what is happening. In the first few months of life we gradually become aware that we live in two realities, the reality of what goes on around us and the reality of what goes on inside us. Learning to distinguish the two is difficult, and if at the same time we do not lay the foundations for a strong sense of self we find it harder in later life to maintain the distinction between inner and outer reality. We might, as extraverts, perceive our outer reality as dark and dangerous, without recognizing that such darkness and danger come from within; or we might, as introverts, find within us threatening voices which we think outer reality has imposed upon us without recognizing that these are voices which we have created ourselves.

Even if we succeed in performing the tasks of identifying inner and outer reality and of structuring a strong sense of self, we still perceive a difference in the degree of reality in our inner and outer reality. For introverts inner reality is more real than outer reality. For extraverts, outer reality is more real than inner reality. Under stress we retreat to the reality in which we feel more secure. Introverts retreat into themselves. Extraverts retreat from themselves into their outer reality. This is why, under the stress which threatens to annihilate the self completely, introverts retreat into schizophrenia and extraverts into mania. That rhyme, *'When in danger or in doubt/Run in circles and shout out'*, is recited with understanding by extraverts and contempt by introverts.

Those of us who cope with life, more or less, have spent considerable time in increasing our competence in our less real reality. As introverts we have consciously acquired social skills, and, as extraverts, we have, equally consciously, familiarized ourselves with our inner world. But there are many introverts who regard outer reality in the way that sixteenth-century Europeans regarded the Antipodes, and many extraverts who regard their inner reality like David, 'a mystery', and not a mystery which they wish to unravel.

Over the past few years Spike Milligan, with great diligence and humour, has been producing succeeding volumes of his autobiography. In these he describes events in minute detail, recounting names and places and conversations, but the one thing that he does not describe in any detail at all are the terrible periods of mania and depression which often came close to destroying him. He mentions them in passing only when necessary for the description of another event. Even less does he try to describe and analyse his inner reality so as to understand it and to link it to the events in his life. In the volume *Where Have All The Bullets Gone?* which covers the period when he was in a military psychiatric hospital, there are only two sentences concerning this inner reality. In 1944 he was on leave in London with his girlfriend:

We sat at night and listened to Harry Parry and the Radio Rhythm Club with Benny Lee. I also remember how her mother made sensational roast beef and Yorkshire pudding for Sunday lunch. I now know that I was, in my mind, living in a dream. I was floating on other people's emotions, and only concerned with my own which were very childlike, naive, and basically, deep down, there was a yearning for recognition.[2]

Spike, despite all his friends and all his millions of fans, thinks of himself as 'a loner', as many extraverts do. They are loners not because they want to be alone – they need to be part of a group just as much as any extravert does – but because they are frightened of other people, and, as a cover for that fear, contemptuous of them.

If you enquire into the childhood of such extravert loners you find that while they might not have had many real friends, they had hosts of imaginary friends. They spent much of their time engaged in fantasies where they were the hero or heroine, embroiled in thrilling adventures under the gaze of legions of admirers.

Wherever possible, these fantasies were acted out. One man, a self-described loner, very depressed and anxious, told me how in his childhood he spent many hours playing a game called 'Owzat', where the player (it could be played by two people, but he played it on his own) threw a dice to represent the runs being made by two cricket teams. The results were recorded in score books and matches won or lost. He created a league of cricket teams, a host of men who became as real to him as his parents (and much nicer) and he enjoyed the omnipotent power of being the high-scoring batsman, the powerful bowler, the intrepid fieldsman, the sagacious umpire, while at the same time controlling all the play and determining its outcome (when we play games on our own we often cheat).

David by fourteen was putting his fantasies into action.

Every experience excited me and it seemed unimportant whether the excitement was fearful or pleasurable, provided that something, anything, was happening. Until I was fourteen, apart from outings with my sister, I did most things on my own. At school I told lies, describing an imaginary circle of friends, because none of the boys I knew appeared to spend as much time on their own as I did. At home, when I went out, I often told more lies, telling my parents that I was meeting a friend when mostly I went alone to the cinemas or parks. Some days, during school holidays, I bought a ticket on the Underground, and for a few pennies I travelled for hours from the beginning to the end of each separate route. Provided that I never left the stations, and merely crossed from one platform to another, it seemed like an interesting way to cure boredom. I forced myself to believe that it was exciting, travelling for five hours in different directions, ending up where I'd begun. I created a private existence, silently entertaining myself, and fantasized about each small event until it developed into a big, exciting drama.[3]

While fantasy is one way that we use in trying to deal with our inner reality, such omnipotent fantasies, wrote Winnicott in his study of the manic defence,

327

are not so much the inner reality itself as a defence against the acceptance of it. One finds in this defence a flight to omnipotent fantasy, and flight from some fantasies to other fantasies, and in this sequence a flight to external reality. This is why I think one cannot compare and contrast fantasy and reality. In the ordinary extrovert book of adventure we often see how the author made a flight to day-dreaming in childhood, and then made use of external reality in this same flight. He is not conscious of the inner depressive anxiety from which he has fled. He has led a life full of incident and adventure, and this may be accurately told. But the impression left on the reader is of a relatively shallow personality, for this very reason, that the author adventurer has had to base his life on the denial of personal internal reality. One turns with relief from such writers to others who can tolerate depressive anxiety and doubt.[4]

Thus speaks a true introvert!

David and Winnicott both illustrate how an extravert usually acquires a good knowledge of practical things – how to do things and how to find things. He may use his knowledge to help others, or, if not greatly troubled by a conscience, to further his own ends. His observations of his external reality may give him a good knowledge, not just about how things behave (how to mend a fuse or steal a car) but how people behave. He understands the how but not the why. Where other people are concerned he may be able to observe, assess and predict with a high degree of success, but, if he has not actively developed his understanding of his own inner reality, he is unable to comprehend the actual, internal, lived experience of the other person. He reasons, and often quite correctly, along the lines of 'If I say that, she'll cry. If I do that, he'll get angry. If I do so and so, she'll give me a present. If I say so and so, he'll punish my brother.' But no real understanding of *why* his mother cries, or is generous, or *why* his father gets angry or punishes his brother. He may think of reasons, but they are simplistic, without real understanding. 'She cries because all women cry a lot.' 'He gets angry because he hates me.'

This kind of understanding of other people is like the

understanding we have of animals. We can observe them, identify their patterns of behaviour, manipulate the conditions of the animals' environment so as to influence their behaviour, but we can never know how animals think and feel. Some people claim that they do, but this is no more than the projection of the mental structures which humans create on to animals whose own mental structures are something completely different and something we can never comprehend.

At one time I used to work with a consultant psychiatrist whose diagnostic skills were world renowned. He certainly did have great skill in assessing people and in influencing their behaviour, but what amazed and appalled me was the way he seemed oblivious to the internal experience of the people he had dealings with. He did great good: he did great harm. It was not just by chance that the patients who interested him the most were those who had earned the diagnosis of psychopath.

A man like this in a position of power has many people who admire him and many who do not. Not everyone likes being treated like a puppet on a string. But extraverts who are unacquainted with their internal reality can relate to others only by trying to control them like puppets. When such extraverts fail to gain power and become instead psychiatric patients, they always earn the condemnatory appellation by the staff of 'manipulative'.

In therapy such an extravert may come to recognize his need to control others. During his stay in a therapeutic community David found learning this very difficult:

> My behaviour in the group seemed to indicate that I acted out a role which I had inherited from my mother. Like her, I wanted to powerfully control other people. I wanted to dominate them. I insisted on being the centre of attention. If they refused to satisfy my demands, then I wanted to hurt them. I wanted to be the best resident, best able to understand my past, best able to communicate, best able to begin a new life, best able to forgive – best able to control.[5]

Often the person creates a fantasy which, if implemented, would fulfil this need to control others. The fantasy which would appeal most to a lonely, rejected child who desperately wants to be a loved and admired member of a group is that of being a parent in a happy family. David described his fantasy:

I idealized married love into a cosy, comfortable relationship; as cosy and comfortable as the apparently ideal families I had met through friends at the Circus Club, or fanciful visions which I created in waking dreams. Love, the love I wanted, possessed a private key which opened a door leading into a private home, where nobody could disrupt my blissful tranquillity, and where I could offer and receive protection. The protection I wanted to offer, and to have accepted, was to be a provider, of care and financial security. I wanted to work hard and prove that I could do what my parents could not. I wanted to be respected and admired for my efforts, and in return I expected to assume all the conventional responsibilities of a Victorian husband. My wife, the one who would help me understand love, would give me what I had never known – a stable home, where I would not be frightened to use my key when I reached the front door, and inside which would be certainty, the certainty that there was always someone who wanted me.[6]

This passage illustrates how sentimentality is the denial of hate, for here a sentimental account of family life denies the fact that family life, no matter how loving the parents and children are, contains plenty of frustration, anger and disappointment. Victorian fathers were tyrants. They damaged and destroyed their wives and children, and they usually ended up as lonely, selfish, feared and unloved old men.

In the grip of such a sentimental fantasy a person may be oblivious of the fact that if we control people we become responsible for them, and many people, especially spouses and children, will cheerfully hand over their responsibilities to the person who wishes to manage their lives. So before long the controller becomes weighed down with burdens, and, with awareness of the burdens, comes resentment and hate.

We can often relieve to some degree our own resentment by complaining and being irritable, and our family has to put up with our behaviour. But hate is a powerful emotion, coming from the deepest recesses of our being. It shows us that we are not the good, civilized person we thought ourselves to be. We hate, and we wish to destroy. You have to have a detailed knowledge of yourself in order to be able to recognize and cope with your own hate. To do this you needed to have a mother who tolerated your hate and hers when you were a baby. Failing that, you need a therapist who can tolerate his own hate as well as yours.

Not everyone is so lucky. If you were born an extravert and if your efforts to create a sense of self were often threatened with failure, if you were not helped to develop an understanding of your inner reality but, rather, shown that you contained a dangerous emotional darkness from which you must flee into outer reality, then hate becomes the danger which you must never recognize but from which you must always flee.

The Manic Defence

Socrates' belief that 'An unexamined life is not worth living' is not one that those people who oscillate between depression and mania would subscribe to. Not until he had made and lost a fortune, nearly died twice by his own hand, and served a gaol sentence for the attempted murder of his wife did David finally gather the courage to seek therapy. Once begun, he was often amazed at what he discovered about himself. He wrote:

> I began to understand that I existed in two extreme emotional states: when something dramatic was happening I felt dynamic and hyperactive; when I felt dormant and useless I fantasized about death.[7]

Thus he summarized briefly and accurately the life of a manic-depressive person.

He first withdrew into the prison of depression when he was thirteen. He did not know it was depression. He thought he was going mad. He had already developed a pattern of living where he escaped from himself into activity in his external reality. He developed this with great skill, working hard to achieve fame and admiration and creating exciting, but solitary, adventures for himself. But,

At night, when I reluctantly switched off my bedroom light, or my torch battery became too dim to read by, nothing felt exciting. I just felt alone. If I'd spent an afternoon with a friend I worried that he, or she, might not want to see me again; or, if I hadn't spent an afternoon with one, why I had no friends. I could not understand why each adventure – whatever it was, even when it made me happy at the time – quickly turned into sad disappointment. The answer seemed to keep finding more things to do.[8]

He became a very successful accountant, but,

However much I earned – and once I was qualified my earnings were always high – I never *had enough*. I could advise clients wisely and, when necessary, cautiously, but I could not exercise self-discipline. I wanted to accumulate capital, but as my income increased, so, too, did my dashes into material possessions. If a month passed and I displayed no new award in my home, I felt defeated. Every month, when my well-trained bank statements or credit card accounts overtook me, I made a fresh start, determined to save, not spend; but then, to thrash worry, I dashed out and bought something . . .

It was not uncommon for me to work until three or four o'clock in the morning on a thrilling idea for expansion, or a demanding client's latest urgent request for advice, gulping a couple of pain-killing tablets every hour to relieve my tension. At night, secreted away with my over-activity while most of the world slept, I became increasingly desperate for continual change. There had to be something new happening. If there was not, life seemed to stand still; and when it stood still, I did not know what to do with myself. Yesterday's success was quickly forgotten. I wanted to be the firm's star, radiating brilliance. When I knew that I needed to 'consolidate', to take time off to enjoy what I had, I did not know how to. Always, at the back of my mind, was the fear that if I did not do immediately what I wanted to do, a dark bout of depression might engulf me in physical and mental isolation.[9]

In the first part of this book I have described how, if a baby is to grow up with a sense of confidence and self-worth, that baby needs to be accepted by his parents as he is and not loved only insofar as he can meet his parents' need that their child should act as a parent to them and, as a dutiful and obedient child, be a credit to them. A child whose developing self is not frequently threatened with annihilation by his parents does not have to go on to develop major defences in order to survive.

The opposite of annihilation can be conceived of not as survival but as omnipotence. This is the opposite chosen by the child who is under major threat, and thus the child goes on to create fantasies of omnipotence and to plan to gain through admiration what he cannot gain through love. Both introvert and extravert children have such fantasies, but in the execution of them extraverts are more likely to succeed. Because they feel alone and threatened, introvert children retreat into the safety of their inner reality, and so do not develop a good understanding of what the world regards as success. Unless they have some special talent which some adult recognizes and fosters, thus giving the child a direction to follow, the introvert child may develop fantasies and practices which take him further and further from ordinary life and into the life of a proud but isolated eccentric.

By contrast, the extravert child, fleeing into his external reality, gains a very good idea of what the world regards as success and sets out to achieve it. He has a keen eye for convention and orthodoxy. At school, if he has sufficient intelligence, he can do well simply by carrying out the teachers' instructions. He is not distracted from incorporating the set syllabus by doubt and wonder, as introvert children are. If he cannot shine academically he can become a spectacular member of a sports team, or, if all that fails, he can abandon the conventions of school and shine instead in the conventions of street life and crime.

The fantasies of omnipotence which a child develops to overcome the threat of annihilation gradually create in the person a sense of grandiosity. This sense, often bolstered by real achievements, can become one of the main characteristics of the person who may be unaware of its significance. As Alice Miller wrote, 'Grandiosity is the defence against depression, and depression is the defence against the deep pain over the loss of the self.'[10]

She went on:

The person who is 'grandiose' is admired everywhere and needs this admiration; indeed, he cannot live without it. He must excel brilliantly in everything he undertakes, which surely he is capable of doing (otherwise he would not attempt it). He, too, admires himself – for his qualities: his beauty, cleverness, talents; and for his success and achievements. Woe betide him if one of these fails him, for then the catastrophe of a severe depression is imminent. It is usually considered normal that sick or aged people who have suffered the loss of much of their health and vitality, or, for example, women at the time of the menopause, should become depressive. There are, however, other personalities who can tolerate the loss of beauty, health, youth, or loved ones, and although they mourn them, they do so without depression. In contrast, there are those with great gifts, often precisely the most gifted, who suffer from severe depression. One is free from depression when self-esteem is based on the authenticity of one's feelings and not on the possession of certain qualities . . .

The collapse of self-esteem in a 'grandiose' person will show clearly how precariously that self-esteem had been hanging in the air – 'hanging from a balloon', a female patient once dreamed. That balloon flew up very high in a good wind but then suddenly got a hole in it and soon lay like a rag on the ground . . . For nothing genuine that could have given strength and support later on had been developed . . .

It is thus impossible for the grandiose person to cut the tragic link between admiration and love. In his compulsion to repeat he seeks insatiably for admiration, of which he never gets enough because admiration is not the same as love. It is only a substitute gratification of the primary needs for respect, understanding, and being taken seriously – needs that have remained unconscious . . .

The grandiose person is never really free, first, because he is excessively dependent on admiration from the object, and, second, because his self-respect is dependent on qualities, functions and achievements that can suddenly fail.[11]

Matthew came to see me very much as a last resort. The psychiatrist on whom he had depended for so long had left the district, and shortly after his departure Matthew had plunged into a deep depression. He was a senior accountant, very honest, upright and conscientious. He did not see how I could help him, but expected that I would impart some facts to him and give him some advice. He intended to learn what I taught him as diligently as he had studied at school and college and to carry out my advice and then, if I was any good at my job, he would no longer be depressed.

He had three anxieties about this. The first was that I was very remiss about giving advice. I gave none, or very vague and woolly stuff like 'Be kind to yourself' or, worse, immoralities like, 'Why not take some time off and do something frivolous and unnecessary?' (People who have to resort to mania and depression in order to survive either never play, or play only to win.)

His second anxiety was that I talked what was obviously nonsense. I seemed to think that his childhood had something to do with his present state. His psychiatrist had never gone on with this sort of nonsense. A ten-minute interview, with an exchange of pleasantries and a checking of his drug prescription was all that that wise doctor needed to do. Why go into these things which happened so long ago?

His third anxiety was that whenever he emerged from his depression he would go along for a while on an even keel, and then he would gradually become more active until he reached a state which he called manic. Dare he risk coming out of this depression?

It was only with difficulty that I got him to tell me of his experience of depression. He described being depressed as feeling that inside him was a hollow space. 'On the outside,' he said, 'I look the same and I can go around doing the things I always do, but inside is this empty space.'

He went on, 'When I'm manic the hollow space is filled in. Then I've got lots of good ideas and things to do.'

Anger to Matthew was complete anathema. He prided himself not only on never losing his temper but on his skill in reasoned argument. All disputes, he considered, could be resolved if people met together and argued calmly and logically. He made no allowance for emotions which, no matter what they are, never fit into neat, logical boxes. He described his depression only in the physical terms of bodily weakness and a tiredness which forced him to stay in bed for days at a time.

It was only when he described a little of those periods which his psychiatrist called manic that he gave some hint of the volcano of rage inside him.

He enjoyed the start of such a period, when he felt whole and full of creative ideas. But then he would find himself doing some things which, in retrospect, he felt were quite worrying.

He described to me how, when, driving his car, he saw other drivers going too fast and so wasting petrol, he would wave them to stop, and then he would speak to them sternly, reminding them of their duty to conserve petrol. He did not tell me how many such drivers threatened physical violence in response to such good advice. I wondered if the person he was really reprimanding was not the other driver, but himself, for 'speeding up'.

I did not offer this interpretation, for he would have found it strange and offensive. Even more so would he have found my interpretations of two other things he did in this period of mania. A recent bombing in England by the IRA left him with the feeling that he should be on the look-out for suspicious people. This he did, and sometimes he would stop a person he thought suspicious and question him about his activities. He uncovered no Irish terrorists, any more than he uncovered and recognized his own anarchic impulses which were close to breaking through and disrupting the peaceful pattern of his life. Again, although ordinarily very careful where money was concerned, he found himself taking the precaution, before going on holiday, of joining both the motoring organizations, the AA and the RAC, even though membership of one is ample protection. His explanation to himself of his action was that he wanted to be sure of getting his wife and children to safety if his car broke down in the wilds of Scotland. Here I felt it inappropriate at that stage to question whether such an action was a reaction formation against the resentment and hate he felt for his family who placed such onerous demands upon him.

David told me of the rage he felt with people who did not obey the rules. 'When we had electricity cuts, I insisted that my family turn off all the lights in the house except the ones they absolutely needed. When I drove home at night and saw other houses with their lights blazing, I felt furious.'

He went on to say, 'When someone makes a mistake I exult. I'm always watching my therapist to see if I can catch him out.'

I asked him what lay behind this.

He said, 'Whenever I see the order and security that someone else has, I feel envious and I want to destroy it. I am filled with destructiveness, terrible destructiveness. I used to think that I was doing everything to preserve my family, but I wasn't.'

Here he echoed Alice Miller when she said of the grandiose person:

> He is envious of healthy people because they do not have to make a constant effort to earn admiration, and because they do not have to do something in order to impress, one way or the other, but are free to be 'average'.[12]

David spoke of how, through therapy, he was gaining an understanding of himself, but he still found within himself a torrent of emotion which he could neither understand nor control. He described himself as being a very good predictor of other people's behaviour. These observational skills, combined with a greater knowledge of how a person's inner reality functions, while increasing his skills in getting along with people, had also increased his skill in finding how to hurt people. He said, 'I pick up something in what a person says and then I say something to that person which hurts. I intend it to hurt. But it's only with people with whom I can have that kind of conversation, when I see things in that other person that I recognize, that I feel there's a real relationship. My family don't like to enter into conversations with me. They say, "Don't psychoanalyse me." I can't be bothered with superficial conversation. It's a waste of time. The only people now I can communicate with are my wife and my therapist.'

What David shows here is how, still, for him, a close relationship must contain hate and hurt as well as love. Children who have been involved in violence always have difficulty in separating love and hate. In adulthood they may be violent towards others, or they may hide their violence under a guise of caring and controlling and inflict their hurts in the name of love, or they may, like David, do all these things.

David's account of his childhood shows that from the beginning he was the victim of violence. His mother was a violent woman, prone to shouting and hurling things, striking her children and threatening to kill herself. She was addicted to barbiturates, the iatrogenic illness of the fifties, and this reduced her self-control even further. When David, as a toddler, showed the usual aggressiveness which all toddlers show he was not guided by his parents into better ways of dealing with anger and envy but punished violently for his own violence. This was done, not just by his parents but by one teacher, who, when he was three, washed out his mouth with soap because he had bitten another child. When he was older he stole a pound note from his mother and destroyed it without understanding why. Later, in a moment of closeness, he confessed to his mother and she promised to keep this as their secret. However, she betrayed him to his father who tied him to the bed and belted him until he bled.

The damage which is done to children by violence is not simply that caused by the infliction of actual violence on the child. There is as well the damage done when the child takes into himself as what the psychoanalysts call 'internal objects' the violent figures of his parents. This is how the poet A.E. Housman described this terrible event.

> *They cease not fighting, east and west,*
> *On the marches of my breast.*
>
> *Here the truceless armies yet*
> *Trample, rolled in blood and sweat;*
> *They kill and kill and never die;*
> *And I think that each is I.*
>
> *None will part us none undo*
> *The knot that makes one flesh of two,*
> *Sick with hatred, sick with pain,*
> *Strangling – When shall we be slain?*
>
> *When shall I be dead and rid*
> *Of the wrong my father did?*
> *How long, how long, till spade and hearse*
> *Put to sleep my mother's curse?*[13]

Matthew's childhood, so he would tell me, was happy. There was one event when he was three that his mother still remembered, but he didn't, so it couldn't be important. This was when he had been admitted to hospital with scarlet fever. In those days parents were not allowed to visit their sick children in hospital. When his mother came to collect him she found that he had lain so long sucking his thumb that a sore had developed inside his mouth. Not long after he had returned home his mother gave birth to his sister.

I tried to put these events into the context of a child's experience. Leaving his parents and going into hospital would have been beyond his comprehension. It would have felt like total abandonment, complete annihilation. The nurses there had obviously made no effective attempt to assuage this sense of overwhelming loss, but left him to lie in the passive state of a child who has given up hope. On his mother's arrival he would have observed her distress, which clearly had to do with something being wrong with him, and probably her distress was exacerbated by his initial lack of response to her, as children in this abandoned state react when reunited with their mother. To this picture I could add only the knowledge that both parents were, in their own way, dominant people. Possibly there was some friction between them about what had happened and what should be done. Without understanding why, he would have felt that he was the cause of this friction.

The violence Matthew experienced was probably not as physically immense as that which David experienced, but in terms of psychic pain it was very great. Then the narcissism which supports us through the vicissitudes of early childhood received another blow. After being the centre of his parents' attention, he was supplanted by another. His mother had betrayed him. Matthew dismissed this interpretation. 'My sister and I get on very well,' he said. He was very glad to have assumed full responsibility for his widowed mother's financial affairs, even though she was not always prepared to follow his advice.

Long before he began his journey into self-discovery David had refused to have anything more to do with his mother. He was ashamed and frightened of her, and even though when in the depths of depression he longed for her, he made no attempt to contact her. The last time he saw her was in a shop, and he passed by without speaking. Four years later she died alone of an overdose of barbiturates.

Matthew and David represent the extremes of a response to parents which has not gone through the mature process of observing our parents with an adult's eye, judging them, and then forgiving them. The extremes are to idealize them, or to treat them with total contempt. They are, in their way, the same response. 'Contempt for parents,' wrote Alice Miller, 'often helps to ward off the pain of being unable to idealize them.'[14] Both responses are a refusal to go beyond idealizing parents to an understanding and acceptance that our parents are fallible human beings who inflict pain on us for which there is no recompense, and so, no longer filled with hate for our parents' failure to be perfect parents, we can feel sad and mourn. Both responses are in obedience to the parental injunction 'Thou Shalt Not Be Aware'.

The Way Out

The lives of those people who go from mania to depression and back again in what seems like an endless cycle of trauma are full of pain and catastrophe. In their extremes they will ask for help, but, even in their extremes, if you said to them, 'I have a magic formula which will ensure that you never get into an emotional state again. You will live the rest of your life on an even keel', they would, if they answered you truthfully, say, 'No, I don't want it.' A life without its highs and lows is not worth living.

When Peter was asked if his therapy was worthwhile, he said, 'I think that when I came out of it, it was much better in the sense that one understood the guilt. One's behaviour didn't promote shame, or indeed guilt either, which was nice. But in a curious sort of way it balanced the books. On the one hand there was a great deal more tranquillity, a great deal more contentment, one felt more even, less bizarre, less of a freak, but on the other hand, the lows had been cut off and so had the highs. A lot of the sparkle had gone. A lot of the excitement. I was, and still am, quite resentful that the upper sort of peaks, of having great enjoyment and perhaps being a bit excessive, if you like, in one's pleasures and so on is no longer there. I suppose I feel less of a person in some ways because a lot of what was there which was me has gone. I think it needed to go and I don't regret it. I mourn it, but I don't regret it. It needed to go, but I'm also resentful of the fact that it has gone because part of me is missing, and it's like part of me has been cut out. And it needed to be and it was right that it should be, but the operation still hurt.'[15]

Many of the people who take Lithium regularly to limit the extent of their mood change feel, as Peter feels, a loss of a vital, creative, lively part of themselves. If, unlike Peter, they have not made their journey into self-understanding, they resent this loss, thus adding to their mountain of resentments, without being, at the same time, able to recognize the necessity of the loss and thus mourn it. Such people may have colluded with their psychiatrists in their diagnosis of a manic-depressive illness, so as to avoid a journey into what for both psychiatrist and patient is the most dangerous territory of all, their inner reality, or they may simply have never been given the opportunity to make this journey. In many of the letters I have had from people who have been given the label of manic-depressive the writer says, 'I have never been offered psychotherapy.'

Life in a therapeutic community, so David found, was quite different from what he had expected. It was far from easy, yet, after a while, he began to realize just how valuable it was. He wrote:

> There, at the unit, if I could work out what I did, and how I felt, and try not to explain it away by blaming my past, was the answer I wanted. Through the members – residents more so than the staff – I could understand myself. They were facing the same problems, experiencing the same angry feelings, and reacting as I did. If I stopped trying to escape from them, perhaps I would feel better . . . I still could not control my feelings, but I was learning to recognize them, and that helped. Bit by bit, despite feeling bad most of the time, I felt I was 'getting there'.[16]

He spoke of discovering the stranger within himself, and the stranger was anger. With that anger was hate, and a wish to destroy.

Hate is part of what it is to be human, but some of us have in our early lives more experiences which provoke our hate than we can master. An immediate way of solving this problem, of not so much mastering hate as running away from it, is to flee into activity in our external world. But when we do this we prevent ourselves from developing the only safeguard human beings have against their own destructiveness.

We destroy those things which we perceive as not being human like ourselves. Thus we can chop down trees, blow up mountains, eat fruit, vegetables, and other animals because, in our perception, they are not human and do not feel as we feel. We even see ourselves as free to destroy creatures who may bear a passing resemblance to us. They may walk and talk and live in groups just like us, but if we don't perceive them as human like us, we can bomb and maim them, exploit them, starve them, and inflict hurt upon them without feeling shame or guilt. We perceive other people as being human like ourselves only when we can make that special leap of the imagination which takes us from our own inner world into theirs.

We are all born with a capacity to hate and to destroy. We are also born with the capacity to know our inner world and to empathize with others. A child brought up in love and acceptance develops all these capacities and can balance one against the other. The empathy balances the hate and keeps the destructiveness in check. But a child who does not have these experiences, but rather has experiences which take from him the right to be himself, is left at the mercy of his hate and destructiveness. He may then defend against the hate and destructiveness with depression, a turning of the hate and destructiveness against himself, and when that becomes too terrifying, to flee from depression and his inner reality to an external reality which may offer temporary shelter but never release from turmoil. For the key to this release lies not in the outside world but in himself.

Chapter Ten

Turning Fear into Schizophrenia

If only we could do for words what manufacturers do for their products, that is, issue instructions about how their products should be used. We are told not to leave our electric blanket switched on when we get into bed, or to change the oil in our car every ten thousand miles. If we could issue instructions about how words must be used, then I would issue the instruction that the word 'schizophrenic' should not be used to mean 'split personality' or 'being inconsistent'.

The kind of person who might be described as having a 'split personality', that is, acting in one role or as one person for a time and then switching to another role, like Dr Jekyll into Mr Hyde, but without the aid of a mysterious potion, is not the kind of person who would ever have the kind of experiences which are rightly called schizophrenic. Rather, this way of experiencing your self as several apparently separate people who are in themselves ordinary and everyday (as in *The Three Faces of Eve*) is a defence available only to extraverts. Unfortunately, from this mistaken notion of multiple selves in one person has come the use of the word 'schizophrenic' to mean 'inconsistent', 'uncertain', 'duplicitous', 'not letting your left hand know what your right hand is doing'.

The notion of 'splitting' which is contained in the word 'schizophrenic' comes from Eugene Bleuler who coined the word 'schizophrenia' to reflect the way a person in the schizophrenic experience seems to be separating his emotions from his ideas. For instance, such a person might say, 'My mother died recently', and instead of looking appropriately sad, might giggle and make a joke, while another event, say, a broken plate, might produce tears. Psychiatrists call this 'inappropriate affect' and regard it as a symptom of the illness of schizophrenia. What Bleuler and his successors did not realize is that while the schizophrenic person's emotional reactions may appear inappropriate to the observer, such reactions are appropriate to and consistent with the way in which that person gives meaning to his world.

We are always in the business of trying to make sense of our world. To do this, we need the events which we are trying to understand to have some consistency and regularity. When our external reality seems to us to be inconsistent and incomprehensible we feel helpless and our self is threatened with annihilation. Extraverts react to such a situation with great passion and activity in order to try to force their external reality into some sort of order and regularity. Introverts retreat into their inner world. Fleeing into their more real reality, extraverts and introverts then attempt a reconstructing and ordering of their world.

Extraverts under immense threat may reconstruct by using massive denial. For instance, instead of grieving for her family destroyed without warning by a terrorist bomb, an extravert woman may say, and believe in the face of all evidence, 'My family have gone away on holiday. They will be home tomorrow', and go on living a life quite ordinary in every respect, except for her denial that her family are dead.

An introvert woman in the same situation may attempt a similar reconstruction of her world, but, having retreated to her inner reality, she finds her external reality so unreal and inconsistent that she can no longer distinguish it from her inner reality of dreams and fantasies. Suppose such a woman has had from her earliest childhood a strong religious faith which included the belief that she had looking after her her own Guardian Angel and that if she was good then this Angel would protect her from all harm. She may never have told anyone that she has held fast to this belief all her adult life. But now that disaster has befallen her, she has to ask herself whether her Guardian Angel has failed her, or whether she has lost the protection of her Angel because she has sinned. To prove to herself that her family has not been destroyed by her own wickedness and that her Guardian Angel is still there caring for her, she may fantasize that her family has been miraculously restored to her by the Angel. This fantasy, like the fantasies we all have which express and try to meet our greatest needs, seems, as she develops it, amazingly real. Only she has lost the ability to distinguish her fantasy from her outer reality. The needs and fears contained in this fantasy are immensely powerful, and suddenly she knows, beyond all shadow of doubt, that the postman, delivering her letters, is her Guardian Angel in disguise, and that the letters, masquerading as sympathy cards and electricity bills, like the voices she hears from her broken television set, are messages of love and hope from her family as well as warnings from her Angel's alter ego, the Devil, about how she should behave if she is to escape a terrible fate. Knowing that her mother is safe in the care of her Angel, she might laugh happily at any mention of her mother's death. Knowing that breaking a plate will earn the Devil's displeasure might cause her to cry in penitence. Such fantasies are to her no stranger than the events which have already overtaken her, but more, they bring her comfort, and she cannot bear to recognize them as fantasies, for to do so would plunge her back into the hell of total helplessness. So she insists, against all argument and evidence, that her fantasies are total and immutable reality. Such fantasies are called the delusions and hallucinations of schizophrenia.

For some people this kind of defence is necessary only for a short period, following a crisis which gradually subsides into something less threatening. But for others, outside reality never becomes sufficiently safe for the defence to be relinquished, and so the person goes on living in a world which bears little resemblance to the external reality which people generally share. This experience of an extremely idiosyncratic world is what is called schizophrenia, and this is the only way that this word should be used.

Schizophrenia has created more ideas and more arguments than any other of the territories to which psychiatry has laid claim. It was the first territory which psychiatrists defined and claimed as their own, and when psychologists and sociologists and renegade psychiatrists like R.D. Laing and Thomas Szasz tried to reclaim it the war to defend the territory was fierce and unforgiving. Even today, when highly respectable psychiatrists produce research results which show the importance of family relationships in schizophrenia, Laing and Szasz are still spoken of by psychiatrists in the same way as the disciples must once have spoken of Judas. We might be able to forgive a stranger who attacked us, but not one of our number who betrayed us.

The literature about the territory called schizophrenia is vast and increasing. Anyone who wants to acquaint himself with it must be prepared to do a great deal of reading. I had time to do that between 1968 and 1971 when I was doing my Ph.D. and was following the progress of two sisters, twins, each of whom needed to retreat into her inner world to avoid the immense stresses in their family. I had known similar teenagers in Sydney, Australia, but this was my first opportunity to get to know the family of such individuals really well. I was also able to begin my observations, which have gone on ever since, of the behaviour of psychiatrists and of the life within a psychiatric hospital.

When I moved to Lincolnshire to establish a department of clinical psychology I could no longer spend many hours a week keeping up with all the research literature on schizophrenia, but I did take time every month to read the *British Journal of Psychiatry* and to follow the development of the arguments which led to ideas which the journal editors at that time would have dismissed as 'unscientific' but are now, in 1986, the basis of serious research and discussion.

Parallel with my reading was my continuing observation of real life in a psychiatric hospital, not just the hospital where I worked, but in the many hospitals where I visited. I met a great many people who had been given the title of 'schizophrenic' and an even greater number of psychiatrists and nurses who had no doubt that the people who were called schizophrenic were ill.

Scientific and 'Practical' Psychiatry

It seems to me that there are two bodies of knowledge about 'schizophrenia'. There is the carefully thought-out, carefully expressed body of knowledge which is formulated within the best tradition of scientific method. The psychiatrists who contribute to this body of knowledge usually work in the big teaching hospitals and universities, places which are very different from the ordinary psychiatric hospital.

It is in the psychiatric hospitals, each a collection of vast, old buildings, once surrounded by a wall, and built originally on the outskirts of a town or city, that the second body of knowledge flourishes. Many of these hospitals are being closed now, and their inhabitants resettled in the community, but the ideas and practices which flourished there have followed the patients into the world outside the hospital. These ideas and practices have been influenced by the changing ideas of the academic psychiatrists (after all, the junior doctors have to pass their examinations, and the clinical tutors have to teach them) but the tried and trusty ideas and practices that had seen good service over many long years have not been discarded for new-fangled notions. The psychiatrists in these 'bins' consider that they have to deal with the real world, not like those academics in their ivory towers.

The two bodies of knowledge had the same beginnings in the work of Kraepelin who first described the symptoms of two mental illnesses, manic-depression and dementia praecox, later called schizophrenia. For Kraepelin, in schizophrenia 'the symptoms were symptoms of an underlying disease process. The patient's life history, his premorbid personality, even his own experience of the illness had no assigned place in the scheme of things. They were an irrelevancy.'[1]

In discussions about schizophrenia it is important to distinguish between that body of knowledge which has developed in the tradition of scientific research and that which has developed in day-to-day practice in psychiatric hospitals. I try to do this, but sometimes when I read of the research reports of drug trials and genetic studies of schizophrenia, mania and depression, I wonder how much the ideas and practices of the second body of knowledge have confounded the carrying out of the research design.

Working within the first body of knowledge are many psychiatrists who reject Kraepelin's concept of the disease process being the only object of interest in the study of schizophrenia. Such psychiatrists, like Andrew Smith in his study of 'General and

Historical Concepts of Schizophrenia', are developing a 'complex developmental psychiatric theory' which includes the 'genetic transmission of a vulnerability to the condition', childhood, relationships with parents, low self-esteem, adverse life events, cultural differences, 'society's tolerance of peculiar behaviour' and the role of institutions. 'In this theory, the illness would be the pathological end of a long process of maladaptation.'[2]

What Andrew Smith is describing here is a theory which encompasses all aspects of human life. Such a theory would need to explain not just why some people become schizophrenic but why the rest do not. Such a theory is indeed complex, far too complex to be understood, much less used, by the practitioners of the second body of knowledge.

· There simplicity is the byword. Psychiatrists practising the second body of knowledge often have their own idiosyncratic methods of diagnosis. One psychiatrist I used to work with would remark that he could always distinguish a woman who was schizophrenic from one who was not by the fact that the woman who was schizophrenic 'doesn't turn me on'. Another psychiatrist assured me that he knew a certain woman was schizophrenic 'by the shape of her eyebrows'. This woman later told me that she always wore make-up which enhanced her similarity to Elizabeth Taylor. She did indeed look like that famous actress who at that time had very distinctively shaped eyebrows, as did many women.

I have often observed that the anti-intellectual stance of many such psychiatrists results in a diagnosis of schizophrenia for any troubled student who happens to be reading philosophy at university. Students are always likely to be the victims of the prejudices many doctors have against people younger than themselves who have not adopted the conventional attitudes and behaviour that the doctors have assumed as part of their becoming accepted members of the medical profession. Envy is as prevalent in the medical profession as it is in the rest of the population.

Even more likely to be the victims of prejudice are those patients who do not share the same nationality as the psychiatrist making the diagnosis. Maurice Lipsedge has updated the work he and Ronald Littlewood did in 1980[3] which showed that West

Indians in Britain are more likely to be diagnosed as schizophrenic than other nationalities and has found that in the intervening years there has been no change. West Indian women are especially likely to be diagnosed as schizophrenic. Lipsedge has also noted that a young West Indian being admitted to hospital has a 40 per cent chance of being diagnosed as having a disease which was unknown fifteen years ago. This is *cannabis psychosis*. The odd thing is that it is extremely rare for a non-West Indian to have this disease, even though many young white people admitted to hospital have used cannabis extensively.[4]

It certainly is not necessary for a patient to display the symptoms of schizophrenia, the hallucinations, delusions, and changes in thinking and speaking, for that patient to be given a diagnosis of schizophrenia. Sometimes these patients are in the process of losing contact with external reality. I have found that such people can talk about what is happening to their thought patterns and in tests like the Rorschach show the process of losing touch with external reality. Very different from them are the people who are given the diagnosis of schizophrenia because they have failed to give up being depressed despite repeated courses of ECT and high doses of the full range of anti-depressants and many of the minor tranquillizers, and those people who are protesting in a not very coherent and orderly way at the injustices of their lives. All too often the diagnosis of schizophrenia means for the psychiatrist 'I don't understand'. The treatment for anyone diagnosed a schizophrenic – doses of the major tranquillizers, the neuroleptics, often by injection – means that the doctors and nurses are no longer so greatly troubled by their patients' grief and protests.

One of the 'symptoms of schizophrenia' is called 'lack of insight'. This 'lack of insight' occurs when the person reaches a point where he can no longer test his experience of inner reality against his experience of his external reality and arrive at some reliable answer. For instance, if, while waiting for a bus, you say to yourself, 'Is that a bus coming, or did I just imagine it?' you can test the match of your two realities. Either the bus itself arrives, or you see that what you thought was a bus was, say, a large lorry. In ordinary life we are always creating hypotheses in our inner reality and testing them against our outer reality (what psychologists call 'reality testing') but to do this successfully we need confidence in our own powers of judgement and an external reality which is fairly consistent and reliable. If external reality is your more real reality you are better equipped to see consistencies in your external reality. If external reality is your less real reality, it is much harder to see it as reliable and consistent, and, under the stress which makes you lose confidence in yourself, you find that external reality becomes more and more strange. So you can choose to retreat to your inner reality and insist, against all arguments by other people, that what you experience there is absolutely and undoubtedly true. This is what is called the symptom of 'lack of insight' in schizophrenia, and what you experience as truth is labelled by others as peculiar ideas, or hallucinations, delusions and paranoia.

There is another 'lack of insight' often diagnosed in psychiatric hospitals. This is where the patient fails to agree with the psychiatrist's assessment of the patient. The psychiatrist arrives at his diagnosis in a way something like this:

PSYCHIATRIST: Harry, the nurses tell me that you went home at the weekend and caused a disturbance. Your parents brought you back to the ward, and instead of settling down you made it necessary for the ward doctor to be called to give you an injection. What have you got to say for yourself?

HARRY: I'm sorry I was a trouble to the staff. I would have taken some extra pills but the doctor and the charge nurse insisted I have an injection. That wasn't necessary. And at home, my father got very angry. He tried to strangle me.

PSYCHIATRIST: Your parents are very worried about you. Now, are you going to behave yourself?

HARRY: It wasn't my fault, but I apologize for my behaviour.

PSYCHIATRIST, writing in Harry's case notes: Pt shows lack of insight.

The practice of psychiatry, like practices of any profession or skill, creates many self-fulfilling prophecies. For many years psychiatrists believed that Kraepelin was right when he said that no one recovered from schizophrenia. Once a schizophrenic, always a schizophrenic. Thousands of people, diagnosed as schizophrenic, obligingly remained schizophrenic for the rest of their lives. It is a feature of human beings that we are very good at behaving in the way that the people around us, especially the people with power over us, want us to behave. Jan Morris found that when she was treated as a woman, she began to behave like a woman.[5] Anyone who has worked in a psychiatric hospital cannot fail to be impressed with how quickly a patient will pick up the movements and habits of the other patients, and anyone who has worked with long-stay patients moving into the community will be impressed with how quickly these movements and habits can be discarded if the new environment encourages change. Luc Compi, writing about 'The Natural History of Schizophrenia in the Long Term', concluded that:

> For everyone who does not link the concept of schizophrenia to an obligatory bad outcome, the enormous variety of possible evolutions shows that *there is no such thing as a specific course of schizophrenia*. Doubtless the potential for improvement of schizophrenia has for a long time been grossly underestimated. In the light of long-term investigations, what is called 'the course of schizophrenia' more closely resembles a life process open to a great variety of influences of all kinds than an illness with a given course.[6]

The World Health Organization has been responsible for a large cross-cultural study[7] of schizophrenia where the idiosyncratic diagnostic methods of psychiatrists were carefully controlled. This study produced some remarkable findings. Historians of medicine have searched all available historical records as widely and as far back in time as possible, and this has shown that while depression is recorded throughout history, that behaviour which is now called chronic schizophrenia is not mentioned in the literature until the beginning of the industrial revolution. The WHO cross-cultural study shows marked differences between industrial and developing countries. In the less developed countries people do show the behaviour which is diagnosed as acute and severe schizophrenia but they are not so likely to go on to become chronic schizophrenics. If you fancy retreating into schizophrenia for a while but don't want to make it a lifetime occupation, the best place to go to be treated is Agra Hospital, a building which does not share the beauty of its neighbour, the Taj Mahal. The place where you are least likely to recover is Aahus Hospital in Denmark. Obviously Western standards of cleanliness have very little regard for recovery from schizophrenia.

The answer to the question why people in the less developed countries are less likely to become chronic schizophrenics than people in developed countries would need to include a wide range of economic and social factors, most of which lie outside the range of this book. Societies differ very much in the tolerance and care they give to their members who fail to conform to the rules of society. Different societies have different family structures and different rules about behaviour within the family. Yet, wherever we are born, Agra or Aahus, Leningrad or London, Tokyo or Topeka, we are faced with the twin tasks of constructing our self and getting along with our families.

Family Relationships

Our families can help us in these tasks by encouraging us and by allowing us to separate more and more from them as we grow up. That this does not seem to happen, or, at least, happens too infrequently, in families with a schizophrenic member has been found in many studies of such families. Dr Julian Leff and his team have been researching this very carefully for a number of years and find that families differ in the number of hostile and critical remarks that are directed at the family member who has become a patient with the diagnosis of schizophrenia and in the degree of involvement the parents have in this patient. Not surprisingly, those adult children whose parents most consistently speak to them kindly and who allow them to be themselves find it easier to return to ordinary life.[8]

So often in families the members are not aware that the criticism which is being flung around is excessive, although the recipient of the criticism feels flayed and frightened. A woman writing about how their schizophrenic daughter had created so many strains and dilemmas in the family said:

> My husband is a scientist of – I suppose one can say – national eminence . . . He thinks that ordinary life has severe enough strains for most people, and an additional strain of a schizophrenic child is almost more than one can take . . . Whenever Ruth is at home he feels continually irritated by her lack of purpose and idleness, and has to hold himself in check. He says she is not the sort of person he would choose to spend time with, or make a friend of. He thinks a fundamental instinct is involved which causes both animals and human beings to peck at oddity, to rid themselves of the one who does not conform. He resents the effects this situation has had on me, the mother, and says that every time I visit Ruth or she comes home, you can scrub 2 or 3 days out of our lives, since it takes time to recover and time to prepare, all like being under a heavy cloud.[9]

It would not be beyond the bounds of possibility that the man described here had always been critical of his wife and daughter. Leff's work is with families where the patient member has been diagnosed as schizophrenic for a year or more. The question is, has the patient's behaviour provoked the hostility, criticism and over-involvement in the parents, or have the parents always mixed their love for the child with some measure of hostility, criticism and over-involvement?

These three attributes can be considered as styles of communication, and one thing that family therapy has shown is that not only does each family have its own system of communicating but that this system is developed early in the family's history and persists with few modifications over the years. A study of infants and their parents carried out in Boston, Massachusetts, in the mid-1950s included an analysis of the communication system within each family. Twenty years later, when the infants were grown up and the parents middle-aged, the study was repeated with a new team of investigators.

When the follow-up team consulted the original reports, not only did the descriptions in them turn out to be strikingly similar to the descriptions they had written after their own visits to the study families, what most impressed them was the large number of cases where the original and follow-up reports used exactly the same words to describe a child's behaviour and his or her interactive dynamics with a parent.[10]

Families rarely objectively observe and discuss the way in which they communicate, nor do they often seek to change their system of communication. As in many organizations, there is no rule for changing the rules. There is a very good reason for this. The world at large is an ever-changing, unreliable place. If the family structure stays the same, then everyone in the family has some point of fixity that keeps chaos and isolation at bay. In our families we tolerate all kinds of cruelties and misunderstandings, rather than face the terror of a world without structure.

As children we soon learn to adapt to the peculiarities of our family, even when those peculiarities cause us pain. Introverts born into families where there is much criticism retreat into impassivity, because they have learned very early in their lives that if they cry or get angry the punishment will increase, and they will suffer a level of painful stimulation with which they cannot cope. The criticizing and punishing parent (and sometimes equally hostile elder siblings) does not realize how much the introverted child is suffering. This is not just because the child does not always give an outward sign of his distress. It is also because the parent through his own upbringing has been forced to deny his own childhood experience and consequently has lost much of his ability to empathize with others. This is demonstrated in the passage quoted above where the father is described as not only having no understanding and sympathy for his daughter but also as using the defence of intellectualism to justify his cruelty to his daughter.

If, at the same time, the parents, or, at least, one parent, clings tightly to the child, refusing to allow the child to develop a separate existence, then the child cannot flee from this pain and suffering. Again love and hate are intermingled, and the child grows up believing that love is not possible without suffering.

One of the striking aspects of those introverts who under great stress retreat into the defence of schizophrenia is the intimate closeness of their relationship with their parents. As children they are not able, as George (Chapter 7) was, to get on their bike, either physically or in imagination, and flee from their parents so as to have some time and space for themselves. They may have been 'loners' as children, but they were never independent loners. Wherever they went in their inner lives, their parents went with them. They never come to feel separate from their parents, and within this connection they feel great concern and responsibility for their parents.

Harry was telling the truth when he told the psychiatrist that his father had tried to strangle him. The psychiatrist dismissed this as a delusion because he was convinced that Harry was an ungrateful, disrespectful son who had gone to university and taken drugs which had made him psychotic. In firm, but kindly, paternalist tones he reminded Harry of his duty to his father. Harry defended himself, but, becoming angry, abruptly left the room. A few minutes later he requested permission to return. The psychiatrist asked him to sit down, but Harry remained standing at a distance, hands by his sides, head bent, and apologized humbly and respectfully for his behaviour and asked for the psychiatrist's forgiveness. The psychiatrist, who came from a country where sons show great respect for their fathers, did not see anything unusual in this scene, but the rest of us present knew that not only was this behaviour not typical of twenty-year-old sons in British working-class families, but that what Harry was doing he had done many times before. In Harry's home the discipline imposed by his father was very strict.

Later, on his own with me, Harry told me a little more about the terrible scene at home where his father had lost his temper and seized him by the throat. Harry had defended himself by hitting his father and then rushing from the room. But he did not want to talk about it. He said, 'That's private', and went on to say of himself, 'They say I'm the black sheep of the family, mother's boy, can't manage on my own.'

· When Harry's father came to the hospital he showed great concern for Harry. Yet he was clearly a man whom I, for one, would hesitate to cross, and, while he spoke to and of Harry in a kindly way, it was also a subtly belittling way. He did not take Harry seriously, even though Harry's situation – about to drop out of university and enter upon the career of a psychiatric patient – was serious indeed.

Perhaps Harry was in the process of sacrificing himself for his family, just as Benjamin had done for his. Benjamin had completed his degree, but after that he found that he could not hold his world together.

Over the years I came to know Benjamin and his family well, but I was not able to help him in any way, except to offer the occasional refuge of my office and a listening ear. In his family he was the simple one who had never lived up to his promise, who needed looking after because he had strange thoughts and sometimes did strange things, like when he sat in a hot bath and slashed his wrist. Yet Benjamin saw his parents, just as he saw me, in all our inadequacies and weaknesses, and he did not reject or criticize us. He smiled at our limitations, just as he smiled when he answered a question about his damaged hand, 'It hurts a lot.'

Eventually Benjamin organized a life for himself where he lived in a bedsitter but came to the hospital two days a week simply, he told me, to save on his heating bills. He did some teaching and writing, but the drugs he was on interfered with his work.

Benjamin said to me, 'I'm having injections of Haloperidol. It makes my parents feel better.'

'If it wasn't for your parents, would you take it?'

'No. It slows me down. For the first two days after the injection I feel terrible. I perk up a bit after that.'

'You're sacrificing yourself for your parents.'

'That's right. I've given up my life for them.'

The content of the communications within a family includes giving information and instructions and recounting stories. All of these involve the process of defining, and the powerful person is the person who makes his definitions prevail. Harry had accepted his family's definition of him as 'the black sheep of the family, mother's boy, can't manage on my own'.

The defining of what a child is comes not just from what the child actually does but from what the parents project on to the child of their own fantasies, hopes and fears. Any baby born into a family is, from birth onward, continually being told whom he is like and what he will do. 'He's going to be a footballer just like his dad', as the baby kicks his legs up. 'She's going to break some hearts', as the baby gives her first smile. No baby looks just like himself. He is always like his granddad, or his uncle, or he has got his mother's eyes and his father's chin.

This is all good fun, and harmless, even helpful, if all the definitions are ones which say that the baby is welcomed, loved and valued. But not all babies are so lucky. Some of us when we were small were defined in such a way that we learned to see ourselves as somehow unacceptable, or evil, or potentially mad. Thus do we carry 'the shadow of the ancestor'.

This is a term used by R.D. Scott and P.L. Ashworth in their study of how one child in a family can be identified and labelled as being like an ancestor who was mad. The parents expected that this child would go mad, and he did.[11] Every family has its own myth about where they come from, what they are like and where they are going. In most families the main rule about the family myth is that it should not be recognized as a myth but believed and acted out as absolute truth. Each family member has a role in the myth, and the group pressure on each member to fulfil his or her assigned role is great. The mother's role might be 'the good mother, devoted to the family' and the father's 'the father who must be obeyed and never argued with'. One child might be 'the clever one', another child 'the cheerful, friendly one', and one 'the odd one out, just like his uncle'.

Turning Fear into Schizophrenia

The kind of research which looks at the attitudes and expectancies of all the family members, and sets this in the context of the family's history is complex and difficult. It is very different from the research into 'the genetics of schizophrenia' where family trees are searched for relatives who could also be diagnosed as schizophrenic or showing some 'schizophrenic' traits. The enthusiasm of some researchers in the search for the schizophrenic gene does, on occasion, allow some prejudice to creep in in the search for affected relatives. In one family I know, where the father and son have been diagnosed as schizophrenic, a cousin, a quiet young man, has been labelled as 'schizoid' and included as evidence for the genetic transmission of schizophrenia because of his unconventional behaviour. He is an active worker in the Campaign for Nuclear Disarmament, a sure sign in the eyes of the psychiatrist concerned of emotional instability!

Research into the genetics of schizophrenia does not take into account the knowledge, perceptions, and fantasies of the family members being studied. Ascertaining 'the facts' is simple: in how many family members is schizophrenia present and what is the genetic link between the affected members? Thus, one such family could be described in the following way:

In this case of schizophrenia the genetic inheritance can be clearly seen in the family tree:

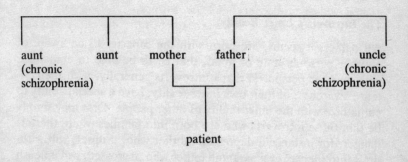

aunt   aunt   mother   father   uncle
(chronic   (chronic
schizophrenia)   schizophrenia)

patient

Researchers looking for the shadow of the ancestor would need to give their findings a story.

The patient, Simon, had an uncle who was a shame and a disgrace to his family. He never worked, but wandered round the country as a vagrant. One Christmas he arrived at his parents' home. Our patient Simon was only six at the time and he remembers being hustled out of the house by his mother, but not before he had caught a glimpse of a tall, dark figure with matted hair and a beard. This image haunted him for ever, especially as he had heard his mother and his aunt, his mother's sister, talking about him, and his aunt said, 'Simon's going to be tall like your husband's brother', and his mother said, 'I pray every day that he doesn't become like his uncle but I fear he might.' Simon did not know that his mother and aunt criticized his father's family because they needed to show that that family was worse than theirs. These two women had an elder sister who, following the death of her illegitimate baby, had thrown herself in the river. She had been pulled out and now languished, unvisited, in a back ward of the local psychiatric hospital. The patient learned of her existence from an elder cousin.

The family myth determines how we relate to one another in our families. Thus it is a powerful factor in our external reality. But we also take it inside us, and it becomes a powerful factor in our internal reality.

The Introvert's Inner Reality

All babies, it seems, are born with the capacity to be aware of another person's state of mind, that is, to be able to empathize with another person. Perhaps introverts generally, with their intense awareness of their own inner reality, have a special ability to empathize with the inner reality of other people. Or it may simply be that those introverts who are born into families where there is danger, for instance a depressed mother who, if upset, will withdraw into silence, or a paranoid father who, if crossed, will unleash his violent temper, have to develop their capacity to empathize with the inner realities of the adults around them so as to protect themselves. Whatever is the case, one striking thing about those introverts who retreat into the defence of schizophrenia is their extraordinary sensitivity to what is happening to the person they are with. Accounts of psychotherapy with schizophrenic clients frequently refer to how the therapist must maintain close attention to the client all the time, for any lapse of attention, no matter if the therapist's 'listening posture' is carefully maintained, will be noted by the client and reacted to as a rejection.

Sometimes the client will comment on what the therapist is thinking or doing, something which the therapist thinks that no one else could possibly know, and that can be extremely disturbing for the therapist. The second time Harry came to see me, when he was talking to me in highly abstract terms which were often difficult for me to follow, he suddenly said, 'This room is your haven.' This hit straight home at me. My office was not a particularly attractive or comfortable room, but it was my own territory. At that time I was feeling under great threat from some powerful people outside my office, so I was often glad to retreat to its safety. Moreover, the threat and anxiety concerned Harry, for in previous years I would have been able to give Harry a great deal of time and perhaps would have been able to work with the counsellors at his university so he could continue his career, but the threats to the future of our psychology service meant that we could not give Harry the help he needed. All the time I was listening to Harry and trying to understand what he was telling me I was angry and grieving that this gentle young man had entered upon a path which, without adequate intervention, would mean that he would either die by his own hand or spend his days like those strange automatons which every day I saw walking past my window. He saw that this room was my haven, and he tried to comfort me.

While Harry saw this in me, and while he tried to help me, he did not realize that making such a comment would shake me. Many people do not like being surprised and shaken like that. Many people prefer that certain aspects of the truth should not be noted and commented upon. Truth is very important to many introverts, for it is only by striving to know the truth, no matter how unpalatable it might be, that any sort of structure and certainty can be found in their external reality. But truth is not a commodity much valued in a conforming society, and introverts like Harry are often punished for their truth telling.

Harry's life had been spent at home and at school and nowhere else. This was why going to university far away from home had been such an unsettling shock to him. In his close-knit family he had not been able to acquire much knowledge of the outside world. He certainly did not have any concepts like 'the structure and reorganization of the National Health Service', or 'the functions of a psychology department', so he would have had no tools for comprehending and assessing my situation in a way which would have been comprehensible to anyone else. If you have this ability to empathize with another person's internal reality, to make good use of it you need to have both a strong sense of your own self and concepts in which to organize what you discover, which are concepts shared with other people. For instance, if I sense that the person to whom I have just been introduced is, under a guise of friendliness, really very angry I can organize this subtle information into, say, a question like 'I wonder what he's angry about?' and, if I feel confident in myself, decide that his anger has nothing to do with me, or, if it has, that he's a fool to get angry with so wonderful a person as me. But if I don't have these concepts, and I have no confidence in myself, what I perceive is anger, danger and confusion.

If we live solely in our inner reality we soon become confused, for in our inner reality we can create so many ideas, and there is no way of making our ideas reliable and true to life because we do not test them against our outer reality. But for an introvert, especially an introvert who lacks confidence in himself, it is not always easy to go out and do this testing.

When your inner reality is more real than your outer reality, you always have a sense of looking out upon the world. It is like living in a room and looking at the outside world through a window. To act upon the world you have to go through this window, and sometimes the window is there like a barrier, so you hesitate,

362

doubting that you can act. It is like standing on the edge of a diving board, wondering how to make the first movement and doubting, not that you won't do it properly, but that any movement is possible. You think, 'Perhaps I only imagine that I'm diving off the board, or perhaps I am diving off the board, only the board and the water aren't real.' The only way to move is to act *as if* the board and the water are real. If you have the courage to pretend a reality, what you do may then become real. You can feel a marvellous exhilaration at having acted upon external reality and found that it was there and real.

But crossing the barrier is so very difficult. Pretending in the reality of something whose reality you do not trust is so very risky. It is much safer to stay inside yourself and not act. If the acting upon the pretence of reality is not followed by exhilaration but by pain and punishment and more confusion (the chaos which threatens your self), then even more will you withdraw and not risk action.

Learning how to knit together inner and outer reality and how to act successfully upon outer reality begins at birth. The first six months of life are not, as many people think, just a space when the baby eats and sleeps; these months are when the child gains his first impressions of what the world is like and how effective he is in engaging the interest of the world and acting effectively in the world. Babies who receive what Winnicott called 'good enough' mothering have no difficulty in attracting the attention of their mothers who behave with sufficient regularity and predictability that the baby comes to experience his external reality as something he can rely on. Such mothers give the baby the opportunity to succeed, or to feel that he has succeeded, in his activities directed to outer reality. The exchanges between a good enough mother and her baby are finely tuned and complicated to describe, but they do not require 'book learning' to acquire. Studies of mothers with their babies in many different cultures show remarkable similarities in the interactions between the mother and baby where the mother is encouraging the baby to be confident in himself and in his actions.

But the starting point is the baby's desire to 'engage the world' as Dr Sanger calls it.[12] Perhaps introvert babies have more difficulty with this than extravert babies. Not wanting to be over-stimulated, they may be quiet babies, often taken for being 'good' by their mothers, who then might leave them alone for longer periods than they would a more demanding baby. Thus right from the start the baby may not have sufficient opportunity to discover his external reality. If added to this the mother is ill or depressed she may not have the energy or enthusiasm to play with her baby and talk to him, and give him those little experiences which leave him with the impression that he can act effectively in his external reality. For a baby 'a win' is anything that has a happy outcome, and this can be anything from catching hold of a rattle to having his nappy changed. Again, for reasons right outside the mother's control, she may be unable to provide her baby with a sufficiently regular and predictable environment which gives the baby con-fidence in his external reality.

It is during this phase of life, when the baby is learning how much he can trust his external reality, that he begins to put together that structure which eventually becomes his self. If some-thing happens which overwhelms this fragile sense of self the infant is flooded with fear, the most terrible experience of his life, so terrible that he spends the rest of his life trying to defend against a repetition of this experience. As Winnicott said:

> What is common in all cases [of schizophrenia] is this, that the baby, child, adolescent or adult *must never again experience* the unthinkable anxiety that is the root of schizoid illness. This unthinkable anxiety was experienced initially in a moment of failure of the environmental provision when the immature per-sonality was at the stage of absolute dependence.[13]

This 'failure of environmental provision' need not be deliberate or even ignorant neglect on the part of the parents. It may be crises quite beyond their control, or some developmental lag on the part of the child. Sanger and his colleagues divide infants into Alpha and Beta infants. The Alpha infants show a better capacity to remember than the Beta infants at the same age, but the Beta infants can, at a later stage, improve their memory function.[14] Thus a combination of factors, none in itself devastating, could create a situation where the infant self is unable to cope.

The 'unthinkable anxiety' is the breaking down of all structures and a falling into chaos. The infant who has suffered this builds up another set of structures, but these do not have firm foundations. The infant no longer trusts the outside world, so the structures he then creates may not relate very much to his outer reality. He may create a set of structures which are totally idiosyncratic, as does the child who earns the diagnosis of 'autistic'. Or he might construct something which serves him well enough through childhood and early adolescence (the 'false self' described by Winnicott and Laing[15]) but fail him when he has to face the stresses of the adult world.

In our first talk Harry said to me, 'I felt that my past and my present and my future didn't make any pattern I could recognize. There were bits, they didn't fit, I couldn't make a pattern.'

He spoke of a law which said it was evil to make barriers between people. I asked him if he was a committed Christian and he said he was 'a committed theologian'. He was well equipped to be a theologian. Later he told me how, 'When I was young I read the Bible under the bedclothes every night.'

Now he said, 'I hate being scrutinized.'

I said, 'It hurts to be scrutinized when the person is also criticizing you. But we need to scrutinize others in order to understand them.'

'I don't scrutinize others,' he put his head down, 'I want them to be free.'

He spoke of the need for stability, purity, which led on to the immense power of God. Stability was pattern, instability was chaos, pain and loss. I included aggression here, in response to fear, but he said he got aggressive only when he was trying to break free. He said, 'I had to forget that loss,' but did not explain what loss he meant. I said, 'When we lose something that was important to us we always feel the pain of that loss,' and he agreed.

He kept talking of how 'I need to have a schedule to organize my time. Then I can sort myself out.'

On the next occasion we met I asked him if I could jot down some of the things he said. These are the notes I made.

'It's like everything all at once and you can't control it.'

'The Jews say that to know everything at once is certain death.' (If he becomes totally powerful and spiritually pure he will die, but the opposite is to be like mud.)

'We can become anything we want to be.'

'The fear is that we don't know what the fear is.' (This was the theme of the book I was writing, but I had not told him about it.)

'As far as I know I could be anybody at any place at any time.' (If you give up the structures of space and time and self you could indeed be anybody at any place at any time.)

'It's like there's no beginning. We construct the time and the place. We construct the scene and we act in it.'

'It's like fears are invented by something that should be there.' (The longing for the security we once knew but now have lost?)

'There must be a written code.' (He sees the need to have some firm, authoritarian rules to keep some order within the freedom to structure. He would not dare overthrow his father's rules.)

'There's no true beginning.'

'I feel very polluted within myself.'

'I long for the things I've lost – my poetic sense, my basic rhythm. I never had them much, that's why I lost them so easily. That's what carries people along.'

'All his utterances are in abstract terms. He ignores my attempts to interpret one of his statements as a metaphor for a real-life situation.'

The next time Harry came he looked a lot better. He had had his hair washed and cut.

He talked about the necessity of structuring his time.

'What's the advantage of having your time structured?' I asked.

'Without structure I'm a shapeless black blob,' he said.

He laughed at this, saying that this was what his friend Jim had said of him, but he went on to explain that as a shapeless black blob he would be reviled and criticized and not accepted as a person.

A black blob is vulnerable and valueless. To protect it Harry needed structures of perfection and purity.

The less real an introvert's external reality becomes, the less he feels that he can deal with it and the more he must retreat from it. But even when we retreat from our external reality we still have to continue finding some structure for it, some kind of explanation. The further we retreat into our inner reality, the less our structures for and explanations of external reality actually match its dimensions. We create structures which those people observing us find to be very strange and idiosyncratic. They call these structures 'ideas of reference', 'delusions', 'hallucinations' and 'peculiar ideas'.

The disease theory of schizophrenia treats these structures as no more than symptoms of the illness and not as being meaningful in themselves. Yet they are part of the structure of meaning in which the person lives and breathes and has his being, and so, if he is to be understood, the meaning of these structures has to be understood. This is not easy, for, unlike the manic extravert whose ideas are simply exaggerations of a shared, common external reality, the introvert pushed to this extreme resorts to ideas which have a meaning which is very private and relates to experiences and feelings which he has never disclosed to anyone else. Moreover, where his ideas do relate to an external, shared experience, he may not be prepared to talk about this, for it may involve matters which his loyalty to his family would prevent him from discussing with strangers. This is why so many people diagnosed as schizophrenic and their families collude with the psychiatrist who holds to the belief that the patient is suffering from a disease of the body whose physical cause and course have not yet been discovered.

The Breakdown of Structure

To be able to give an account of anything we have to be able to see that thing in contrast to something else. Like that old saying, 'What does he know of England who only England knows?'

To give an account of what it is like to be depressed you have to have known what it is to be not depressed. There are many people who are depressed but who cannot give an account of it because they have been depressed ever since they were small children and thus do not know that there is another, more pleasant state of being. Similarly, if your external reality has always been strange then you cannot give an account of it in contrast to a more real external reality. Moreover, even with the firmest, clearest vision of a co-ordinated external and internal reality it is extremely difficult to give an account of *just how* we structure the world of meaning in which we live. As we can think only in structures, we cannot get outside structures to describe them.

Since so many of the people who have been forced to defend themselves with what is called schizophrenia have never known a time when their vision of their external reality appeared as quite real and similar to that of the people around them, we have very few accounts of what it is to have the whole structure of your world threatened to such a point that you have to defend yourself with new and idiosyncratic structures. However, one person who could give an account of what happened to her was Jessica.

Andy phoned me at home one Sunday evening. 'Something's happened to Jessica. She's started acting very strangely. She's hearing voices, I think, I can't make sense of what she's saying. Our GP came to see her and he got a psychiatrist and now she's going into hospital.'

He was very upset. I tried to reassure him that she would be well

368

looked after. I described the hospital procedures and told him how best to find out how she was and what decisions the staff made about Jessica. Over the next few weeks he kept in touch with me, and when Jessica was discharged having had the usual treatment for schizophrenia he phoned to ask if Jessica and he could come to see me. I agreed, and some time later phoned him to arrange a time. Jessica answered, her old self. Yes, she would like to come and talk. She thought it could be very helpful.

They arrived, a handsome couple in their late forties. They had been together for just five years, and each had a personal history of various relationships, marriages and alliances. Jessica now occupied her time with various small tasks which supplemented their income, but she still spoke with all the authority of a woman who had held senior posts in a large organization and had discharged her duties there competently and responsibly.

'When I was working,' she said, 'I would see how inefficient the firm was because people didn't work together co-operatively. I would draw up plans to overcome these problems – models of co-operative organization – but I could never get them implemented. My colleagues would say, "You can get people to work together because you're you, but your plans won't work generally." So eventually I decided to get out and I came here to live.'

I was interested in Jessica's emphasis on co-operation. Was this more than an interest in sensible social organization. Was it a denial of aggression within herself?

'Only to a certain extent,' she said. 'I'm a fighter when I have to be. When I was a child I fought my father all the time. I remember it caused a laugh at the time one day when he'd made me so angry I said that when I grew up I'd come back and murder him.'

She spoke of herself as being a passionate woman, full of strong sexual feelings. She spoke of affairs, and how hurt she was that although Andy shared her house he did not share her bed. Nevertheless, she had thought that they had a good relationship. They shared lots of interests and enterprises, they talked together a great deal, they pooled their knowledge and experience in ways which she found delightful and stimulating. She judged that all these benefits outweighed the times they argued.

An argument with Andy could be a dangerous activity for a woman. Even though he was now a much more peaceful, contented man than he had been in his youth, he had, he felt, been pursued and unjustly tortured by a monstrous regiment of women – his mother, wives, girlfriends, female colleagues – and he had developed a fine line of abuse about women generally which any woman standing in earshot could not help but feel was directed at her. So Jessica, over the years of being at the receiving end of Andy's sharp tongue, had gradually lost confidence in herself.

'In the five years we've been together,' she said, 'I've come to feel increasingly bad about myself.'

However, even with this she had felt that she could see and assess their relationship quite clearly and she had confidence in her judgement. Then something happened which showed her that she could not. She discovered that Andy was having an affair with a woman neighbour. Each day when he was supposed to be going about his various tasks he was disappearing into this woman's house. Jessica was shattered.

'I felt I could no longer trust my judgement in anything. This is what is so important. I have to be able to trust my judgement and to act on it. My judgement isn't just from my head, my intellect, but from here,' she pressed her hands against the region of her heart and stomach. 'It has to come from here out, on what is out there, and I have to be able to trust it so I can act. If I don't trust my judgement I don't know how to act. When Andy criticized me he would attack my judgement and that was what was so devastating. He would say that I was wrong in my judgement of other people – people who were important to me. He'd question my motives. He'd make out that my motives were bad, that I wanted to hurt him, when I knew they weren't. I didn't want to injure him, but he said I did. My father did the same to me as a child. He wanted to tell me that I was bad, wicked. I would tell him that I wasn't but he wouldn't believe me.'

The news of Andy's defection brought more than the pain of rejection. Her confidence in her judgement, the process whereby she structured and evaluated her world, was shattered. Now she was in danger of annihilation.

'I was filled with the most terrible sense of dread. It was the most horrible experience. I felt that something terrible was about to happen. It was something I was going to do, or something was going to happen to me. I thought I had killed Andy and buried him in the garden. I thought that Andy and Alex were going to live together in my house and I would have to live with her husband. I went out into the garden and stayed there because I thought nothing bad could happen to me there. Then I went next door. My neighbour there is a very good woman and I thought nothing bad could happen if I stayed with her. Then I felt that that wouldn't work, so I went out into the marketplace. I thought if I was in such a public place then people would see and nothing terrible could happen to me there. To others all this running about seemed quite crazy, but to me it made sense at the time.'

Along with these desperate attempts to avoid the greatest danger came thoughts of omniscient power. 'I thought I understood the most complex mathematical concepts. It frightened me having so much knowledge. In the past I felt I was blocked in every direction. Now I felt I had changed. I had got rid of all the blocks. I was free to go in any direction.'

'Is that how you feel now, that you've changed?'

Jessica looked at me, her lips tightening. 'There are some things which I see now are not important. But, no, nothing's changed.'

Eighteen months later she had revised her opinion. She said that it had 'not been a bad experience. Just what I needed really. You have fixed pictures in your unconscious and you don't have access to them, although they exert a strong influence. In that experience of madness everything gets well and truly mixed up. That was good for me.'

She contrasted this experience where her structures fell apart

371

with other experiences in her life where all her structures came together in a complete and wonderful whole, and she entered into periods of what mystics call 'union' or 'enlightenment'. That such experiences of increased awareness are generally more common than is generally recognized has been shown by the work of the zoologist Alister Hardy and his colleagues in the Religious Experience Unit at Oxford[16] and by David Hay.[17]

In such experiences our structures are not so much destroyed as abandoned. Having our structures destroyed makes us helpless; abandoning our structures, we feel brave and strong. To be able to abandon our structures we have first to be able to recognize them as structures. Once you know, either through teachings such as Zen, or through your own experience, such as many introverts have, that everything you perceive is a structure which you have created, nothing thereafter seems very real. You know that there is for you always the possibility of falling helplessly into chaos, which is then followed by desperate reconstructing, and at the same time the possibility of abandoning your structures, changing in an infinite number of ways, and having one of the most glorious experiences which life can offer. This is one of the reasons why many of the introverts who have entered upon the schizophrenic experience decide not to relinquish it.

Linking the Inner and Outer Realities

Many people who have had a schizophrenic experience have reported that even in the extremes of this experience part of them remains separate, 'watching the parade go by'. Manfred Bleuler, who for fifty years was the director of the Burghölzli clinic in Zurich, wrote:

Even though older schizophrenics seldom laugh, they do smile on occasions. After years of illness they can still discuss their symptoms in detail, banter them about as if they were nothing but their whimsical ideas, and then adapt themselves in keeping with the effect of all this on the conversational partner. One patient remarked with regard to his symptoms: 'It was partly my own choice, and partly it was repugnant to me.' Schizophrenics learn no longer to live in the world of delusions, but to live with it; they no longer allow themselves to be driven by their madness, but they work through it as part of themselves, in shaping their own will and manner of living, by considering and applying normal, healthy traits of human behaviour.[18]

Unfortunately, in our society anyone who is in the midst of a schizophrenic experience can very quickly become a person of little value. In a traditional psychiatric hospital, once a person is given the diagnosis of schizophrenia, that person is immediately slotted into routine care. Doctors and nurses greet a diagnosis of schizophrenia with relief, for with that they know what to do. The person is given one of the major tranquillizers and very soon becomes quieter, more reasonable, and the strange behaviour disappears. The nurses usually treat the patient with great kindness, for they see the person as condemned to lifelong illness, and as the illness has a physical cause, it is not the patient's fault. But this kindness is in itself a denigration of the person. He is seen as damaged and inferior, not someone to be taken seriously.

Anyone diagnosed as schizophrenic by a psychiatrist who believes that schizophrenia is a physical illness is unlikely to be given the chance to talk to a psychotherapist. Despite the extensive reports by many psychotherapists successfully working with people in the schizophrenic experience, many psychiatrists believe that psychotherapy is detrimental to someone with such a diagnosis. The only reason I met Harry was because the psychiatrist considered that all Harry's problems stemmed from his taking drugs at university. As he explained to me, 'If I thought Harry was schizophrenic I would not have asked him to see you.' When it became clear from what Harry and his elder brother told me that Harry had begun his retreat into his inner world many years before, I was placed in a quandary, for if I imparted this to the psychiatrist he might insist that I stop seeing Harry. This is one of the issues which arise again and again for psychologists working in a traditional psychiatric hospital.

In such hospitals now many psychologists are concerned with

helping those people who are regarded as chronic schizophrenics to leave the hospital and live in the community. Such people are often strange and difficult, and they are regarded as being of little importance by many psychiatrists and administrators. One consultant I knew, an otherwise kind and caring man, would refer to the inhabitants of his back wards as 'the dregs'. Many administrators see them as no more than objects to be counted and moved from one place to another. Any individuality is discounted and ignored. Such doctors and administrators do not attempt to make that empathetic leap of the imagination into the world of the person enclosed in the schizophrenic experience.

It is not easy to do, even with the best will in the world.

Imagine that you are in a dark, circular room which has no doors or windows. The walls and ceiling of this room form a continuous television screen, and from the screen come changing, vibrant, intriguing, exciting, dangerous, fearful images and sounds so strong that they seem to fill the entire space.

Captivated by all this you are not much aware that you have ingested a tranquillizing drug. But now the enveloping screen with all its images starts to shrink. It does not disappear completely, but it reduces to the size of an ordinary television screen. It is not switched off. It stays there, the images flickering on the screen.

You hear someone talking to you. Off to one side you see a small window open on to the external world. You are frightened to go over to it because you are so unsure of yourself. There is someone out there trying to reach you. The more you trust the person who is trying to reach you, the more you are drawn to the window. The better the world looks outside your window, the more windows you open up, until the television screen vanishes in the bright light.

But if the outside world brings you pain and suffering, you can always slam the windows shut and retreat to the safety and comfort of your television screen. It may not be much, but it is your own.

The person who is poised between the window and the television screen has to decide whether to face the implications of what it is to be known as a schizophrenic in our society. It is not merely the public shame of being labelled as mad. There are the practical issues of having lost a job, or failed to graduate, or having been divorced by your spouse, or having lost your few friends to their careers and their marriages. The options open to you, working at something well below your capabilities, joining the unemployed in their fruitless job-seeking, working on the monotonous and trivial tasks in the hospital's Industrial Rehabilitation Unit, sitting in the ward's day room, or the hospital corridor or canteen, drinking tea in the ex-patients' drop-in centre, or drifting from bus station to park bench and back again while you wait for your landlord to let you into your room again, are not likely to engage your interest or boost your self-confidence. It is no wonder that you keep the television in your head for company.

Many such people know that their private thoughts are not sufficient company and that their future is unacceptably bleak. It would not be surprising if someone in this situation became depressed, and, of course, many do. Amongst those people who have been diagnosed as schizophrenic there is a higher rate of suicide than in the general public. Amazingly, those psychiatrists who believe that schizophrenia is a physical disease have argued that the disease process of schizophrenia is incompatible with the disease process of depression. Thus, if you catch schizophrenia you cannot catch depression. Accordingly, when someone who was diagnosed as schizophrenic insisted on showing the powerful emotions of being depressed, the diagnosis would be changed to 'schizo-affective illness'. Denying that someone is capable of becoming depressed is, in effect, to deny that person's humanity. The same thing happens to mentally handicapped people. They are supposed by many people to be always carefree and happy, incapable of sadness and mourning.

The idea that schizophrenia is an illness located inside the adolescent or adult person has prevented many psychiatrists from studying infant development. Yet it is in those early months that the basic structures of self and relationships with others are laid down.

For instance, it seems that a baby is born expecting 'reciprocity in interactions. This expectancy forms the basis for the learning of an important skill: how to play the speaker's and listener's roles in dialogue. Known as *turn-taking*, its mastery is essential to the ability to communicate effectively with others. (Imagine how hard it would be to tell anyone anything if you didn't know when it was your turn to speak and your turn to listen.) This is why an infant has been primed to expect his building block, reciprocity, in exchanges. And why, when that reciprocity is provided, not only do the child's turn-taking skills blossom early and fully but his other, related communication skills do as well. It is also why a baby eventually turns away from a partner who can't or won't conduct interactions on a reciprocal basis.'[19]

A great deal of research has been devoted to the study of 'schizophrenic thought disorder'. Schizophrenia has been seen by many psychologists as 'fundamentally a cognitive disorder in which language disturbance is part of an inability or failure to regulate one's thoughts'. This theory, like the theory of the disease of schizophrenia, locates the problem as being in the individual. One psychologist working in this area, David Rutter, decided that instead of examining individual monologues he would look at what goes on in conversations. He found that 'in conversations, just as in monologues, the problem for schizophrenic patients was much less the *cognitive* processes of regulating and organizing their thoughts than the *social* processes of expressing and communicating those thoughts in a way which the listener could understand and follow. Where the difficulty really lay was in taking the role of the other and it is that which seems to be the key.'[20] That is, the problem is in turn-taking.

When we have been trained to think and work in a particular way, and when the conclusions we drew from our early childhood experiences are reinforced by this training, we find it extremely hard to change. It is no wonder that those people who had the kind of upbringing which made them conventional and obedient and who then entered a profession, psychiatry, which demands that its members conform obediently to its rules and beliefs, have great difficulty in accepting ideas and practices which challenge what they have learned. Moreover, if the schizophrenic experience is defined as an illness, in the cure of which only psychiatrists have expertise, then the consultant psychiatrist becomes a powerful person. It is not easy to give up power.

The neuroleptic drugs, the major tranquillizers, which have been developed to reduce the horrors which the schizophrenic experience can produce, are prescribed for many more people than those diagnosed as schizophrenic, and such drugs provide considerable wealth for the drug industry. These neuroleptic drugs certainly deaden and restrain the emotions, but they also destroy that part of the mid-brain which controls movement, thus producing uncontrollable facial and body movements. Anyone for whom these drugs are recommended, particularly on a long-term basis, should be informed of the implications of taking the drug so they can decide what degree of risk they are prepared to run. The only way in which we can ever gain self-confidence is for us to make our own decisions. This means that the people around us must let us make our own decisions.

It is impossible to separate the individual's schizophrenic experience from the economics and politics of the society where the individual lives. You can indulge your anxiety and panics, your obsessions and compulsions, your depression, and even your mania, provided you don't run foul of the law and remain in the privacy of your home, but once you choose schizophrenia as your defence society will not let you be. Whether you emerge unscathed from your schizophrenic experience depends as much on what society decides to do with you as on what you decide to do for yourself.

Those two profound experiences, depression and schizophrenia, are more than just the experiences of troubled individuals. Just as the experience of depression addresses itself to all the moral issues of life, so the experience of schizophrenia addresses all the issues of becoming and being an individual in relation to a group.

We can, in cowardice, turn away from the people enduring the experience of schizophrenia, insisting as we do that what they are suffering is nothing but a physical illness and that they are now a lower order of the species, incapable of even understanding their illness, much less making decisions about it. Or we can have the courage to try to understand what these people experience, and, in that understanding, come to understand ourselves, not in just what we think and do, but how our thoughts, feelings and actions are structured and how these structures were created in our interactions with others.

Julian Leff, in his *Schizophrenia: Notes for Relatives and Friends*,[21] recommends that 'the schizophrenic person' should be treated with patience and tolerance and allowed to lead a life separate from his family. To this I would add that those of us who go through the schizophrenic experience should not be deprived of the right to make our own decisions.

Turning Fear into Courage

Chapter Eleven

Turning Fear into Courage

There is an old Chinese saying, *One disease, long life; no disease, short life*.

Which means that if you know your weaknesses, you will live sensibly and wisely, and protect yourself from danger. But if you don't know your weaknesses you will delude yourself that you are safe and well when you are not, or you will think that danger lies in one direction when it lies in another. The end result of such ignorance is that, at best, you fail to become the person that you might have been, and, at worst, you suffer terribly.

We all have weaknesses, even those who claim to have none. We cannot avoid having weaknesses, for there is no way of living, no philosophy of life, which means that you always do the right thing, make the right decision, succeed at everything you do, and never get into danger. A right action towards one person is usually a wrong action towards another (the more attention you pay to your children, the less to your spouse). All decisions have good implications and bad implications (deciding to work hard at your job to provide well for your family means that your family gets less of your time and attention). There are not enough hours in the day for us to perform every task we undertake at the highest possible level of achievement, or even merely competently. There is no part of the earth's surface where the inhabitants are safe from the vagaries of nature, and, now, the incompetence if not the malice and aggressiveness of men (and one or two women; alas, when women get into power they can be as insensitive and cruel as men).

In weakness we feel fear. So fear is always with us.

We cannot eradicate fear. But we can learn to deal with fear so that we are no longer overwhelmed by it, or forced to maintain expensive, life-sapping defences against it.

How can we deal with fear?

Knowing and Naming

All sensible men and women, and most of us are, are fairly good at identifying threats to our physical wellbeing and at doing something about them. We might not be very good at dealing with the major threats to our existence – nuclear war, nuclear radiation, worldwide pollution, starvation, colossal national debts – but we are quite good at seeing that our children get safely to school and that our car is in running order. What we are not very good at doing is identifying and dealing with threats to our person, the self which is our essential being. This is the fear which is too fearful even to be acknowledged.

The most terrible fear we can experience is the fear that our identity, our self, is about to be annihilated. We sense ourselves falling into chaos, into emptinessness, a withering away, a disappearing, a wiping out. Where there was once a person will be a nothingness. We defend ourselves with whatever comes to hand. Some people even kill their bodies in order to preserve their self.

We can kill our own body, but we cannot annihilate our self. Our self can be annihilated only by other people.

Other people can annihilate us only if we give them the power to do so.

It is as if we give the other person a knife and say, 'Now kill me.'

The way we give other people the power to annihilate us is to see other people as more powerful than us, as more valuable than us, as better than us, as having the right to criticize us, to talk down to us, to insult us, to deprive us, to punish and to injure us.

We give other people the power to annihilate us when we do not value ourselves.

If we value ourselves we are not impressed by the claims to power that other people make. If we value ourselves we see ourselves as being as valuable as all other people. If we value ourselves we see ourselves as the equal of all other people. If we value ourselves we accept helpful advice, but we do not accept destructive criticism, or allow ourselves to be belittled, or insulted, or deprived, punished or injured.

Remember the children's rhyme, *Sticks and stones can break my bones but names will never hurt me*.

Tragically, most of us were taught as children that we were not good enough. We grew up not valuing ourselves, and thus are for ever giving to other people the power to annihilate us.

Other people do try to annihilate us. They may not wish to wipe us out as a person, but they do want us to know our place, not argue, be obedient, accept their definition of reality and abandon ours. We can go along with what they want, and be, if not annihilated, never ourselves. Or we can decide things for ourselves.

There are two problems about deciding things for yourself. First, it means you can't blame anyone else when things turn out badly. (But you can take the credit when things turn out well.) Second, other people can get very angry with you for not doing what they want.

Valuing yourself is a risky business.

Which risk is preferable? The risk of making your own decisions or the risk of not valuing yourself.

Valuing Yourself

Undoing the training of our early years, when we learned that we weren't good enough, that we had to be good to earn the right to exist, and never even think about, much less question, why and how we were taught this, is not easy. If you have spent all the years you remember feeling that somehow you have to prove yourself by your achievements, or that you have to earn the right to breathe by working hard in devoted service to others, for if you don't prove yourself to be brave, or a winner, or a hard worker, some vast hand will come down from Heaven and pick you off the face of the earth like a flea off a dog's back, and cast you into nothingness, if this is how you have spent your life, then deciding that you are simply going to *be* and that you accept your being is a revolution in thought that you aren't likely to achieve in the twinkling of an eye.

Though some people do do it, just like that. They say to

themselves, 'I'm not going to go on carrying this load of shit that other people have dumped on me over the years. I'm dropping it now.' And they do. They are free, just being themselves.

But some people, I find, don't even know what I am talking about when I say, 'Just be yourself.'

So we have to begin by asking, 'Do we have the right to exist?'

If we exist, we have the right to exist.

We do not have to ask anyone's permission to exist.

We do not have to thank our parents for creating us, for we did not ask to be born. We can appreciate the love and care our parents gave us, but if they demand that we owe them a debt of gratitude which our lifetime will never be long enough to repay, then they are demanding that we give up our self for them, and that is a price no parent has the right to demand. We do not owe our parents a debt of gratitude, and our children do not owe us a debt of gratitude. When we talk of love we should be clear what we mean.

We can say, 'I love you' and mean, 'I love you because I want to feed off you. You must meet my needs. You must do what I want. I will not love you unless you do what I want.' Or we can mean, 'I love you because you are you. My life is better because you exist. I wish you well in every aspect of your being, even if what is well for you will not always include me.'

The first kind of love destroys; the second preserves, accepts, supports and creates.

Accepting yourself means accepting the self that you have. Accepting yourself means giving up shopping around for an alternative self, a better model, which will meet all your ridiculous demands for perfection.

Self Selection

At last Safeways
Has made a notable contribution
To everyday philosophical thought.

SELF SELECTION is their theory, put forward
In bold caps, beside the oranges,
And who could resist it?

Who would not be pleased to carry home
A better-adjusted, seamless,
Selfless self: decisive yet flexible,

Loving yet integral; cheerful
But not offensively so?
A self with poise,

Who knows a mot juste
From a put-down;
A complaint from a whine.

A brave self. A self
Who worries more about world starvation
Than his dandruff.

But what to do with the old self?
Drown it in a bucket? Leave it
Under the counter, where the boxes are?

It would follow you home.
You would feel it creeping back
Under your waistcoat.

It knows you hate change.[1]

There are a lot of people who are for ever trying to get rid of their hateful old self and find a new self which matches up to their impossibly high standards. They have not realized that this activity is as likely to succeed as if they decided that they didn't like having brown eyes and were determined to trade them in for blue.

They have not realized that that part of themselves which they despise, the darkness into which they have cast all those parts of themselves which their family told them were bad, is the source of their creativity, freedom and individuality.

It is possible to take your old self and, caring for it deeply, polish up its performance. Make it less prone to self-criticism and more self-rewarding. Help it give up all those pathetic self-conceits put on to hide the bits of itself that you don't like and so come to delight in being itself.

You are yourself and you care for yourself.

It is sad that so often it takes a great deal of pain and suffering for us to realize that we must care for ourselves.

Joy endured tremendous pain and anxiety in the months that followed the revelations about what Jack had done. Yet, some time later when I went to visit Joy and Jack I was surprised to see her looking relaxed and calm. She told me, 'All my life I thought I had to make it right for everybody else before I could make it right for myself. Now I've learned that I don't have to be responsible for everyone. I'd always thought that I had to do everything perfectly because I was responsible for everyone. Now I know I'm not, and I can take the time to look after myself. So now, when I need a rest, I go and sit in the garden.'

People who want to swap their old self for a new one think that this is like trading in your old car for a new one. You can show your new self off to the neighbours, but life still goes on as before, only better. They don't realize that changing your self changes everything.

Accepting yourself changes you. Accepting yourself changes your relationship with others.

Your Relationships With Others

When we don't accept ourselves we live in fear of other people. We are afraid they will hurt us. We are afraid they will leave us. The people who can hurt us most are the ones we do not want to lose. We hang on to the people we love, all the time expecting that they will leave us, for if we are as bad as we think we are, then of course they will go.

We hang on to people by trying to control them. We pretend that we aren't trying to control the people we need. We tell ourselves that we know what is best for other people. We tell ourselves that we are responsible for other people. We tell ourselves that we are very good at caring. And all the time we are hanging on like grim death, and our tight grip damages the people that we love. We will not let ourselves see *'How selfhood begins with a walking away/And love is proved by letting go.'*[2]

Not valuing yourself means that you have never grown up. You have never walked away. You are still trying to please your parents, if not the actual people who conceived you, then the representations of parents that you carry around inside you. You are still trying to be good and obedient.

Someone once remarked that the Soviet Union is a school from which no one ever graduates. The Russians are certainly very good at being good. If they weren't so good at being good they would value their dissidents much more. But they stick very obediently to their society's rules. They are not the only people who have never graduated to adulthood no matter how old they become, and who have chosen the security of permanent childhood instead of the freedom of being themselves. The world is full of people who are good at being good and who, like obedient high school children, prefer security to freedom.

But such a security is an illusion, for no amount of goodness and obedience can preserve you from danger and disaster. Even when the illusion of safety is being maintained, such people cannot enjoy a contented life, for, as anger always follows unacknowledged fear, they are always feeling angry with those people who don't keep to the rules. There is envy there, too, for those people who don't keep to the rules.

But, of course, there is a reward for not accepting yourself, for always feeling that you have to work hard to be good and never being quite good enough, so you can never stop trying and thus never really grow up. You had to meet your parents' needs, and now your children can meet yours.

I see many examples of parents expecting that their needs should be met by their children in the letters which I receive from the readers of *Chat* magazine. For instance, knowing how small children tend to dawdle behind their parents when they are out walking, and how worrying and aggravating this can be to parents, I wrote a piece about some research which was done by two psychologists in America. They watched children and mothers in a shopping mall, and estimated the height of each child, the height of each mother, and the distance each child walked behind his mother. Their calculations showed that each child walked at a distance from which he could see the whole of his mother, thus distinguishing her from all the other people in the mall. If the child moved closer to his mother, all he could see was skirts and shoes, and the ubiquitous jeans and trainers, and that way mother easily got lost.

I was quite pleased with what I had written, thinking that it would help parents be more patient and understanding with their small children. But, no. I got letters from readers who were mothers telling me that what I should have said was that mothers should put their children in walking reins. Walking reins are a leather or plastic harness which fits over the child's chest and to which is attached a lead. The mother can then control her child as she would her dog. Walking reins make the mother feel safe.

Walking reins meet the mother's needs. Her child can't wander off and fall under a bus or be abducted, or take up her time in searching and waiting, or explore things which she does not want him to explore.

Walking reins do not meet the child's needs. They prevent the child from learning through trial and error (the only kind of learning that is of any practical use) the complex social skill of being with other people while walking and observing. The child is prevented from learning this skill, but he will certainly learn something else. It may be undying rage at the mother who so inhibits him, and the moment he is free he will try to escape. Twenty years later his mother wonders why he never comes back home. Or it may be the belief that it doesn't matter what mischief he gets into, mother will get him out of it. Twenty years later she wonders why she is still paying his debts and sorting out his divorces. Or he might come to believe that he cannot exist without her and that he has no right to try. Twenty years later she wonders why he stays in his bedroom, not speaking to anyone except her and the nurse who gives him his monthly injection.

As parents, one of the needs we have is that our children should have a secure and happy life. Even those parents who have no difficulty in letting their children be themselves and who do not expect their children to make up to them what they missed out in childhood, still would like to see their adult children enjoying life. As parents, most of us spend a great deal of time teaching our children things which we hope will stand them in good stead in their adult lives. Why is it then that we can see a connection between being given pocket money and a money box when you are four and being able to manage your financial affairs when you are twenty-four, but we cannot see a connection between being punished for exploring when you are four and not wanting to go anywhere on your own when you are twenty-four?

The answer is that we refuse to see in our children what we refuse to see in ourselves.

We do not want to admit that childhood is not a happy time. Sheldon Kopp called it a nightmare,[3] and a nightmare it is, in that you are small and weak in a strange new world, and helplessly dependent upon giants who can be the most wonderful people and the most terrifying people, and you don't know why. There are times when you are happy, but this is always when you are being yourself, discovering the world, or with people who will let you be yourself and even, best of all, let you win. The rest of the time, when you have to be what other people want you to be, which is quiet, clean and tidy, eating properly, sleeping properly, grateful, unselfish, not answering back, doing as you're told, in all, *being good*, then, at best, you are getting by, and, at worst, you are lost in a world of terror. This terror haunts you for the rest of your life.

Everybody knows this terror. If someone says he doesn't, he is lying. He may just be lying to others in order to maintain his pride. Or he may be lying to himself, which is the most self-destructive thing anyone can do.

389

Beyond Fear

We can go on struggling and being defeated by fear all on our own, or we can decide to go beyond the fear by holding and helping one another.

Holding and Helping One Another

It is other people who threaten to annihilate us and to plunge us into the greatest fear.

It is other people who can protect us and help us survive our greatest fear.

When you have had a life full of punishments and disappointments you find it hard to ask for help. Years ago, before the invention of credit cards, shops used to carry a sign *Do not ask for credit as a refusal often offends*. Many people spend their lives avoiding being offended in this way.

When you have had a life full of punishments and disappointments you carry so much pain inside you that you cannot bear to see another person's pain, because that makes you all the more aware of your own.

So many of us will not ask for help, and many of us, when asked, will turn away. We give money to charity, but we will not listen to what those nearest to us might say.

Some of us, fortunately, learn wisdom.

George said, 'The wrong sort of religion can be extremely dangerous. But the right sort of religion, that's searching for God in oneself. I think that that is concerned with relationships with people, and if these are right, then it's in these experiences that we find God. Religion can be so devastating to people, and it can be so enriching if we can find the right path. When people are tied to the rules of their religion, like I was tied, they are crippled by their religion. If you can get over this rule-keeping, then, somehow, you can grow up. I haven't achieved wholeness in myself yet, but what I have learned is that other people matter. The parish has been so good to me. They've looked after me. I realize now that we minister to one another. It's not the pastor and the parish. It's all of us, together.'

What is the right kind of relationship, one that helps and holds?

A psychologist who had, as she put it, 'survived depression' said:

> From my GP's non-intrusive but sustained interest and con-
> cern, I have learnt something of the critical importance of
> constructively encouraging rather than undermining people's
> own efforts, in the misplaced zeal to be 'helpful'. I also
> appreciate how vital it can be to have someone just to go on
> being there and wanting to know, month after month, and
> year after year, if need be. Quite apart from the quality of the
> relationship, the continuity of regular contact with someone I
> could trust and could still seem to relate to me as a whole and
> viable person, when all I felt like was a heap of disconnected
> bits was crucial in keeping the disconnections from actually
> happening.[4]

A psychotherapist, who no doubt knew all the intellectually compelling concepts and systems of the various schools of psychotherapy, looked back over her experience of depression and wrote:

> What I really needed was someone who I could feel was on my
> side in trying to sort out my problems; someone who did not
> need to prove his or her professional competence by coming
> up with a neat solution, or hide behind a professional role that
> cut me off from the person; someone who did not have to put
> my parents' point of view, or that of society, or have to protect
> someone else's interests. Such a person could, I feel, have
> given me the security within which to look at why I had
> become depressed, and I am sure I would have come out of it
> a lot sooner as a result.[5]

What these two people are describing is something which is more than everyday communications which go on between people, but not something which requires special training to produce 'experts'. It is something we all can do for one another, if we take the time to listen to and observe other people and our own selves. This way we can help one another to go beyond fear.

Beyond Fear

To go beyond fear we have to accept ourselves and to let other people be themselves and to accept them as they are.

To go beyond fear we have to accept that we have to take life on trust. There are many people who feel that there must be some Grand Design about Life, the Universe and Everything which human beings are capable of understanding, because if there wasn't 'Life would be meaningless'. What such people have not realized is that the worry about life being meaningless if there isn't a Heaven, or a Law of Karma, or a Judgement Day, all as real and certain as the sun, is the fear of falling into chaos and nothingness, that is, the fear of the annihilation of the self. If we realize this, we find that all the ambiguities about life and death are not so bewildering and frightening.

When we accept ourselves we are not frightened by the ambiguity of life and death, but see it as something delightfully intriguing, and the source of our freedom. When we accept ourselves we are not frightened by freedom.

When we accept ourselves we no longer fear annihilation. We might still fear death, for there are people we don't wish to lose, and when you are enjoying life you don't want to die.

But if we have the courage to face death and ambiguity, then what we find is that death is death, the solution to all problems, the end to all suffering, and ambiguity is nothing but a welcoming sea which, if we cast ourselves upon it, will bear us up in hope and understanding and inexplicable joy. Pain may come before we cast ourselves on the sea, but in the end there is nothing to be afraid of.

All is all, and everything is everything, and we are part of it all, and we belong.

Appendices

Appendices

Source Notes

1. The Nature of Fear

1. See R. J. Lifton, *Home from the War*, Simon and Schuster, New York 1973.
2. See D. Rowe, *The Construction of Life and Death*, Wiley, Chichester 1982.
3. D. Adams, Pan, London 1980.
4. In *Crossing the Water*, Faber, London 1971.
5. Charlotte Lessing, July 1985.
6. P. Mollon, 'Shame in relation to narcissistic disturbance', *British Journal of Medical Psychology*, 57, 1984, pp. 207–14.
7. See T. Doi, *The Anatomy of Dependence*, trans. J. Bester, Kodansha International Ltd, Tokyo 1981.
8. *The Mind Box*, Everyman Series, BBC TV, 2 February 1985.
9. Quoted in *Family Circle*, from *Fizz*, July 1985.
10. *Observer*, 14 April 1985.
11. D. Rowe, *Living With the Bomb: Can We Live Without Enemies?* Routledge, London 1985, p. 38.
12. *The First Relationship: Infant and Mother*, Fontana, London 1977, p. 9.
13. *ibid.*, p. 41.
14. *Collected Papers*, Hogarth Press, London 1978, p. 151.
15. *ibid.*, p. 150.
16. Stern, *op. cit.*, p. 119.
17. *op. cit.*, p. 303.
18. Stern, *op. cit.*, p. 65.
19. S. Kakar, *Shamans, Mystics and Doctors*, Oxford University Press, New Delhi 1982, pp. 197–201.
20. *The Child, the Family and the Outside World*, Penguin, Harmondsworth 1964, p. 77.
21. *ibid.*, p. 78.
22. *ibid.*, p. 90.
23. *op. cit.*, p. 120.
24. *Collected Papers*, p. 150.

2. Fear Denied

1. R. Scott, 'They hounded him to death', *Daily Mail*, 25 June 1985.
2. *Men*, BBC Books, London 1984, p. 19.

3. Learning How to Deny

1. *Conceptions of Modern Psychiatry*, Tavistock, London 1955, pp. 59–61.
2. *The Child, the Family and the Outside World*, Penguin, Harmondsworth 1964, p. 62.
3. *Collins Concise English Dictionary*, Williams Collins Sons and Co. Ltd, Glasgow 1978, p. 551.
4. Quoted by A. Miller, in *For Your Own Good*, Faber, London 1983, p. xviii.
5. Basil Blackwood, Oxford 1985, pp. 1–2.
6. *ibid.*, p. 2.
7. *Thou Shalt Not Be Aware*, Pluto Press, London 1985, p. 92.
8. Routledge, London 1985.
9. A. Miller, *op. cit.*, p. 98.
10. M. Mehr, *Steinzeit* (Stone Age), Berne 1981, quoted in A. Miller, *op. cit.*, p. 45.
11. *op. cit.*, p. 130.
12. A. Miller, *For Your Own Good*, Faber, London 1984, p. 192.
13. Pocket Books, New York 1979.
14. Volcano Press, Inc., San Francisco 1978.
15. *The Late, Late Show*, Eire TV, 1985.

4. A Bodily Solution?

1. Routledge, London 1983.
2. J. Aubertin, personal communication, 24 August 1985.
3. *Wounded Healers*, ed. V. Rippere and R. Williams, Wiley, Chichester 1985, p. 168.
4. Tavistock, London 1982.
5. In *Wounded Healers*, p. 136.
6. Wiley, Chichester 1985.
7. G. A. Marlett and D. J. Rohsenow, 'The think-drink effect', *Psychology Today*, 15, 1981, pp. 61–4, quoted in Snyder *et al*, *op. cit.*, p. 226.
8. C. H. McGaghy, 'Drinking and Deviance Disavowal: The case of child molesters', *Social Problems*, 16, 1968, pp. 43–9, quoted in Snyder *et al*, *op. cit.*, p. 229.

9. Snyder *et al*, op. cit., p. 229.
10. 'Is Alcoholism a Disease?' *New Society*, 21 February 1986, p. 318.
11. *ibid.*, p. 319.
12. *ibid.*, pp. 319–20.
13. Hamlyn, London 1981.
14. *Hunger Strike*, Faber, London 1986, p. 13.
15. *ibid.*, p. 14.
16. *The Second Sin*, Routledge, London 1984, quoted in S. MacLeod, *The Art of Starvation*, Virago, London 1984, p. 63.
17. *op. cit.*, p. 66.
18. *Hunger Strike*, p. 149.
19. *ibid.*, p. 36.
20. *ibid.*, p. 69.
21. *op. cit.*, p. 25.
22. *Hunger Strike*, p. 89.
23. *op. cit.*, p. 49.
24. *Hunger Strike*, p. 89.
25. *ibid.*, p. 66.
26. *ibid.*, p. 66.
27. *ibid.*, p. 152.
28. Women's Therapy Centre, London, and Women's Therapy Centre Institute, New York.
29. Anorexic Aid, The Priory Centre, 11 Priory Rd, High Wycombe, Buckinghamshire, England; National Association of Anorexia Nervosa and Associated Disorder, Box 271, Highland Park, Illinois 60035, USA.
30. 'Stress link with cancer', *Guardian*, 24 February 1986.
31. 'Psychological influences on immunity', *Psychosomatics*, in press, 1987, and 'Marital quality, marital disruption, and immune function', *Psychosomatic Medicine*, in press, 1987.

5. The Alternatives

1. A. Scull, *Museums of Madness*, Penguin, Harmondsworth 1972, p. 13.
2. Interview, *Bulletin of the Royal College of Psychiatrists*, 10, March 1986, p. 44.
3. *Asylums*, Penguin, Harmondsworth 1980.
4. H. Maudsley, *Responsibility in Mental Disease*, Kegan Paul, London 1984, p. 154.
5. 'Books for asylum doctors', *Bulletin of the Royal College of Psychiatrists*, 10, February 1986, p. 23.
6. *Aliens and Alienists*, Penguin, Harmondsworth 1980.

7. *The Complete Letters of Sigmund Freud to Wilhelm Fliess, 1887–1904*, 7 August 1901, ed. J. M. Masson, Harvard University Press, Cambridge, Massachusetts, 1985.
8. *Depression: The Facts*, Oxford University Press, Oxford 1981, pp. v, vi.
9. 23 December 1977, p. 3.
10. D. Wigoder, *Images of Destruction*, Routledge, London, 1987, p. 9.
11. *Royal Air Force News*, 18 October 1986, p. 13.
12. *Wounded Healers*, ed. V. Rippere and R. Williams, Wiley, Chichester 1985, pp. 15, 20.
13. 22 March 1986, p. 1.
14. Volcano Press, Inc., San Francisco 1978, pp. 6, 64.
15. *Thou Shalt Not Be Aware*, Pluto Press, London 1985, p. 162.
16. 'Confusion of tongues between adults and the child', paper read before the International Psycho-analytic Congress, September 1932, quoted in J. M. Masson, *Freud, The Assault on Truth*, Faber, London 1984, p. 147.
17. D. Wigoder, *op. cit*, pp. 52, 54.
18. *op cit.*, p. 297.
19. A. Miller, *For Your Own Good*, Faber, London 1984, p. 265.
20. *Collected Papers*, Hogarth Press, London 1978, p. 124.
21. G. Claridge, *Origins of Mental Illness*, Basil Blackwell, Oxford 1985.
22. P. Toynbee, *Part of a Journey*, Collins, London 1981.
23. Personal communication, 21 September, 1985.

7. Turning Fear into Obsessions and Compulsions

1. *Living With the Bomb: Can We Live Without Enemies?* Routledge, London 1985.
2. D. Rowe, *The Construction of Life and Death*, Wiley, Chichester 1982, pp. 132–7.
3. Thrane, G. 'Shame and the construction of the self', *Annual of Psychoanalysis*, 1979, 7, pp 321–41.
4. P. Mollon, 'Shame in relation to narcissistic disturbance', *British Journal of Medical Psychology*, 57, 1984, pp. 207–14.
5. *Poems*, Oxford University Press, London 1948, p. 110.

8. Turning Fear into Depression

1. Jackie, Val and Peter from the transcript of interviews for *The Mind Box*, Everyman Series, BBC TV, 1985.
2. See D. Rowe, *Depression: The Way Out of Your Prison*, Routledge, London 1983.

3. Bailliere, Tindall and Cassell, London, p. 31.
4. G. Brown and T. Harris, *The Social Origins of Depression*, Tavistock, London 1973.
5. 'A psychotherapist looks at depression', *British Journal of Psychiatry*, 143, 1983, p. 431.
6. *Wounded Healers*, ed. V. Rippere and R. Williams, Wiley, Chichester 1985, p. 74.
7. T. Doi, *The Anatomy of Self*, Kodansha International Ltd, Tokyo 1986, p. 149.
8. Faber, London 1974, p. 138.
9. *Wounded Healers*, p. 175.
10. S. Kopp, *No Hidden Meanings*, Science and Behaviour Books, Palo Alto, California 1975.
11. *The Mind Box*, 2 February 1985.
12. *Wounded Healers*, p. 19.

9. Turning Fear into Mania

1. *Origins of Mental Illness*, Basil Blackwell, Oxford 1985, p. 103.
2. M. J. Hobbs in association with Michael Joseph, London 1985, p. 161.
3. D. Wigoder, *Images of Destruction*, p. 132.
4. 'The Manic Defence', in *Through Paediatrics to Psycho-analysis*, Hogarth Press and the Institute of Psychoanalysis, London 1982, p. 130.
5. D. Wigoder, *op. cit.*, p. 94.
6. *ibid.*, p. 144.
7. *ibid.*, p. 74.
8. *ibid.*, p. 133.
9. *ibid.*, p. 147, 123.
10. *The Drama of the Gifted Child*, trans. Ruth Ward, Faber, London 1979, p. 56.
11. *ibid.*, pp. 56, 58, 60.
12. *ibid.*, p. 59.
13. 'The Welsh Marches', in *The Shropshire Lad*, Jonathon Cape, London, 1972, p. 33.
14. *The Drama of the Gifted Child, op. cit.*, p. 129.
15. *The Mind Box*, 2 February 1985.
16. D. Wigoder, *op. cit.*, p. 226.

10. Turning Fear into Schizophrenia

1. J. Hoenig, 'The concept of schizophrenia: Kraepelin – Bleuler – Scheiner' in *Contemporary Issues in Schizophrenia*, ed. Alan Kerr and Philip Snaith, Gaskell, London 1986, p. 52.
2. *ibid.*, p. 14.
3. *Aliens and Alienists*, Penguin, Harmondsworth 1980.
4. See D. Cohen, *Psychology News*, 45, 1986, p. 3.
5. *Conundrum*, Faber, London 1974, p. 138.
6. *Contemporary Issues in Schizophrenia*, p. 449.
7. World Health Organization, *Schizophrenia: An International Follow-up Study*, Wiley, Chichester 1979.
8. J. Leff, 'Recent research on relatives' expressed emotion', *Contemporary Issues in Schizophrenia*, pp. 339–45.
9. Published by the National Schizophrenia Fellowship, Surbiton, Surrey, 1974, quoted in P. Barnham, *Schizophrenia and Human Value*, Basil Blackwell, Oxford 1984, p. 190.
10. L. Sander, 'A twenty-five-year follow-up of the Pavenstedt Longitudinal Research Project, its relation to early intervention', in J. D. Call, E. Galenson and R. L. Tyson, eds, *Frontiers in Infant Psychiatry*, Basic Books, New York 1983, pp. 225–34, quoted in S. Sanger and J. Kelly, *The Magic Square*, Bantam Press, New York 1986, p. 120.
11. 'The shadow of the ancestor: a historical factor in the transmission of schizophrenia', *British Journal of Medical Psychology*, vol. 42, no. 1, 1969, pp. 13–32.
12. S. Sanger and J. Kelly, *The Magic Square*, Bantam Press, New York 1986, p. 39.
13. 'Clinical regression compared with defence organization', in *Psychotherapy in the Designed Therapeutic Milieu*, ed. Eldred and Vanderpool, Little, Brown and Co., Boston 1967, quoted in M. Davis and D. Wallbridge, *Boundary and Space*, Penguin, Harmondsworth 1983, p. 60.
14. *op. cit.*, p. 177.
15. 'Ego distortion in terms of true and false self' in *The Maturational Processes and the Facilitating Environment*, International Universities Press, New York 1985, pp. 140–52, and R. Laing, *The Divided Self*, Penguin, Harmondsworth 1970.
16. *The Spiritual Nature of Man*, Oxford University Press, Oxford 1979.
17. *Exploring Inner Space*, Penguin, Harmondsworth 1981.
18. *The Schizophrenic Disorders: Long-term Patient and Family Studies*, Yale University Press, New Haven 1978, p. 216, quoted in P. Barnham, *op. cit.*, p. 172.

19. S. Sanger and J. Kelly, *op. cit.*, p. 22.
20. 'Language in schizophrenia: the structure of monologues and conversations', *British Journal of Psychiatry*, 146, 1985, pp. 399–404.
21. *Schizophrenia: Notes for Relatives and Friends*, National Schizophrenia Fellowship, Surbiton, Surrey, 1985.

11. Turning Fear into Courage

1. C. Bensley, 'Self Selection', *Moving In*, Harry Chambers/Peterloo Poets, Liskeard, Cornwall, 1984.
2. C. Day-Lewis, 'Walking Away', *Listener*, 3 February 1983, p. 15.
3. *No Hidden Meanings*, Science and Behavior Books, Palo Alto, California 1975.
4. *Wounded Healers*, ed. V. Rippere and R. Williams, Wiley, Chichester 1985, p. 44.
5. *ibid.*, p. 158.

Select Bibliography

L. Armstrong, *Kiss Daddy Goodnight*, Pocket Books, New York 1979

S. Butler, *The Conspiracy of Silence*, Volcano Press, San Francisco 1982

G. Claridge, *Origins of Mental Illness*, Basil Blackwell, Oxford 1985

M. Davis and D. Wallbridge, *Boundary and Space*, Penguin, Harmondsworth 1983

T. Doi, *The Anatomy of Dependence*, trans. J. Bester, Kodansha International Ltd, Tokyo 1981

T. Doi, *The Anatomy of Self*, trans. M. A. Harbison, Kodansha International Ltd, Tokyo 1986

A. Hardy, *The Spiritual Nature of Man*, Oxford University Press, Oxford 1979

D. Hay, *Exploring Inner Space*, Penguin, Harmondsworth 1981

M. Herbert, *Caring for Your Children*, Basil Blackwood, Oxford 1985

A. Kerr and P. Snaith, eds., *Contemporary Issues in Schizophrenia*, Gaskell, London 1986

S. Kakar, *Shamans, Mystics and Doctors*, Oxford University Press, New Delhi 1982

S. Kopp, *No Hidden Meanings*, Science and Behavior Books, Palo Alto, Ca., 1985

J. Leff, *Schizophrenia: Notes for Relatives and Friends*, National Schizophrenia Fellowship, Surbiton, Surrey, 1985

R. J. Lifton, *Home from the War*, Simon and Schuster, New York 1973

R. Littlewood and M. Lipsedge, *Aliens and Alienists*, Penguin, Harmondsworth 1980

S. Macleod, *The Art of Starvation*, Virago, London 1984

J. M. Masson, *Freud: the Assault on Truth*, Faber, London 1984

A. Miller, *The Drama of the Gifted Child*, trans. R. Ward, Faber, London 1983

A. Miller, *For Your Own Good*, trans. Hildegarde and Hunter Hannum, Faber, London 1983

A. Miller, *Thou Shalt Not Be Aware*, trans. Hildegarde and Hunter Hannum, Pluto Press, London 1985

P. Mollon, 'Shame in relation to narcissistic disturbance', *British Journal of Medical Psychology*, 57, 207–14, 1984

J. Morris, *Conundrum*, Faber, London 1974

S. Orbach, *Fat Is a Feminist Issue*, Hamlyn, London 1981

S. Orbach, *Hunger Strike*, Faber, London 1986

V. Rippere and R. Williams, eds., *Wounded Healers*, Wiley, Chichester 1985

D. Rowe, *The Experience of Depression*, Wiley, Chichester, 1978; second edition Fontana, London (forthcoming)

D. Rowe, *The Construction of Life and Death*, Wiley, Chichester 1982

D. Rowe, *Depression: The Way Out of Your Prison*, Routledge, London 1983

D. Rowe, *Living with the Bomb. Can We Live without Enemies?*, Routledge, London 1985

S. Sanger and J. Kelly, *The Magic Square*, Bantam Press, New York 1986

R. D. Scott and P. L. Ashworth, 'The shadow of the ancestor: a historical factor in the transmission of schizophrenia', *British Journal of Medical Psychology*, 42, 1, 13–32, 1969

A. Scull, *Museums of Madness*, Penguin, Harmondsworth 1972

C. R. Snyder, R. L. Higgens and R. J. Stucky, *Excuses: Masquerades in Search of Grace*, Wiley, New York 1985

D. Stern, *The First Relationship: Infant and Mother*, Fontana, London 1977

H. S. Sullivan, *Conceptions of Modern Psychiatry*, Tavistock, London 1955

T. Szasz, *The Second Sin*, Routledge, London 1984

P. Toynbee, *Part of a Journey*, Collins, London 1981

D. Wigoder, *Images of Destruction*, Routledge, London 1987

D. Winnicott, *The Child, the Family and the Outside World*, Penguin, Harmondsworth 1964

D. Winnicott, *Collected Papers*, Hogarth Press, London 1978

D. Winnicott, *The Maturational Processes and the Facilitating Environment*, International Universities Press, New York 1985

World Health Organization, *Schizophrenia: an International Follow-up Study*, Wiley, Chichester 1979

Index

Index

Index

The Successful Self

Freeing our Hidden Inner Strengths

Dorothy Rowe

Is it possible to be truly successful as a person? Or must we, as most of us do, continue to live our lives feeling in some way trapped and oppressed, frustrated, irritable, haunted by worries and regrets, creating misery for ourselves and others?

In *The Successful Self* leading psychologist Dorothy Rowe, author of *Beyond Fear*, shows us how to live more comfortably and creatively within ourselves by achieving a fuller understanding of how we experience our existence and how we perceive the threat of its annihilation.

She demonstrates how to develop the social and personal skills we lack, retaining the uniqueness of our individuality while becoming an integral part of the life around us and learning how to value and accept ourselves.

With characteristic originality, clarity and unfailing wisdom, Dorothy Rowe enables us to revolutionise our own lives and the lives of others in the process of becoming a Successful Self.

'Dorothy Rowe stands out amongst psychologists for her clear insight into human experience: her writing is refreshingly free from the dubious theoretical constructs and jargon ideas which plague this subject' Oliver Gillie, *Independent*

'A very brightly written book that intriguingly makes you question something most of us discuss: do we really like ourselves? Then it goes on to help us do so' Mavis Nicholson

A FONTANA ORIGINAL

Choosing Not Losing

The Experience of Depression

Dorothy Rowe

'I remember feeling very isolated. For a while I became convinced that I was set apart. Everyone seemed so well and confident. I marvelled that they were able to get through the day.'

Depression is the greatest isolation we can experience, a prison which we build for ourselves. Just as we build it, however, so we can unlock the door and let ourselves out.

In *Choosing Not Losing*, eminent psychologist Dorothy Rowe draws on her experiences with a number of patients who were referred to her for treatment. Their stories show that the lives of even those in the depths of depression can change.

A sympathetic and immensely valuable book, full of insight into the often strange and moving world of suffering inhabited by the depressive, *Choosing Not Losing* will give hope to all who read it.

FONTANA PAPERBACKS

Katharina Dalton

Once a Month

Once a month, with demoralising regularity, over fifty per cent of women feel tired, confused, irritable and incapacitated due to the effects of premenstrual tension. Many others are indirectly affected – husbands, children, colleagues, workmates and friends.

Premenstrual syndrome is responsible for the timing of half of all criminal offences in women, for half of all suicides, accidents in the home and on the roads, hospital admissions, incidents of baby battering and alcoholic bouts. These are the calculable effects – how much greater are the less obvious changes in a woman's daily life, in her behaviour, appearance and health?

The problems might seem insurmountable – but are they? This book is a popular and easily understood account of menstrual difficulties by a doctor with many years of professional and research experience in their causes and treatment. Katharina Dalton shows that in most cases women can treat themselves, and that in severer cases progesterone treatment can be highly effective. It is a book which many readers – male as well as female – will find informative, sympathetic, helpful and above all practical in relieving the suffering caused by prementrual syndrome.

Liz McNeil Taylor

Living with Loss

Death is a subject we try to ignore until it happens to someone we love. Liz Taylor's husband, Adam, died suddenly, aged only forty-three, leaving her to suffer the isolation of a widow (or widower) in a society where social life is based on couples and death is unmentionable.

She discusses honestly the problems of money, sex and the children, and her strong and conflicting emotional reactions to the tragedy. She describes how she learned to come to terms with her grief, despair and anger, to take full responsibility for her family and her own life, and how eventually she learned to laugh again.

Drawing on this personal knowledge and on interviews with other bereaved people, she has created a survival handbook for the widowed, showing how best to heal oneself and how to get the most from the organizations and resources which can help the bereaved to build a new life.